INTRODUCTORY THANKSGIVINGS
IN THE LETTERS OF PAUL

INTRODUCTORY THANKSGIVINGS IN THE LETTERS OF PAUL

BY

PETER THOMAS O'BRIEN

WIPF & STOCK · Eugene, Oregon

Wipf and Stock Publishers
199 W 8th Ave, Suite 3
Eugene, OR 97401

Introductory Thanksgivings in the Letters of Paul
By O'Brien, Peter T.
Copyright©1977 by O'Brien, Peter T.
ISBN 13: 978-1-60608-811-1
Publication date 6/11/2009
Previously published by E. J. Brill, 1977

TABLE OF CONTENTS

Preface IX
List of Abbreviations XI

Introduction 1
   1. Problem and Procedure 1
   2. Previous Research on Pauline Thanksgiving . . . 4

PART ONE

INTRODUCTORY THANKSGIVINGS OF THE FIRST CATEGORY: THANKSGIVING AND PETITIONARY PRAYER CONJOINED

I. Thanksgiving and Joyful Intercession: Phil. 1:3-11 . . 19
   1. Thanksgiving from a Full Heart: Vv. 3-6 . . . 20
   2. Intercession for Love and Discernment: Vv. 9-11 . 29
   3. Concluding Remarks 37
   Appended Note 41

II. Thanksgiving and Intercession for an Individual: Phm. 4-6 47
   1. Thanksgiving for Philemon's Love and Faith: Vv. 4f. 50
   2. Intercession concerning Philemon's Generosity: V. 6 54
   3. Conclusions 58

III. Thanksgiving—Intercession—Thanksgiving: Col. 1:3-14 62
   1. Thanksgiving in Colossians 62
   2. Language and Style of Col. 1:3-14 67
   3. The Limits of the Thanksgiving Period 71
   4. Thanksgiving: Faith-love-hope and the Gospel: Vv. 3-5 75
   5. Intercession for Knowledge and Godly Conduct: Vv. 9-14 82
   6. General Conclusions 100

PART TWO

INTRODUCTORY THANKSGIVINGS OF THE SECOND CATEGORY: THANKSGIVING PRAYERS ALONE

IV. Thanksgiving for God's Grace Given : 1 Cor. 1:4-9 . . 107
    1. Thanksgiving for God's Grace : V. 4 108
    2. Riches in Christ : V. 5 116
    3. A Testimony Confirmed : V. 6 120
    4. Awaiting the Parousia : V. 7 123
    5. Preserved Blameless : V. 8 126
    6. God is Faithful : V. 9 130
    7. Conclusions 134

PART THREE

MIXED CATEGORIES OF INTRODUCTORY THANKSGIVINGS

V. The Three-Fold Thanksgiving of 1 Thess. 1:2ff. . . . 141
    1. Limits and Structure of the Period 143
    2. Thanksgiving for Work, Toil and Patience : Chap. 1:2-5 146
    3. Receiving God's Word aright : Chap. 2:13 . . . 153
    4. Thanksgiving, Petition and a Wish-Prayer : Chap. 3:9-13 156
    5. Conclusions 164

VI. The Two Thanksgivings of 2 Thess. 1:3ff., and 2:13f. . 167
    1. Links with the Introductory Thanksgiving of 1 Thessalonians 167
    2. Limits of the Periods 169
    3. Thanksgiving for Remarkable Growth : Chap. 1:3-4 171
    4. A Two-fold Intercession : Chap. 1:11-12 177
        a. Worthy of their calling 178
        b. Right resolutions and actions 179
        c. Purpose : the glory of Christ and His people . . 181
    5. Thanksgiving for God's Activity from all Eternity : Chap. 2:13f. 184
    6. Conclusions 193

TABLE OF CONTENTS

VII. Thanksgiving for a Church Unknown to Paul : Rom. 1:8ff.   197
1. General 197
2. Limits of the Passage 200
3. Thanksgiving for a Faith Proclaimed Far and Wide : V. 8 202
4. An Oath—the Guarantee of Thanksgiving and Intercession : V. 9 210
5. A Psalmist's Prayer-Sigh : V. 10 216
6. Reasons for a Visit to Rome 221
7. The Function of the Paragraph 224
8. Paul's Thanksgiving and Petitionary Prayer . . . 229

PART FOUR

AN INTRODUCTORY *BERAKAH*

VIII. The Introductory *Berakah* of 2 Cor. 1:3ff. 233
1. A *Berakah* instead of a Thanksgiving 233
2. The Limits of the Paragraph 235
3. Praise for God's Comfort : Vv. 3-4 236
4. Relationship of the *Berakah* to Vv. 5-7 . . . 247
5. The *Berakah* and Paul's Affliction in Asia . . . 248
6. Intercession and Thanksgiving in V. 11 250
7. The Function of the Paragraph (1:3-11) . . . 254
8. Praise, Petition and Thanksgiving 257

IX. Conclusions 259
1. Varied Nature of the Letters 259
2. Extent of the Thanksgiving Periods 261
3. Manifold Function of the Introductory Thanksgivings 261
4. Language 263
5. Prayers of Thanksgiving and Petition 265

Bibliography 273
Index of Passages Cited 287
Index of Authors 305

PREFACE

This book began as a doctoral dissertation and was accepted by the University of Manchester in 1971. My sincere thanks are due to Professor F. F. Bruce under whose supervision the thesis was originally written. His high standards of scholarship are a challenge to any student of the New Testament while his many kindnesses over the years have been a source of encouragement to me.

Sections of the work have been rewritten in the light of further reflection and by way of interaction with more recent literature on the subject. However, I have resisted the temptation to expand an already lengthy manuscript. I am especially grateful to Professor R. P. Martin of Fuller Theological Seminary, Pasadena, U.S.A. for his constructive criticisms of the manuscript while it was being prepared for publication.

To my colleagues on the staff of Moore Theological College, Newtown, N.S.W., especially the Principal, Canon D. B. Knox, and also to Bishop D. W. B. Robinson who first introduced me to the complex area of *studia Paulina*, my debt is great. I would like to record my appreciation to Mrs. Elaine Vaughan for her typing assistance at various stages of the book's preparation; and I cannot omit to express my thanks to the Sydney Diocesan Book Society and to friends in Sydney who have materially supported the printing of the volume.

I am grateful to the Editors of *New Testament Studies* for permission to incorporate in the book material previously published in my article, 'Thanksgiving and the Gospel in Paul', *New Testament Studies* 21 (1974-75), pp. 144-155.

My loving thanks are due to Mary, my wife, to whom this book is dedicated and without whose help it would not have been written. David, Stephen, Elizabeth and Sarah, our children, will be pleased that it has finally been completed.

Finally, 'thanks be to God through our Lord Jesus Christ'.

Newtown (Sydney), Australia PETER T. O'BRIEN
July, 1977

LIST OF ABBREVIATIONS

ABR	Australian Biblical Review
AG	Arndt, W. F., and Gingrich, F. W., edd., *A Greek-English Lexicon of the New Testament and Other Early Christian Literature* (ET, Cambridge, 1957)
ATR	Anglican Theological Review
AV	Authorised Version
BJRL	Bulletin of the John Rylands Library
Bl.-D.	Blass, F., and Debrunner, A., *A Greek Grammar of the New Testament and Other Early Christian Literature*, ed. R. W. Funk (ET, Cambridge, 1961)
CBQ	Catholic Biblical Quarterly
ed.	editor
EQ	The Evangelical Quarterly
ET	English Translation
EvTh	Evangelische Theologie
EVV	English Versions
Exp	The Expositor
ExT	The Expository Times
HTR	The Harvard Theological Review
Interp	Interpretation
JBL	Journal of Biblical Literature
JJS	Journal of Jewish Studies
JTS	Journal of Theological Studies
LXX	Septuagint version
mg	margin
MM	Moulton, J. H. and Milligan, G., edd., *The Vocabulary of the Greek Testament* (London, 1930)
MS	Manuscript
n.d.	no date
NEB	The New English Bible
NovT	Novum Testamentum
N.S.	New Series
NTS	New Testament Studies
RB	Revue Biblique
RGG	*Die Religion in Geschichte und Gegenwart*, Galling, K., ed. (Tübingen, ³1956-1965)
RSV	The Revised Standard Version of the Bible
RThPh	Revue de Théologie et de Philosophie
RThR	The Reformed Theological Review
SJTh	Scottish Journal of Theology
ST	Studia Theologica
Str.-B.	Strack, H. L., and Billerbeck, P., *Kommentar zum Neuen Testament aus Talmud und Midrasch*, Vols. 1-4 (München, 1922-1928)

TDNT	*Theological Dictionary of the New Testament* (ET of *Theologisches Wörterbuch zum Neuen Testament*) (trans. and ed. by G. W. Bromiley, 1964-1974)
ThViat	*Theologia Viatorum*
TLZ	*Theologische Literaturzeitung*
TU	*Texte und Untersuchungen*
TynB	*Tyndale Bulletin*
TZ	*Theologische Zeitschrift*
UPZ	*Urkunden der Ptolęmäerzeit I*, ed. U. Wilcken (Berlin, 1927)
ZNW	*Zeitschrift für die neutestamentliche Wissenschaft*
ZThK	*Zeitschrift für Theologie und Kirche*

INTRODUCTION

1. *Problem and Procedure*

It is apparent to anyone reading Paul's letters that the apostle, in his introductions, frequently recorded his thanks to God for the faith, love, etc., of the addressees and offered petition for them. At first sight it would appear that the introductory passages in which the writer describes his thanksgivings and intercessions were not without significance. It is all the more surprising, therefore, to note that some commentators dismiss these paragraphs with a brief sentence or two, anxious to pass on to the 'weightier' sections of Paul's epistles.

In 1939 Paul Schubert's important monograph, *Form and Function of the Pauline Thanksgivings*, was published in Berlin. In his study of the forms Schubert examined the structures of Paul's opening thanksgiving periods [1] and sought to assess their place in the letters they introduced. Unfortunately, Schubert's monograph has not had the influence it deserved (partly due, no doubt, to the Second World War), and it is only in more recent times that commentaries and similar studies of the forms have taken the work into account.[2]

The following problem immediately presents itself: What place and function did these introductory paragraphs have? And, further: Why did the apostle, in his introductions, mention that he gave thanks and offered petition for the addressees? Were such reports mere literary devices by which Paul, in keeping with the epistolary style of the period, introduced the basic themes of each letter? Or were they included since they reflected the public prayers of the apostle, and, ultimately, fixed elements in early Christian services of worship?

---

[1] The terms 'introductory thanksgiving', 'thanksgiving passage' and 'thanksgiving period' are used to denote the *paragraph* commencing with the εὐχαριστέω-formula. 'Thanksgiving report' is employed to refer to the sentence(s) of the paragraph which report Paul's thanksgiving (*vis-à-vis* the petitionary prayer report or personal details), while 'thanksgiving' connotes the *actual* prayer (lying behind such a report).

[2] See the recent survey of previous epistolary research by W. G. Doty, *Letters in Primitive Christianity* (Philadelphia, 1973).

Before some of these questions can be answered an exegetical examination of the paragraphs needs to be carried out. The following investigation, then, which is primarily an exegetical study, attempts to determine the place of the introductory thanksgivings within their respective Pauline letters, and examines the prayers found within these introductory paragraphs.

In order to illuminate the Pauline texts reference has been made to the Old Testament (particularly the LXX) and other Jewish writings (e.g., the Qumran texts and the rabbinic literature), as well as to papyrus letters and other material in the Greek world. Yet the investigation is not, in the first instance, a background study. Nor is the work a complete examination of Pauline thanksgiving on the one hand, or petitionary prayer on the other. In the final chapter certain conclusions are drawn concerning Paul's introductory prayers of thanksgiving. But a comprehensive inquiry into Pauline thanksgiving would require a careful assessment of all paraenetic or exhortatory references to the giving of thanks (and these have been treated elsewhere),[3] as well as an examination of other contexts where the εὐχαριστέω word-group did not appear but where the idea of thanksgiving was present. Paul's petitionary prayers appear in paraenetic, didactic or speculative contexts as well as in the introductory thanksgiving paragraphs, while wish-prayers (or benedictions) are scattered throughout the letters. Apart from the wish-prayers of 1 Thess. 3:11-13 our research has been restricted to an examination of petitions in the introductory periods. Thus no comprehensive inquiry into Pauline petition has been made and although it has been suggested that this type of prayer was an important weapon in Paul's apostolic armoury, for a full assessment contexts such as Rom. 8, where the Spirit is mentioned in relation to prayer, would have to be examined.

A word of explanation is needed in connection with the letters that have been studied, and the order in which the introductory passages have been investigated. The introductory thanksgivings of the Pastoral Epistles (1 Tim. 1:12ff.; 2 Tim. 1:3ff.) have not been treated, for, apart from the question of authorship, these paragraphs do not contribute anything of significance to our study. The remaining letters

---

[3] In Appendix A of my thesis, *Introductory Thanksgivings in the Letters of Paul* (Manchester University, 1971), pp. 445-469.

in the *corpus Paulinum* [4] (with the exception of Galatians which has no introductory thanksgiving) have been dealt with, although Ephesians, which contains a long introductory eulogy (1:3-12 or 14), a thanksgiving report (1:15f.), and an intercessory prayer report (1:17-19), has been treated elsewhere.[5] For, apart from the questions of authorship, destination, etc., no detailed exegetical examination of Eph. 1:3-19 has been possible. A full treatment of this passage, together with a thorough examination of its relationship with the rest of the letter, constitutes a separate subject for research. Thus any conclusions reached on the basis of our preliminary enquiries are used only as supplementary evidence in the investigation.

Secondly, the order in which the paragraphs have been studied has been determined by structural considerations, not chronological ones. It would be customary to examine the introductory thanksgiving of 1 Thessalonians first, since this is the first extant thanksgiving passage of the apostle we possess. But this period, with its special problems, has a mixed structure and our inquiry into the passage is postponed until the first category of introductory thanksgiving (with its seven basic elements) and the second type of period (with its causal ὅτι-clause) are investigated. Thus the introductory passages of Philippians, Philemon and Colossians are treated first. 1 Cor. 1:4-9, as an example of the second type of structure is then dealt with, before the mixed thanksgiving periods of 1 Thessalonians, 2 Thessalonians and Romans are reviewed. Finally the introductory eulogy of 2 Cor. 1 (the function of which is similar to those passages where the εὐχαριστέω-formula appears) is studied. Since there is no chronological development in the structures of the periods (e.g., from a simple to a complex form), nor a progression of thought in Paul's prayers, it is considered that such a sequence is legitimate. Further,

---

[4] The Pauline authorship of Romans, 1 and 2 Corinthians, Galatians, Philippians, Colossians, 1 and 2 Thessalonians and Philemon has been assumed.

[5] See my forthcoming article, 'The *Berakah* and Introductory Thanksgiving of Eph. 1:3-19'. Ephesians is the only letter in the Pauline corpus that commences with both a *berakah* and an introductory thanksgiving. On the one hand, the writer has carefully maintained the distinction between the εὐλογητός-formula, used of blessings in which he himself participated, and εὐχαριστέω, the thanksgiving term that related to *Fürdank* for God's work in the lives of the addressees. On the other hand, he has included, rather unusually, both a *berakah* and an introductory thanksgiving in the one letter, thus making it different from all others in the Pauline corpus. The person most likely to have done this, in our judgement, was Paul himself.

by examining the paragraphs in this order comparisons can more easily be made.

Finally, these introductory periods of Paul's letters consist of personal and apostolic details, didactic material and so on, as well as thanksgiving and petitionary prayer reports. Although we have sought to assess the place of each period within its letter, our verse-by-verse examination has been confined to the prayer reports, and thus to the actual prayers lying behind them.

2. *Previous Research on Pauline Thanksgiving*

The subject of thanksgiving, like the more general theme of prayer, has been a neglected area of New Testament research. Since 1900 the number of articles or monographs on Pauline thanksgiving has been slight and, apart from Schubert's *Form and Function of the Pauline Thanksgivings*, no full-scale contribution of major importance on this motif has been produced.

The first monograph on Pauline prayer to appear was Alfred Juncker's short but seminal study, *Das Gebet bei Paulus* (Berlin, 1905).[6] Though consisting of only thirty-two pages, Juncker's work raised many fundamental issues about Pauline prayer (e.g., the influence of the Psalter on Paul's prayers, and prayer to God as Father—a new element in Paul the Christian's praying). On the specific matter of thanksgiving Juncker noted that the apostle gave thanks for manifold blessings: 'für die Errettung, die Gott den Gläubigen in Christo ein für allemal gegeben hat... für die mancherlei Tröstungen... für das Hoffnungsgut... für die erfreulichen religiös-sittlichen Zustände der Gemeinden...'.[7] Juncker observed that praise and thanksgiving stood in the foreground of Paul's prayers—though they were frequently linked with petition—and this was because of 'der absoluten Abhängigkeit seines und jedes Christen ganzen Seins von Gott'.[8] Like von der Goltz [9] before him, Juncker distinguished '*das persön-*

---

[6] Cf. G. P. Wiles. *The Function of Intercessory Prayer in Paul's Apostolic Ministry with Special Reference to the First Epistle to the Thessalonians* (unpublished Ph.D. thesis, Yale University, 1965), p. 229. Apart from von der Goltz's study (see below) there seems to have been nothing of real significance prior to Juncker's work.

[7] *Gebet*, p. 4.

[8] *Ibid.*, p. 22.

[9] E. von der Goltz, *Das Gebet in der ältesten Christenheit* (Leipzig, 1901), p. 105.

liche Dankgebet' from the 'huldigenden, ehrfurchtsvollen Lobpreise'. Contrary to the rabbinic prayers where *berakoth* were frequently found, 'spielen bei Paulus die Termini "Danken" und "Dank" eine hervorstechende Rolle'.¹⁰

Theodor Schermann's lexicographical study entitled '*Εὐχαριστία und εὐχαριστεῖν* in ihrem Bedeutungswandel bis 200 n. Chr.', which appeared in *Philologus, Zeitschrift für das klassische Altertum* 69 (Leipzig, 1910), pp. 375-410, because of his particular interest in liturgy, concentrated on the use of εὐχαριστέω and its cognates in the Apostolic Fathers and their successors. On Pauline prayer Schermann correctly noted that the apostle used the thanksgiving terminology in a variety of ways but he did not develop this. G. H. Boobyer, *"Thanksgiving" and the "Glory of God" in Paul* (Leipzig, 1929), made an investigation of εὐχαριστία in the sense of praise or general thanksgiving to God with particular reference to 2 Cor. 1:11; 4:15 and 9:11f. He did not deal with thanksgiving as a prayer offered to God 'on the occasion of, and in return for, some particu ar benefit received'.¹¹ In the above-mentioned passages 'an actual material increase of the δόξα θεοῦ (was) occasioned by the εὐχαριστία of the Christians'.¹² Paul put thanksgiving into a place of surprising prominence. He did this because of the effect it had upon God. According to Boobyer :

'... thanksgiving increases the glory of God.
The thanksgiving of God's children gives him
greater power. By it, his dominion over Satan,
over all κύριοι, over the στοιχεῖα, and the
ἀρχαί will become yet stronger; and his final
triumph when Christ "shall deliver up the
Kingdom to God, even the Father", "that God
may be in all", more complete'.¹³

Note R. Deichgräber's assessment, *Gotteshymnus und Christushymnus in der frühen Christenheit* (Göttingen, 1967), pp. 11f.

¹⁰ Juncker, *Gebet*, p. 23.

¹¹ "*Thanksgiving*", p. 1. Prior to Boobyer's work E. Lohmeyer had examined the introductory greetings of the Pauline letters, concluding that their background was to be sought in early Christian worship; 'Probleme paulinischer Theologie. I. Briefliche Grussüberschriften', *ZNW* 26 (1927), pp. 158-173.

¹² *Ibid.*, p. 4.

¹³ *Ibid.*, p. 84.

For J.-A. Eschlimann, *La Prière dans saint Paul* (Lyon, 1934), Pauline prayer was characterised by joyful gratitude. His requests were humble, confident (for they rested upon divine faithfulness), filial, free and supernatural. The occasions on which the apostle gave thanks or encouraged others to do so were manifold, while the objects were as wide as petition. Paul could hardly conceive of prayer without thanksgiving, and he used the εὐχαριστέω terminology as a joyful reminder of one's entire dependence on God's grace.[14]

The great merit of Günther Harder's work, *Paulus und das Gebet* (Gütersloh, 1936), a most comprehensive study on Pauline prayer, lay in his treatment of the Old Testament and Jewish antecedents [15] of Paul's prayers. In both style and content the LXX Psalter, in particular, had left its stamp. Christian prayer [16] was distinctive in three ways: it was 'im Geist', 'durch Christus' and 'zum "Herrn"'. Harder noted Paul's frequent use of εὐχαριστέω and its cognate εὐχαριστία: 'sie bedeuteten eine Neuprägung des Apostels, den neuen Begriff für die neue Sache, das Dankgebet der Erlösten'.[17] Pauline thanksgivings, offered διὰ Χριστοῦ were 'die *typisch endzeitlichen* Gebete'.[18] In contrast to many thanksgivings in the ancient world Paul's were wonderfully simple. He knew to whom he prayed—to the Father of the Lord Jesus Christ. As a Christian he knew what he gave thanks for, viz., God's eschatological act in Christ, love, faith, godly power in weakness, and so on. These were thanksgivings offered 'im Reich Christi' [19] for definite and specific blessings received.

As already noted the most important formal and functional investigation of εὐχαριστέω and its cognates in the Hellenistic and Jewish world was the study of Paul Schubert, *Form and Function of the Pauline Thanksgivings* (Berlin, 1939). Noting that most of Paul's letters began with a thanksgiving he observed that the introductory thanksgivings exhibited certain identical formal and functional traits.[20] He sought to determine in detail the extent and significance

---

[14] *Prière*, p. 109.
[15] *Paulus*, pp. 4-129.
[16] *Ibid.*, pp. 163-214.
[17] *Ibid.*, p. 38.
[18] *Ibid.*, p. 184 (author's italics).
[19] *Ibid.*
[20] *Form*, pp. 1-9.

of these resemblances and to define the purpose of the thanksgiving passages within the letters they introduced.²¹

So using the opening thanksgiving of the letter to Philemon as a basis, Schubert compared the syntactical structures of each of these introductory thanksgivings which follow the epistolary greetings. He found that there were two basic types. The first, type Ia, ²² began with the principal clause in which εὐχαριστέω τῷ θεῷ (or its equivalent) was the characteristic phrase and was followed by one, two or three participles which modified the principal verb, εὐχαριστέω. These participles were always in the singular or plural of the nominative masculine, indicating that the writer (sometimes in conjunction with his associates) was the subject of the action expressed. The participle(s) was/were followed by a 'final' ²³ clause, introduced by ἵνα, ὅπως or εἰς τό with the infinitive. This final clause was subordinate to the participles.²⁴

The second basic category, type Ib,²⁵ also began with the εὐχαριστέω-phrase,²⁶ but instead of being followed by participles, was succeeded

---

²¹ *Ibid.*, pp. 10-39.

²² Eph. 1:15ff.; Phil. 1:3ff.; Col. 1:3ff.; 1 Thess. 1:2ff. (the final clause in the thanksgiving period of 1 Thessalonians is not taken up until 3:9ff. For the special problems relating to this see Schubert, *ibid.*, pp. 16ff.; Wiles, *Function*, pp. 131f.; and chapter V below); Phm. 4ff. Schubert considered 2 Cor. 1:11 to be an 'inverted' instance of type Ia (p. 46); see the exegesis below.

²³ 'Final' is not used in the technical sense of 'telic' = purpose (clause). Rather it refers to the clause which terminates the thanksgiving periods.

²⁴ While stressing the epistolary nature and function of the opening thanksgivings, Schubert denied their liturgical form. If the latter were present we should be able to observe structural traces of 'liturgical tripartition, "God, the minister and the people" '; *Form*, p. 38.

²⁵ 1 Cor. 1:4ff.; cf. Rom. 1:8; 1 Thess. 2:13; 2 Thess. 1:3; 2:13. These latter instances belong to the mixed category, although the verses cited do contain the causal ὅτι-clause.

²⁶ Schubert did not examine formally or structurally the introductory periods which began with εὐλογητός (2 Cor. 1:3ff.; Eph. 1:3ff.) or χάριν ἔχω (1 Tim. 1:12ff.; 2 Tim. 1:3ff.). The latter he omitted because he considered the Pastorals to be non-Pauline and because the passages did not contribute anything further to the study. He did however draw attention to texts such as Rom. 6:17; 7:25: 1 Cor. 15:57; 2 Cor. 2:14; 8:16; 9:15 when noting the use of χάρις τοῖς θεοῖς (ἔστω) and χάριν ἔχω in various Hellenistic documents; *Form*, pp. 159f. Concerning the opening of 2 Corinthians Paul 'chose the more liturgical, and less personal εὐλογία' (εὐλογητὸς ὁ θεός κτλ. 1:3-11). The reason 'must be looked for in the particular epistolary situation which called forth this letter'; *ibid.*, p. 50. While the latter statement is correct, the observation about the 'less personal εὐλογία' is not. The introductory period of 2 Corinthians is the *most personal* of all Paul's introductions. See chapter VIII.

by a causal ὅτι-clause which was subordinate to the εὐχαριστέω-clause. The final element in this thanksgiving type was a consecutive clause, introduced by and subordinate to the ὅτι-clause.[27]

The first category, while being more elaborate and more personal, was employed by Paul a greater number of times, though Schubert noted that there were several instances of mixed types.[28] Although the Pauline thanksgiving periods were introductory to the letters we are not to consider that their function was unimportant or negligible. Even the omission from Galatians argued the same point. The separate thanksgiving paragraphs showed a 'close relationship of basic structure',[29] and even though each had peculiar characteristics of style, contents, etc., they were not to be regarded as meaningless devices. They were a functional element in each letter. And that function, according to Schubert, was: 'to indicate the occasion for and the contents of the letters which they introduce'.[30]

To avoid obtaining false results through deliberate and arbitrary parallel-hunting Schubert then proceeded to analyze formally all other uses of εὐχαριστέω and its cognates in the Hellenistic world. Thus the non-Pauline writings of the New Testament, the LXX (with its important introductory thanksgiving at 2 Macc. 1:11ff.), Philo (who emphasized the value and necessity of thanksgiving), the papyrus letters and the inscriptions were examined.

In conclusion the author declared:

> 'Direct exegesis of the Pauline thanksgivings
> with reference to their respective letters
> reveals beyond the shadow of doubt their strictly
> epistolary form and function. The reference to
> the extra-Pauline Hellenistic epistolary thanks-
> givings confirms the exegetical judgement convincingly'.[31]

From this study of thanksgiving the author concluded that Paul 'was not just a Jew who was "exposed" to Hellenistic "influences", but that he was an indigenous Hellenist... Ἑλληνίστης ἐξ Ἑλληνιστῶν'.[32]

---

[27] Note J. M. Robinson's criticisms mentioned below, pp. 10ff.
[28] Rom. 1:8ff.; 1 Thess. 1:2ff.; 2 Thess. 1:3ff.
[29] Schubert, *ibid.*, p. 25.
[30] *Ibid.*, p. 27.
[31] *Ibid.*, p. 183.
[32] *Ibid.*, p. 184.

Before evaluating Schubert's work, which forms the point of departure for the following investigation, and criticisms levelled against it, reference is made to A. Hamman's study, *La Prière. I. Le Nouveau Testament* (Tournai, 1959), an examination of prayer and liturgy in the Bible in which ninety pages were devoted to Pauline prayer.[33] Hamman considered that thanksgiving was almost 'un synonyme de vie chrétienne'[34] and in particular was an important theme in Colossians. It played a much larger role in the New Testament than in the Old Testament where the praising of God frequently occurred. Hamman considered 'le Christ ait infléchi l'usage juif, en transformant la bénédiction en action de grâces'.[35] For Paul this permanent state of the Christian, i.e., thanksgiving, was based on God's grace ($\chi\acute{a}\rho\iota\varsigma$) in Christ (1 Cor. 1:4; 2 Cor. 1:11; 4:15; Phil. 4:6; 1 Thess. 5:18).

The apostle used $\epsilon\dot{\upsilon}\chi a\rho\iota\sigma\tau\acute{\epsilon}\omega$ with reference to salvation in general (e.g., Col. 1:12; 2 Thess. 2:13; cf. Rom. 6:17; 2 Cor. 2:14; 9:15), but on the other hand it was also applied to gifts in particular: the work of evangelisation (1 Thess. 2:13), for the faith of communities (Rom. 1:8; Eph. 1:15), faith and love (Eph. 1:16; Col. 1:4; 2 Thess. 1:3; Phm. 5), for faith, love and hope (1 Thess. 1:2f.), and so on.

To date the most comprehensive examination of Pauline intercessions is the monograph of G. P. Wiles, entitled *Paul's Intercessory Prayers* (Cambridge, 1974).[36] While acknowledging the difficulty of classifying the prayer material, which includes reports about prayers as well as actual petitions, the author grouped the intercessory material of the seven 'generally recognized Pauline epistles' into the following categories:

(1) intercessory wish-prayers (e.g., Rom. 15:5f., 13; 1 Thess. 3:11-13);
(2) intercessory prayer-reports (e.g., Rom. 1:9f.; Phil. 1:4, 9-11);
(3) paraenetic references to intercessory prayer—requests for and exhortations to such prayer (e.g., Rom. 12:12; 15:30-32; 2 Cor. 1:11); and
(4) didactic and speculative references to intercessory prayer (e.g., Rom. 8:15f., 26f.; Gal. 4:6).

---

[33] *Prière*, pp. 245-334.
[34] *Ibid.*, p. 291.
[35] *Ibid.*, p. 292.
[36] A revision and expansion of his 1965 thesis (see p. 4).

The possible backgrounds in Jewish practice and Christian worship were discussed though Wiles' primary concern was to show, by careful exegetical study, that Paul's intercessions were not simply formal liturgical expressions but were intimately related to the basic concerns of the letters in which they occurred. The author showed how the vocabulary of prayer was related to the pastoral situation and how closely Paul's missionary work and his intercessory prayers were integrated with each other. Wish-prayers and prayer-reports tended to epitomize the dominant message of the letters in which they appeared. There was no limit to the intercessions for Paul's converts: he desired that they experience every blessing and attain entire sanctification; he wished to see an attitude of reconciliation and loving unity among the members of each church; he longed that each congregation be involved in his apostolic ministry—especially in prayer on his behalf as he prays for them.

While not particularly concerned with the theme of thanksgiving as such Wiles noted the frequent links between Paul's assurances of unceasing intercessory prayer and his assurances of thanksgiving for his various addressees. The author did, however, examine the intercessory prayer reports within the thanksgiving periods, particularly in connection with their function (pp. 175-229), and reference is made to the relevant comments in the exegetical sections that follow.

It is now necessary to assess Schubert's work in the light of recent criticisms. His formal and functional examination has proved to be the point of departure for other formal studies [37] on the *corpus Paulinum*. At the same time not all of his conclusions have been accepted. J. M. Robinson [38] and D. J. McFarlane,[39] among others,

---

[37] E.g., J. T. Sanders, 'The Transition from Opening Epistolary Thanksgiving to Body in the Letters of the Pauline Corpus', *JBL* 81 (1962), pp. 348-362; T. Y. Mullins, 'Petition as a Literary Form', *NovT* 5 (1962), pp. 46-54; Mullins, 'Disclosure. A Literary Form in the New Testament', *NovT* 7 (1964), pp. 44-50; C. J. Bjerkelund, *Parakalô* (Oslo, 1967); and J. L. White, 'Introductory Formulae in the Body of the Pauline Letter', *JBL* 90 (1971), pp. 91-97. For further references see the literature cited by T. Y. Mullins, 'Ascription as a Literary Form', *NTS* 19 (1972-1973), pp. 194f., and Doty, *Letters, passim*.

[38] In his important article, 'Die Hodajot-Formel in Gebet und Hymnus des Frühchristentums', *Apophoreta: Festschrift für Ernst Haenchen*, ed. W. Eltester and F. H. Kettler (Berlin, 1964), pp. 194-235, Robinson examined the *hodayah* and *berakah* forms with reference to the prayers and hymns of Judaism and early Christianity. He considered that these two terms were interchangeable (cf. J.-P. Audet, 'Literary Forms and Contents of a Normal Εὐχαριστία in the First Century', in *Studia Evangelica*

have correctly pointed out that there was more interaction between the Hellenistic and Judaistic worlds than was assumed when Schubert wrote. Certainly the latter's conclusion that Paul, because of his use of the Hellenistic thanksgiving form, 'was not just a Jew who was "exposed" to Hellenistic "influences", but that he was an indigenous Hellenist... 'Ελληνίστης ἐξ 'Ελληνιστῶν' does not follow.[40] There are good reasons for believing with Fitzmyer and Delling,[41] that the *structure* of the Pauline thanksgiving periods was Hellenistic while the *contents* (apart from their specifically Christian elements) showed the influence of Jewish thought.

Secondly, although Schubert acknowledged Paul's indebtedness to this Greek epistolary convention, he was the first to admit that Paul was no 'slavish imitator' [42] of any such literary form, for he recognised that Paul's structures in these thanksgiving periods were highly developed and sophisticated. McFarlane, on the contrary, considered that Paul inserted into the general epistolary pattern his thanks-

---

1, ed. F. L. Cross *et al.* (Berlin, 1959), p. 646, who believed the Jewish benediction to have been 'the true parent of the Christian εὐχαριστία'), and that early Christianity was familiar with prayers opening in a form analogous to the Qumran *Hodayoth*. *Contra* Schubert, Robinson (pp. 201f.) noted that there was ample evidence in 1 QH and other Jewish literature to show that Schubert's introductory thanksgivings, esp., type Ib with its causal ὅτι-clause, did not spring from a 'specifically pagan Hellenistic, non-Jewish origin' (*Form*, p. 168). The *Tefillah* was a good example in Jewish prayers of the linking of petition with thanksgiving (or praise); cf. Schubert's first category, type Ia.

[39] *The Motif of Thanksgiving in the New Testament* (unpublished M.Th. thesis, St. Andrews University, 1966). McFarlane agreed with F. X. J. Exler, *The Form of the Ancient Greek Letter* (Washington, D.C., 1923), that Paul made use of a general epistolary pattern that was widespread in his time. But this pattern did not include the introductory thanksgiving.

[40] Schubert, *Form*, p. 184. But against Schubert the apostle's following the Greek epistolary style at this one point can only demonstrate that, as a Jew, he was exposed to Hellenistic influences.

[41] J. A. Fitzmyer, 'New Testament Epistles', in *The Jerome Biblical Commentary*, ed. R. E. Brown, *et al.* (London, 1968), pp. 223-226, agreed with Schubert's general conclusions about Paul's following the letter style of the period. He noted that although the prayer 'resembles the Greco-Roman letter form, the sentiments uttered in it are often phrased in characteristic Jewish "eucharistic" formulas and sometimes recall the Qumran Hôdayôt' (p. 225); cf. G. Delling, *Worship in the New Testament* (ET, London, 1962), pp. 51ff.

[42] *Form*, p. 119. Note also Doty's comment about Paul's sense of freedom in literary matters, *Letters*, p. 22.

giving period, an element of great importance.[43] Its roots were not sufficiently explained by a Hellenistic epistolary form because the introductory thanksgiving was not as widespread as Schubert claimed, and since Paul's thanksgivings were recitals rather than wishes. But it is doubtful whether McFarlane has overthrown Schubert's basic point [44] that in the *form* (including the structure) and *function* of these periods Paul was following and developing the current letter style.

Thirdly, Schubert's study, as the title implied, was only an examination of the 'Form and Function' of Paul's introductory thanksgivings, and although certain exegetical issues were raised and discussed, notably the *crux interpretum* of Phil. 1:3, ἐπὶ πάσῃ τῇ μνείᾳ ὑμῶν,[45] his work was not an exegetical examination of these introductory passages. His research did not lead him to investigate the language or ideas of the thanksgiving periods, their possible background in the Old Testament or Judaism, nor the relationship of each passage to the letter it introduced.[46] Sanders was thus right when he stated that Schubert 'thoroughly cleared the ground *for further study*'.[47] McFarlane's warnings and Robinson's breaking fresh ground have been helpful in drawing attention to the wider background of Paul's thanksgivings.

Fourthly, it is undoubtedly true that Schubert has rendered a valuable service to New Testament scholarship in drawing attention to the epistolary forms and function of the introductory Pauline thanksgivings. But when due allowance is made for this formal approach, noting that the purpose of the thanksgiving periods was

---

[43] *Motif*, p. 20.

[44] Bjerkelund, *Parakaló*, has corroborated many of Schubert's conclusions. His full-scale formal study has shown that the apostle's παρακαλέω-sentences (like the εὐχαριστέω-sentences) had a literary form and function. Paul derived the form from secular rather than Jewish Greek. Bjerkelund noted that the παρακαλέω-form was found frequently in the private letters of the papyri, as well as in more official documents, where there was some degree of intimacy. Often the παρακαλέω-clause was linked with a thanksgiving period. While he frequently expressed his indebtedness to Schubert, Bjerkelund (p. 21) suggested Schubert's work had not had the influence one might have expected because he did not relate the thanksgiving periods to the παρακαλέω-sentences.

[45] *Form*, pp. 71-82. Even this detailed inquiry was to determine 'the structure of the εὐχαριστῶ-period' (p. 71).

[46] Schubert, *ibid.*, p. 183. He did, however, acknowledge the need for such research.

[47] Sanders, *loc. cit.*, p. 348; our italics.

to introduce the basic theme of the letter, it still leaves unanswered many questions about the *thanksgivings* as prayers. In drawing our attention to the literary nature of these passages Schubert has given the impression that Paul's thanksgiving reports were *mere* literary devices. One is left wondering whether Paul actually gave thanks (or offered petition) for the churches concerned at all.

We know that the apostle had the various churches on his mind and heart when he wrote his letters. As he thought about these small congregations, some of which he knew personally and others which he had heard about from the reports of his colleagues, he would give thanks to God for the various gifts they had received or the progress in Christian maturity they had made. Further, it was not unnatural to think of him as interceding for them on those very points which he raised in each of the letters. As the apostle wrote his prayers were introduced indirectly. Direct prayers were recast as wish-prayers or as prayer reports describing the thanksgivings or intercessions of the writer. It was the readers who were being addressed while references to God would occur in the third person.[48] The apostle had at hand the Greek epistolary form of introductory thanksgiving that could be suitably used, but that form has not controlled the content of these thanksgiving periods.[49]

The following suggestions, drawing upon Schubert's researches, yet adding to them and modifying them to a considerable extent, may be made :

1. The thanksgiving and petitionary prayer reports are evidence of the apostle's deep *pastoral and apostolic concern* for the addressees. This deep concern is shown not only by Paul's actual prayers but also by his telling the recipients of his thanksgivings and intercessions for them. Though strong, and on occasion even severe, words may follow in the bodies of the letters the addressees would be in no doubt about their apostle's deep love for them.

2. Paul's thanksgiving periods have a *didactic function*. It need not be assumed that the thanksgivings and intercessions described in these passages are reports of complete prayers. Perhaps they are summaries of the actual prayers which the apostle offered to God. We may assume that these summaries contain the essential points

---

[48] Cf. Wiles, *Function*, pp. 12f.

[49] The variations within the introductory thanksgiving paragraphs, in spite of the many structural similarities, make this clear.

of the petitions and thanksgivings. But whether the reports in these periods are of complete prayers or not the apostle instructs the recipients, either by way of recall to previous teaching or by fresh guidance, about what he considers to be important. In 1 Thessalonians his thanks are for the outworking of the faith, hope and love of the recipients (1:3ff.). When the letter was first read to the assembled congregation they would no doubt have been reminded of elements in the apostle's first preaching in their city. The grounds for his thanksgiving are vital issues, directly related to the gospel. So too when Paul gives thanks for the active participation of the Philippians in the ministry of the gospel, he is in fact instructing that church on a matter which he considers most important. In several of these thanksgiving passages the ultimate basis is seen to be the faithfulness of God. Thanksgiving is addressed to Him and is based on His activity in the hearts of the believers—an activity that will continue even to the parousia. If the individual congregations know that their apostle gives thanks in his own prayers along such lines, they may be sure that such issues are vital, and further, the prayer reports may serve as a model for their own giving of thanks when remembering fellow-believers before God.

A similar didactic function is to be noted in the intercessory prayer reports, found within some of these thanksgiving periods. The apostle prays that the Philippians may grow in knowledge and spiritual insight as well as abound in love (Phil. 1:9-11), for he desires to see these things take place in their experience. And by recording such petitions the readers would realize the importance of these issues—matters which their apostle utters in the presence of God.

3. Closely related to the preceding is the *paraenetic purpose* of the introductory thanksgivings. Schubert himself had noted this but did not take up the point and develop it. Further, his noting of it seems to have been prompted by his desire to show that the thanksgiving periods mentioned the basic theme or themes of the letters concerned. With one or two exceptions each of the introductory thanksgivings prefigures one or more paraenetic thrusts of the letters as they have come down to us. This is particularly, though not exclusively, true of the intercessory prayer reports within these passages. A good example of this is found in Phil. 1:9-11 : Paul's petition is for the growth in love of the Philippians (cf. 2:1-11; 4:1-3), in knowledge and discernment (cf. 4:8f.), so that they may be pure and blameless for the day of Christ (cf. 2:14-16).

4. Finally, with Schubert, we note in these periods an *epistolary function*, i.e., to introduce and indicate the main theme(s) of the letters.

In the exegetical studies of the introductory thanksgivings which follow these suggestions will be examined in order to determine what support they have from the texts themselves.

PART ONE

INTRODUCTORY THANKSGIVINGS OF
THE FIRST CATEGORY :
THANKSGIVING AND PETITIONARY PRAYER CONJOINED

CHAPTER ONE

THANKSGIVING AND JOYFUL INTERCESSION:
PHIL. 1:3-11

The first Pauline thanksgiving period to be examined, Phil. 1:3-11, occurs at the beginning of a letter which reflects the warmth of the apostle towards a congregation which over the years had remained close to him. Here is a glowing thanksgiving period that refers to Paul's sense of close fellowship with his Philippian friends. The thanksgiving report of vv. 3-6 is unusually earnest. Paul 'dwells long and fondly on the subject' [1] of his thanksgiving repeating words and accumulating clauses in the intensity of his feeling. Not only does the apostle offer heart-felt thanks to God for those who had been loyal partners with him in the gospel from the very first; he also assures them that his intercessions on their behalf are always made with joy (v. 4). So great is his longing to be reunited with them that he yearns for them with the affection of Christ Himself (vv. 7f.). Although Paul cannot be with them at the moment—he is a prisoner writing under the shadow of probable execution—he knows that God will complete the work He had begun in their lives (v. 6), and thus with this assurance the apostle prays that their 'love may abound more and more... to the glory and praise of God' (vv. 9-11).

The repetition of words and the accumulation of clauses in the paragraph make for one or two difficulties of interpretation (as Lightfoot,[2] Lohmeyer [3] and Gnilka [4] have noted). These are treated in the exegetical comments below. But there is certainly no problem in

---

[1] J. B. Lightfoot, *Saint Paul's Epistle to the Philippians* (London, ³1873), p. 80.

[2] *Ibid.*

[3] E. Lohmeyer, *Die Briefe an die Philipper, an die Kolosser und an Philemon* (Göttingen, ¹³1964; 9th edn. onwards revised by W. Schmauch, 1953), pp. 14f., saw the structure of vv. 3-6 in three double lines which were separated by participles (μετὰ χαρᾶς τὴν δέησιν ποιούμενος, and πεποιθὼς αὐτὸ τοῦτο). Each of the three double lines spanned a separate period of time—the first, vv. 3 and 4, referred to the present; the second, v. 5, pointed back to the past; while the third, v. 6, looked forward into the future. But it is generally agreed that aesthetic considerations have unduly influenced Lohmeyer's structural analysis.

[4] J. Gnilka, *Der Philipperbrief* (Freiburg-i.-Br., 1968), pp. 42ff.

deciding where the thanksgiving paragraph ends—at v. 11.[5] The period with its thanksgiving report (vv. 3-6), personal details (vv. 7f.) and intercessory prayer report (vv. 9-11) thus extends from vv. 3-11.

1. *Thanksgiving from a Full Heart: Vv. 3-6*

In this introductory thanksgiving, an example of Schubert's first category (Ia), the principal clause introduced by εὐχαριστέω, v. 3, dominates the paragraph. Gratitude to God is the thought uppermost in Paul's mind as he begins to pen this letter. His thanksgiving, like most of his other prayers, is directed to God [6] (τῷ θεῷ μου), i.e., the Father. For the apostle this is no vague or casual reference to whatever gods there might be. It is to the one true God [7] that he offers his

---

[5] This is clear for the following reasons: first, recent form-critical studies have indicated that 'the transition from the *eucharistō* period at the opening of a Pauline letter to the body of the letter is more formally structured than Schubert realized'; so Sanders, *JBL* 81 (1962), p. 348. He has shown the presence of a distinct paraenetic form (with up to seven basic elements), which was often introduced by παρακαλέω, and which was used: to introduce new material, to indicate when an argument took a new turn, or to change the subject under discussion (cf. Bjerkelund, *Parakalô*, pp. 13-23). At Phil. 1:12f. a clause in this form appears. The body of the letter has been reached and the apostle proceeded to inform his readers of the effects of his arrest on the progress of the gospel. Secondly, in many introductory thanksgivings the thought moves to an eschatological climax. It is clearly discernible here at vv. 10f. (so Schubert, *Form*, p. 4). Thirdly, the words εἰς δόξαν καὶ ἔπαινον θεοῦ are a doxology giving a fitting conclusion to the period.

[6] E. Orphal, *Das Paulusgebet* (Gotha, 1933), pp. 5-7, 147-149. He considers 131 prayers to be addressed to God, eighty-three to Christ. But Orphal casts his net too wide and includes in his list many passages which are not prayers. References are found in Harder, *Paulus*, pp. 173f. and Hamman, *Prière*, pp. 264-280, esp. pp. 264f. See also E. Delay, 'A qui s'adresse la prière chrétienne?', *RThPh* 37 (1949), pp. 189-201.

No prayer of thanksgiving is offered to Christ (except 1 Tim. 1:12, where Paul gave thanks 'für eine *besondere* Gnade, für seine Berufung zum Apostel', J. Wobbe, *Der Charis-Gedanke bei Paulus* (Münster, 1932), p. 91)—note especially the contrast in Rom. 14:6—although it is sometimes mentioned that thanksgiving is to be offered 'through Him' (when διά is always used): Rom. 1:8; 7:25; 1 Cor. 15:57 (?); Col. 3:17; see further W. Thüsing, *Per Christum in Deum* (Münster, ²1969), pp. 164ff., esp. pp. 174ff.

[7] 'Le Dieu de la prière paulinienne est le Dieu de l'Ancien Testament, Yahvé, le Dieu unique, créateur du ciel et de la terre... Les titres que Paul lui donne sont habituellement empruntés à l'Ancien Testament'; Hamman, *Prière*, pp. 265f. Von der Goltz, *Gebet*, p. 90, observes that even after his conversion Paul prayed to the same God, the God of his people; see L. Cerfaux, *Christ in the Theology of St. Paul* (ET, London, 1959), p. 515.

thanksgiving and, stressing the consciousness of a personal relation to Him, he adds the pronoun 'my' (μου).[8] This phrase, with one exception, is used by the apostle in prayers or prayer reports,[9] and he has probably drawn from the wells of the Psalter [10] for it. The person thanked for the progress of the Philippians is the God of the psalmists, known to Paul through Jesus Christ as 'Father'.

The adverb which follows, 'always' (πάντοτε),[11] modifies the principal verb εὐχαριστέω and indicates the frequency with which the apostle gave thanks. It ought to be realised, however, that by using this word 'always' Paul was not referring to unceasing prayer. To speak of prayer by this and similar terms [12] was part and parcel of the style of ancient letters.[13] A measure of hyperbole is also to be noted in the apostle's language.[14] When Paul states he gave thanks 'continually'

---

[8] Lightfoot, *Philippians*, p. 80. E. Stauffer, 'θεός' (in NT), *TDNT* 3, pp. 100-119, esp. p. 111, states : 'The countless attestations of living prayer in the NT are so many testimonies to the personal God in whom early Christianity believed'.

[9] Rom. 1:8; 1 Cor. 1:4(?); Phil. 1:3; 4:19; Phm. 4. 2 Cor. 12:21 is not in a prayer context.

[10] Pss. 3:7; 5:2; 7:1, 3, 6; 13:3; 18:2, 6, 21, 28, etc. Cf. E. Lohse, *Colossians and Philemon* (ET, Philadelphia, 1971), p. 192. Harder, *Paulus*, pp. 67f., notes that in the pagan world of Paul's day it was the practice to increase the number of names and epithets in one's address to the gods. This sprang from uncertainty and scepticism. But Paul, like the Psalter, showed restraint. The names and epithets he used were relatively few.

[11] Πάντοτε is used with εὐχαριστέω in the introductory periods at 1 Cor. 1:4; Phil. 1:4; Col. 1:3; 1 Thess. 1:2; 2 Thess. 1:3; 2:13; and Phm. 4. At Rom. 1:9 and 1 Thess. 1:2 (cf. 2:13) the synonym ἀδιαλείπτως is used probably for the sake of stylistic variety since πάντοτε also occurs. Πάντοτε is used in other prayer contexts at Rom. 1:10; Eph. 5:20; and 2 Thess. 1:11.

[12] Cf. προσκαρτερέω, Rom. 12:12; Col. 4:2; cf. Acts 2:42, 46; 6:4; ἐν παντὶ καιρῷ, Eph. 6:18; οὐ παυόμεθα, Eph. 1:16; Col. 1:9; νυκτὸς καὶ ἡμέρας, 1 Thess. 3:10; 2 Tim. 1:4 (see Delling, *Worship*, p. 111); ἀδιαλείπτως, Rom. 1:9; 1 Thess. 1:2; 2:13; 5:17; cf. ἀδιάλειπτον, 2 Tim. 1:3.

[13] It was a Jewish practice as well as a pagan one; cf. 1 Macc. 12:11. See also R. Kerkhoff, *Das unablässige Gebet* (München, 1954), who treats the subject of unceasing prayer in detail.

[14] So Harder, *Paulus*, pp. 8-19, esp. p. 9. There are, in Judaism, examples of persons spending lengthy periods of time in unbroken prayer, but that they should be singled out shows them to be rare exceptions; cf. 2 Macc. 13:12, where a man spent three days in unbroken prayer. The idea of incessant prayer in the sense of unceasing repetition of the same prayer (with the aim '*fatigare deum*') is far from Paul, though late Judaism knew the thought; b.Ber. 32a.

he means that he did not forget them in his regular times of prayer.[15] Although the customary three hours each day of Jewish prayer are to be borne in mind, it ought not to be concluded that the apostle's prayers were limited to such periods. There is evidence to suggest that Paul, like his Master, broke the confines of religious custom in the times of his prayers, as well as in the language and content.[16]

In the following words of v. 4, 'for you all' (ὑπὲρ πάντων ὑμῶν), Paul refers to the addressees about whom the thanksgiving [17] is offered. The apostle is grateful to God for the whole Philippian congregation— for all without exception. The temporal phrase and the participial clause, ἐν πάσῃ δεήσει μου ... τὴν δέησιν ποιούμενος denote the intercessory [18] prayer of the writer, the details of which are then spelled out in the ἵνα-clause of v. 9. This use of a participle indicating intercessory prayer is one of the characteristics of the first category of introductory thanksgiving (Ia). In this passage, somewhat unusually, a phrase of manner, μετὰ χαρᾶς, is added. Paul makes his petition 'with joy'.[19] And the jubilant note struck here at the beginning rings throughout the whole letter.

Next, two phrases showing the cause for Paul's thanksgiving (ἐπὶ πάσῃ τῇ μνείᾳ ὑμῶν, v. 3, and ἐπὶ τῇ κοινωνίᾳ ὑμῶν εἰς τὸ εὐαγγέλιον, v. 5), as well as the causal clause of v. 6 (πεποιθὼς αὐτὸ τοῦτο, ὅτι ...), are to be noted. Accordingly, there are three reasons why Paul thanked God for the Philippians: because of their remembrance of him, because of their fellowship in the gospel and

---

[15] The point is not 'zu jeder Zeit' but 'im jedem Gebet'; Harder, *Paulus*, p. 16. Von der Goltz, *Gebet*, pp. 102-104, considers that phrases such as ἐπὶ τῶν προσευχῶν (μου or ἡμῶν), Rom. 1:10; Eph. 1:16; 1 Thess. 1:2; Phm. 4; ἐν ταῖς προσευχαῖς, Col. 4:12; and ἐν πάσῃ δεήσει μου, Phil. 1:4; together with the adverbs of time mentioned above, all refer to the customary hours of prayer. Cf. J. Jeremias, *The Prayers of Jesus* (ET, London, 1967), p. 79.

[16] *Ibid.*, pp. 78-81.

[17] The reference is to the thanksgiving for all, rather than the intercession for all, since Paul was at that moment thinking of their good deeds; Lightfoot, *Philippians*, p. 81. Lightfoot correctly points out that there is 'a studied repetition' of the word 'all' in this epistle (cf. 1:2, 7, 25; 2:17; 4:21). 'It is impossible', he adds, 'not to connect this recurrence... with the strong and repeated exhortations to unity which the epistle contains'.

[18] Μνείαν ποιούμενος is the most common phrase used in these opening paragraphs (cf. προσευχόμενοι, Col. 1:3). Here δέησιν ποιούμενος is simply a stylistic variation, for Paul had already used μνεία (in a different sense) in v. 3.

[19] Lohmeyer, *Philipper*, p. 16, comments: μετὰ χαρᾶς in naheliegender sachlicher Beziehung, vielleicht auch in bewusstem Wortspiel auf εὐχαριστῶ'.

because he was convinced that the God who had begun a good work in them would complete it on the day of Christ Jesus.

Most *Neutestamentler* consider that in this passage the apostle spelled out *only two reasons* for the thanks which he offered to God. His first ground for thanksgiving was their fellowship in the gospel while the second was the conviction that God would complete in them the work He had begun. In other words, the phrase ἐπὶ πάσῃ τῇ μνείᾳ ὑμῶν, which we consider to be a reference to the Philippians' remembrance of Paul, is understood by most exegetes as signifying Paul's remembrance of the Philippians, particularly in his prayers. However, on grammatical, linguistic and contextual grounds (see the appended note) [20] it seems best to understand the phrase as a reference to the Philippians' remembrance of Paul by means of their monetary support on several earlier occasions. Ἐπὶ πάσῃ τῇ μνείᾳ ὑμῶν thus spells out the first of three reasons for Paul's giving of thanks.

The second ground for Paul's thanksgiving to God is found in v. 5: 'thankful for your partnership in the gospel (ἐπὶ τῇ κοινωνίᾳ ὑμῶν εἰς τὸ εὐαγγέλιον) from the first day until now'. This clause has been understood in various ways. For example, κοινωνία is taken in a passive [21] sense, and the phrase is translated 'your participation in the gospel', being almost equivalent to 'your faith'. But it seems

---

[20] See below, pp. 41-46.

[21] H. Seesemann, *Der Begriff KOINΩNIA im Neuen Testament* (Giessen, 1933), pp. 73f., 79, who champions this view, writes: 'so muss der Ausdruck κοινωνία εἰς τὸ εὐαγγέλιον ihr "Anteilhaben am Evangelium" = ihre "enge Beziehung zum Evangelium" bedeuten'. And again: 'κοινωνία εἰς τὸ εὐαγγέλιον ist also Umschreibung für "Glauben", den Paulus sonst fast regelmässig in den Dankgebeten seiner Briefeingänge erwähnt'. In support he refers to Rom. 1:8; Col. 1:4; 1 Thess. 1:3; 2 Thess. 1:3; and Phm. 5f. Seesemann, who is followed by others (e.g., F. Hauck, 'κοινός', *TDNT* 3, pp. 789-809, esp. p. 805, refers to his interpretation with approval; and G. Friedrich, *Die kleineren Briefe des Apostels Paulus: Der Brief an die Philipper* (Göttingen, [10]1965), p. 99), understands the εἰς-clause as equivalent to another genitive on the grounds that two genitives together (ἐπὶ τῇ κοινωνίᾳ ὑμῶν τοῦ εὐαγγελίου) would have been easily misunderstood; cf. Bl.-D., paras. 269 (1) and (2). Paul does not write τῇ τοῦ εὐαγγελίου but εἰς τὸ εὐαγγέλιον. Seesemann also considers that v. 6 supports his interpretation for it is an expansion of the phrase under review, rather than, as we have suggested, a separate basis for Paul's thanksgiving. A. R. George, *Communion with God in the New Testament* (London, 1953), p. 182, inclines to Seesemann's view, while R. P. Martin, *The Epistle of Paul to the Philippians* (London, 1959), p. 48, cuts the knot when he comments that 'the two main interpretations of *koinōnia* here fuse together'.

better, for several reasons,[22] to understand κοινωνία in an active sense, so that the phrase ἐπὶ τῇ κοινωνίᾳ ὑμῶν εἰς τὸ εὐαγγέλιον means 'your co-operation (in aid of) the gospel'.[23] A comparison is made with Rom. 15:26 and 2 Cor. 9:13 where κοινωνία εἰς ... is used.[24] The meaning is not to be restricted exclusively to the monetary support given by the Philippians to the apostle, but

> 'denotes co-operation in the widest sense, their participation with the Apostle whether in sympathy or in suffering or in active labour or in any other way. At the same time their almsgiving was a signal instance of this co-operation, and seems to have been foremost in the Apostle's mind'.[25]

---

[22] First, Seesemann asserts that Paul is not accustomed to give thanks for the 'achievements' of the addressees, such as financial assistance or general co-operation, in the opening paragraphs of his letters ('Paulus dankt niemals für subjektive Leistungen der angeredeten Christen, sondern er dankt stets für objektive Wirkungen Gottes an ihnen'; *op. cit.*, p. 74). But this assertion begs the question. The introductory Philippian thanksgiving may be the *one* instance where this is so. Further, at least one interpretation—indeed, the most likely one—of the bases of Paul's thanks to God in the introductory paragraph of 1 Thessalonians (1:3) is that the apostle was thankful for their 'work which sprang from faith', their 'toil which came from love', and their 'steadfastness which arose from hope'. In one sense these were achievements ('*Leistungen*') which sprang out of faith, love and hope, for which the apostle gave thanks to God. This, in principle, was no different from the Philippian thanksgiving.

Secondly, the 'passive' view treats the word εὐαγγέλιον as a reference to the content of the gospel. So Hauck, *TDNT* 3, p. 805, considers the phrase under review to designate 'the inward and undisturbed participation of the Philippians in the *saving message of Christ*' (our italics). But this is unlikely. An examination of the other instances of εὐαγγέλιον in the letter to the Philippians, i.e., chaps. 1:7, 12, 16, 27 (twice); 2:22; 4:3, 15, reveals that on most occasions, if not all, the substantive is a *nomen actionis*, describing the involvement of either Paul or the Philippians in the furtherance of the gospel. The contexts of chap. 1 suggest that this important word ought to be understood in terms of an activity directed to Gentiles. The term is not used here of the content and message of the gospel.

[23] Lightfoot, *Philippians*, p. 81; cf. M. Dibelius, *An die Thessalonicher I. II. An die Philipper* (Tübingen, ³1937), *ad loc.* N. Turner, *Grammatical Insights into the New Testament* (Edinburgh, 1965), p. 91, following M. Zerwick, *Biblical Greek* (ET, Rome, 1963), paras. 107-109, thinks we ought to take εἰς τὸ εὐαγγέλιον as something more than '*in furtherance of* the gospel'. The εἰς has the idea of movement or development towards a goal. So we ought to translate the phrase as 'fellowship *as a contribution towards* the preaching of the gospel'.

[24] Κοινωνία is often taken in an exclusively financial sense, meaning 'alms' or 'acts of charity', cf. 2 Cor. 8:4; Rom. 12:13; 1 Tim. 6:18; and Heb. 13:16. There is also evidence in the papyri to show that εἰς was used in connection with contributions and payments of accounts, e.g., 'for the rent'; MM, pp. 186f. On Paul's use of κοινωνία to refer to the collection, see K. F. Nickle, *The Collection* (London, 1966).

[25] Lightfoot, *Philippians*, p. 81; cf. J. H. Michael, *The Epistle of Paul to the*

Gnilka is right when he observes that the references to εὐαγγέλιον in this epistle show the word to be 'fast personifiziert', but he unnecessarily limits the meaning of the term here when he refers to it as the 'Akt der Verkündigung'.[26] The second reason, therefore, for Paul's thanksgiving to God was the Philippians' co-operation with him in his ministry of the gospel to Gentiles. This co-operation is to be understood in a wide sense. It is not to be restricted to monetary assistance, though this was obviously in the apostle's mind having been referred to in chap. 1:3. It probably includes the idea of their actual proclamation[27] of the gospel message to outsiders, their suffering along with Paul for the gospel's sake,[28] as well as their intercessory activity[29] on his behalf, an activity which the apostle knew they were engaged in, at the time of his writing to them.[30]

The third and ultimate ground for Paul's thanksgiving to God in this paragraph is expressed in the words of v. 6, πεποιθὼς αὐτὸ τοῦτο ὅτι κτλ. (a causal participial construction). The first two grounds stress the 'achievements' of the recipients, while the final basis emphasizes the activity of God. But there is no ultimate distinction as the following will make clear.

Philippians (London, 1928), pp. 11f. L. M. Dewailly, 'La part prise à l'Évangile (Phil., I, 5)', *RB* 80 (1973), pp. 247-260, has recently suggested that κοινωνία here has an active and dynamic quality and refers to the part (understood in a general way) the Philippians shared in the gospel up to the time of the letter's being written.

[26] *Philipperbrief*, p. 44. If Gnilka had not restricted the meaning of κοινωνία ... εἰς τὸ εὐαγγέλιον in this way but, with many other commentators, had included the notion of financial help (regardless of how he interpreted ἐπὶ πάσῃ τῇ μνείᾳ ὑμῶν of 1:3) there would have been one less reason for using drastic surgery on this epistle.

[27] Gnilka, *ibid.*, p. 45, correctly points out that one ought not to press the expression 'from the first day until now', as though the Philippians became missionaries at the very moment they believed.

[28] So P. Benoit, *Les Épîtres de S. Paul : Aux Philippiens, à Philémon, aux Colossiens, aux Éphésiens* (Paris, ³1959), ad loc. Cf. chaps. 1:30; 4:14f.

[29] W. Michaelis, *Der Brief des Paulus an die Philipper* (Leipzig, 1935), p. 13. Cf. chap. 1:19.

[30] Not only did the Philippians and Paul share the conflict and suffering; they also shared the grace of God. Paul said : 'you are partakers with me of grace' (1:7). Although the precise significance of this phrase is not certain (it is probably best to understand the μου of συγκοινωνούς μου τῆς χάριτος as an objective genitive, linked with συγκοινωνούς rather than with χάριτος. Thus, the phrase is rendered, 'you all are partakers with me of grace'; so most commentators), it seems to indicate that the Philippians shared with Paul the absolute grace of God, manifested particularly in his commission as an apostle to Gentiles (cf. Rom. 1:5; Eph. 3:2 and 8).

To express his certainty the apostle uses the perfect participle of the verb πείθω. As an example of the present perfect tense it expresses present certainty or conviction,[31] and is correctly translated by the RSV as 'I am sure'. These words are dependent on the principal verb εὐχαριστέω.[32] The αὐτὸ τοῦτο, as the object of πεποιθώς, does not point back to v. 5 as though the reason for the certainty was their past co-operation. Rather, it refers to what follows.[33] Paul gave thanks because of a certain conviction: that 'He who began a good work in you will bring it to completion at the day of Christ Jesus'.

The 'good work'[34] is to be understood in a broad sense pointing to that work of grace in their lives which began with their reception of the gospel. The reference in chap. 2:13, to God's being at work in them both to will and to work for His good pleasure, supports this. It is confirmed by other references where Paul points to the time when God's grace began to work in the lives of the converts (cf. 1 Cor. 1:4; Col. 1:5; 1 Thess. 1:5f.; Phm. 5f.), and it is particularly supported by Gal. 3:3 where the same two verbs are used,[35] the first to describe entry into the Christian life. Nevertheless, the Philippians' co-operation with the apostle in the grace of his ministry in spreading the gospel among the Gentiles was an evident sign to Paul that this good work had indeed begun. He knew of God's creative and sustaining activity through the actions displayed by them towards the progress of the gospel. In this sense, then, the third cause is related to the preceding two. The 'achievements' of the Philippians sprang out of that prior action of God among them. But their 'achievements' also demonstrated that God was currently at work in their midst.

---

[31] Bl.-D., para. 341; A. T. Robertson, *A Grammar of the Greek New Testament in the Light of Historical Research* (Nashville, 41923), p. 881; AG, p. 645.

[32] In that sense it is similar to ποιούμενος of v. 4, though the latter is a temporal participle, while πεποιθώς is causal.

[33] As in Rom. 9:17; Eph. 6:22; and Col. 4:8. At Phil. 1:6 it is an example of the recitative ὅτι introducing a clause in which the content of the certainty is specified. Yet the participle πεποιθώς describes the reason(s) Paul had in mind when he offered thanks to God. So the grammatically recitative ὅτι is logically a causal ὅτι; Schubert, *Form*, p. 45; *per contra* Bl.-D., para. 290 (4); and E. Haupt, *Die Gefangenschaftsbriefe* (Göttingen, 71902,), *ad loc.*

[34] Dibelius, *Philipper*, p. 53, sees in the phrase ἔργον ἀγαθόν a play 'auf die pekuniare Hilfeleistung'.

[35] Ἐναρξάμενοι πνεύματι νῦν σαρκὶ ἐπιτελεῖσθε; cf. J. D. G. Dunn, *Baptism in the Holy Spirit* (London, 1970), p. 108: 'ἐνάρχομαι at Gal. 3:3 and Phil. 1:6 can only refer to "the moment of becoming a Christian"'.

In selecting the verb πέποιθα—a favourite one in this epistle [36]—the apostle chose a word frequently used by the Psalmists in their prayers, and we shall not miss the mark in thinking that the prayers of the Psalter [37] have in some measure influenced the apostle. It is perhaps not without significance that there is no personal object to the verb, as though the apostle's confidence might have been placed in the Philippians' ability to continue to the end. Further, although the apostle's certainty was based on God's faithfulness, he did not use the normal Old Testament expression: πέποιθα ἐπὶ τῷ κυρίῳ. In v. 6 Paul wished to emphasize that his certainty was grounded, not on God in some general way, but on His creative and sustaining activity. This he did by using the ὅτι-clause and by designating God as ὁ ἐναρξάμενος (where the name of God is omitted).[38]

Perhaps the ideas of creation and calling, such as are found in Deutero-Isaiah, were not far from the apostle's mind. There Yahweh was spoken of as the First and the Last.[39] He was the Creator [40] not only of a 'work' that might in terms of Gen. 1 and 2 be called 'good' but also of Israel. Creation and calling were closely linked in Deutero-Isaiah, where it could be seen that the First and the Last had not only created Israel, His servant, but also called her (esp. Isaiah 44:1-6).[41] And as the First and the Last Yahweh might be relied upon to complete the work He had begun. It was with such confidence that the apostle wrote. The One who had begun the new creation, that good work in them, by calling them to Himself would bring it to completion at the day of Jesus Christ.[42]

---

[36] Apart from chap. 1:6 it is found in chaps. 1:14, 25; 2:24; 3:3 and 4.

[37] In the Psalms and later works God was regularly seen to be the One in whom the Psalmist had certainty (so in Ps. 25:2 (LXX 24), ὁ θεός μου ἐπὶ σοὶ πέποιθα; cf. Pss. 2:11; 11:1; 57:1; 118:8; 125:1, etc.). The verb πέποιθα indicating trust or conviction was never found with God as the subject. This was only possible of men. Further, the word was only used in connection with the circle of believers, binding together those who are equals 'in the Lord'; so Lohmeyer, *Philipper*, p. 19.

[38] Cf. Gnilka, *Philipperbrief*, p. 46; M. R. Vincent, *A Critical and Exegetical Commentary on the Epistles to the Philippians and to Philemon* (Edinburgh, 1897,) p. 7. Lohmeyer, *Philipper*, p. 20, as might be expected, detects a liturgical style.

[39] Isaiah 41:4; 44:6 and 48:12.

[40] Isaiah 40.20, 28; 41:20; 42:5; 43:1, 7, 15; 45:7 (twice), 8, 12, 18 (twice); 54:16 (twice); where ברא is used.

[41] See also Isaiah 42:5f.; 43:1 and 7.

[42] Cf. 1 Cor. 1:8f. and 1 Thess. 5:24, two prayer contexts where God's calling and completing work is mentioned.

It has been recognized by many that Paul's introductory thanksgivings usually end with an eschatological climax. For Schubert the eschatological note was helpful in determining, on most occasions (the introductory thanksgivings of Romans and Philemon are the only exceptions), where the thanksgiving periods ended. And it was observed above that although the limits of the Philippian thanksgiving period were clearly defined on formal grounds, the reference to the day of Christ in v. 10, with its following doxology, shows that this thanksgiving passage fits the general pattern.

However, in Phil. 1:3-11 there are two references to the 'day of Christ (Jesus)'. That in v. 10 occurs at the conclusion of the reported intercessory prayer. Paul's request to God was that they 'may be pure and blameless for the day of Christ'. The earlier instance of a parousia reference is found in v. 6, at the conclusion of Paul's actual thanksgiving: 'I am sure that he who began a good work in you will bring it to completion [43] at the day of Jesus Christ'.

It may be correctly said that the parousia underlay much of Paul's thinking. And, therefore, it would not be unusual for the subject of thanksgiving to be related to the coming of the Lord. But in Phil. 1:6 thanksgiving is not directly linked with that coming. Rather, it is based on the faithfulness of God and in particular on His ability to finish that work which He had begun. At v. 10 Paul was directly concerned with the Philippians' progress in Christian love and maturity during the remainder of this present age, while in v. 6 the stress is not so much on the Philippians' progress towards or blamelessness for that day [44] (though this thought is not entirely absent), but on the faithfulness of God in completing that good work on the day of Christ. [45]

---

[43] E. de W. Burton, *Syntax of the Moods and Tenses in New Testament Greek* (Edinburgh, ³1898), para. 60, considers ἐπιτελέσει to be a 'progressive future', i.e., the action 'will be in progress in future time'. C. F. D. Moule, *An Idiom Book of New Testament Greek* (Cambridge, 1953), p. 10, is doubtful about this. But Vincent, *Philippians and Philemon*, p. 8, is correct when he comments: 'The sense is pregnant; will carry it on toward completion, and finally complete'.

[44] *Contra* D. E. H. Whiteley, *The Theology of St. Paul* (Oxford, 1964), p. 246, who groups vv. 6 and 10 with chap. 2:16. The emphases in the two verses of the thanksgiving period are different. This point is also brought out by the different prepositions Paul used, viz., ἄχρι ἡμέρας Χριστοῦ Ἰησοῦ, 1:6, and εἰς ἡμέραν Χριστοῦ, 1:10. The latter stresses preparation and fitness for the test on the last day.

[45] W. Kramer, *Christ, Lord, Son of God* (ET, London, 1966), pp. 174-176, observes that in only three passages—all of which are in Philippians (1:6, 10; and 2:16)—is

2. Intercession for Love and Discernment: Vv. 9-11

The final element in the introductory thanksgiving of Philippians —the intercessory prayer of vv. 9ff.[46]—is the climax of the period. In vv. 7 and 8 there is an interruption. Paul no longer mentioned or reported his prayer, as he had done in vv. 3-6. Instead, he spoke directly to the church with a remarkable warmth and affection.[47] Although we know of the close relations between the apostle and the Thessalonian community and the joy which that church gave to him, the expressions in Phil. 1:7f. show a depth not plumbed elsewhere. His longing to be reunited with these converts was so great that he could say he yearned for them with the affection of Christ Himself.[48]

At v. 9 Paul took up the threads of his prayer report of vv. 3-6,[49] mentioning the content of his intercession for the Philippians. Here προσεύχομαι (v. 9) is meant to recall the words τὴν δέησιν ποιούμενος of v. 4.[50] The grammatical object of προσεύχομαι is τοῦτο, and this in

---

Christ associated with a statement about the parousia. Normally Paul uses *Lord* in such contexts.

[46] In the thanksgiving periods there is greater variety of form from this point onwards, i.e., the structures of the intercessory prayer reports show greater flexibility than those of the thanksgiving reports. These intercessory prayer reports have been recently examined by Wiles, *Prayers*, pp. 175ff.

[47] The presence of vv. 7 and 8 in this introductory thanksgiving tells against the passage as a whole being a liturgical unit. The church is addressed directly in the second person. The words are not those of a prayer report. Instead, the apostle told the Philippians about his deep affection for them.

[48] R. Bultmann, *Theology of the New Testament* 1 (ET, London, 1952), p. 222 (cf. Gnilka, *Philipperbrief*, p. 50), considers σπλάγχνα by metonymy, stands for love. Christ is expressing His love through the personality of Paul; note Lightfoot, *Philippians*, p. 83, and Martin, *Philippians*, p. 64. For a recent discussion see R. Jewett, *Paul's Anthropological Terms* (Leiden, 1971), pp. 323ff.

[49] Schubert, *Form*, p. 14. Lohmeyer, *Philipper*, p. 31, states that the request is closely joined to the preceding sentence by 'and'. But this is doubtful. Certainly the petition of vv. 9-11 may be regarded as an outlet for Paul's feelings mentioned in vv. 7f., but the καὶ τοῦτο προσεύχομαι is linked to vv. 3-6. So rightly, Friedrich, *Philipper*, p. 100; Vincent, *Philippians and Philemon*, p. 11, and K. Barth, *The Epistle to the Philippians* (ET, London, 1962), p. 20.

[50] *Contra* Schubert, *Form*, p. 14, and H. Greeven, *Gebet und Eschatologie im Neuen Testament* (Gütersloh, 1931), pp. 136ff. The former considers that προσεύχομαι is designed to recall the reader's attention to εὐχαριστέω, τὴν δέησιν ποιούμενος and πεποιθώς, as it expresses the combined meanings of these verb forms. The latter understands προσευχή and its cognate προσεύχομαι as referring to general intercourse

turn points to what follows. The ἵνα-clause expresses not the aim or purpose of Paul's praying, but rather the content of the prayer or the objects requested by the apostle in his petition.[51]

The substance of this request is that the Philippians' love may become richer and richer. The word ἀγάπη was used by the apostle in many contexts. It sometimes appeared in his thanksgiving passages, not only as the object of his intercessory prayer for his addressees but also as one of the causes or reasons for which he gave thanks.[52] On a straight count it can be seen that the apostle normally used the term and its cognates of love towards one's neighbour.[53] Some commentators have therefore understood ἀγάπη in the present context as referring to a reciprocal love of the Philippians one towards another.[54]

---

with God. But against these views it is to be noted that every instance of προσεύχομαι in the thanksgiving periods refers to petitionary prayer—it is significant that the occurrences are found only in type Ia and the mixed types. Further, the following ἵνα-clause expresses the content of the petition(s). Therefore, προσεύχομαι can only refer back to δέησιν ποιούμενος.

[51] There is no material difference between this use of the word 'object' (so C. Spicq. *Agape in the New Testament* 2 (ET, St. Louis, 1965), pp. 276-284; and H. Greeven, 'εὔχομαι', *TDNT* 2, p. 807. Lightfoot, *Philippians*, p. 84; and Vincent, *Philippians and Philemon*, p. 11, refer to the ἵνα denoting the 'purport' of the prayer, but the meaning is the same), and what is meant by 'content' when used by other commentators (cf. Lohse, *Colossians and Philemon*, p. 193, with reference to Phm. 6). However, if it is borne in mind that vv. 9-11 are not the words of the prayer as Paul actually prayed them, but a report to the Philippians about his prayer, then it is more precise to speak of the ἵνα-clause as *reporting* the content or object of the intercessory prayer.

[52] In the latter contexts it sometimes occurs as the middle member of a triad, along with πίστις and ἐλπίς; Col. 1:4f.;1 Thess. 1:3; and outside prayer passages at 1 Cor. 13:13; 1 Thess. 5:8; cf. also Rom. 5:1-5; Gal. 5:5f.; Eph. 4:2-5; see A. M. Hunter, *Paul and his Predecessors* (London, ²1961,) pp. 33ff.

[53] E. Stauffer, 'ἀγαπάω' (in NT), *TDNT* 1, pp. 50f., states: 'Paul speaks only rarely of love for God'. Rather, 'his true interest is concentrated on brotherly love... Neighbourly love, once a readiness to help compatriots in the covenant people of Israel, is now service rendered to fellow-citizens in the new people of God'.

[54] The reasons are as follows: (1) Paul did not give thanks to God for the love of the Philippians—a basis for thanksgiving found in other letters. (2) In the Philippian community there were tendencies towards disunity and fault-finding which needed to be corrected (4:1ff.). In chap. 2:1ff., where the apostle exhorted the Philippians to humility, he urged them to show love one towards another. (3) If Paul admonished the Philippians later in the letter about their lack of brotherly love, then we might have expected him to have offered earnest prayer for them on this matter. (4) It appears that Paul in this prayer was repeating the idea of 1 Thess. 3:12 where he prayed for an increase in the love of his readers, each for the other.

But here the term ἀγάπη ought not to be restricted either to love for God or love towards man. The love spoken of by the apostle is to be understood in the most comprehensive way.[55] Obviously it includes brotherly love and prepares the way for the later words of correction. But it ought not to be limited to this. There is no implied rebuke in this prayer as some have suggested. The apostle did not say that the Philippians lacked this love. His earnest desire was that it would increase to overflowing, suggesting that it was already present in their lives—even in some measure. Their gifts to him, their continued sharing with him in the spread of the gospel were clear evidences that their brotherly love had made considerable progress. Further, to suggest that there is an implied rebuke in this prayer report is to indicate that either Paul prayed to God along these lines (i.e., with a rebuke concealed in the petition—an idea which is absurd), or that his prayer report differed considerably from the actual petition itself. Neither is satisfactory when it is borne in mind that this prayer of intercession has been offered 'with joy' (μετὰ χαρᾶς, v. 4), an adverbial phrase used only in conjunction with intercessory prayer in the Philippian passage.

The strongest reasons for taking ἀγάπη in a broad sense come from the context itself. In the apostle's request of v. 9 'love' has no object,[56] although the object is clearly defined in 1 Thess. 3:12.[57] It would seem that in the Philippian passage Paul was less interested in the object of the love than its source. In addition to this the apostle's treatment went far beyond that of 1 Thess. 3:12, for in the petition under review he dealt with love's influence in the intellectual and moral sphere.[58]

The apostle used the verb περισσεύω to describe the increase of this love. It was a favourite one with him, being used on four

---

[55] So with most commentators, e.g., F. W. Beare, *The Epistle to the Philippians* (London, 1959), p. 54. Note the detailed treatment of Spicq, *Agape* 2, pp. 276-284.

[56] Lohmeyer, *Philipper*, p. 31, and Spicq, *Agape* 2, ad loc.

[57] It is 'love to one another and to all men' (RSV).

[58] Spicq, *Agape* 2, p. 277, in his definitive treatment of love in the New Testament comments on this passage: 'Verses 9, 10 and 11 of the first chapter are the New Testament's most profound and precise treatment about the influence of *agape* from the intellectual and moral point of view, in this world or in the next. Eight words show the extent of its domain: knowledge, insight, judgement, uprightness, blamelessness, holiness, glory, and praise of God'. Lohmeyer, *Philipper*, p. 31, who understands the terms in a general sense, writes: 'So sind es vermutlich überlieferte Begriffe einer besonderen missionarischen oder allgemein urchristlichen Sprache'.

occasions in this epistle.⁵⁹ It meant 'to be rich, abundant, overflow', and was applied by Paul to many aspects of Christian perfection where the idea of growth or progress was in mind. This is especially so of ἀγάπη (cf. 1 Thess. 3:12) which perhaps more than any other grace is made to grow.⁶⁰ In Phil. 1:9 Paul prayed that the love of the addressees may enter into and operate within the domain of 'knowledge and all insight'. The idea of direction is also present.⁶¹ Although the verb περισσεύω can mean 'to overflow' it does not mean this in the sense of 'beyond all measure', and so to give this elative force Paul added ἔτι μᾶλλον καὶ μᾶλλον.⁶² His earnest desire was that there be no limit to the growth or increase of the Philippians' love, and to stress the idea of continuous growth the progressive present tense, περισσεύῃ, was used.

This love was to go on increasing ἐν ἐπιγνώσει καὶ πάσῃ αἰσθήσει. The two nouns are governed by the one preposition ἐν, indicating that the love spoken of was to grow in the direction of and sphere of both knowledge and insight. Ἐπίγνωσις was used by Paul frequently in his epistles, and was an object of his intercessory prayers at the conclusion of the introductory thanksgiving periods of the four Captivity Epistles.⁶³ The term does not appear in prayer requests outside these four letters. It is a disputed point as to whether Paul intended a different meaning from γνῶσις when he used the term ἐπίγνωσις.⁶⁴ Usually ἐπίγνωσις is closely connected with 'the know-

---

⁵⁹ Phil. 1:9, 26; 4:12, 18.

⁶⁰ When περισσεύω is used intransitively of persons, the thing in which the abundance is said to consist is expressed by the genitive (Luke 15:17) or ἐν with the dative (Rom. 15:13; 1 Cor. 15:58; 2 Cor. 8:7; Col. 2:7). But when the verb is used intransitively of things and is followed by ἐν with the dative it is best to regard this as the sphere in which the thing operates; see AG, pp. 656f.; Bl.-D., para. 172; and Robertson, *Grammar*, p. 510.

⁶¹ Spicq, *Agape* 2, *ad loc.*, emphasizes the sphere, while K. Sullivan, 'Epignōsis in the Epistles of St. Paul', *Studiorum Paulinorum Congressus* 2 (Rome, 1963), p. 408, apparently following Barth, *Philippians*, p. 21, understands the prayer in terms of their love abounding and attaining its object *en epignōsei*. Michael's view, *Philippians*, p. 20, that knowledge and insight are essential elements in Christian love, does not precisely represent Paul's thought here, however true it may be.

⁶² So Bl.-D., para. 246; cf. 1 Thess. 4:9 and 10.

⁶³ Eph. 1:17; Col. 1:9f.; Phm. 6. For the significance of this, see below, pp. 85f.

⁶⁴ Various suggestions have been made concerning the function of ἐπί: that it is intensive (J. B. Lightfoot, *Saint Paul's Epistles to the Colossians and to Philemon* (London, ⁹1890), p. 136: 'The compound ἐπίγνωσις is an advance upon γνῶσις, denoting a larger and more thorough knowledge'); or directive (J. Armitage Robinson, *St Paul's Epistle*

ledge of Christ and conformity to his likeness, which, in turn, is the substance of *God's self-revelation*.⁶⁵ Bultmann considers that in many, though not all, New Testament instances, ἐπίγνωσις like its cognate ἐπιγινώκω has become 'almost a technical term for the decisive knowledge of God which is implied in conversion to the Christian faith'.⁶⁶ The theoretical element is always present—the idea of a mental grasp of spiritual truth ⁶⁷—yet it is understood that Christian knowledge carries with it a corresponding manner of life (as in Phil. 1:9ff.).

Paul's view of knowledge was largely determined by the Old Testament.⁶⁸ To know God meant to be in a close personal relationship with Him because He had made Himself known. There was the element of an obedient and grateful acknowledgement of His deeds on behalf of His people. The knowledge of God began with a fear of Him, was linked with His demands, and often was described as knowing His will. In the Old Testament, as well as in the writings of Paul, knowledge was not a fixed *quantum* but rather something that developed in the life of the people as they were obedient.⁶⁹

In Phil. 1:9 ἐπίγνωσις has neither definite article nor object, and is to be understood in the comprehensive sense ⁷⁰ of knowing God through Christ in an intimate way. The intellectual element is present, so that as love increases the knowledge of God and Christ is more penetrating.

---

to the Ephesians (London, ²1909), p. 249. His conclusion is that 'γνῶσις is the wider word and expresses "knowledge" in the fullest sense: ἐπίγνωσις is knowledge directed towards a particular object, perceiving, discerning, recognizing' (p. 254)), or that it has no special significance (R. Bultmann, 'γινώσκω', *TDNT* 1, p. 707). There seems to be no rule that will apply in all circumstances.

⁶⁵ C. F. D. Moule, *The Epistles of Paul the Apostle to the Colossians and to Philemon* (Cambridge, 1957), p. 161.

⁶⁶ *TDNT* 1, p. 707.

⁶⁷ How much the Christian vocabulary in general owes to pagan 'Gnostic' thought is a disputed point. The extant documentary evidence for Gnosticism cannot be dated earlier than Christianity with any certainty, though interestingly enough the Dead Sea Scrolls show some affinities with it. It is quite possible that Paul and other Christian writers spoke of knowledge with a reference to incipient gnosticism—not in agreement but in conscious distinction from it. Christian knowledge was not to be confined to an inner circle of the elite. Every Christian possessed it, and was to possess it in greater measure, as the object of the above-mentioned prayer makes plain.

⁶⁸ So Bultmann, *TDNT* 1, p. 707, and J. Dupont, *Gnosis* (Paris, 1949).

⁶⁹ Both Bultmann and Dupont stress this point.

⁷⁰ Lohmeyer, *Philipper*, p. 31; Spicq, *Agape* 2, p. 278.

To this intimate knowledge of God Paul added 'and all insight', πάσῃ αἰσθήσει. The love of the Philippians was to increase in this sphere also. Αἴσθησις [71] is a *hapax legomenon* in the New Testament. It might be translated 'tact' [72] as it is the capacity for practical concrete judgement. The addition of πᾶς does not indicate it is 'all discernment' (RSV) in the sense of full power of discernment. Rather, it points to insight for all kinds of situations as they arise. Paul's prayer, then, was not that some fresh elements such as knowledge and insight might be introduced into their love as though these were two separate ingredients that were lacking or deficient. The object of the prayer was that the love of God within the addressees might increase beyond all measure, and that as it increased it might penetrate more deeply into that personal relation with God through Christ as well as into all types of situations involving practical conduct.

The purpose [73] of this love increasing in knowledge and tact was that they might be able to distinguish the really important issues in their corporate lives, and to act on the basis of such distinctions. Δοκιμάζω has the meaning of 'to put to the test, examine'.[74] In particular it was used of testing metals and money. A more general use was of testing oxen for their usefulness, Luke 14:19. The verb then had reference to the result of the examination, and came to mean 'to accept as proved, approve'. Such is the meaning here. It not only includes the function of examination and evaluation but also that of choice. Τὰ διαφέροντα means not 'the things which differ', but 'the things which excel',[75] i.e., those things which differ by surpassing

---

[71] On the use of αἴσθησις outside the Bible see G. Delling, 'αἰσθάνομαι', *TDNT* 1, pp. 187f. In Proverbs, where 22 out of 27 LXX occurrences are found, αἴσθησις is that practical understanding which is keenly aware of the circumstances of an action, manifesting itself particularly in discretion of speech (Prov. 5:2; 14:7; 15:7).

[72] Martin, *Philippians*, p. 65; Gnilka, *Philipperbrief*, p. 52; E. Käsemann, *New Testament Questions of Today* (ET, London, 1969), p. 214, says it should be translated 'the feeling for the actual situation at the time'.

[73] Burton, *Moods*, para. 409, considers εἰς expresses purpose; cf. Barth, *Philippians*, p. 21, and Michael, *Philippians*, p. 22; while Spicq, *Agape* 2, p. 280, favours a consecutive interpretation. A. Oepke, 'εἰς', *TDNT* 2, p. 430, seems to prefer this because of his comment on the parallel passage, Rom. 12:2.

[74] AG, p. 201. In the LXX δοκιμάζω is regularly used of the proving of man's heart by God, e.g., Pss. 17:3 (LXX 16); 26:2 (25); 66:10 (65); Prov. 8:10; 27:21; Jer. 9:7; 11:20, etc. For a treatment of δοκιμάζω and its cognates in Paul (and particularly in Phil. 1:9-11) see G. Therrien, *Le discernement dans les écrits pauliniens* (Paris, 1973), esp. pp. 165ff.

[75] So most commentators. This participle, according to MM, p. 157, is used

others, cf. Rom. 2:18. The phrase εἰς τὸ δοκιμάζειν ὑμᾶς τὰ διαφέροντα can also be understood against the religious background of Judaism. The Jew was to choose what was essential on the basis of the Law.[76] But the Philippians who were in Christ were to make such choices [77] on the basis of an ever increasing love—a love which penetrated more deeply into the knowledge of God and the treasures of Christ, and imparted to the Christian a keener and more delicate moral sense for specific situations.

The second ἵνα-clause of the prayer report (v. 10) is probably to be understood in terms of both purpose and result.[78] Paul's prayer dealt with fitness and preparedness for the second coming. It was that they might be 'pure' or 'sincere' on the positive side [79] as well as 'blameless' on the negative side.[80] As their love increased, enabling them to choose what was vital, so they would be ready for the day of Christ.

The preposition εἰς used by Paul in the phrase εἰς ἡμέραν Χριστοῦ does not simply denote a time limit meaning 'until'. It is better to translate it 'in view of' or 'against' the day of Christ, since the ideas of preparation for the scrutiny of that great day as well as the ability to stand its test are suggested by the word in this context.[81] Paul's prayer indeed spanned the present age, but its aim was that the Philippians would not only *reach* the final day, but also that they might *be pleasing* to God on the occasion of the great assize.

The final object of Paul's intercessory prayer is found in v. 11: 'that you may be filled [82] with the fruit of righteousness which comes

---

specifically in one of the papyri in the sense of 'essential' or 'vital' (cf. Moffatt's translation 'a sense of what is vital').

[76] Lohmeyer, *Philipper*, p. 32, stresses this.

[77] In v. 10 the subject changes from ἀγάπη to 'you', i.e., the Philippian Christians.

[78] Spicq, *Agape* 2, p. 276, however, regards the second ἵνα as introducing another object of the prayer; cf. Wiles, *Prayers*, p. 210.

[79] In the New Testament εἰλικρινής is used only here and in 2 Peter 3:1. The cognate noun is found in 1 Cor. 5:8; 2 Cor. 1:12; 2:17. Both the adjective and the substantive denote moral purity, hence the translation 'pure' or 'sincere'; cf. Lohmeyer, *Philipper*, p. 33, and F. Büchsel, 'εἰλικρινής', *TDNT* 2, pp. 397f.

[80] 'Απρόσκοπος can be understood transitively 'not causing others to stumble' (cf. 1 Cor. 10:32, and note Rom. 14:20f.), or intransitively 'without stumbling' (Acts 24:16). Chrysostom takes it in both senses. If the former is correct then the reference is to the influence on others for good.

[81] So Vincent, *Philippians and Philemon*, p. 14; Michael, *Philippians*, p. 24.

[82] Beare, *Philippians*, p. 55, takes the participle as a middle and translates: 'Bringing forth a full harvest'; cf. NEB, 'reaping the full harvest of righteousness'. But most

through Jesus Christ'. Although some exegetes consider the statement defines the 'pure and blameless' of v. 10 more fully,[83] and while there is much to be said in favour of this, our preference is to understand the words as parallel with 'pure and blameless'.[84] 'Filled with the fruit of righteousness' is not a further definition of 'pure and blameless' but a quality or characteristic that the apostle wishes to see in the Philippians together with purity and blamelessness. The adjectives εἰλικρινεῖς and ἀπρόσκοποι point to an all-round fitness and preparedness for the last day. But Paul desires that they not only be acquitted; he also prays that they may be filled with a crop of godly deeds and actions—the result of a right relationship with God.

Commentators have differed in their interpretation of καρπὸν δικαιοσύνης. There are basically two alternatives: to understand righteousness itself as the fruit, i.e., fruit which consists in being right with God; or, to take fruit as referring to ethical characteristics (which are described in Gal. 5:22) that are evidence of such a right relationship. Many commentators interpret δικαιοσύνης as a genitive of definition: the Philippians are to bring forth righteousness.[85] The qualifying phrase, τὸν διὰ Ἰησοῦ Χριστοῦ, appears at first sight to support this view. Our preference, however, is to interpret καρπὸν δικαιοσύνης along the lines of the 'fruit of the Spirit' (Gal. 5:22), i.e., the display of ethical qualities such as love joy, peace, longsuffering, etc.[86] Paul's emphasis here is that such a crop can only be given and produced through Jesus Christ.

---

commentators, and grammarians such as Bl.-D., para. 159 (1); Robertson, *Grammar*, pp. 483, 485; and N. Turner, *Syntax*, Vol. 3 of J. H. Moulton, *A Grammar of New Testament Greek* (Edinburgh, 1963), p. 247, do not see any real difficulty in the accusative case with the passive. The verb 'to fill' does in fact occur with the accusative rather than the genitive in the LXX; Exod. 31:3.

[83] Vincent, *Philippians and Philemon*, p. 14; and Gnilka, *Philipperbrief*, p. 53.

[84] Michael, *Philippians*, p. 25: 'Grammatically the words are parallel with *transparent and no harm to anyone*'.

[85] E.g., Michaelis, *Philipper, ad loc.*; P. Ewald, *Der Brief des Paulus an die Philipper* (revised by G. Wohlenberg) (Leipzig, 4/1923), *ad loc.*; G. Schrenk, 'δικαιοσύνη', *TDNT* 2, p. 210; and Gnilka, *Philipperbrief*, p. 53, understand it as either a genitive of apposition or a qualifying genitive. Cf. Barth, *Philippians*, p. 22.

[86] J. A. Ziesler, *The Meaning of Righteousness in Paul* (Cambridge, 1972), pp. 151 and 203, interprets the phrase along these lines (i.e., as a genitive of origin), because of its meaning at Prov. 11:30; Amos 6:13 and Jas. 3:18. Michael, *Philippians*, p. 25, though understanding the fruit in terms of ethical characteristics considers the Old Testament use of this phrase to be of no help in interpreting this passage; *per contra* Lohmeyer, *Philipper*, p. 34.

The first half of the ἵνα-clause in v. 10 looks forward to the future state of the Philippians at the day of Christ. The clause of v. 11 has a side-glance at the parousia, for Paul's prayer is that they may be *filled* with these godly Christian virtues—an activity only completed on the last day. But the object of this section of the prayer relates primarily to their present experience.[87] Paul prayed along such lines for he desired that in the present they might be of one mind, in humility count others better than themselves, do things without grumbling and questioning, have love for one another, and follow those things that are lovely, just and worthy of praise. These are some of the elements in the 'fruit of righteousness'.

The apostle Paul began the thanksgiving period with the report of a prayer of thanks to God. In vv. 9-11 it passed over to an intercessory prayer for the Philippians. The prayer report is then closed in a typical Jewish and Christian fashion with a doxology (or more accurately with the report of a doxology), using the words εἰς δόξαν καὶ ἔπαινον θεοῦ.[88] These final words have the impress of liturgical style, and do not simply apply to the final words of Paul's intercessory prayer.[89] Instead they are to be seen as the fitting conclusion to the entire thanksgiving period, i.e., vv. 3-11. The apostle concluded his prayer report on a note of praise.

3. Concluding Remarks

The introductory thanksgiving of Phil. 1:3-11 consists of a thanksgiving report (vv. 3-6), an intercessory prayer report (vv. 9-11) and a deep, warmhearted statement of the apostle's concern for the addressees (vv. 7, 8). Expressions of thanksgiving, personal affection, pastoral concern, supplication and praise are all closely woven together in a paragraph which introduces the mood and style of what is to come.[90]

The *epistolary purpose* of the thanksgiving period, then, is clearly in evidence. Although the paragraph arises naturally out of the situation of apostle and congregation it functions as a prologue setting

---

[87] Martin, *Philippians*, pp. 66f.

[88] Note the discussion in Thüsing, *Per Christum*, pp. 181ff.

[89] So most commentators. Doxologies are frequently used at the conclusion of Old Testament and Jewish prayers: 2 Sam. 22:50; Pss. 21:13; 35:28; 41:13, etc. Note the use of the phrase at 1 QSb 4:25.

[90] Wiles, *Prayers*, p. 204; cf. Jewett, *Terms*, p. 21.

the tone and anticipating some of the major themes and motifs which bind the whole letter together.[91] Thus, for example, the note of joy [92] which rings throughout the epistle (χαίρω is used at 1:18; 2:17f., 28; 3:1; 4:4 (twice), 10; χαρά at 1:25; 2:2, 29; 4:1) has already been struck in the opening words of the prayer report where Paul mentions his 'joyful' intercession for the addressees (1:4). The intimate sense of fellowship Paul has with his friends at Philippi, which becomes clear as the letter proceeds, is already evident in the thanksgiving report (vv. 4-6) and the statement about his earnest longing to be reunited with them (vv. 7f.). Didactic and paraenetic themes (see the following discussion) are prefigured in vv. 3-11, while a reference to the financial help the Philippians had given to Paul, certainly one important reason why the letter was written, is made in the phrase ἐπὶ τῇ κοινωνίᾳ ὑμῶν κτλ. (1:5), even if it has not already been alluded to, as we have suggested, at v. 3, ἐπὶ πάσῃ τῇ μνείᾳ ὑμῶν. Such help was bound up with the proclamation of the gospel—a point which the apostle develops more fully in chap. 4:10-20.

The *didactic thrust* of the paragraph and its *paraenetic function*, as might be expected, are closely related. For Paul the anticipation of significant theological ideas in Phil. 1:3-11 and the prefiguring of exhortatory thrusts cannot ultimately be separated even if for the sake of convenience we may distinguish them. Theology and ethics are inter-related. Where themes of the first are anticipated we might expect the same of the second, and such indeed is the case. Important theological terms, some of which seem to have been part and parcel of Paul's missionary preaching, are prefigured in the opening para-

---

[91] The question as to whether Philippians is a single letter or an editorial compilation cannot be discussed here in detail. Various anomalies (e.g., the sudden break and change of tone at 3:1ff.; the contrast between 1:15-18 and 3:2f., 18f.; the break after 4:9; and the apparent delay in Paul's acknowledgement of the Philippians' gift) have given rise to several different theories about the letter's composition. Interestingly enough the major themes of the thanksgiving can be parallelled in *all parts* of the letter as it has come down to us. Wiles, *Prayers*, pp. 195ff., having surveyed the problem of the letter's integrity, concluded: 'none of the difficulties raised against accepting the epistle as a unity appear to be insurmountable, nor does the evidence seem sufficient to bear the burden of proof for dividing the letter' (p. 197). For the literature and a survey of the debate see the standard introductions as well as T. E. Pollard, 'The Integrity of Philippians', *NTS* 13 (1966-1967), pp. 57-66; R. Jewett, 'The Epistolary Thanksgiving and the Integrity of Philippians', *NovT* 12 (1970), pp. 40-53; and Wiles.

[92] Note too the related motif of assurance or confidence which occurs first in the thanksgiving report (1:6) and then in the body of the letter at chaps. 1:14, 25; 2:24; 3:3 and 4.

graph, chap. 1:3-11. So the word εὐαγγέλιον, which is used to describe a preaching activity directed to Gentiles (as such the word is a *nomen actionis*), rather than the content of the message, occurs twice in the period (vv. 5 and 7) and then turns up a further seven times (1:12, 16, 27 (twice); 2:22; 4:3, 15). The opening references in the thanksgiving paragraph prepare the way for the further treatment in chap. 1:12f. and so on. The theme of fellowship or partnership, a significant theological motif in the epistle, is mentioned in Paul's thanksgiving report (κοινωνία, 1:5) to denote Philippian co-operation with the apostle in his ministry of the gospel to Gentiles (cf. συγκοινωνός, 1;7). The ideas reappear in the body of the letter to denote the Philippian participation in the Spirit (κοινωνία πνεύματος, 2:1)—as such it is one of the bases for Paul's exhortatory appeal for unity and humility—and to signify Paul's fellowship in Christ's sufferings (3:10), as well as Philippian partnership in giving and receiving (συγκοινωνέω, 4:14; κοινωνέω, 4:15). References to the day of Jesus Christ have appeared in both the thanksgiving and intercessory prayer reports (1:6, 10), suggesting that the apostle was concerned about the Philippians' accountability on that final day (cf. 2:15f.; 4:1). The motif of righteousness [93] is touched upon in v. 11 of the intercessory prayer report and then turns up again, with varying meanings, at chap. 3:6ff. Thus, some of the theological ideas, mentioned in the opening paragraph, are taken up and expounded in the body of the letter. By way of recall to teaching previously given or by fresh instruction Paul informed the recipients of things he considered 'vital' (τὰ διαφέροντα, 1:10).

The intercessory prayer report, in particular, has a *paraenetic or exhortatory function* and points the way to themes in the letter which follow. Paul was concerned that the Philippians show love towards one another for personal discords had arisen between members of the church (cf. 2:1ff.; 4:2ff.). His request to God that their love might increase beyond all measure (1:9ff.) while emphasizing the source of the love and its comprehensiveness nevertheless includes the notion of brotherly love. In Paul's intercessory prayer report there is a heavy emphasis on knowledge (ἐπίγνωσις, v. 9) and discernment or the ability to choose the things that are vital (εἰς τὸ δοκιμάζειν ὑμᾶς τὰ διαφέροντα, v. 10); in other words the Philippians are to have a right Christian mental attitude to the things around them. The Jew might

---

[93] The term καρπός which occurs at chap. 1:11 turns up again at chaps. 1:22 and 4:17.

choose what was essential on the basis of the attainable standards of the Law—and the antagonists of the Philippians may well have pressed this point. However, the addressees were to make such choices on the basis of an ever-increasing love, a love which penetrated more deeply into the knowledge of God and the treasures of Christ. Paul knows this secret of judging what is vital,[94] as he later points out: 'For his sake I have suffered the loss of all things... But one thing I do... I press on toward the goal for the prize of the upward call of God in Christ Jesus' (3:8, 13f.). He now prays that his Philippian friends may choose what is vital, and he anticipates his later exhortations of chap. 2:5 and esp. chap. 4:8f. where the addressees are encouraged to follow those things which are honourable, just, pure and holy.

In the light of the abovementioned remarks the *pastoral care* of Paul for the Philippians stands out clearly. Not only is this so in vv. 7f. where the expressions show a depth not plumbed elsewhere in the *corpus Paulinum* as he tells the addressees that his desire to be reunited with them is so great that he yearns for them with the affection of Christ Himself, but also in the actual thanksgiving where the intensity of feeling is clear from the repetition of words and the accumulation of phrases. Indeed, this thanksgiving is the fullest one found in these periods. His pastoral care shines forth at every point in the intercessory prayer as the apostle looks forward to the day of Christ, when the Philippians will stand 'pure and blameless, filled with the fruit of righteousness'.

Concerning Paul's *actual prayers* of thanksgiving and petition it is noted that the latter springs out of the former. This has been demonstrated above, grammatically and exegetically, and although the intercessory prayer of vv. 9-11 is the outlet of Paul's feelings as expressed in vv. 7f., it is linked with and based upon the thanksgiving of vv. 3-6. According to the exegesis above the adverbial phrase of v. 3 (ἐπὶ πάσῃ τῇ μνείᾳ ὑμῶν) mentions the most specific reason for Paul's thanks—a reference to the gift of money. Its meaning would have been clear and unmistakable to the recipients of the letter. The second ground for Paul's thanksgiving (ἐπὶ τῇ κοινωνίᾳ ὑμῶν εἰς τὸ εὐαγγέλιον, v. 5) has a wider reference, including the concrete instances in its scope, while the third basis (πεποιθὼς αὐτὸ

---

[94] Wiles, *Prayers*, p. 210.

τοῦτο, ὅτι..., v. 6), rises to the heights of eschatological hope for the full perfection of the Philippians. These three causal phrases form a well-rounded unit and move to a climax. The last reason is the ultimate ground showing that Paul's thanksgiving is based on the faithfulness of God, a basis which will be discerned in other prayers of thanksgiving of the apostle.

Paul has expressed his confidence in God's creative and sustaining work. He is sure that the One to whom he gives thanks will bring to completion, on the day of Christ, that work which He has begun. He then intercedes along these lines with the day of Christ in mind. These requests are ultimately based on the faithfulness of God. But so was his thanksgiving. And in each he looks forward to the parousia. In the thanksgiving he anticipates that day when God will finish His work. In the intercessory prayer he looks forward to the day of Christ, when the Philippians will stand 'pure and blameless, filled with the fruit of righteousness'.

Although Paul's prayers prefigure thrusts of a paraenetic and didactic nature, they are broader in scope, particularly the intercessory prayer, than the Philippians' immediate needs. Ἀγάπη, as has been shown, is to be understood comprehensively with an emphasis on the source of the love. It includes the aspect of brotherly love, but is wider in scope than this. Ἐπίγνωσις, too, as Lohmeyer pointed out, has no object and is to be understood in a comprehensive sense of knowing God through Christ in an intimate way.

Two observations may be made about Paul's prayers for the Philippians: first, they spring directly out of the needs of the Philippian congregation (as the apostle understood them). But his intercessions are not restricted to these necessities. The requests catch up the particular needs within a broader framework. The apostle is concerned not simply about the deficiencies of the moment but the Philippians' full maturity in Christ, a life consistent with the gospel and a fitness and perfection for the last day, as well.

Appended Note

The Meaning of Phil. 1:3, ἐπὶ πάσῃ τῇ μνείᾳ ὑμῶν

In the exegesis above it was suggested that the phrase, ἐπὶ πάσῃ τῇ μνείᾳ ὑμῶν, of Phil. 1:3 was to be understood as a cause or ground for Paul's thanksgiving (and so translated 'for all your remembrance of me'), rather than as a temporal expression denoting the frequency with which Paul prayed (= 'on every remembrance of you', i.e., in my prayers). Most exegetes, however, accept the temporal understanding of the phrase and so the reasons for taking a different line need to be set forth.

In the modern period T. Zahn and A. von Harnack [95] seem to have been the first to put forward the causal view. James Moffatt's translation reads 'for all your remembrance of me', but J. H. Michael in the Moffatt Commentary, while arguing that this could be the correct rendering and admitting that it 'gives excellent sense',[96] disagreed with the translation on the grounds that it did not represent Paul's meaning, being inconsistent with his use of μνεία in the other introductory thanksgivings. Schubert examined the point in detail in 1939 giving lengthy reasons for the causal interpretation,[97] but by and large this has been neglected or simply dismissed.

The *temporal* [98] understanding of the phrase ἐπὶ πάσῃ τῇ μνείᾳ ὑμῶν has been accepted by scholars on one or more of the following grounds: (1)' *Ἐπί* with the dative is to be understood as meaning 'at' or 'in', in a predominantly temporal sense.[99] (2) The phrase ἐπὶ πάσῃ τῇ μνείᾳ ὑμῶν cannot mean 'on every remembrance' pointing to isolated intermittent acts, for to express this Paul would have omitted the article and written ἐπὶ πάσῃ μνείᾳ ὑμῶν.[100] (3) It is considered that ὑμῶν as a subjective genitive with μνεία is against usage, and 'would require

---

[95] T. Zahn preferred the causal view in his *Introduction to the New Testament* 1 (ET, Edinburgh, 1909), pp. 529 and 534, and drew attention to his treatment of the passage in *Zeitschrift für kirchliche Wissenschaft und kirchliches Leben* 6 (Leipzig, 1885), pp. 185-202, esp. p. 185. A. von Harnack, in a review article of E. Loening's *Die Gemeindeverfassung des Urchristenthums* (Halle, 1889) in *TLZ* 14 (1889), cols. 417-429, esp. col. 419, argued in favour of the causal interpretation, because of the epistolary situation and especially because of the proximity of ἐπισκόποις καὶ διακόνοις to ἐπὶ πάσῃ τῇ μνείᾳ ὑμῶν. Ewald, *Philipper, ad loc.*, took the same view. More recently Turner, *Insights*, p. 91, allowed the possibility of ὑμῶν being objective or subjective, or both! See his comment on p. 207 of his *Syntax*.

[96] *Philippians*, p. 10.

[97] *Form*, pp. 71-82. In the following discussion I am indebted to many of Schubert's insights.

[98] I.e., taking ὑμῶν as an objective genitive so that the phrase has reference to Paul's remembrance of the Philippians in his prayers.

[99] Bl.-D., para. 235 (5). G. B. Winer, *A Grammar of the Idiom of the New Testament* (ET, Philadelphia, ⁷1872), p. 392, notes that ἐπί in Phil. 1:3 has reference to time. But the interpretation is contradicted on the following page.

[100] Lightfoot, *Philippians*, p. 80.

a definite mention of the object of remembrance'.[101] (4) The thought that Paul is moved to remembrance *only* because of the exhibition of their care for him is regarded as unsuitable.[102] So the temporal interpretation is preferred. (5) If a causal explanation is followed then its position is unusual and there are too many causal modifiers dependent on the principal verb εὐχαριστέω. The sentence is unnecessarily overloaded.

But these arguments are not as strong as they appear. (1) Although ἐπί is used in a temporal sense in the opening Pauline thanksgivings, on each occasion the case which follows the preposition is the genitive.[103] Conversely, ἐπί is used with the dative case on three other occasions in these passages, and in each instance the phrase is used in a causal sense.[104] The examples are : 1 Cor. 1:4, 'I give thanks to God always for you because of the grace of God (ἐπὶ τῇ χάριτι τοῦ θεοῦ) which was given you in Christ Jesus'; 1 Thess. 3:9, 'For what thanksgiving can we render to God for you, for all the joy which we feel for your sake (ἐπὶ πάσῃ τῇ χαρᾷ ᾗ χαίρομεν δι᾽ ὑμᾶς) before our God?'; and finally in the Philippian thanksgiving period itself, v. 5, 'thankful for your partnership in the gospel (ἐπὶ τῇ κοινωνίᾳ ὑμῶν εἰς τὸ εὐαγγέλιον), from the first day until now'. To my knowledge the causal interpretation of the above three passages has never been in dispute. Equally relevant is the fact that in extra-Biblical Hellenistic sources the construction εὐχαριστέω ἐπί τινι is the most commonly used prepositional phrase to express the cause for which thanks are offered.[105] Indeed, when ἐπί with the dative is used after εὐχαριστέω it *always* expresses the ground for thanksgiving.[106]

(2) Lightfoot's contention, that the phrase ἐπὶ πάσῃ τῇ μνείᾳ does not mean 'on every remembrance' pointing to isolated intermittent acts because of the presence of the article after πᾶς, is open to question. Admittedly most grammarians agree with Lightfoot that when πᾶς

---

[101] This objection was brought forward by Vincent, *Philippians and Philemon*, p. 6.
[102] *Ibid*.
[103] Ἐπὶ τῶν προσευχῶν μου (or ἡμῶν) in Rom. 1:10; Eph. 1:16; 1 Thess. 1:2; and Phm. 4.
[104] Zerwick, *Greek*, para. 126, cf. p. 184.
[105] E.g., Philo : *Heres* 31; *Spec*. I. 67, 283, 284; II. 185; Josephus : *Ant*. I. 193; Perg. Inscr. 224A, 14; *UPZ* 59, 10f.; Hermas Simil. 9 : 14:3; cf. Schubert, *Form*, pp. 77, 129, 141, 166. Περί τινος, ὑπέρ τινος and ἔν τινι are found to express cause on only a few occasions.
[106] I know of no instance in the extra-Biblical Hellenistic sources where ἐπί τινι after εὐχαριστέω indicates anything other than the cause for thanksgiving.

means '*every* it is used with an anarthrous noun',[107] but the distinction between an anarthrous and an articular noun with πᾶς in the New Testament is not very clear.[108] At 2 Cor. 1:4 Blass-Debrunner translate ἐπὶ πάσῃ τῇ θλίψει ἡμῶν (where a contrast with τοὺς ἐν πάσῃ θλίψει is in mind) as 'all tribulation actually encountered'. Schubert relates their interpretation of 2 Cor. 1:4 to Phil. 1:3, and renders the latter: 'I thank God for every (actual) expression of your remembrance of me'.[109] Thus, there is an allusion to the recent money gift as well as to their help on previous occasions.[110] Now while the evidence for this interpretation is not conclusive, it may be allowed as possible because of the imprecise use of the article with πᾶς in the New Testament. At least the temporal interpretation is not demanded, and if other arguments for the causal view prove weighty then this may be regarded as supplementary evidence.

(3) The third reason for rejecting the causal interpretation concerns ὑμῶν when used with μνεία. Vincent considers: 'To make ὑμῶν the subjective genitive "your thought of me", with an allusion to their gift, is against usage, and would require a definite mention of the object of remembrance'.[111] But against this the following points are to be noted: first, although μνεία in the sense of 'remembrance' (not with the meaning 'mention' when used with ποιεῖσθαι, for in such a phrase the genitive is always objective) is usually found with the objective genitive of the person, on occasion a subjective genitive appears.[112] 'Your remembrance of me' would not be wholly against usage. Secondly, it is not obvious, with Vincent, why there should have been any definite mention of the object of remembrance. The allusion would have been quite clear to Paul and his addressees, the Philippians. So whatever way ὑμῶν is construed, subjective or objective, the adverbial phrase is allusive and suggestive rather than explicit. Other points, therefore, must be brought into consideration.

(4) Paul's being moved to remembrance only because of the Philippians' care for him is considered unsuitable. But this is *not the*

---

[107] Moule, *Idiom Book*, p. 93. However, Moule has no discussion of 2 Cor. 1:4.

[108] Turner, *Syntax*, p. 200.

[109] *Form*, p. 74; cf. Bl.-D., para. 275 (3).

[110] L. Morris, 'Καὶ ἅπαξ καὶ δίς', *NovT* 1 (1956), pp. 205-208, has demonstrated on philological grounds that in Phil. 4:16 Paul referred to *several* gifts of money sent to him at Thessalonica.

[111] *Philippians and Philemon*, p. 6.

[112] Bar. 5:5 is an example of the subjective genitive with μνεία; Schubert, *Form*, p. 80.

only reason for which the apostle gave thanks to God. He was thankful for their concern for him (tangibly expressed in their gifts), because of their participation in the gospel, and because he was convinced God's work in their lives would be brought to fruition. No exegete who takes the adverbial phrase in a causal sense suggests that this is the only reason for which the apostle gave thanks.[113] Instead, ἐπὶ πάσῃ τῇ μνείᾳ ὑμῶν expresses the first of three grounds for thanksgiving to God.

(5) Some consider that if ἐπὶ πάσῃ τῇ μνείᾳ ὑμῶν is understood causally, there would be too many causal modifiers dependent on the principal verb, εὐχαριστέω, making the sentence unnecessarily clumsy. But if the clause is interpreted in a temporal sense there is an accumulation of temporal phrases in direct succession (viz., ἐπὶ πάσῃ τῇ μνείᾳ ὑμῶν; πάντοτε; ἐν πάσῃ δεήσει μου and μετὰ χαρᾶς τὴν δέησιν ποιούμενος), making the sentence even more clumsy. On the causal interpretation, however, although there are three causal elements dependent on the principal verb εὐχαριστέω, they do not accumulate; instead they are well balanced.[114]

(6) The circumstances of the letter. It has been thought by many that one of the reasons for Paul's writing his letter to the Philippians was to acknowledge the gift of money which he had received from this church at the hands of Epaphroditus. This transaction is explicitly referred to in chap. 4:10-20. That it should have appeared so late in the letter, as well as the delay in sending it, has posed a problem which New Testament exegetes have tried to solve in various ways. One suggestion is that this section, chap. 4:10-20, is a fragment of another letter sent to thank the Philippians for their gift soon after the arrival of Epaphroditus. This letter of thanks, minus the salutation, was then attached to a copy of the letter despatched with Epaphroditus on his return to Philippi. But as noted above [115] it is not necessary to resort to such hypotheses. There are

---

[113] On grammatical grounds alone it is necessary to interpret ἐπὶ τῇ κοινωνίᾳ ὑμῶν κτλ. in a causal sense, regardless of how πεποιθὼς αὐτὸ τοῦτο be understood.

[114] Schubert considered that if the phrase was taken in a temporal sense it 'would be the *only major* structural peculiarity within the entire syntactical area (sc. of the Pauline thanksgivings)..., comprising both types Ia and Ib'. This he considers is 'decisive' against its being so understood; *ibid.*, p. 74. Jewett, *NovT* 12 (1970), pp. 40-53, follows Schubert in taking ἐπὶ πάσῃ τῇ μνείᾳ ὑμῶν in a causal sense; cf. Martin, *Philippians*, pp. 59f.

[115] See p. 38.

many verbal parallels between the introductory thanksgiving (1:3-11) and this section where Paul thanks the Philippians for their gifts (4:10-20).[116] If in the latter section, where there was specific reference to the financial assistance, particular terms and ideas are found, it does not seem unreasonable to assume that where those terms and ideas have been introduced (1:3-11) there was an anticipatory reference to the gift of money.

Furthermore, although it has been suggested that the apostle gave thanks for the financial help, it is not considered that this was the most important reason for his thanksgiving. In the concluding section, chap. 4:10-20, although Paul was appreciative of the manifold help the Philippians had rendered to him, he politely told them that he had learned in whatever circumstances he found himself to be content.[117] Ultimately he did not seek any gift of money that may have provided a continuous supply of food for him (4:17). He was more concerned about the spiritual growth of the Philippians. Thus the allusion to the gift in chap. 1:3 prepares the way for the more detailed treatment in chap. 4:10-20.

---

[116] Cf. the following references: chap. 1:3 with 4:10 and 18; chap. 1:5 with 4:14, 15; chap. 1:7 with 4:10, 14 and 15.

[117] These verses show a certain tenseness on the apostle's part, but perhaps this is due to reserve or even embarrassment over money matters in general. We need not resort to the suggestions of Michael, *Philippians*, p. 209, that Paul was clearing up resentment on the Philippians' part, brought about through something that he had written in the 'first letter of thanks'.

CHAPTER TWO

THANKSGIVING AND INTERCESSION FOR AN INDIVIDUAL: PHM. 4-6

The thanksgiving passage of the letter to Philemon, vv. 4-6, as might be expected, is the shortest of all in the Pauline corpus. It comprises a mere forty-seven words, and is approximately one seventh of the letter. This thanksgiving period is short, not only because Philemon [1] is the briefest of all the Pauline letters, but also because it is formally and functionally more closely related [2] to the ordinary private and personal letters [3] of the time—related in a way that the other letters in the Pauline corpus,[4] addressed either to communities or groups of communities, are not.

---

[1] B. Rigaux, *The Letters of St. Paul* (ET, Chicago, 1968), p. 118, on the basis of v. 19, considers the letter to Philemon to have been the only one penned by Paul himself, while W. G. Kümmel, *Introduction to the New Testament* (ET, London, 1966), p. 178, interprets the verse as a reference to the apostle's own autograph (cf. 1 Cor. 16:21; Gal. 6:11; Col. 4:18; 2 Thess. 3:17), which authenticated the letter.

[2] The thanksgiving passages in the papyrus letters are generally briefer than those in the Pauline letters.

[3] Most scholars have recognized that Philemon stands near the ancient private letter; so P. Wendland, *Die urchristlichen Literaturformen* (Tübingen, ².³1912), pp. 280f.; note also J. L. White's work cited by Doty, *Letters*, p. 22. This fact, however, does not indicate that the letter is purely a piece of private correspondence; cf. O. Roller, *Das Formular der paulinischen Briefe* (Stuttgart, 1933), p. 147. Kümmel, *Introduction*, p. 176, states that Philemon is 'like Paul's longer epistles, no private correspondence, but the fruits of early Christian missionary work'. See also A. Suhl, 'Der Philemonbrief als Beispiel paulinischer Paränese', *Kairos* 15 (1973), pp. 267-279.

[4] The precise nature of the letter to Philemon and the reasons for its inclusion in the canon have been the subject of discussion among scholars for some time—not least since 1935 when Professor John Knox published his important little book, *Philemon among the Letters of Paul* (Chicago). Knox considered that Philemon was included in the Pauline corpus by one who played a prominent part in its publication—Onesimus, the runaway slave mentioned in this letter who, according to tradition, later became bishop of Ephesus.

The letter, according to Knox, was addressed primarily to Archippus, Onesimus' owner. It is he rather than Philemon who is referred to in the second person singular from vv. 4 to 24 of the letter, for it was in Archippus' house that the church met. Philemon was overseer of the churches of the Lycus valley. He lived at Laodicea and

Furthermore, this thanksgiving passage is most simple in form. It is not fully developed, having no pronominal phrase (such as ὑπέρ σου), while there is only one causal participial clause (ἀκούων σου τὴν ἀγάπην κτλ.), and but one object of intercessory prayer (v. 6).

Most commentators treat the passage under review as extending from vv. 4-7,[5] with Paul's request in connection with Onesimus

---

Paul arranged that the letter should reach Philemon first. The latter would then use his influence with Archippus to ensure that Onesimus be released from slavery and be free to assist Paul in his ministry.

In spite of Knox's many penetrating insights (esp. his comments concerning the reason for the epistle's inclusion in the canon, and whether or not Paul's request for/concerning Onesimus was accepted), his thesis has not found general acceptance among New Testament scholars (partial agreement with Knox has been expressed by H. Greeven, 'Prüfung der Thesen von J. Knox zum Philemonbrief', *TLZ* 79 (1954), cols. 373-378) and according to Kümmel, *Introduction*, p. 246, 'shatters on the natural exegesis of Phlm. 1, 2 and Col. 4:17'. Philemon's name appeared first in v. 1, and this, together with the phrase κατ' οἶκόν σου (v. 2), tells against Archippus as being the one primarily addressed; so Moule, *Colossians and Philemon*, pp. 16f. (Even in the second edition (London, ²1960), pp. 51ff., Knox has not effectively answered this).

The idea that the letter to Philemon (which according to Knox is the 'letter from Laodicea' of Col. 4:16) should be read aloud in the church of Colossae in order to put pressure on Archippus, Onesimus' owner is impossible. In his letter to Onesimus' owner Paul has exercised discretion and tact, graciously making his request, rather than exercising any authority by way of demand (U. Wickert, 'Der Philemonbrief—Privatbrief oder apostolisches Schreiben?', *ZNW* 52 (1961), pp. 230-238, correctly points out that Paul did not write as a private individual to Philemon, but as an apostle. However, he errs when he considers that Paul asserted his apostolic authority and made Philemon accede to his demands. This is the very thing Paul does not do). To suggest that such a letter now be read to the assembled church at Colossae would be entirely inconsistent with this exercise of tact (so Lightfoot, *Colossians and Philemon*, p. 279, who put the matter clearly : 'Why should a letter, containing such intimate confidences, be read publicly in the Church, not only at Laodicea but at Colossae, by the express order of the Apostle? The tact and delicacy of the Apostle's pleading for Onesimus would be nullified at one stroke by the demand for publication'. Cf. P. N. Harrison, 'Onesimus and Philemon', *ATR* 32 (1950), p. 280; and F. F. Bruce, 'St. Paul in Rome. 2. The Epistle to Philemon', *BJRL* 48 (1965), p. 95).

Further, the inclusion of other Christians' names in the salutation (vv. 1f.) and benedictions (vv. 3 and 25) is due to the apostle's courtesy. The body of the letter (vv. 4-22) is addressed to a private individual. It is reasonable to infer from the preservation of the letter in the canon that Paul's request to Philemon about Onesimus was granted. Otherwise, the letter would probably have been destroyed. The contents of vv. 4-22 may well have been known to others, after Philemon received Onesimus back and possibly even released him for service with Paul (see below, p. 56).

[5] So M. Dibelius, *An die Kolosser, Epheser, an Philemon* (Tübingen, 3rd edn. revised by H. Greeven, 1953), p. 101; Vincent, *Philippians and Philemon*, p. 177; G. Friedrich,

beginning at v. 8. Accordingly, the thanksgiving period concludes with v. 7. But this is not strictly correct. The thanksgiving period extends from vv. 4-6, reaching its climax in the final clause of v. 6 which is introduced by ὅπως. V. 7 is a smooth and effective transition from the thanksgiving passage to the main purpose of the letter, a purpose which Paul promptly set forth in vv. 8ff.[6] It is important to note that v. 7 is not a report of Paul's prayers for Philemon but is rather a statement of the apostle telling the recipient why he had been refreshed and comforted. In this simple transition important ideas from both the thanksgiving and the body of the letter are mentioned (or anticipated),[7] e.g., ἀγάπη, cf. vv. 5 and 9; παράκλησις cf. vv. 9 and 10; σπλάγχνα, cf. vv. 12 and 20; οἱ ἅγιοι, cf. v. 5; ἀναπαύομαι, cf. v. 20; and ἀδελφός, cf. v. 20.[8]

This thanksgiving passage has no eschatological climax although Lohmeyer and Wickert, perhaps in the interests of uniformity, considered the phrase εἰς Χριστόν of v. 6 to point to such a theme.[9] Furthermore, there is no doxological ending to the passage. J. T. Sanders, following and developing a suggestion of J. M. Robinson, considered that as it was a Jewish custom to begin and end a prayer with a *berakah*, and since *berakoth* (and their variants *hodayoth*) had been attested at the beginning of New Testament prayers, we might also expect *berakoth* as well as doxologies to conclude the thanksgiving periods.[10] According to Sanders, Paul did not end with a doxology but closed his passage with a 'joygiving' (v. 7). Because of the apostle's rather loose usage of words built on the root χαρ- there was no material difference between rejoicing and giving thanks.

Die kleineren Briefe des Apostels Paulus : *Der Brief an Philemon* (Göttingen, [10]1965), p. 192; H. M. Carson, *The Epistles of Paul to the Colossians and Philemon* (London, 1960), p. 105; and Moule, *Colossians and Philemon*, p. 140.

[6] Cf. Schubert, *Form*, p. 5. Lohmeyer, *Kolosser und Philemon*, p. 179, rightly observed that the thanksgiving passage concluded at the end of v. 6 : 'Mit diesen Worten ist der Dank im strengen Sinne beendet; die eine Doppelzeile, die noch folgt, steht nicht mehr unmittelbar unter ihm, sondern spricht von den menschlichen Beziehungen'.

[7] Cf. Bjerkelund, *Parakalô*, pp. 118 and 124.

[8] So Knox, *Philemon*, pp. 18f., who follows Schubert.

[9] Lohmeyer, *op. cit.*, p. 179; Wickert, *loc. cit.*, p. 231, writes : 'Bei εἰς Χριστόν Phlm. 6 dürfte also der Gedanke an den Richter mitschwingen'. Schubert, *Form*, p. 5, while admitting there is no eschatological note in the thanksgiving reports of either Romans or Philemon, adds : 'no thanksgiving is without some eschatological allusion'. Even so this is no help in determining the *limits* of the period.

[10] Sanders, *JBL* 81 (1962), p. 358, following Robinson in *Apophoreta*, pp. 194-235.

Thus v. 7 is a concluding thanksgiving which ends the period. But this appears to be straining the evidence unduly in an effort to fit the thanksgiving periods into a liturgical mould.[11]

1. *Thanksgiving for Philemon's Love and Faith : Vv. 4f.*

Although the passage under discussion is simple in form the basic structural elements of the more elaborate thanksgiving passages are present.[12] It is an example of type Ia. The passage is dominated by the one finite verb, εὐχαριστέω, in its sole principal clause. Although Timothy's name is joined with Paul in the salutation, the latter alone is the subject of the principal verb. This is in contrast to the thanksgiving of the companion letter to the Colossians where Timothy is linked with Paul in the giving of thanks (1:3), εὐχαριστοῦμεν τῷ θεῷ κτλ. The following elements are the object of the principal verb, τῷ θεῷ (together with its personal pronoun μου), and the temporal adverb πάντοτε which modifies the principal verb. These elements are identical with those in the Philippian thanksgiving and are to be understood accordingly. Paul's giving of thanks for an individual was addressed to the same God, for He was responsible not only for blessings received by communities but also for those which graced individuals. Furthermore, such thanksgiving was offered to God regularly. Whenever the apostle prayed in his daily prayers [13] he gave thanks for the love and faith of Philemon.

Consistent with the general pattern of the Pauline introductory thanksgivings the principal verb in that of Philemon, εὐχαριστέω, is followed by several participles—in this case, two: μνείαν σου ποιούμενος and ἀκούων σου τὴν ἀγάπην κτλ. They are grammatically dependent on the finite verb indicating that Paul is the subject of the actions expressed. It was the apostle who made intercession for Philemon [14] whenever he prayed, for it was he who had heard

---

[11] A stronger case can be made out for a doxological ending to the thanksgiving periods of 1 Corinthians and Philippians (see pp. 130, 37). But there is neither *berakah* nor *hodayah* at the conclusion of this introductory thanksgiving of Philemon.

[12] See above, p. 7.

[13] See the treatment of Phil. 1:4, pp. 21f.

[14] In the phrase μνείαν σου ποιούμενος where the personal pronoun σου is added, somewhat unusually, Paul stressed that in his prayers he remembered Philemon. Normally the phrase περὶ ὑμῶν (or its equivalent) is used in the thanksgiving paragraphs of type Ia and the mixed types (though see Rom. 1:9, μνείαν ὑμῶν ποιοῦμαι). In Phm. 4

of Philemon's love and faith. The first participial clause, which is linked with ἐπὶ τῶν προσευχῶν μου, is a temporal one. The object of the intercession is not taken up until v. 6 when the final clause, which is grammatically dependent on μνείαν σου ποιούμενος, is introduced by ὅπως.[15]

The second participial clause ἀκούων σου τὴν ἀγάπην κτλ., v. 5, is a causal one giving the ground or basis for Paul's thanks to God. Paul had received a good report about the conduct of the addressee. This news caused him to express his thanksgiving to God. The causal participle ἀκούων [16] is found on two other occasions in the introductory thanksgiving passages, as introducing the basis or ground for thanksgiving: ἀκούσαντες τὴν πίστιν ὑμῶν κτλ. (Col. 1:4), and ἀκούσας τὴν καθ' ὑμᾶς πίστιν κτλ. (Eph. 1:15)—interestingly enough to churches unknown to Paul (assuming a 'circular letter' hypothesis for Ephesians). However, no significance for the letter to Philemon ought to be drawn from this (i.e., that Philemon was unknown to Paul) as Dibelius [17] and Knox [18] suggest. Information probably came from Epaphras (Col. 1:7f.; 4:12), rather than from Onesimus, about Philemon's good standing in the Christian faith.

The apostle had heard about Philemon's 'love and faith'. But how are these words to be interpreted, and what are the respective objects of these two Christian graces? On such questions exegetes have been divided, giving answers along the following lines:

First, πίστις is taken to mean 'faithfulness' or 'reliability' (cf. 3 John 5), so that both ἀγάπη and πίστις are directed towards both

---

the personal pronoun σου is a simple substitute for the above-mentioned phrase, thus directing attention to the intercessory prayer; Greeven, *Gebet*, p. 137.

[15] Lightfoot, *Colossians and Philemon*, p. 332, states that 'all established principles of arrangement are defied in the anxiety to give expression to the thought which is uppermost for the moment'. But the structural pattern of this thanksgiving is similar to that of the other passages. The only change is the order of ἀγάπη and πίστις.

[16] Spicq, *Agape* 2, p. 303, notes that the present participle expresses continuity and duration. 'It suggests that St. Paul had received up-to-date information about Philemon from more than one source, or even that he was getting regular reports about him'. In the greater number of thanksgiving passages where there is a causal participial clause the verb is in the past tense (either aorist, Eph. 1:15, and Col. 1:4, or perfect, Phil 1:6).

[17] *An die Kolosser, Epheser, an Philemon*, p. 103.

[18] *Philemon*, p. 45. Cf. Greeven's comment: 'So wird auch Phm 5 ἀκούων als Zeichen dafür anzusehen sein, dass bisher kein persönliches Band zwischen Paulus und dem eigentlichen Briefempfänger bestanden hat', *TLZ* 79 (1954), col. 376.

the Lord Jesus and all God's people.[19] So the NEB translates 'for I hear of your love and faith [20] towards the Lord Jesus and towards all God's people'.

Secondly, some take 'love' and 'faith' as being intimately linked (and render them as 'piety' or 'godliness') in an attitude which is shown to the Lord on the one hand and God's holy people on the other.[21] Advocates of this interpretation point out that love towards the Lord Jesus is closely linked with faith, because it is from faith that love grows, and by faith love is nourished. Further, the love which is shown towards the brethren is still love in the context of faith. The change of preposition from πρός to εἰς is then said to stress a difference in the relationships, to the Lord as object on the one hand, and to fellow believers in a like relationship on the other.[22]

The third interpretation sees in v. 5 an example of chiasmus (abba) in which Philemon's love is directed towards all God's people and his faith to the Lord Jesus.[23] According to this view it is then possible to take πίστις in the usual Pauline sense of 'trust' in the Lord Jesus.

---

[19] So A. Schlatter, *Die Briefe an die Galater, Epheser, Kolosser und Philemon* (Stuttgart, 1949), p. 312; Vincent, *Philippians and Philemon*, p. 178; J. Moffatt, *Love in the New Testament* (London, 1929), p. 173; and Bruce, *BJRL* 48 (1965), p. 81.

[20] Bruce, *ibid.*, has translated more accurately with 'loyalty'.

[21] Dibelius, *An die Kolosser, Epheser, an Philemon*, p. 103, who is followed by Kramer, *Christ*, p. 47; cf. Spicq, *Agape* 2, pp. 303f.; and Carson, *Colossians and Philemon*, pp. 105f., who are followed by Sullivan, *loc. cit.*, p. 409.

[22] Spicq, *Agape* 2, p. 304; Sullivan, *loc. cit.*, p. 409; and Carson, *Colossians and Philemon*, p. 106. Lightfoot, *Colossians and Philemon*, p. 333, is not an advocate of this interpretation, but he still sees a distinction between the prepositions. Πρός is used 'of the faith which aspires *towards* Christ, and εἰς of the love which is exerted *upon* men'. It is interesting to observe that there is no general agreement about the significance of the distinction. Rather, it is better to regard the change as simply a stylistic variation.

[23] Among grammarians this is favoured by Bl.-D., para. 477 (2); Robertson, *Grammar*, p. 1200 (though see his article 'Philemon and Onesimus: Master and Slave', *Exp.* 8, 19 (1920), p. 35); and among commentators by Lightfoot, *Colossians and Philemon*, pp. 332f.; Lohmeyer, *Kolosser und Philemon*, p. 177; Moule, *Colossians and Philemon*, p. 141, seems to prefer the chiastic interpretation; Friedrich, *Philemon*, p. 192; J. Müller, *The Epistles of Paul to the Philippians and to Philemon* (London, 1955), p. 176; cf. also Stauffer, *TDNT* 1, p. 50; Greeven, *Gebet*, p. 177; R. Bultmann, 'πιστεύω' (in NT), *TDNT* 6, p. 212; and J. Jeremias, 'Chiasmus in den Paulusbriefen', *ZNW* 49 (1958), pp. 145-156, esp. p. 146.

Our preference is to understand the verse chiastically, for the following reasons: first, chiasmus is common in the New Testament,[24] and may be said to play a considerable role in the writings of Paul. Jeremias rightly sees Semitic influence in the New Testament use of chiasmus [25] (cf. Psalm 1:6). Secondly, in the letter to Philemon the usual order of graces (for which the apostle gave thanks) is reversed. Paul normally placed πίστις before ἀγάπη. This reversal can be explained in terms of the situation which called forth the letter.[26] At the time of writing the apostle's attention was focussed on Philemon's love. The word appears again in vv. 7 and 9, and Paul's request in connection with Onesimus was made on the basis of that Christian love.[27] The apostle was setting down his thoughts in the sequence in which they occurred to him. Having mentioned Philemon's love, Paul referred to his faith. This led on to the object of the faith which in turn directed one's thoughts to the range and comprehensiveness of the love, i.e., it had been shown in the past to all God's holy people. Thirdly, this interpretation is consistent with the introductory thanksgiving of the companion letter to the Colossian Christians, 'because we have heard of your faith in Christ and of the love which you have for all the saints' (1:4). The variation in order can be adequately accounted for along the lines suggested above, while the change in prepositions, from πρός to εἰς, is to be seen as stylistic.[28]

---

[24] Even though Blass-Debrunner consider it is not frequently used in the New Testament, they admit its presence in Phm. 5; see para. 477 (2).

[25] Jeremias, *loc. cit.*, is at one with N. W. Lund, *Chiasmus in the New Testament* (London, 1942), on this point of Semitic influence. However, he severely criticises (p. 145) Lund for observing chiasmus in large units of the New Testament (e.g., Matt. 5-7 and 1 Cor. 12-14).

[26] There is some textual support (D 69 1739 pesh.) for placing πίστις before ἀγάπη, but this change of early scribes was made in the interests of uniformity. Lohmeyer, *Kolosser und Philemon*, p. 177, rightly comments that the mention of ἀγάπη first betrays 'eine leise Anspeilung auf die briefliche Lage'.

[27] In v. 7 ἀγάπη is used with the same connotation as at v. 5. In v. 9 where Paul made his appeal to Philemon many commentators consider ἀγάπη was used in a broader and different sense than in the two preceding references. It is considered to mean 'love absolutely' or love as a 'principle' (so Lightfoot and others) without any reference to Philemon's love. But although Paul did appeal to Philemon on the basis of Christian love, he certainly had in mind the demonstration of it by the latter to the brethren. Philemon now had a further opportunity of showing it by granting Paul's request. (See below, p. 56, for a discussion of the nature of that request). Cf. Wiles, *Prayers*, p. 218.

[28] Cf. Moule, *Idiom Book*, p. 68; Turner, *Syntax*, p. 256; and Lohse, *Colossians and*

According to this view ἀγάπη in the thanksgiving passage of Philemon is not to be understood as comprehensively as when used in the Philippian counterpart (1:9). The very mention of the objects is to that extent a limitation, and even if the first line of interpretation, mentioned above, be preferred ἀγάπη would still have reference to two objects. In the Philippian passage ἀγάπη appears in the intercessory prayer report. The apostle's request was that their love might increase beyond all measure. In that particular context a wide reference might well have been expected.[29] In the thanksgiving passage of Philemon ἀγάπη appears, not in the context of an intercessory prayer report, but as one of the grounds for Paul's thanks to God. The apostle had been inspired by the news he had received about Philemon's charity. If the tense of the participle ἀκούων be pressed, then it appears that Paul had been getting up-to-date information or regular reports about Philemon's progress in the Christian life. Presumably the apostle was told precise facts, which he interpreted as evidences of Philemon's love to the brethren on the one hand, and Christian belief in the Lord Jesus on the other. Such ἀγάπη and πίστις were indeed grounds for thanksgiving to God.

2. *Intercession concerning Philemon's Generosity : V. 6*

The final and climactic element of the introductory thanksgiving passage of Philemon is the intercessory prayer report of v. 6.[30] As in the Philippian passage so too in that of Philemon the close link between thanksgiving and intercessory prayer is to be observed. The ὅπως-clause, indicating the substance of Paul's prayer (v. 6), is to be taken with μνείαν σου ποιούμενος (v. 4).[31] But this temporal participial clause is dependent on the principal verb εὐχαριστέω. Grammatically and logically the intercessory prayer springs out of the prayer of thanksgiving. Paul could not give thanks for the love and faith of his colleague Philemon without making intercession for him. The two types of prayer were part of the same religious act.[32]

Philemon, p. 193. Nowhere else in the New Testament is πρός used with πίστις as directed to Christ. The nearest parallel to it is 1 Thess. 1:8, ἡ πίστις ὑμῶν ἡ πρὸς τὸν θεὸν ἐξελήλυθεν (cf. 2 Cor. 3:4, πεποίθησιν ... πρὸς τὸν θεόν).

[29] See above, p. 31.
[30] Schubert, *Form*, pp. 12, 54f.
[31] So most commentators.
[32] 'Wenn Paulus des Philemon im Gebet gedenkt, so ist sein Herz nicht nur von

The intercessory prayer reports of these paragraphs show a greater flexibility in form than do the other elements of the periods, and the passage in Philemon is no exception. As already noted this is probably due to the different epistolary situations which called forth the various letters.³³

The exact meaning of v. 6 is difficult to determine. This is because there are several exegetical problems within the intercessory prayer report. First, what is the meaning of ἡ κοινωνία τῆς πίστεώς σου ? The following are some of the suggestions that have been made : (a) 'the kindly deeds of charity which spring from your faith',³⁴ (b) 'the communication (to others) of your faith',³⁵ (c) 'your fellowship with other Christians created by faith',³⁶ (d) 'communion (with Christ) by faith—i.e., faith-communion with Christ',³⁷ (e) 'the faith in which you participate', i.e., your share in the faith,³⁸ and (f) 'the participation of other Christians in your faith',³⁹ Secondly, how is εἰς Χριστόν to be understood ? Thirdly, is it to be connected with ἐνεργής, with παντὸς ἀγαθοῦ or with ἐπιγνώσει ? Finally, how is ἐν ἐπιγνώσει to be interpreted, and who is to attain to the *knowledge* in question— Philemon himself or those who notice and profit from his 'fellowship of faith' ?

C. F. D. Moule, having outlined some of the difficulties of the verse and the attempts made at its solution, observed : 'Unless and until further ἐπίγνωσις is given to Christian interpreters, the answers

---

Dank gegen Gott erfüllt, sondern mit dem Dankgebet verbindet sich die Bitte', Friedrich, *Philemon*, p. 193.

³³ Schubert, *Form*, p. 62.

³⁴ So Lightfoot, *Colossians and Philemon*, p. 333, taking κοινωνία as especially referring to 'contributions, almsgiving'; Robertson, *Exp.* 8, 19 (1920), p. 36, understands κοινωνία as 'generosity'.

³⁵ Vincent, *Philippians and Philemon*, p. 179, considers the idea grows directly out of εἰς πάντας τοὺς ἁγίους; cf. L. S. Thornton, *The Common Life in the Body of Christ* (London, n.d., ? 1942), p. 38.

³⁶ Lohmeyer, *Kolosser und Philemon*, p. 178, and J. M. Nielen, *Gebet und Gottesdienst im Neuen Testament* (Freiburg-i.-Br., 1937), p. 145; cf. E. W. Koch, 'A Cameo of Koinonia. The Letter to Philemon', *Interp* 17 (1963), p. 184. According to Lohmeyer πίστεως is a genitive of origin. He appeals to Phil. 1:5 in support.

³⁷ Dibelius, *An die Kolosser, Epheser, an Philemon*, p. 103. Seesemann, *KOINΩNIA*, pp. 79ff., considers such an interpretation is consistent with a correct exegesis of Phil. 1:5 ! Cf. Hauck, *TDNT* 3, p. 805.

³⁸ C. H. Dodd, *Colossians and Philemon* (London, 1929), *ad loc.*

³⁹ J. Y. Campbell, '*KOINΩNIA* and its cognates in the New Testament', *JBL* 51 (1932), pp. 370ff. So also Moffatt's translation.

to these questions must remain obscure'.[40] Thus the following suggestions are only tentative :

Κοινωνία is understood in an active sense, not simply of almsgiving, although this is obviously covered, but in a wider sense referring to 'generosity' or 'liberality';[41] τῆς πίστεως is treated as a genitive of origin indicating the source from which the kindness comes. So the translation would be : 'I pray that your generosity which springs from your faith (i.e., in the Lord Jesus)...' Πίστις has the same meaning as in v. 5, although the phrase in v. 6 throws the emphasis on the practical expression of the faith rather than on the faith itself or its object.

According to this view ἐνεργής is to be understood as 'effective' rather than 'active', for the liberality of Philemon, according to Paul's statements in vv. 5 and 7, had already been 'active'. The intercessory request of the apostle was that Philemon's liberality (and not that of others) might lead him effectively [42] into a deeper understanding [43] of all the blessings that belonged to him in Christ. Ἐνεργὴς γένηται is to be taken with ἐν ἐπιγνώσει παντὸς ἀγαθοῦ. In the Philippian intercessory prayer report ἐπίγνωσις was used without modifier or object. But here, as often when ἐπίγνωσις is employed, the object [44] is mentioned, παντὸς ἀγαθοῦ. This is understood to refer to 'every

---

[40] Moule, *Colossians and Philemon*, p. 143. Because of the difficulties George, *Communion*, p. 183, does not commit himself to any alternative; cf. V. Taylor, *Forgiveness and Reconciliation* (London, 1941), p. 132; and Wiles, *Prayers*, pp. 221-225.

[41] See the exegesis of Phil. 1:5 above, pp. 23ff.

[42] There may well be a hint that Paul wished Philemon's liberality to be specially effective in the case of Onesimus. Commentators and exegetes have differed in their views about what Paul actually requested of Philemon. One difficulty lies in the interpretation of v. 21, εἰδὼς ὅτι καὶ ὑπὲρ ἃ λέγω ποιήσεις. The majority of scholars consider Paul wants Philemon to forgive Onesimus and treat him as a Christian brother; so F. V. Filson, *A New Testament History* (London, 1965), p. 278; Kümmel, *Introduction*, p. 246. T. Preiss, *Life in Christ* (ET, London, 1957), p. 36, thinks that Onesimus is to be sent home for the service of the gospel, and not in order to be re-instated as a domestic slave. But others, rightly we believe, interpret v. 21 as a request of the apostle for Onesimus to be returned to him for the service of the gospel; so A. Jülicher, *An Introduction to the New Testament* (ET, London, 1904), p. 125; Lohmeyer, *Kolosser und Philemon*, p. 191; Knox, *Philemon*, pp. 24ff.; Harrison, *loc. cit.*, pp. 275f.; Bruce, *BJRL* 48 (1965), p. 96; and Wiles, *Prayers*, pp. 216, 221.

[43] Ἐν marks the sphere in which something takes place, cf. 2 Cor. 1:6; Col. 1:29; so Vincent, *Philippians and Philemon*, p. 180.

[44] Eph. 1:17; 4:13; Col. 1:9f.; 2:2; 1 Tim. 2:4; 2 Tim. 2:25; 3:7; Tit. 1:1; Heb. 10:26; 2 Pet. 1:2, 8; 2:20.

blessing' which belongs to Philemon as a Christian.⁴⁵ In the present context ἐπίγνωσις conveys both the ideas of understanding and experience. The apostle's prayer was not simply that Philemon might understand or appreciate the treasures that belonged to him, but that he might also experience them. It is necessary to use two English words to translate this one Greek word, and therefore we render it by 'understanding and experience'.⁴⁶

These Christian blessings of which the apostle has spoken do not belong to Philemon alone. They are for all who are incorporated 'into Christ' and include Paul himself.⁴⁷

One difficulty of the above-mentioned interpretation is the phrase εἰς Χριστόν. Lohmeyer, Wickert and Suhl treat this as an eschatological thrust in the passage, Wickert maintaining it has special reference to Christ as 'Richter'. Others such as Dodd and Moule treat the phrase as meaning 'bringing us into (closer) relation to Christ'.⁴⁸ Lightfoot understands εἰς Χριστόν as having reference to Christ as the goal. He considers that the phrase ought not to be connected with τοῦ ἐν ἡμῖν, but with the main statement of the sentence, ἐνεργὴς γένηται κτλ. Lightfoot then paraphrases: 'as thou attainest to the perfect knowledge of every good thing bestowed upon us by God, looking unto and striving after Christ'.⁴⁹

---

⁴⁵ Lohmeyer, *Kolosser und Philemon*, p. 179, maintains that πᾶν ἀγαθόν is a frequent designation for the will of God (so in Paul: Rom. 2:10; 5:7; 7:13, 19; 9:11; 12:2, 9, 21; 13:3; 14:16; 15:2; Gal. 6:10; 1 Thess. 5:15). He draws a parallel between the function of the Law for a Jew and the place of faith here for the Christian. Both are to be active in the believer, so that he may find out and do God's will (πᾶν ἀγαθόν). It is doubtful whether many of Lohmeyer's references are to the will of God at all and, further, his case stands too heavily on a particular interpretation of εἰς Χριστόν which is questionable; see Moule, *Colossians and Philemon*, p. 143.

⁴⁶ Cf. F. F. Bruce's rendering, 'the experience and appreciation of every blessing', *An Expanded Paraphrase of the Epistles of Paul* (Exeter, 1965), ad loc. Bultmann, *TDNT* 1, p. 708, considers the phrase ἐπιγνώσει παντὸς ἀγαθοῦ to mean 'a recognition of all that is given to the believer', while Sullivan, loc. cit., p. 409, interprets it as 'a clear understanding of all the blessings of the Christian situation'.

⁴⁷ Reading ἐν ἡμῖν, with A C D and some of the Fathers, rather than ἐν ὑμῖν. It is quite probable that an early scribe, not fully grasping the meaning of Paul's statement, changed ἡμῖν to ὑμῖν, wishing to apply the words to Philemon and his household. Cf. the RSV and NEB rendering 'us'; so also Lightfoot, *Colossians and Philemon*, p. 334.

⁴⁸ Dodd, *Colossians and Philemon*, ad loc.; Moule, *Colossians and Philemon*, pp. 142f.

⁴⁹ *Colossians and Philemon*, pp. 332 and 334. Vincent, *Philippians and Philemon*, p. 181, connects the phrase with ἐνεργὴς γένηται and understands it as 'unto Christ's glory', i.e., the advancement of His cause.

According to our suggestion the phrase εἰς Χριστόν refers to incorporation and is almost equivalent to ἐν Χριστῷ. It is perhaps not without significance that where the person of Jesus is referred to in v. 5 κύριον Ἰησοῦν is used, while the corporate reference in v. 6 is to εἰς Χριστόν.[50] One can understand why Paul would have employed this expression, for in the ὅπως-clause of v. 6 he had already used the preposition ἐν twice (ἐν ἐπιγνώσει and τοῦ ἐν ἡμῖν) before penning the phrase in question. Ἐν Χριστῷ following hard upon ἐν ἡμῖν would sound harsh. So the synonymous phrase εἰς Χριστόν has been chosen. Paul's intercessory prayer report may thus be paraphrased : 'I pray that your generosity, which arises from your faith may lead you effectively into a deeper understanding and experience of every blessing which belongs to us as fellow-members in the body of Christ'.

3. Conclusions

It was suggested above that the introductory thanksgiving of Philemon was important because of its being the only such passage in the Pauline corpus where petition and thanksgiving for an individual were closely conjoined. Further, it may be observed that with one or two qualifications the varied function of the introductory Pauline thanksgivings is present in this 'private' passage of Philemon.

First, the *epistolary purpose* is noted—to introduce and indicate the main themes of the letter. The occasion of the letter and its contents are hinted at in vv. 3-6. The usual formal pattern of the introductory thanksgivings, with only slight variations, has been followed. The paragraph (if v. 7 be included) is designed to prepare the way for the specific matter with which the letter is primarily concerned. 'It is the overture in which each of the themes, to be later heard in a different, perhaps more specific, context, is given an anticipatory hearing'.[51] Terms (or their cognates) such as προσευχή, ἀγάπη, κοινωνός (cognate with κοινωνία), ἀγαθός, παρακαλέω (cognate with παράκλησις), σπλάγχνα and ἀναπαύομαι reappear in the body of the letter. The apostle had celebrated the generous character of the slave owner's relationships with his fellow-Christians. Paul too

---

[50] Kramer, *Christ*, p. 140, translates the phrase by 'in Christ'. Cf. also E. Percy, *Die Probleme der Kolosser- und Epheserbrief* (Lund, 1946), p. 125.

[51] Knox, *Philemon*, p. 19.

had been encouraged by this love, and he now has a favour to ask. So he leads on to the request about Onesimus—the subject which prompted the writing of the letter.

Secondly, the *didactic aim* is also in evidence. Certainly the apostle was not seeking to instruct a local congregation (not even the church that met in Philemon's house) about important issues in thanksgiving and petitionary prayer. The greater part of this letter (including the thanksgiving period) was addressed, in the first instance, to Philemon alone. Nevertheless the didactic intent was not absent even when this is taken into account. Paul has shown that he regularly gave thanks to God for his dear friend and fellow-worker. And this he did whether he was making a tactful request or not. If the above-mentioned suggestions for the exegesis of v. 6 be correct then Paul has interceded for his fellow-worker along the lines of a deeper experience of Christ's blessings through the exercise of his Christian generosity. From the actual thanksgiving it can be seen that faith in the Lord Jesus and love to God's people are important issues. The same may be said from the petitionary prayer of a deeper grasp and experience of Christ's blessings to His people. So Philemon is instructed by the apostle in a context where 'love', 'faith', 'knowledge', 'generosity' and 'the saints' are important.

Thirdly, from both the thanksgiving and the petitionary prayer the *pastoral concern* of the apostle shines clearly. And that pastoral concern was for a fellow-worker in Paul's ministry of the gospel to Gentiles. Philemon had not only been converted through the agency of Paul,[52] but had also participated in that same ministry of the gospel. He had refreshed the hearts of God's people and Paul had been encouraged because of it.

Fourthly, in a strict sense the *paraenetic function* is absent, and this is because of the nature of the letter—addressed to an individual. The introductory thanksgiving does not point to or amplify any paraenetic material in the body of the letter, for there is no such material in the remaining twenty verses. Nevertheless a general exhortatory motif is not entirely absent. Philemon, having read the thanksgiving passage of vv. 3-6, would have been encouraged to

---

[52] Most commentators, with Knox a significant exception, understand καὶ σεαυτόν μοι προσοφείλεις of v. 19 as a reference to Philemon's owing his conversion to Paul. Such a view demands that Philemon must have met the apostle outside the Lycus valley, where the latter was not known personally (Col. 2:2). Perhaps such an encounter took place on a visit to Ephesus.

continue in his exercise of faith and love, particularly with reference to Paul's request about Onesimus.[53] Also, having read the report of Paul's intercessory prayer he would have been stirred to enter into a deeper appreciation of his heritage as a Christian. Thus the various functions of the thanksgiving period, outlined in the introduction, can (with certain modifications) be observed in this passage also.

Concerning *Paul's actual prayers* it has been noted that Paul's intercession was for Philemon. According to the suggested exegesis of v. 6, Paul's petition did not directly concern others, but related specifically to the *same* person for whom thanks had been given. This is similar to the other intercessory prayers within these paragraphs. The only difference here is that there is but one addressee for whom thanks were given and for whom intercession was made.

Further, it has been shown that grammatically and logically the petition was linked with Paul's thanksgiving.[54] The reference to 'liberality which arises from Philemon's faith' was meant to remind one of the love shown to God's people on the one hand, and the faith directed to the Lord Jesus on the other—for it was out of this 'faith' that the practical expression flowed. Paul's thanksgiving was related to Philemon's situation, as the apostle understood it from the reports he had received. These kind acts of his fellow-worker were interpreted by the apostle as evidence of Philemon's love and faith. The petitionary prayer was related to these, and thus it too sprang from the situation. Yet its scope was broader than this. Paul was concerned about the immediate needs;[55] but his concern was not so tied to those needs that he failed to see the necessity for 'presenting every man mature in Christ'. Ultimately the petitionary prayer was related to Philemon's full growth as a Christian.[56]

---

[53] V. P. Furnish, *Theology and Ethics in Paul* (Nashville, 1968), pp. 94f., considers that Paul's thanksgiving sections, particularly that of Philemon, which commend the readers' past performances in indicative statements, 'point forward to the imperatives which are expressed further on'. If this is correct it shows that the thanksgiving paragraphs have an exhortatory function.

[54] In the *Tefillah* petitions are closely linked with praises or benedictions, but this is generally not the case in the Qumran literature. The only instance where the two are closely linked is in the closing benediction, 1 QS 11:15f.

[55] See Harder's brief treatment, *Paulus*, pp. 201ff. W. A. Beardslee's statement, in *Human Achievement and Divine Vocation in the Message of Paul* (London, 1961), p. 109, that Paul's prayers in his letters were general, is misleading.

[56] Paul's petitionary prayers were directed primarily to spiritual objects, 'Dingen des Heils', C. Schneider, 'Paulus und das Gebet', *Angelos* 4 (Leipzig, 1932), p. 21 (e.g.,

grace, peace, love, faith, joy, hope, salvation, knowledge, wisdom, thanksgiving, etc.). But prayers for earthly matters were not excluded. Note the injunction of Phil. 4:6, and Paul's petitions about his travel (Rom. 1:10; 1 Thess. 3:10f.; cf. Phm. 22), though the latter group were intimately bound up with his apostolic ministry to Gentiles; cf. Harder, *Paulus*, pp. 78, 115; von der Goltz, *Gebet*, pp. 115f.; and J. Burnaby, 'Christian Prayer', *Soundings*, ed. A. R. Vidler (Cambridge, 1966), pp. 223f.

CHAPTER THREE

THANKSGIVING—INTERCESSION—THANKSGIVING: COL. 1:3-14

I. *Thanksgiving in Colossians*

Thanksgiving plays an important role in the Epistle to the Colossians.[1] Εὐχαριστέω and its cognates, εὐχάριστος and εὐχαριστία, appear no fewer than six times in the space of four short chapters.[2] Paul used these terms more frequently each page than any other Hellenistic author, pagan or Christian.[3] These words, together with χάρις when it has the meaning of 'thanksgiving' or 'thankfulness', occur forty-six times [4] and are fairly evenly distributed throughout the letters of the Pauline corpus, appearing in every epistle except Galatians and Titus.

In Colossians the emphasis on thanksgiving is accented, for if ἐν [τῇ] χάριτι of chap. 3:16 be included in the count, then there is a reference to this Christian activity seven times in ten pages of the Nestle Greek New Testament. In Romans, 1 Corinthians, and 2 Corinthians, which are considerably longer letters, the count is seven, eight and seven times respectively. However, in Romans and 1 Corinthians three examples of εὐχαριστέω, used to express gratitude on a conversational or colloquial level,[5] ought to be omitted from

---

[1] Hamman, *Prière*, p. 292.

[2] Εὐχαριστέω: 1:3, 12; 3:17; εὐχάριστος: 3:15; εὐχαριστία: 2:7; 4:2.

[3] Schubert, *Form*, p. 42. Eschlimann, *Prière*, p. 110, understands thanksgiving as 'la plus haute expression de la prière paulinienne; cf. Schneider, *Angelos* 4 (1932), p. 19; Juncker, *Gebet*, p. 23. Philo of Alexandria (who follows Paul in relative frequency) used εὐχαριστέω and an unusually large number of derivatives over one hundred times. He placed a 'big emphasis upon the value and necessity of εὐχαριστία' (so Boobyer, "*Thanksgiving*", p. 31), emphatically declaring that man's entire religious duty may be described as 'thanksgiving'; cf. Schubert, *Form*, pp. 122ff., esp. p. 125.

[4] Εὐχαριστέω: Rom. 1:8, 21; 14:6 (twice); 16:4; 1 Cor. 1:4, 14; 10:30; 11:24; 14:17, 18; 2 Cor. 1:11; Eph. 1:16; 5:20; Phil. 1:3; Col. 1:3, 12; 3:17; 1 Thess. 1:2; 2:13; 5:18; 2 Thess. 1:3; 2:13; Phm. 4; εὐχαριστία: 1 Cor. 14:16; 2 Cor. 4:15; 9:11, 12; Eph. 5:4; Phil. 4:6; Col. 2:7; 4:2; 1 Thess. 3:9; 1 Tim. 2:1; 4:3, 4; εὐχάριστος: Col. 3:15; χάρις: Rom. 6:17; 7:25; 1 Cor. 15:57; 2 Cor. 2:14; 8:16; 9:15; Col. 3:16; 1 Tim. 1:12; 2 Tim. 1:3.

[5] Rom. 16:4; 1 Cor. 1:14; 14:18.

this analysis. The net result is that thanksgiving was most frequently referred to by Paul (apart from Colossians) in 2 Corinthians—seven times in all. But since these instances are spread over twenty-three pages of the Nestle edition, it may be concluded that thanksgiving appears in Colossians twice as often as in 2 Corinthians and three times more frequently than in the other letters of the Pauline corpus.[6]

More important for our purposes, however, are the contexts in which εὐχαριστέω and its cognates appear and the significance given to the terms in those contexts. As might be expected, the apostle Paul gave thanks to God for the Colossian Christians in the introduction of his letter, chap. 1:3ff. The principal verb of v. 3, εὐχαριστοῦμεν, dominates the paragraph which introduces the basic themes of the letter. As in the thanksgiving periods of Philippians and Philemon, so in Colossians the intercessory prayer report of the apostle sprang out of the opening thanksgiving. One of Paul's requests was that these Christians, though unknown to him personally, might 'walk worthily of the Lord', v. 10. In the participles which follow, 'bearing fruit', 'increasing' (v. 10), 'being strengthened' (v. 11) and 'giving thanks' (v. 12), the apostle defined more precisely what it meant to 'walk worthily of the Lord'.[7] The thanksgiving was offered to 'the Father', and the grounds were that He 'has qualified us to share in the inheritance of the saints in light. He has delivered us from the dominion of darkness and transferred us to the kingdom of His beloved Son, in whom we have redemption, the forgiveness of sins' (vv. 12-14). The striking fact is that nowhere else in the Pauline corpus does an intercession pass into a thanksgiving (though cf. 2 Cor. 1:11). The passage has moved from thanksgiving (v. 3) to intercession (v. 9) and back to thanksgiving again. The re-introduction of the first element stresses the significance of thanksgiving and indicates its presence was not due to the apostle's *simply* following some epistolary style of the period.

In chap. 1:3 Paul, probably in conjunction with his associates, had been giving thanks to God. At v. 12, in answer to his intercessions, the Colossians were to offer thanksgiving to the Father because of

---

[6] However, statistics such as these can mislead. It might be argued, for example, that chaps. 10-13 of 2 Corinthians constitute a separate Pauline letter, with thanksgiving being mentioned four times in as many chapters. Further, the total number of occurrences is not exceedingly large, and perhaps not sufficient for obtaining reliable conclusions.

[7] Schubert, *Form*, p. 93. See the exegesis below, pp. 88ff.

His actions on their behalf. This giving of thanks in v. 12 (as elsewhere in Colossians) was related to the filial consciousness.[8] In the blessings the Colossians and Paul had received from God they recognized the Father's bounty and knew themselves to be His sons.

At chap. 2:6f. Paul told the Colossians that they had received a tradition.[9] That tradition was none other than Christ Himself. He was a more than adequate safeguard against the 'tradition of men' (v. 8). But they were to continue in Him (v. 6). This they would do by being 'rooted and built up in him', 'established in the faith', and 'abounding in thanksgiving' (περισσεύοντες ἐν εὐχαριστίᾳ, v. 7). Firmness and strength of faith, coupled with thanksgiving, describe the Christian way of life.

At chap. 3:5 Paul turned to a practical application of the teaching given in the earlier sections of the letter. In fact, the whole passage (3:5-4:6) which precedes the personal notes (4:7ff.) is best understood as a catechetical 'form' in which distinctive catchwords 'put off' (3:5), 'put on' (3:12), 'be subject' (3:18) and 'watch and pray' (4:2) introduce paragraphs dealing with Christian ethical conduct. The remaining references to thanksgiving are found in this catechetical section, the first three in the paragraph headed by the catchword 'put on' (3:12-17), the last in that introduced by the rubric 'watch and pray' (4:2-6). Thanksgiving (εὐχάριστοι γίνεσθε, v. 15) was inculcated among those who had been called into the body of Christ. As members of that body they had been reconciled to God through the death of His Son. Christ's peace was to arbitrate in their midst. Indeed, they who 'were once estranged and hostile in mind, doing evil deeds' (1:21) had much to thank God for. Such an attitude was a worthy response to His grace. They might do more, for as the word of Christ dwelt in them richly and as they taught and admonished one another, so they ought to sing [10] to God, thankful for what He had done (v. 16).

---

[8] This is true, in general, of Pauline thanksgiving. So Hamman, *Prière*, p. 294: 'L'action de grâces dans la prière est le fruit de la filiation divine, c'est l'attitude de l'enfant en face de son Père, dans une réciprocité fondée sur la grâce'. The point is emphasized in Colossians.

[9] Παραλαμβάνω and its correlative παραδίδωμι are equivalent to the Hebrew קבל and מסר, technical terms common in Judaism, which describe the receiving and handing down of the oral tradition. Cf. the *locus classicus*, Ab. 1:1.

[10] Recent study on New Testament hymnody has shown that the theme of thanksgiving to God for His mercy in Christ was a common one running through many hymns. See Robinson, in *Apophoreta*, pp. 194-235; R. P. Martin, *Worship in the Early Church*

The paragraph with its general injunctions is summed up in the words: 'And whatever you do, in word or deed, do everything in the name of the Lord Jesus, giving thanks to God the Father through him' (v. 17). Thanksgiving was to be the accompaniment of every activity.[11] It was to be offered to the Father through Christ,[12] just as all actions were to be done in His Name. There are few exhortations in the New Testament which are as comprehensive as this one. That thanksgiving is an important component is highly significant, and underlines what has already been observed about its being an integral part of the Christian life.[13]

The final reference to thanksgiving in Paul's letter to the Colossians occurs within the context of prayer: 'Continue steadfastly in prayer, watching therein with thanksgiving' (4:2).[14] The Colossian Christians were to persevere in petitionary prayer, a point stressed by προσ-καρτερεῖτε on the one hand, and γρηγοροῦντες on the other. The latter word seems to have been used regularly in catechetical contexts,[15] and in the present passage is normally understood to refer to attention and engagement in prayer as opposed to a humdrum and lethargic praying. It has, however, been interpreted in a more technical sense of the children of light being awake and renouncing the sleep of this world of darkness, with the mind directed towards Christ's coming and the consummation of the hope.[16] It is interesting to recall that in the introductory period the salvation of the readers was described

---

(London, 1964), pp. 135ff.; and J. T. Sanders, *The New Testament Christological Hymns* (Cambridge, 1971).

[11] Delling, *Worship*, pp. 123f., points out that in the pagan world although thanks to the gods were expressed publicly (as found on inscriptions) the public only shared in it from the outside, as it were, so that the thanksgiving was in effect a private affair. In Colossians the corporate nature of thanksgiving is stressed.

[12] Thanksgiving is 'through Christ' at Rom. 1:8; 7:25 and possibly 1 Cor. 15:57. Cf. Thüsing, *Per Christum*, pp. 164ff., esp. pp. 174ff., and see on Rom. 1:8.

[13] Greeven, *Gebet*, p. 180, considers Paul's short form of exhortation to thanksgiving, in which the basis is not expressly mentioned, to be the most profound.

[14] Eschlimann, *Prière*, pp. 96-98, comments that thanksgiving often anticipates petition, while essentially request is ordered to thanksgiving.

[15] F. F. Bruce in E. K. Simpson-F. F. Bruce, *Commentary on the Epistles to the Ephesians and the Colossians* (London, 1957), p. 297; cf. E. G. Selwyn, *The First Epistle of St. Peter* (London, 1946), pp. 439ff.

[16] E. Lövestam, *Spiritual Wakefulness in the New Testament* (Lund, 1963), pp. 75ff., following Lohmeyer, *Kolosser und Philemon*, p. 161. So too more recently R. P. Martin, *Colossians: The Church's Lord and the Christian's Liberty* (Exeter, 1972), pp. 135f., following Conzelmann, inclines to this view.

in the categories of light and darkness; they were freed from the dominion of darkness in this world and were, in Christ, sharers of the inheritance of the saints in light (1:12ff.).

If this understanding be correct, then the Colossians as a response to their deliverance from darkness into a realm of light were to ensure that they did not fall into the sleep of this world—a hindrance to or even destruction of prayer. At the same time, prayer was an expression of and means for such wakefulness. Prayer and the light-darkness motifs appeared in the introductory thanksgiving. According to the above interpretation their presence is found once more in Paul's final Colossian reference to thanksgiving.

We conclude our introductory remarks on thanksgiving by suggesting that the reason for the emphasis on this Christian activity is to be sought in the situation which called forth the letter. Prior to their conversion the Colossian Christians had been estranged from God 'hostile in mind, doing evil deeds' (1:21). As Gentiles they had been without hope. But now through the preaching of Paul's associates God's mystery, formerly hidden for ages and generations, had been made known. Further, it had special reference to Gentiles—indeed the mystery was that 'Christ is in you (even in you Gentiles) as the hope of glory' (1:27). The Colossians now had a hope, so secure that it was laid up for them in heaven, where Christ was seated, and where their thoughts and aspirations were to ascend. As baptized persons they had been transferred from a kingdom of darkness to one of light. This baptism was not some preliminary initiation which had then to be supplemented by other rites if one were to proceed along the path to $\tau\epsilon\lambda\epsilon\iota\omega\sigma\iota\varsigma$. Already they had a share in the realm of light. No longer need they fear planetary or other intermediate powers which controlled the lines of communication between God and man.[17] The Christ whom they served had not only created things in heaven and on earth (including whatever principalities or powers there might be). He had also reconciled all things to Himself through His death

---

[17] Cf. F. F. Bruce, 'St. Paul in Rome. 3. The Epistle to the Colossians', *BJRL* 48 (1966), p. 275. On the nature of the Colossian heresy and its relation to second century Gnosticism see the commentaries, esp. Lohse, *Colossians and Philemon*, pp. 127-131, and J. Lähnemann, *Der Kolosserbrief. Komposition, Situation und Argumentation* (Gütersloh, 1971). The present writer agrees with those scholars who understand the heresy as an incipient form of gnosticism—a fusion of Jewish elements (of a native Phrygian variety) with a philosophy of non-Jewish origin.

on the Cross. Thus, with true gratitude they ought to give thanks to God the Father for His actions on their behalf.

2. *The Language and Style of Col. 1:3-14*

The language and style of the Colossian thanksgiving period have occasioned different—indeed, contradictory—comments from New Testament exegetes. Conzelmann considered the style to be 'feierlich', the speech that of 'gottesdienstlichen Gebets'.[18] Bornkamm, who in company with many other German scholars rejects the Pauline authorship of the letter, saw in vv. 3-8 an overloaded sentence with seven participial expressions, four relative sentences, three καθώς-clauses, as well as unusual prepositional and genitival expressions.[19] Masson noted in the laborious style the hand of a redactor tearing at the primitive text and making various additions.[20] Lohmeyer could refer to the richness of the expressions,[21] while Beare, commenting on vv. 6 and 7, noted that the true text weaves back and forth on itself, and although there is an 'external awkwardness' it has a 'verve and vigour which suggests the atmosphere of living speech'.[22]

But most of the stylistic features found in the thanksgiving period [23]

---

[18] H. Conzelmann, *Die kleineren Briefe des Apostels Paulus* : *Der Brief an die Kolosser* (Göttingen, ¹⁰1965), p. 134; cf. E. Norden, *Agnostos Theos* (Stuttgart, 1956 (= ⁴1923)), pp. 252f.; Percy, *Probleme*, pp. 16-66; Lohse, *Colossians and Philemon*, pp. 12ff., and pp. 84-91, 'The Language and Style of Colossians'.

[19] G. Bornkamm, 'Die Hoffnung im Kolosserbrief zugleich ein Beitrag zur Frage der Echtheit des Briefes', *TU* 77 (1961), p. 56.

[20] C. Masson, *L'Épitre de Saint Paul aux Colossiens* (Paris, 1950), p. 93.

[21] Lohmeyer, *Kolosser und Philemon*, p. 21.

[22] F. W. Beare, 'The Epistle to the Colossians', *The Interpreter's Bible* 11, p. 153.

[23] In Col. 1:3-14 there are two New Testament *hapax legomena*, προακούω (v. 5) and ἀρεσκεία (v. 10); two words (σύνδουλος, v. 7; 4:7; and κλῆρος, v. 12) not found elsewhere in the Pauline corpus; and five terms (ἀπόκειμαι, v. 5; αἰτέομαι, v. 9; δυναμόω, v. 11; κράτος, v. 11; and ἄφεσις, v. 14), which occur only in Ephesians and/or the Pastorals, but not elsewhere in the corpus. Ἱκανόω in v. 12 is considered to have a different meaning from that in 2 Cor. 3:6—the only other New Testament instance of the word.

Other features are : an expression in which cognate words are joined together—ἐν πάσῃ δυνάμει δυναμούμενοι, v. 11; the doubling up of terms by means of synonyms, e.g., προσευχόμενοι καὶ αἰτούμενοι, v. 9, and εἰς πᾶσαν ὑπομονὴν καὶ μακροθυμίαν, v. 11; the heaping together of dependent genitives, e.g., ἐν τῷ λόγῳ τῆς ἀληθείας τοῦ εὐαγγελίου, v. 5; εἰς τὴν μερίδα τοῦ κλήρου τῶν ἁγίων, v. 12; and εἰς τὴν βασιλείαν τοῦ υἱοῦ τῆς ἀγάπης αὐτοῦ, v. 13; and the use of ἐν to join a substantive to an expression on which it is

can be observed throughout the whole of the letter. Thus there are thirty-four [24] *hapax legomena* in the epistle, twenty-eight words not found in the Pauline corpus (excluding 2 Thessalonians and the Pastorals), and fifteen words common to Colossians and Ephesians alone. Cognate expressions are scattered throughout the rest of the letter, while synonyms are used together quite frequently. The dependent genitive occurs at least ten times in the letter,[25] while the linking of a dependent substantive to the previous phrase by means of ἐν is to be observed outside the thanksgiving period.[26]

The language and style, as well as theological considerations, have convinced some scholars that Colossians was not written by Paul.[27] We do not wish to enter into this question in detail, but note that, in general, the different linguistic manner can partly be explained in terms of the liturgical language (esp. 1:15-20), and partly by the polemical purpose of the epistle. Some peculiarities of language and manner of expression are found in those sections where the apostle attacks the heresy, or at least develops his own thought with a glance at it. The omission of well-known Pauline theological concepts (such as righteousness, justification, law, salvation, revelation, and the near omission of the Spirit) does not prove anything since similar observations can also be made about other Pauline letters (as Lohmeyer has shown).[28] On the other hand, stylistic peculiarities of Paul, such as pleonastic καί after διὰ τοῦτο (1:9), οἱ ἅγιοι αὐτοῦ (1:26), ἐν μέρει (2:16) = 'with regard to', and πᾶν ἔργον ἀγαθόν (1:10), are present in Colossians.[29] The traditional view of the Pauline authorship, with a Roman provenance, in spite of the difficulties still seems

---

dependent, e.g., τὴν χάριν τοῦ θεοῦ ἐν ἀληθείᾳ, v. 6; τὴν ὑμῶν ἀγάπην ἐν πνεύματι, v. 8; and εἰς τὴν μερίδα τοῦ κλήρου τῶν ἁγίων ἐν τῷ φωτί, v. 12.

[24] For the following statistics see Lohse, *Colossians and Philemon*, pp. 84-91; cf. Percy, *Probleme*, pp. 16-66.

[25] Col. 1:5, 12, 13, 20, 24, 27; 2:2 (twice), 11, 12.

[26] Col. 1:29; cf. 2:4, 15; 3:4.

[27] See for example Lohse's recent treatment, *op. cit.*, pp. 177ff.

[28] *Kolosser und Philemon*, pp. 12f. Ἀποκάλυψις is not used in 1 Thessalonians and Philippians; δικαιοσύνη appears in 1 Corinthians only at 1:30, but not at all in 1 Thessalonians; δικαιόω occurs in neither 1 Thessalonians, Philippians nor 2 Corinthians; νόμος does not appear in 2 Corinthians, πιστεύω only at chap. 4:13 in an Old Testament citation, and so on. See Zahn, *Introduction* 1, pp. 521f., who has noted thirty *hapax legomena* in Galatians.

[29] Kümmel, *Introduction*, p. 241.

the most satisfactory solution to the present writer, and accordingly this position is followed.³⁰

It was noted in discussing the Philippian thanksgiving period that terms and ideas, particularly those of a paraenetic nature appeared in the body of the letter. This is even more pronounced in the Colossian counterpart. So the following words and/or their cognates, found in the thanksgiving passage, occur in the body of the letter: εὐχαριστέω of 1:3 and 12 (εὐχαριστία in 2:7; 3:17; 4:2; εὐχάριστοι, 3:15; ἐν [τῇ] χάριτι, 3:16); πάτηρ 1:3 and 12 (3:17), all in a context of thanksgiving; προσεύχομαι 1:3 and 9 (4:3 and προσευχή, 4:12); πίστις 1:4 (1:23; 2:7, 12 and especially 2:5, τῆς εἰς Χριστὸν πίστεως ὑμῶν), cf. πιστός 1:7 (4:7, 9), used of Epaphras; ἀγάπη 1:4 (2:2; 3:14), cf. ἀγαπάω of 3:19; ἅγιοι 1:4 and 12 (1:22, 26; 3:12); ἐλπίς 1:5 (1:23, 27; cf. 3:1-4); εὐαγγέλιον 1:5 (1:23); αὐξάνω 1:6 and 10 (2:19); ἐπίγνωσις and ἐπιγινώσκω 1:9, 10 (2:2; 3:10); Ἐπαφρᾶς 1:7 (4:12); πληρόω 1:9 (1:25; 2:10; 4:17 and πλήρωμα 1:19; 2:9; πληροφορέω 4:12 in an intercessory prayer context; πληροφορία 2:2; ἀνταναπληρόω 1:24); θέλημα 1:9 (4:12 in a prayer context); σοφία 1:9 (1:28; 2:3, 23; 3:16; 4:5); σύνεσις 1:9 (2:2); περιπατέω 1:10 (2:6; 3:7; 4:5); δύναμις 1:11 (1:29); δόξα 1:11 (1:27 twice; 3:4); μακροθυμία 1:11 (3:12). To these may be added two parallel expressions ἐν παντὶ τῷ κόσμῳ (1:6) and ἐν πάσῃ κτίσει τῇ ὑπὸ τὸν οὐρανόν (1:23); while a possible reference to baptism in chap. 1:13f. would find a parallel in chap. 2:11-15. The idea of deliverance from the realm of darkness and from alien control (1:13f.) seems to prepare the way for the words about Christ's creation and reconciliation of such forces.

It is undoubtedly true that too much ought not to be read into some parallels (e.g., four occurrences of δόξα may not be significant) since one might expect in the space of four chapters a repetition of certain terms and ideas. But when due allowance is made for this, we are still left with a large number of significant themes. Some terms, such as ἀγάπη, μακροθυμία and περιπατέω introduce exhortatory thrusts [31] which appear in chap. 3, but others are more directly theological and point to the Colossian heresy. Thus, there may be a good case for understanding the apostle's use of ἐπίγνωσις

---

[30] For the arguments advanced in favour of the traditional view see D. Guthrie, *New Testament Introduction. The Pauline Epistles* (London, 1961), pp. 167ff., and Kümmel, *Introduction*, pp. 240ff.

[31] Cf. Greeven, *Gebet*, pp. 170f. Wiles, *Function*, p. 86, notes the paraenetic anticipation of chaps. 3 and 4 in the intercessory prayer report of vv. 9-14.

as a means of contrast with the much sought-after γνῶσις of the false teachers.[32] Certainly the accumulation of expressions and ideas like τὴν ἐπίγνωσιν τοῦ θελήματος αὐτοῦ, τῇ ἐπιγνώσει τοῦ θεοῦ and ἐν πάσῃ σοφίᾳ καὶ συνέσει πνευματικῇ points to the important theological statement that in Christ all the treasures of wisdom and knowledge are hidden (2:2). Ἐλπίς, to be understood as the object of hope in chap. 1:5, was a significant term and formed part of the subject-matter of the gospel message as first proclaimed in Colossae. The word in Paul's introductory thanksgiving pointed forward to the remarkable statement of chap. 1:27 where Christ's presence among the Gentiles—the subject of the mystery in Colossians—was the glorious hope which they possessed. The universal spread of the gospel is mentioned in the thanksgiving report as well as in the body of the letter. Paul's significance as an eschatological figure was bound up with this (1:6 and 23).[33] The important theme of deliverance from alien powers is handled at the point where the thanksgiving period passes into the hymn. In the passage the ministry of Epaphras is commended in strong terms, and this theme is taken up in chap. 4.

Although the terms μυστήριον and ἐκκλησία do not occur in the thanksgiving passage related concepts are present, e.g., 'wisdom' and 'knowledge' which are significant motifs in the introduction point to these two terms (note esp. 2:2, εἰς ἐπίγνωσιν τοῦ μυστηρίου τοῦ θεοῦ, Χριστοῦ). Τὴν ἐπίγνωσιν τοῦ θελήματος αὐτοῦ is a broad expression, the meaning of which is expanded as the epistle unfolds, and for the Colossian Christians will mean a recognition that Christ is the subject of the mystery, the One who is Lord of both the cosmos and the church.

To sum up : 1. The language and style of the thanksgiving passage are similar to that found in the rest of the letter. At first sight the language appears to be general, but it is in fact related to the Colossian heresy, sometimes by way of deliberate contrast.

---

[32] Bruce, *Colossians*, p. 185.

[33] Dibelius, *An die Kolosser, Epheser, an Philemon*, p. 22, considers πάσῃ κτίσει in the phrase τοῦ κηρυχθέντος ἐν π. κ. κτλ. (1:23) a 'rhetorische Übertreibung'. More accurate, however, is the suggestion of Bruce, *Colossians*, p. 213, that Paul is 'perhaps indulging in a prophetic prolepsis'. J. Munck, *Paul and the Salvation of Mankind* (ET, London, 1959), pp. 36ff., considers the universal terminology of similar passages (esp. Rom. 10:18) points to Paul's eschatological significance. He correctly states that the apostle's 'work is more important than that of all the figures in Old Testament redemptive history, because he has been appointed by God to fill the key position in the last great drama of salvation' (p. 43).

2. Many terms and ideas which are introduced in the passage are taken up and developed in the body of the letter.

3. Many exhortatory thrusts of the letter are foreshadowed in the introductory paragraph, as also are important theological and doctrinal motifs.

3. *The Limits of the Thanksgiving Period*

Up to this point it has been assumed that the introductory thanksgiving of Colossians extends from vv. 3-14. But this is not accepted by all scholars. The problem is to determine where the passage ends. Schubert had noted that the conclusions to the periods were not as clearly marked as the beginnings,[34] and although Sanders, Mullins and Bjerkelund have thrown further light on aspects of the periods their researches have not been of any help in determining more precisely where the passage under review actually ends. There seems to be no lack of climaxes to the period—v. 14; v. 20; v. 23 and chap. 2:3.[35]

All scholars are agreed that the Colossian thanksgiving extends from vv. 3-8 at least. The issue is to determine how far beyond this point the intercessory prayer proceeds, and whether or not the hymn of vv. 15-20 is to be included. Eduard Norden, the first scholar to submit Col. 1:15-20 to a comprehensive form-critical analysis, observed old traditional material in the passage which came originally from Jewish circles influenced by Greek ideas.[36] Significant for our purposes, however, is that Norden considered the hymn commenced, not at

---

[34] *Form*, pp. 4ff.

[35] Schubert conceded that the passage could end at v. 14, but preferred to see the climax in vv. 21-23 where there was a noticeable heightening of eschatological ideas and terminology; *op. cit.*, p. 6; cf. Dibelius, *An die Kolosser, Epheser, an Philemon*, p. 1; Bruce, *Colossians*, p. 184. Bjerkelund, for his part, saw the passage extending to chap. 2:3. The following section is introduced by τοῦτο λέγω ἵνα...—the positive counterpart of which commences in chap. 2:6ff.; *Parakalô*, pp. 179ff. Although it is conceivable that Paul's introduction extends to chap. 1:23 or even to chap. 2:3, it is incorrect to think that vv. 21-23 are the report of Paul's intercessory prayer which concludes the period. Further, although chaps. 1:21-2:3 may be of interest from a form-critical point of view in determining where the body of the letter begins, they are outside the scope of our inquiry, i.e., to examine the content and function of Paul's thanksgivings and petitionary prayers.

[36] *Agnostos Theos*, pp. 250ff. Regarding the vast amount of literature on this hymn see Lohse, *Colossians and Philemon*, pp. 41ff.

v. 15, but with the words τῷ πατρὶ τῷ ἱκανώσαντι... of v. 12. He observed in vv. 12-14 a participial construction (τῷ ἱκανώσαντι κτλ.) and an accumulation of relative clauses (ὃς ἐρρύσατο, ἐν ᾧ ἔχομεν)—both of which were characteristic of liturgical or hymnic texts.

Lohmeyer drew attention to the unusual fact that nowhere else did a Pauline intercession pass into a thanksgiving or a summons to thanksgiving, and had asked the reason for the apostle's altering his practice here.[37] Bornkamm developed Norden's thesis a step further through his particular interpretation of the introductory εὐχαριστοῦντες in v. 12.[38] He considered that in this context εὐχαριστία had the concrete meaning of homology or confession. The words which followed were the community's confession of faith in Christ, rendered in hymnic form, 'which later acquired its settled, although, within wide limits, variable liturgical form in the prefaces of the ancient liturgies'.[39]

Thus, according to Bornkamm's thesis, put forward in 1942, we are to insert a semi-colon and quotation marks after εὐχαριστοῦντες (v. 12), and see vv. 12-20 as a unit, with the words εἰς πᾶσαν ὑπομονὴν καὶ μακροθυμίαν of v. 11 concluding Paul's intercessory prayer report.

Käsemann, who understood the passage in a baptismal rather than a eucharistic context (so Bornkamm), considered that the connexion between v. 12 and what followed, in the light of Bornkamm's thesis, was 'nothing less than mandatory'. He noted, in addition to Norden's comments, that τῷ πατρί, used without further qualification, would fit especially well into a liturgy.[40] Käsemann enlisted Harder's support to show that εὐχαριστέω could well refer to a liturgical act of thanksgiving or confession.[41] Behind vv. 15-20, according to Käsemann, lay a pre-Christian hymn. The author of the letter to the Colossians had worked over this original gnostic hymn, so that the myth of the Primal Man in a Jewish-Hellenistic form, which lay at

---

[37] *Kolosser und Philemon*, p. 38.

[38] 'Das Bekenntnis im Hebräerbrief', *Studien zu Antike und Urchristentum* (München, 1959), pp. 188-203; cf. E. Käsemann, 'A Primitive Christian Baptismal Liturgy', *Essays on New Testament Themes* (ET, London, 1964), pp. 149-168, esp. p. 153.

[39] Bornkamm, *Studien*, p. 197; Käsemann, *Essays*, p. 154; cf. N. A. Dahl, 'Anamnesis. Mémoire et Commémoration dans le Christianisme Primitif', *ST* 1 (1948), p. 86 : 'Tout le passage (*sc.* vv. 12-20) est gouverné par εὐχαριστοῦντες'.

[40] *Essays*, p. 153.

[41] Harder, *Paulus*, pp. 38ff. Käsemann, *Essays*, p. 154, correctly noted that εὐχαριστέω did not merely signify the personal thanksgiving of the believer. But this does not mean that εὐχαριστέω = 'to confess Christ in a liturgy'.

the heart of the passage, had been reshaped in a Christian context. According to Käsemann, the concepts of vv. 12-14, which were not Pauline, 'hark back... to the language of the LXX and revive many of its liturgical and cultic formulations'.[42] The words showed that the setting of the hymn (vv. 15-20) was that of a baptismal liturgy.

Eduard Lohse, first in an article in the *Festschrift* for Ernst Haenchen,[43] and more recently in the *Meyer Kommentar* on Colossians, strongly supported Norden's divisions. He entitled the section (1:12-20) 'Lobpreis und Hymnus',[44] interpreting the participle εὐχαριστοῦντες in an imperatival sense. It was only loosely linked with the preceding words.[45] Lohse thus agreed with the structural divisions of Norden, Bornkamm and Käsemann, at the same time enlisting further support.[46]

To the present writer, such a division has two serious weaknesses. First, it is not at all clear why εὐχαριστοῦντες ought to be understood in an imperatival sense,[47] or why it is only loosely linked with the preceding words. The four participles καρποφοροῦντες, αὐξανόμενοι, δυναμούμενοι and εὐχαριστοῦντες define more precisely what it means to 'walk worthily of the Lord'. There is no need, *a priori*, to separate εὐχαριστοῦντες from the preceding three participles, as Lohse does without adequate explanation.

Secondly, Bornkamm's understanding of εὐχαριστοῦντες as a technical term to introduce a confession is doubtful. Although

---

[42] *Essays*, pp. 154f.

[43] 'Christologie und Ethik im Kolosserbrief', *Apophoreta*, pp. 156-168.

[44] Translated as 'Thanksgiving and Hymn' in *Colossians and Philemon*, p. 32; cf. F. Hahn, *Der urchristliche Gottesdienst* (Stuttgart, 1970), p. 68.

[45] He appealed to D. Daube's article, 'Participle and Imperative in 1 Peter', in Selwyn, *1 Peter*, pp. 467-488, and *The New Testament and Rabbinic Judaism* (London, 1956), pp. 90-105, in support, as well as referring to examples from the Qumran literature; *Colossians and Philemon*, pp. 32f.

[46] K.-G. Eckart, 'Exegetische Beobachtungen zu Kol. 1, 9-20', *ThViat* 7 (1959-1960), p. 106, treated the whole section (vv. 9-20) as 'eine dreiteilige Taufliturgie mit einer Eingangsparänese (9-12), die in der Aufforderung zum Bekenntnis gipfelt (12), dem bekennenden Lobpreis der Getauften (13.14) und einem Christushymnus (15-20), der eine christliche Überarbeitung eines älteren nichtchristlichen Hymnus ist'. He is correct in seeing traditional expressions in vv. 9-12, but has failed to convince scholars that vv. 9-20 are a single 'Taufliturgie'. Further, in failing to recognize the author's epistolary style (vv. 9ff. are joined with the preceding words) he has questionably considered vv. 9-12 to be a *liturgically formulated piece* of paraenesis; see Lohse's criticisms, *Colossians and Philemon*, p. 31.

[47] The imperatival infinitive is found in paraenetic material where there is a series of injunctions, not simply one admonition as here.

εὐχαριστέω was used in a wider sense than the mere giving of thanks for *personal* benefits received, and probably in some measure overlapped with εὐλογέω and ὁμολογέω (see the discussion of εὐλογητός at 2 Cor. 1:3, pp. 237-239), it is questionable whether it referred to the community's confession of faith in Christ. Further, if this had been the intention of the author then two words (ὁμολογέω and ἐξομολογέω) [48] lay close at hand to express such ideas.[49]

For the purposes of determining the content and function of Paul's thanksgivings and intercessory prayers the issue is simply: Should vv. 12-14 be understood with the preceding words? Or ought they to be regarded as part of the hymnic passage of vv. 15-20? [50] Norden and those who follow his divisions prefer the latter alternative on the grounds of the liturgical language of vv. 12-14. They are obliged to make a division at the end of v. 11, for reasons that we have suggested are tenuous. Furthermore, Käsemann and others are still bound to separate vv. 12-14 from the hymn, for they recognize that the subject of the actions in vv. 12 and 13 is the Father, while the hymn of vv. 15-20 is in praise of the cosmic Christ.

The former alternative, however, is preferable. The mere presence of liturgical phrases does not bind vv. 12-14 to the following hymn.[51]

---

[48] Note Deichgräber's criticisms of Bornkamm's interpretation of εὐχαριστοῦντες, *Gotteshymnus*, pp. 145f.

[49] Other criticisms have been levelled at Käsemann's view of the whole section being 'an early Christian baptismal liturgy'. So H. Hegermann, 'Die Vorstellung vom Schöpfungsmittler im hellenistischen Judentum und Urchristentum', *TU* 82 (1961), pp. 88-157, esp. pp. 90f., H. J. Gabathuler, *Jesus Christus: Haupt der Kirche—Haupt der Welt* (Zürich, 1965), pp. 52f., and Deichgräber, *Gotteshymnus*, pp. 78, 144f., consider that we do not know sufficient about early Christian liturgies to be able to make pronouncements with the certainty that Käsemann does. Nevertheless, Bornkamm and Dahl hold the unity of vv. 12-20 without subscribing to a baptismal setting for the passage; Bornkamm, *Studien*, p. 196, argues that the hymn introduced by εὐχαριστοῦντες leads us to expect a 'Thanksgiving prayer' which finds its setting at the communion service (cf. Did. 10:7); so also Dahl, *loc. cit.*, pp. 68ff.; note R. P. Martin's discussion, 'An Early Christian Hymn (Col. 1:15-20)', *EQ* 36 (1964), p. 203.

[50] Lohmeyer, *Kolosser und Philemon*, pp. 41ff., apparently in the interests of maintaining a structure of two seven-line stanzas placed in juxtaposition, with each introduced by a three-line stanza, made a division between vv. 12 and 13. He considered vv. 13-29 to be 'die Ordnung eines urchristlichen Gottesdienstes'. This opened with a thanksgiving prayer (v. 12), which in turn followed directly upon an intercession for the assembled church. Most scholars, however, have rejected Lohmeyer's structural analysis (cf. Käsemann).

[51] Conzelmann, *Kolosser*, pp. 136f., has pointed to the pronounced stylistic change between vv. 14 and 15: 'Bisher hatten wir Prosa (des Bekenntnisstils), jetzt Poesie;

It would be possible with Deichgräber to consider the words as 'ein ad hoc formuliertes Prosagebet',[52] and separate from the following passage. Perhaps a case can be made for seeing the terms as pre-Pauline, and Käsemann may be right in noting that ῥύεσθαι, μεθιστάναι, φῶς, μέρις and κλῆρος were known in a baptismal context.[53] But the experience of being transferred from a power of darkness to a kingdom of God's beloved Son, and of a redemption that was related to the forgiveness of sins, would have been again and again the occasion for joyful thanksgiving and praise. Further, if these motifs had been used in a baptismal context (and we have no certain means of knowing), and were in fact pre-Pauline, then it is quite understandable for the author of Colossians to remind the recipients of these truths, so as to inculcate joyful thanksgiving to the Father. It is considered that the evidence does not permit one to go beyond this.

We are thus led to conclude that the thanksgiving period of Colossians extends from vv. 3-14.[54] It does not have a well-rounded and clear-cut climax, but passes almost imperceptibly from the form of a prayer to that of a creed or hymn. The final words of the period show evidence of liturgical style which may have been associated with baptism, but which in their present context are the basis of thanksgiving to the Father.

4. *Thanksgiving : Faith-love-hope and the Gospel : Vv. 3-5*

The introductory thanksgiving of Colossians differs from the two previously examined in that the report of Paul's thanksgiving and

---

bisher Begriffe der Gemeindesprache, jetzt kosmologische Terminologie; dort Sprach das Wir der Gemeinde'. One wonders why there has been so much disagreement among scholars if there is such a marked change as Conzelmann suggests! There *is* a change from the form of a prayer to that of a creed or hymn, but it is almost imperceptible.

[52] *Gotteshymnus*, p. 82; cf. Gabathuler, *Jesus Christus*, p. 53. Although Martin, *Colossians*, pp. 34ff., treats vv. 12-20 as a unit, he correctly recognizes that the 'opening words are connected with what has gone before and form part of the apostle's prayer' (p. 37).

[53] Dunn, *Baptism*, p. 152, considers any reference to baptism in v. 13 is 'purely subsidiary'.

[54] With reference to vv. 15ff. Moule, *Colossians and Philemon*, p. 58, observes: '*At this point, references to prayer and thanksgiving merge into a description of Christ*' (Moule's italics).

intercessory prayer concerns a church which (apart from some individuals; cf. ὅσοι of Col. 2:1) was not known to him personally.

Immediately after the salutation Paul reported his thanksgiving to God for the good news he had received about the Christians at Colossae. The passage (an example of Schubert's category Ia) is introduced by the principal verb εὐχαριστοῦμεν (v. 3). Here the first person plural is used—as in the Thessalonian correspondence, 1 Thess. 1:2; 2:13; 3:9; 2 Thess. 1:3; 2:13—not as an epistolary plural,[55] nor because Paul stood at a distance from the Colossians,[56] but since he was writing on behalf of Timothy, and perhaps others, as well as himself.[57] When, later in the chapter, he wished to emphasize his own ministry as an apostle to the Gentiles and its eschatological significance, he changed to the first person singular (vv. 23ff. οὗ ἐγενόμην ἐγὼ Παῦλος διάκονος κτλ.).

Paul's prayer of thanksgiving was directed to 'God the Father of our Lord Jesus Christ', v. 3. This phrase, different from the customary object of the verb of thanksgiving—it is normally either 'God' (1 Cor. 1:4; 1 Thess. 1:2; 2 Thess. 1:3) or 'my God', the more personal form (Rom. 1:8; Phil. 1:3 and Phm. 4)—appears at first sight to be a stereotyped expression taken over from the worship of the early church. The general title was used in prayer with εὐλογητός (2 Cor. 1:3; 11:31; Eph. 1:3; cf. 1 Peter 1:3), εὐχαριστέω (Eph. 1:17), as a summons to a doxology in Rom. 15:6 and as the source of 'grace and peace' in Phm. 3.[58]

There is, however, a textual problem in the words [59] and the more

---

[55] Lohse, *Colossians and Philemon*, p. 14; but cf. Bl.-D., para. 280.

[56] Lohmeyer, *Kolosser und Philemon*, p. 21.

[57] Lightfoot, *Colossians and Philemon*, p. 229, states 'there is no reason to think that St Paul ever uses an "epistolary" plural referring to himself solely'. Cf. Roller, *Formular*, pp. 169ff.; W. F. Lofthouse, 'Singular and Plural in St. Paul's Letters', *ExT* 58 (1946-1947), pp. 179-182; 'I and We in the Pauline Letters', *ExT* 64 (1952-1953), pp. 241-245; and Turner, *Syntax*, p. 28. (But Paul seems to use an epistolary plural at 2 Cor. 1:4, ἡμᾶς, where he refers to God's continual comfort).

[58] Kramer, *Christ*, p. 93, considers that the phrase has 'its fixed place in thanksgiving'—for Kramer thanksgiving covers eulogy and doxology also—and was a formula which Paul took over with its original setting. G. Schrenk (with G. Quell), 'πατήρ', *TDNT* 5, p. 1008, notes that πατὴρ τοῦ κυρίου 'adds to and defines θεός. But there is always something lofty about the double name, and it is of liturgical derivation'. Cf. Lohse, *Colossians and Philemon*, p. 15.

[59] D* G and Chrysostom insert τῷ before πατρί, while ℵ A I Ψ and many other authorities insert καί instead, thus reading τῷ θεῷ καὶ πατρὶ κτλ.

difficult reading, τῷ θεῷ πατρὶ τοῦ κυρίου ἡμῶν Ἰησοῦ Χριστοῦ,[60] is to be followed. We thus translate the phrase with Moule, 'God, who is the Father of our Lord Jesus Christ'. Paul gave thanks to God in words probably used in early Christian worship but by omitting the article before πατρί he stressed that the God to whom thanksgiving was offered is the One whom Jesus reveals to us in His character as Father.[61]

In the time of Jesus *abba* ('father') was an everyday family word. Although it and *imma* ('mother') were originally the first sounds which a child stammered, the words were not restricted to children's talk, being used by grown-up sons and daughters to address their parents. No Jew would have dared to address God in this manner,

---

[60] The rarity of the phrase argues in its favour and it is the reading from which the variants can be explained. An expression, quite as unusual, is found in chap. 3:17, τῷ θεῷ πατρί—again in the context of thanksgiving—where the manuscript evidence is even more decisive; cf. Moule, *Colossians and Philemon*, pp. 48f.

[61] On the general subject of God as Father, see E. Lohmeyer, *The Lord's Prayer* (ET, London, 1965), pp. 32-62; Schrenk, *TDNT* 5, pp. 945-1014; W. Marchel, *Abba, Père! La Prière du Christ et des Chrétiens* (Rome, ²1971); and Jeremias, *Prayers*, pp. 11ff.

In the Old Testament God was spoken of as Father on only fifteen occasions (Deut. 32:6; 2 Sam. 7:14; 1 Chron. 17:13; 22:10; 28:6; Pss. 68:5; 89:26; Isa. 63:16 (twice); 64:8; Jer. 3:4, 19; 31:9; Mal. 1:6; 2:10). As Father and Creator He was not thought of as ancestor or progenitor. Further, His Fatherhood was related to Israel in an unparallelled way. Israel, as God's first-born, had been chosen out of all peoples (Deut. 14:1f.). The new factor here was her election, manifest in God's saving action in the Exodus. The depth of this relationship and the seriousness of the demands involved in it were brought out by the prophets who stated again and again that Israel repaid God's fatherly love with ingratitude. Most of the prophetic statements concerning God as Father point to the contradiction between Israel's sonship and its godlessness.

In the literature of ancient Palestinian Judaism, Jeremias claims that there is no evidence that *abba* was used by the individual as a personal address to God. Contrary to what has been commonly asserted 'Father' was not a frequent designation for God in the Judaism of the time of Jesus, for there are in fact few instances before the New Testament period. When God was spoken of as Father in Palestinian Judaism the saying was usually understood in a collective sense. There are a few instances which link the individual to God and these represent an essential deepening of the relationship with Him. Once the divine fatherhood was understood in a personal way, it followed that He could be addressed as 'Father' in prayers. However, the evidence shows that the Jewish Palestinian community prayed to God as Father in the words אבינו מלכנו and although the individual occasionally spoke of God as his heavenly Father, אבי שבשמים, the addition of 'who is in heaven', as well as the obsolete form אבי, with its time-honoured and solemn sound, expressed the distance felt to exist between God and man, even when God was described as 'my Father'. To date no instance of 'my Father' as a personal address to God has been found in Palestinian Judaism.

but Jesus did so habitually in His prayers—a significant exception was the cry from the cross : 'My God, my God, why hast thou forsaken me?' (Mark 15:34; Matt. 27:46), where He was quoting from Psalm 22:1. In His use of *abba* Jesus spoke with God simply, intimately and directly, as a child speaks with his father. The term expressed a special relationship with God. Significant too, is Matt. 11:25ff., where in His cry of joy, Jesus addressing God as Father, expressed His certainty that He was in complete possession of divine knowledge because of the Father's revelation. So Jeremias adds : 'In Jesus' prayers... *abba* is not only an expression of obedient trust (Mark 14:36) but also at the same time a word of authority'.[62]

The striking fact is that in the Lord's Prayer the Son authorized His disciples to repeat the word *abba* after Him. The Aramaic-speaking church retained *abba* as a form of address to God. So precious was the word and so rich were its associations that it was preserved in its original form in the Greek-speaking communities of the Pauline mission (Gal. 4:6; Rom. 8:15). The term 'Father' could now be used by Paul and his converts in a most personal way. Thus when the apostle offered thanks to God as Father for the Colossians' love and faith, though he used an expression of early Christian worship in his address, it contained a wealth of meaning now made known through the 'Lord Jesus Christ'.

Πάντοτε, the third element in the thanksgiving structure is to be taken with περὶ ὑμῶν, and both are connected, not with the following προσευχόμενοι,[63] but with the principal verb εὐχαριστοῦμεν.[64] The translation is then : 'We give thanks... for you always in our prayers'. Thus, the frequency with which thanksgiving was offered to God is mentioned.

Προσευχόμενοι, the first of two participles dependent on the principal verb, fulfils the same function as μνείαν ποιούμενος of Phm. 4 and δέησιν ποιούμενος of Phil. 1:4. The three expressions were used interchangeably, even synonymously, by the apostle (cf. Phil. 1:9 where προσεύχομαι reintroduces the original idea expressed through δέησιν ποιούμενος, of v. 4).[65] In this context προσευχόμενοι has

---

[62] *Op. cit.*, p. 63.

[63] As Lohmeyer, *Kolosser und Philemon*, p. 22; Harder, *Paulus*, p. 16; and Carson, *Colossians and Philemon*, p. 30, suggest.

[64] So among others T. K. Abbott, *A Critical and Exegetical Commentary on the Epistles to the Ephesians and to the Colossians* (Edinburgh, 1897), p. 195.

[65] See above, pp. 29f.

particular reference to petitionary prayer, the object of which will be spelled out in vv. 9ff. Thus Paul and his associate(s) who offered thanksgiving to God for the Colossians also interceded for them.

The reasons for Paul's thanksgiving are expressed by means of the causal participial clause of v. 4, ἀκούσαντες τὴν πίστιν ὑμῶν κτλ.[66] (cf. πεποιθώς, Phil. 1:6, and ἀκούων, Phm. 5). 'Ακούσαντες, by itself, does not indicate that Paul did not know the Colossians, but rather that he had received news, presumably from Epaphras, about their faith and love. We do know, however, from chap. 2:1f. that the church was unknown to the apostle, even though individual members like Philemon had met him.

Within the causal clause of vv. 4f. we note the grounds for Paul's thanksgiving to be the familiar Christian triad—faith, love and hope. However, in this context as Professor Bruce notes 'the three are not completely co-ordinated'.[67] Only πίστιν and ἀγάπην are direct objects of the verb ἀκούσαντες, while ἐλπίδα is found within the prepositional phrase introduced by διά.

The faith of the Colossians is ἐν Χριστῷ Ἰησοῦ. While there is good authority in the LXX for the use of ἐν with πίστις and πιστεύω to denote the object to which faith is directed,[68] it is probably best to understand the preposition as indicating the sphere in which the faith moves.[69] Paul is thought to have expressed the object of faith with the

---

[66] *Contra* Beare, *Colossians*, p. 151, who states that the participle may be taken as causal *or* temporal.

[67] *Colossians*, p. 180. The three are not co-ordinated in Eph. 1:15, 18. 'Faith' and 'love' (according to some MSS) were grounds for thanksgiving while 'hope' appeared as an object of the intercessory prayer. In fact, hope is not specifically the ground of any Pauline thanksgiving. The nearest thing to it is 1 Thess. 1:3, where the apostle gave thanks for the recipients' 'patience which sprang from their hope' in the Lord Jesus Christ. However, the idea of hope was not far from the prayers of the apostle. In language reflecting the LXX Psalter he addressed a wish-prayer to the 'God of hope' (Rom. 15:13), i.e., the One who gives hope, or in whom man can hope, asking that the Roman Christians might increase in hope through the power of the Holy Spirit, while in another petition he referred to the God who has given a good hope (2 Thess. 2:16).

[68] Jer. 12:6; Ps. 78 (LXX 77):22. A. Deissmann, *Paul* (ET, New York, ²1927), pp. 161f., interprets Christ as the object of faith, noting that there is little distinction between ἐν and εἰς in popular Greek.

[69] So many commentators including Moule, *Idiom Book*, p. 81, and *Colossians and Philemon*, p. 49. Spicq, *Agape* 2, p. 243, reads too much into the phrase when he states: 'the expression also includes the thought of all the goods of salvation obtained by faith through the permanent intercession of Jesus'. Other examples of ἐν after πίστις are: Gal. 3:26; 5:6; Eph. 1:15; 1 Tim. 1:14; 3:13; 2 Tim. 1:13; 3:15.

genitive (Gal. 2:16; 20, 3:22; Rom. 3:22, 26; Phil. 3:9) or with the prepositions πρός (Phm. 5) or εἰς (Col. 2:5). Here the Colossian Christians exercise their faith as those who have been incorporated into Christ. Indeed they have already been addressed as 'the saints and faithful brethren in Christ (ἐν Χριστῷ) at Colossae'.

Their love sprang from their faith and so was mentioned next. In Philemon the apostle had noted his co-worker's love in the first instance for this was uppermost in his mind and on the basis of it he made his request in connexion with Onesimus. Here the customary word order is followed. The object of their love is πάντας τοὺς ἁγίους i.e., all of God's holy people. The technical term, οἱ ἅγιοι is used, not to designate Jewish Christians generally, or the primitive Jewish church of Judea, but Christians generally,[70] and in this instance those of Colossae and perhaps of the other churches in the Lycus valley as well. The addition of πάντας [71] accentuates the breadth of the Colossians' love.

The relationship of faith and love to the third member of the triad hope, as we have noted, is somewhat unusual. The faith which the Colossians have as men and women in Christ and the love which they showed to God's holy people were based upon the hope laid up for them in heaven. Some commentators, finding such an idea unusual, link διὰ τὴν ἐλπίδα κτλ. directly with the principal verb 'we give thanks' and see in the phrase the reason for Paul's gratitude: 'We give thanks for you... because of the hope which is laid up for you in heaven'.[72] But this is unlikely for the following reasons: first, although the grounds for thanksgiving can be expressed by a preposition, it is usually ἐπί with the dative case, but never διά in either biblical or extra-biblical Greek.[73] Secondly, the phrase διὰ τὴν ἐλπίδα

---

[70] Note, however, D. W. B. Robinson's article, 'Who Were the "Saints"?', *RThR* 22 (1963), pp. 45-53.

[71] The phrase 'all the saints' has almost become a fixed expression, used frequently in prayer contexts. In fact, apart from a greeting (Rom. 16:15), a salutation (Phil. 1:1), and a statement where Paul indicates that he is less than the least of all saints—without exception (Eph. 3:8), the remaining instances in the Pauline corpus are found in reports of Paul's prayers: Eph. 1:15; 3:18; 6:18; 1 Thess. 3:13; Phm. 5.

[72] Abbott, *Ephesians and Colossians*, pp. 195f.; P. Ewald, *Die Briefe des Paulus an die Epheser, Kolosser und Philemon* (Leipzig, 1905), p. 295; Beare, *Colossians*, p. 152.

[73] Apart from the use of the ὅτι-clause to express the grounds for thanksgiving, ἐπί with the dative is the usual construction. On a few occasions Philo (*Heres* 174; *Cong*. 96; *Mut*. 222f.) used other prepositions (e.g., ὑπέρ), when expressing the cause

is too distant from the principal verb for this interpretation to be likely. Thirdly, in order to overcome this second criticism Beare regards the words ἀκούσαντες τὴν πίστιν ... τοὺς ἁγίους of v. 4 as parenthetical. But this is incorrect. In this participial clause *the* reason for the apostle's thanks is mentioned. To regard the clause as parenthetical would involve understanding the participle in a temporal sense—something that is inconsistent with all other parallels in the thanksgiving periods.

Hope in this context is not the hope of reward.[74] Nor is it like faith and love which are here subjective. Rather, it has the concrete meaning 'the object of hope' (*Hoffnungsgut*).[75] It is said to be 'laid up... in heaven'—a phrase expressing certainty. No power, human or otherwise, can touch it. Hope was a significant motif in this epistle. The reference in this context prefigured those in chap. 1:23 and 27, and the related ideas of chap. 3:1-4. At v. 23 hope was an essential ingredient of the gospel preached at Colossae, while v. 27 shows that because Christ dwelt in them (even as Gentiles) they had a glorious hope. Yet Christ Himself was that hope.[76]

In Col. 1:4f. the apostle was making use of an early triad of Christian graces. These were possibly not Paul's creation, but may have been a sort of compendium of the Christian life current in the early apostolic church. A. M. Hunter suggests that the formula may have derived from Jesus Himself.[77] This passage will then represent Paul's own exegesis of the triad.

In vv. 6-8 there is a digression in which, although still in the thanksgiving period, Paul moved from a report of his actual thanks-

---

of thanksgiving (cf. Schubert, *Form*, pp. 122ff.; AG, pp. 328f.). But I can find no instance of διά to express such grounds. See p. 43.

[74] So correctly Percy, *Probleme*, pp. 477f., with whom Lohse, *Colossians and Philemon*, p. 17, agrees.

[75] So most commentators.

[76] Bornkamm, *TU* 77 (1961), pp. 56ff., with reference to the non-Pauline authorship of Colossians, considers that ἐλπίς as the 'object of hope' in chap. 1:5 is unusual in Paul. Further, he detects in Col. 1:26f. not hope in the sense of historical eschatology but a 'gnostic spherical thought'. However, in neither chap. 1:26f. nor chap. 3:4 are there spherical conceptions. There is rather evidence of a genuine eschatological tension. It is perhaps not without significance that Bornkamm, in his article, makes no reference to Rom. 8:24f. (a passage in one of the *Hauptbriefe*!) where the connotation 'object of hope' is certainly present (cf. Gal. 5:5); see Kümmel's criticisms of Bornkamm in his *Introduction*, p. 243.

[77] *Paul*, pp. 33ff.; Bruce, *Colossians*, p. 180.

giving to a report about the spread of the gospel and a commendation of the ministry of Epaphras. It is difficult to determine whether the actual thanksgiving ends with the words 'because of the hope laid up for you in heaven', or after the phrase 'the gospel which has come to you'. Perhaps a final decision is not important. Either way the links with the important theological term εὐαγγέλιον are clear. Hope was an essential element of the gospel. Based on that hope were faith and love—for which the apostle gave thanks. His thanksgiving, then, was indirectly based on the gospel or, more accurately, on God's activity in the gospel. In Philippians we noted that the Christian graces arose from the work of God. The same truth applies here. So thanksgiving was not only directed to God the Father. Its basis lay in what He had already done.

Here, as in the Philippian thanksgiving passage, εὐαγγέλιον is almost personalized. The 'gospel' had come to the Colossian Christians and remained with them having a firm place in their lives.[78] Like the seed in the parable of the sower it continued to produce a vigorous fruit, not only among the Colossians themselves (v. 10) but also in all the world (ἐν παντὶ τῷ κόσμῳ). This gospel which had been universally attested stood in direct contrast to the παραδόσεις of the false teachers.

Linked with this dynamic spread of the gospel was Paul's strong commendation of the ministry of Epaphras. As the evangelist of Colossae Epaphras had represented Paul there (v. 7) [79] and preached in his stead.

5. *Intercession for Knowledge and Godly Conduct : Vv. 9-14*

The second major section of the thanksgiving period commences at v. 9, διὰ τοῦτο καὶ ἡμεῖς κτλ. This is the seventh and final element of the Colossian passage, and as the intercessory prayer (vv. 9-14) is its climax. In vv. 6-8 Paul had digressed, no longer reporting his actual thanksgiving. In v. 9 he took up the threads of his prayer report of vv. 3-5. A fresh syntactical beginning is made with the words διὰ τοῦτο κτλ. in order to link the petition with the thanks-

---

[78] This is the significance of τοῦ παρόντος εἰς ὑμᾶς, as Chrysostom made clear : οὐ παρεγένετο, φησί, καὶ ἀπέστη, ἀλλ' ἔμεινε καὶ ἔστιν ἐκεῖ, quoted by Abbott, *Ephesians and Colossians*, p. 197.

[79] Reading ὑπὲρ ἡμῶν with P46 ℵ*A, etc. rather than ὑπὲρ ὑμῶν.

giving. A similar device is used at Phil. 1:9 and 2 Thess. 1:11. Logically and syntactically the petitions were based on the preceding thanksgivings. This point is stressed in the Colossian passage in a most remarkable way. For the writer picked up and used terms, which were not grammatically necessary, but which accented the dependence of the petition on the thanksgiving.

So the words διὰ τοῦτο καὶ ἡμεῖς ... οὐ παυόμεθα ὑπὲρ ὑμῶν προσευχόμενοι (v. 9) correspond with and point back to εὐχαριστοῦμεν ... πάντοτε περὶ [80] ὑμῶν προσευχόμενοι of v. 3.[81] Other points of correspondence can be observed between the intercessory prayer and the thanksgiving prayer (vv. 3ff.). So ἀφ' ἧς ἡμέρας (v. 9) is akin to ἀφ' ἧς ἡμέρας (v. 6); ἠκούσαμεν (v. 9) to ἀκούσαντες (v. 4); τὴν ἐπίγνωσιν (v. 9) to ἐπέγνωτε (v. 6); καρποφοροῦντες καὶ αὐξανόμενοι (v. 10) to καρποφορούμενον καὶ αὐξανόμενον (v. 6); τῇ ἐπιγνώσει (v. 10, cf. v. 9) to ἐπέγνωτε (v. 6); εὐχαριστοῦντες (v. 12) to εὐχαριστοῦμεν (v. 3); πατρί (v. 12) to πατρί (v. 3); τῶν ἁγίων (v. 12) to τοὺς ἁγίους (v. 4); while πνευματικῇ of v. 9 corresponds to ἐν πνεύματι of v. 8 and τοῦ κλήρου ... ἐν τῷ φωτί v. 12 may well overlap in meaning with ἐλπίς as the 'object of hope'. The meanings of the above-mentioned terms are not identical, but the correspondence and word-play are obvious. It remains only to note the use of πᾶς [82] in the passage : εἰς πάντας τοὺς ἁγίους (v. 4); ἐν παντὶ τῷ κόσμῳ (v. 6); ἐν πάσῃ σοφίᾳ καὶ συνέσει πνευματικῇ (v. 9); εἰς πᾶσαν ἀρεσκείαν, ἐν παντὶ ἔργῳ ἀγαθῷ (v. 10); and ἐν πάσῃ δυνάμει ... εἰς πᾶσαν ὑπομονὴν καὶ μακροθυμίαν [83] (v. 11).

---

[80] Bl.-D., para. 229 (1), have noted that περί and ὑπέρ overlap in meaning. In the thanksgiving periods they are interchangeable.

[81] Correctly noted by Lohse, *Colossians and Philemon*, p. 24.

[82] Lohse, *ibid.*, p. 4, has drawn attention to the extraordinary frequency with which the word 'all' and related terms appear in Colossians : chaps. 1:4, 6, 9-11, 15-20, 28; 2:2f., 9f., 13, 19, 22; 3:8, 11, 14, 16f., 20, 22; 4:7, 9, 12.

[83] Norden, *Agnostos Theos*, pp. 240ff., 347f., has discussed the πᾶν formula of doxologies and hymns in relation to a Stoic background. The term πᾶς is frequently found in the thanksgiving passages, but its presence is not stereotyped. In Phil. 1:3f. Paul stressed that he gave thanks for all without exception, while in 1 Cor. 1:4ff. the accent was on the goodness of God who had enriched the Corinthians in every way. The repetition of πᾶς in Col. 1:3ff. points, on the one hand, to the universality of the gospel and, on the other, to Paul's concern for the full maturity of the Colossians (cf. 'that you may be *filled*', v. 9; Paul's aim in 1:28 and Epaphras' prayer of 4:12). Note Wiles' comments regarding the 'extravagant quality' of Paul's requests, a quality that is typical of his prayer style, *Prayers*, p. 60.

The ἡμεῖς of v. 9 stresses the identity of the ones who intercede with those who have given thanks. From the day he learnt of their progress in the Christian faith the apostle not only offered constant thanksgiving to God the Father; he matched it with regular intercession for them. Αἰτούμενοι is used synonymously with προσευχόμενοι and not as a specific request in contrast to general prayer, for προσεύχομαι in the thanksgiving passages, as has already been shown, is used of petitionary prayer. The addition of αἰτούμενοι indicates that the apostle prayed to God with great intensity so that his request might be granted.[84]

The content or object [85] of the prayer report is expressed by means of the ἵνα-clause of v. 9. In his report Paul mentioned that his petition had been for a sensitivity to God's will consisting in an understanding of what was spiritually important.[86] This would result in conduct pleasing to the Lord, i.e., a harvest of good deeds and growth in understanding. The power that would enable them to act in such a manner exercising patience and longsuffering was derived from God's glorious might. At the same time they would give thanks to the Father for an eternal inheritance, deliverance from the power of darkness, and the forgiveness of sins.

In describing what he prayed for Paul touched on his complaint against the Colossians. The idea of 'fulness' recurs frequently in the epistle, and it seems that the false teachers boasted that they offered the fulness of truth and spiritual maturity, while Epaphras had only instructed the Colossians in the first steps.[87] But Paul and his colleagues had consistently prayed (cf. 4:12) that the Colossians might receive fulness of blessing, and he indicates in the prayer that unfolds what that fulness was. By means of the passive πληρωθῆτε the apostle, in typical Jewish fashion, showed it was God [88] who supplied in abundance [89] this knowledge.

---

[84] Lohse, *Colossians and Philemon*, p. 25. The verbs have an exact parallel in Mark 11:24, 'Whatever you ask in prayer (προσεύχεσθε καὶ αἰτεῖσθε), believe that you receive it, and you will'.

[85] Rather than the purpose, so Robertson, *Grammar*, p. 993; Lohmeyer, *Kolosser und Philemon*, p. 32; Lohse, *Colossians and Philemon*, p. 25. See Wiles, *ibid*., pp. 173f.

[86] Moule, *Colossians and Philemon*, p. 47.

[87] Beare, *Colossians*, p. 156.

[88] G. Delling, 'πληρόω', *TDNT* 6, p. 291; Lohse, *Colossians and Philemon*, p. 25. On the use of the passive of a verb 'to fill' followed by an accusative rather than a genitive case, see p. 36. Masson, *Colossiens*, p. 93, understanding ἐπίγνωσις as a process rather than a measurable quantity considers Paul's requests to have been: 'that you

Once again ἐπίγνωσις is found within the context of an intercessory prayer report.[90] However, in the Colossian passage not only is the term found twice (vv. 9f.) but the cognate verb is used in the thanksgiving report (v. 6) as well. Indeed, because the Colossians had come to know (ἐπέγνωτε)[91] God's grace they might be expected to grow in ἐπίγνωσις. Knowledge as one of the important objects of the intercessory prayer reports in the Captivity Epistles has been noted occasionally, but rarely interpreted. We suggest the following reasons for such an emphasis:

First, Cerfaux considers that the importance given to knowledge (which is not unrelated to love) in these letters is due to its relationship to the mystery. This mystery, which was Paul's gospel, had its accent on the salvation of Gentiles. Statements of the mystery, according to Cerfaux, were given in a special liturgical style, with its superfluities, its accumulation of synonymous expressions and its successions of relatives and participles. Paul endeavoured to plumb the depths of this secret which surrounded the person and work of Christ and to pass this knowledge on to others. Knowledge of the mystery now played a great part in the life of the Christian.[92] He was bound to advance in this knowledge, and such progress involved every facet of the Christian's life. Cerfaux's interpretation partly explains the use of ἐπίγνωσις in the letter to the Colossians and in Ephesians (if we accept, with Cerfaux, the Pauline authorship and Roman provenance of that letter). But it does not adequately account for the appearance of ἐπίγνωσις in the prayer reports of Philippians and Philemon.

Secondly, this accent on knowledge can be partly accounted for by Paul's own circumstances.[93] In prison (be it Ephesus, Caesarea or Rome!) knowing that he might not be able to visit and strengthen the churches to whom he wrote, he saw the need for them to increase in the knowledge of God and His will, and with this God's mystery, Christ.

---

may come to maturity *in respect of* the knowledge'. But Rom. 15:14, πεπληρωμένοι πάσης τῆς γνώσεως, shows that to be filled with knowledge was a Pauline conception; Moule, *Colossians and Philemon*, pp. 52f.

[89] On the ideas of 'fulness' and 'abundance' in Paul's prayers, see pp. 30ff., 116f., 162f., 172f.

[90] Cf. Eph. 1:17; Phil. 1:9; Phm. 6.

[91] Bultmann, *Theology* 1, p. 67, rightly points out that ἐπέγνωτε τὴν χάριν τοῦ θεοῦ ἐν ἀληθείᾳ, v. 6, refers to conversion to the Christian faith.

[92] Cerfaux, *Christ*, pp. 404ff., suggests it was in the churches of Asia that Paul became used to speaking of the gospel as a mystery.

[93] Cf. Lightfoot, *Colossians and Philemon*, pp. 135f.

Thirdly, the requirements of the churches demanded a deeper and fuller exposition of the gospel in order to combat fresh dangers and heresies that were arising. Thus, for example, Paul's treatment of the church and Christ as Lord of the cosmos in the letter to the Colossians was to refute the heresy that was making inroads into that community. His use of ἐπίγνωσις here might be by way of contrast with the much-canvassed *gnosis* of the heretics. But with such fuller expositions a deeper grasp and understanding was required of the believers if they were to cope with the dangers. So the apostle prayed that God might fill them with understanding.

The object of the Colossians' knowledge is τοῦ θελήματος αὐτοῦ, while the words which follow, ἐν πάσῃ σοφίᾳ καὶ συνέσει πνευματικῇ, define what this means, i.e., the 'perception of God's will consists in wisdom and understanding of every sort, on the spiritual level'.[94] Even a cursory reading of these and the following words shows that the source of these ideas was the Old Testament. Thus ἐπίγνωσις, τοῦ θελήματος αὐτοῦ, σοφία καὶ σύνεσις and their conjunction with πνεῦμα find clear Old Testament parallels.[95] Furthermore, similar ideas appear in the writings of the Qumran community.[96] God, apart from whose will nothing happens, gives knowledge (1 QS 11:17f.; 3:15) and reveals secrets (1 QHab 11:1; 1 QS 5:11; 1 QH 4:27). Knowledge, insight and wisdom (where שכל, בינה, and חכמת גבורה are the Hebrew equivalents of ἐπίγνωσις, σύνεσις and σοφία) were understood by the community of Qumran as gifts of God which He had imparted by His Spirit

---

[94] So Moule, *Colossians and Philemon*, p. 53. This fits the context better than the view of Abbott, *Ephesians and Colossians*, p. 202, and Dibelius, *An die Kolosser, Epheser, an Philemon*, p. 7, appealing to Bl.-D., para. 219 (4) in support, that ἐν introduces the manner in which πληρωθῆτε is carried out. However, they are right in linking the prepositional phrase with the preceding, rather than with περιπατῆσαι ἀξίως τοῦ κυρίου. Dibelius also notes the paraenetic thrust in the words.

[95] On knowledge see pp. 32f.; will: Ps. 103 (LXX 102):7; 143 (142):10. Wisdom and knowledge derive from God's Spirit, cf. Exod. 31:3; 35:31, 35; Deut. 34:9; 1 Chron. 22:12; 2 Chron. 1:10f.; Job 12:13; Dan. 1:17; Ecclus. 39:6, 9f.; Isa. 11:2. Note too the fourth benediction of the *Tefillah*. See Harder, *Paulus*, pp. 118f.; Lohmeyer, *Kolosser und Philemon*, pp. 32f.; Lohse, *Colossians and Philemon*, pp. 25f.; and esp. K. G. Kuhn, *Achtzehngebet und Vaterunser und der Reim* (Göttingen, 1950), pp. 13f.

[96] Noted in detail by J. Coppens, ' "Mystery" in the theology of Saint Paul and its parallels at Qumran', *Paul and Qumran*, ed. J. Murphy-O'Connor (London, 1968), pp. 149-152. Coppens considers it is knowledge of the mystery which is expressed by ἐπίγνωσις in Col. 1:9. In the context of the letter as a whole 'knowledge of the mystery' is probably included in the phrase, though not stated in so many words. For parallels to Qumran see Lohse, *ibid*.

(1 QS 4:3ff., where רוח דעה is used; cf. 1 QSb 5:25). The author of the Hymns, perhaps the Teacher of Righteousness, praises God as אל הדעות and says:

> 'I, the Master, know Thee O my God,
>   by the spirit which Thou hast given to me,
>   and by Thy Holy Spirit I have faithfully hearkened
>   to Thy marvellous counsel' (1 QH 12:11f.; cf. 14:25).

'Ἐπίγνωσις in the Philippian intercessory prayer report had no object and was to be understood comprehensively. In the Colossian counterpart although the object of this knowledge was specified, τοῦ θελήματος αὐτοῦ is itself comprehensive, being made clear by the following words, 'in wisdom and understanding of every kind'. Thus, Paul's prayer, with a glance at the particular issue at hand, was that the Colossian Christians might be filled with a comprehensive knowledge of God (τοῦ θελήματος αὐτοῦ)—since they had already experienced the grace of God (v. 6)—and a clear grasp of its ramifications. Paul prepared the way for further instruction on knowledge in this intercessory prayer report. At the same time he has indicated that apart from the activity of God on their behalf (πληρωθῆτε) they would not know as they ought to, nor grasp what he had to say in the following sections of the letter. We agree that πάσῃ should apply to both σοφίᾳ and συνέσει, while πνευματικῇ, being in an emphatic position, indicates that the wisdom and understanding are on a spiritual level. This was in contrast to the wisdom of the heretical teachers, which at best was only a show (λόγον σοφίας, 2:23), an empty counterfeit calling itself φιλοσοφία (2:8). Although there are no explicit references to the Holy Spirit in this letter (apart from 1:8), His activity is not far away and in the present context it is correct to see that the wisdom and insight mentioned, come through the agency of the Spirit.

Although there is perhaps greater emphasis on knowledge and wisdom in this petitionary prayer report than in any other in the Pauline corpus (though cf. Eph. 1:17-19; 3:16-19)—and this includes a strong intellectual element to enable them to combat error—in true Hebraic fashion it leads to right action and conduct. The Colossians are to walk worthily of the Lord so as to please Him in every way.[97] Περιπατῆσαι is an infinitive of purpose,[98] indicating

---

[97] Percy, *Probleme*, p. 126, aptly remarks: 'der richtige Wandel als Ergebnis der richtigen Erkenntnis erscheint'.

[98] This fits the context better than consequence (so Lightfoot, *Colossians and*

that the knowledge for which Paul prayed was designed to lead to right behaviour. The verb is equivalent to the Hebrew התהלך/הלך which is found frequently in the Qumran texts to describe the activity, of those who walk in 'the ways of darkness' (e.g., 1 QS 3:21), or, of those who showing themselves to be true sons of light walk before God in an upright manner (1 QS 1:8). The latter 'walk according to God's will' (1 QS 5:10; 9:24),[99] refusing to please themselves (contrast CD 3:12). Like the men of Qumran the Colossian Christians are to live in a manner that is worthy of the One whom they confess as Lord.

'Αρεσκεία [100] is found on only one other occasion in the Greek Bible, Prov. 29:48. However, its cognates occur more frequently, so that the phrase ἀρεστὸν ἐνώπιον θεοῦ (or its equivalent) [101] can refer to those actions that are pleasing to God. The verb is found in the Pauline corpus on fourteen occasions, with reference to the necessity of pleasing God (or, of pleasing others as a result of one's obedience to God) rather than pleasing oneself.[102] There is no doubt that in the context of this intercessory prayer and in the light of the apostle's use of the cognate verb, ἀρεσκεία refers to pleasing the Lord [103]—and that in all things.

If the infinitive περιπατῆσαι indicates the purpose for which they are to be filled with a knowledge of God's will, then the four participles

---

Philemon, p. 137; and Abbott, *Ephesians and Colossians*, p. 203). Robertson, *Grammar*, pp. 1086f., considers it to be epexegetical, but admits: 'It is but a step from the explanatory or epexegetical inf. to that of design. Indeed, the epexegetical inf. sometimes is final, a secondary purpose after ἵνα'. Bl.-D., para. 337 (1), consider, somewhat questionably, the aorist refers to the new life of the Christian. This has already taken place (v. 6), so that Paul is not praying for the conversion of the Colossians. The aorist points to the anticipated fact of walking worthily without reference to the process.

[99] Examples cited by Lohse, *Colossians and Philemon*, p. 27.

[100] In Classical Greek ἀρεσκεία was customarily used in a bad sense to denote 'obsequiousness'. There is the occasional example where the word was used in a higher sense (for examples see AG, p. 105; A. Deissmann, *Bible Studies* (ET, Edinburgh, 1901), p. 224; and MM, p. 75). Philo often employed the term in the higher sense with reference to God, sometimes explicitly and on other occasions where the context shows this is what was meant (for references see Lohse, *Colossians and Philemon*, pp. 27f.).

[101] Exod. 15:26; Lev. 10:19; Deut. 12:8; Prov. 21:3; Isa. 38:3, etc.

[102] Rom. 8:8; 15:1, 2, 3; 1 Cor. 7:32, 33, 34; 10:33; Gal. 1:10 (twice); 1 Thess. 2:4, 15; 4:1; 2 Tim. 2:4. Contra W. Foerster, 'ἀρέσκω', *TDNT* 1, p. 455.

[103] *Contra* Foerster, *TDNT* 1, p. 456 (who considers it is not clear to whom the pleasing attitude is directed), and Lohmeyer, *Kolosser und Philemon*, p. 34 (who understands it of pleasing men, so that it explains the preceding phrase 'to walk worthily of the Lord').

which follow, καρποφοροῦντες, αὐξανόμενοι (v. 10), δυναμούμενοι (v. 11) and εὐχαριστοῦντες (v. 12), define more precisely what it means to 'walk worthily of the Lord'.[104] These participles refer to the logical subject of περιπατῆσαι (i.e., the Colossians) not to πληρωθῆτε, although they would normally be in the accusative rather than in the nominative case.[105]

The phrase καρποφοροῦντες καὶ αὐξανόμενοι recalls the words in the thanksgiving passage about the powerful spread of the gospel, and although in v. 6 the middle καρποφορούμενον is found, there is no difference in meaning from the active of v. 9.[106] The gospel had borne fruit and spread throughout the whole world and in particular at Colossae. With Chrysostom and several modern commentators 'fruitbearing' is to be understood as a crop of good deeds (cf. Phil. 1:11), while the growth of the gospel points to the increasing number of converts.[107] But in his intercessory prayer the apostle indicated that the words were not only to be applied to the gospel but to its recipients as well. This is reminiscent of the interpretation of the parable of the sower (in its Markan form; 4:1-9, 13-20). Interestingly enough in both the parable and Paul's two uses fruit-bearing is mentioned before the growth.[108]

---

[104] Schubert, *Form*, p. 93.

[105] *Contra* Harder, *Paulus*, p. 203. The word-order favours their conjunction with περιπατῆσαι, while the nominative case with the infinitive is not unknown in the New Testament, e.g., Matt. 19:21; some MSS of John 7:4; Acts 18:15; Rom. 1:22; 9:3; 2 Cor. 10:2; Phil. 4:11; Heb. 5:12; 11:4. Fortunately there is no material difference in meaning since the subject of the prayer, the Colossians, is the same, as is the purpose, 'to walk worthily of the Lord'.

[106] Lightfoot, *Colossians and Philemon*, p. 133, considered the force of the middle was intensive, denoting inherent energy. But it is extremely doubtful whether such a distinction is intended; see Turner, *Syntax*, p. 55. On occasion in the New Testament the middle of other verbs is used in place of the active; cf. Bl.-D., para. 316; Moule, *Colossians and Philemon*, p. 50.

[107] Chrysostom comments: καρποφορούμενον διὰ τὰ ἔργα, αὐξανόμενον τῷ πολλοὺς παραλαμβάνειν, τῷ μᾶλλον στηρίζεσθαι ... (quoted by Lohse, *Colossians and Philemon*, p. 20). See my article, 'Thanksgiving and the Gospel in Paul', *NTS* 21 (1974-1975), pp. 144-155. Martin, *Colossians*, p. 32, has suggested that *every good work* has 'a reference to the church's missionary task'. *Increasing* could then denote 'the church's expansion in the world as "the knowledge of God" in the gospel is made known'.

[108] In the Old Testament the conjunction of פרה ורבה is frequent, being found, in the first instance, in the creation narrative, Gen. 1:22, 28. Other examples are Gen. 8:17; 9:1, 7; Jer. 3:16; 23:3. But the LXX rendering is always with the verbs αὐξάνομαι and πληθύνομαι, and never with καρποφορέω which is the equivalent of the rabbinic phrase עשה פריות. It is interesting to observe that fruitfulness is mentioned before the increase in the Old Testament.

The whole clause ἐν παντὶ ἔργῳ ἀγαθῷ καρποφοροῦντες καὶ αὐξανόμενοι τῇ ἐπιγνώσει τοῦ θεοῦ, v. 10, has been interpreted by commentators in two different ways. Some understand τῇ ἐπιγνώσει τοῦ θεοῦ as an instrumental dative. The participles καρποφοροῦντες and αὐξανόμενοι, it is considered, ought not to be separated in v. 10 any more than in v. 6.[109] Thus ἐν παντὶ ἔργῳ ἀγαθῷ modifies both participles. The basic idea is that spiritual growth is fostered by the knowledge of God and manifests itself in an abundance of good works.

The second alternative, which we prefer, is to see in the clause an instance of the verbal arrangement chiasmus, so that ἐν παντὶ ἔργῳ ἀγαθῷ is to be taken with καρποφοροῦντες, while τῇ ἐπιγνώσει τοῦ θεοῦ (a dative of reference) is joined to αὐξανόμενοι.[110] Accordingly Paul is asking that the fruit of good works might appear in greater abundance in their lives—and this because of the seed sown in their midst—while they continue to make progress in the knowledge of God.

It is not essential, with proponents of the first view, to consider that καρποφοροῦντες and αὐξανόμενοι must be kept together. If the *Sitz-im-Leben* of the parable (Mark 4:1ff.) was the ministry of Jesus,[111] then Paul's treatment could be a development of this, on the one hand applying the words to the gospel which he and his associate Epaphras preached (vv. 6f.), and on the other hand relating the terms to the recipients of that gospel, at the same time defining more precisely what was meant by each of the two ideas.[112] Fruit-bearing and increasing were marks of the gospel. He prayed that fruit-bearing and increasing might be characteristics of the Colossians themselves

---

[109] So Lohmeyer, *Kolosser und Philemon*, p. 35, states: 'Diese beiden Partizipien sind nach 1, 6 auch als grammatische Einheit zu fassen, welche durch zwei nominale Endungen umrahmt wird'. Cf. Beare, *Colossians*, p. 157, and Lohse, *Colossians and Philemon*, p. 29.

[110] Lightfoot, *Colossians and Philemon*, pp. 135, 137, separates the two verbs, but unlike others understands τῇ ἐπιγνώσει as an instrumental dative, which represents the knowledge of God as 'the dew or the rain which nurtures the growth of the plant'. Bruce, *Colosssians*, p. 186, favours the second view.

[111] Beare, *Colossians*, p. 157, considers that the image of the vine, familiar to readers of the Old Testament as a symbol of the people of God (Isa. 5:1-7; Ps. 80:14ff.) lies behind these words. But such a background, true though it may be in a general sense, does not explain the application of the words to the message in v. 6. Indeed, no Old Testament parallel can be found to this. פרה ורבה is always applied to people or animals.

[112] Moule, *Colossians and Philemon*, p. 51, admits that 'increasing' must be given 'a slightly different turn in v. 10'. Bruce, *Colossians*, p. 181, speaks of 'development' from the parables.

—the fruit of good works and an increase in the knowledge of God.[113] The four participles which define the walking worthily are all in the present tense and stress the notion of progress. Paul thus implied that the Colossian Christians would receive further knowledge as they were obedient to the knowledge of God they had received.[114]

The third participial clause, ἐν πάσῃ δυνάμει δυναμούμενοι κτλ., v. 11, indicates how the conduct, worthy of the Lord, was to be achieved. The standards set before the Colossians were far higher than those of the false teachers. And nothing short of God's almighty power, at work within them, would enable them so to live as to please Him in all things.

The apostle, in prayer contexts particularly, stressed two aspects of God's power: first, that in calling and equipping him as an apostle to the Gentiles; and secondly, that power of God which indwelt the Christian community enabling them to walk in a way that was pleasing to Him. So Paul gave thanks to the One who had empowered him by appointing him to his ministry (1 Tim. 1:12). He also learnt that God's power was perfected in weakness (2 Cor. 12:9; cf. Eph. 1:18f.). In the passage under review the second theme, God's power at work in the Christian community, was in mind.[115] The present participle δυναμούμενοι [116] suggests a steady accession of strength, while the prepositional phrase ἐν πάσῃ δυνάμει, which in true Semitic style includes the cognate noun, signifies that it was nothing less than God's indwelling power at work.

Κατά [117] τὸ κράτος indicates that the power to be distributed to the Colossians corresponds to the divine might from which it comes.[118]

---

[113] There is probably little difference between ἐπίγνωσις τοῦ θεοῦ and ἐπίγνωσις τοῦ θελήματος αὐτοῦ. If anything the stress of the former is on the object, that of the latter on the scope of the knowledge.

[114] Bruce, *Colossians*, p. 186.

[115] It was not power in a general sense as Harder, *Paulus*, p. 71, claims.

[116] The power of God is a prominent motif in Colossians and Ephesians; cf. Col. 1:29; 2:12; Eph. 1:19; 3:7, 16, 20; 6:10.

[117] Κατά in the sense of 'corresponding to' is found in petitions and thanksgivings; e.g., Phil. 4:19; Eph. 1:19; 3:16. The source may well have been the Psalter for it seems to have influenced later Jewish prayers, e.g., Prayer of Manasses 14; Dan. 3:42; so Harder, *Paulus*, p. 45. In each case God's power, grace or glory is seen as the source of blessing to the recipient. At the same time the supply corresponds to the riches of the divine attribute and is more than adequate for the needs.

[118] Lightfoot, *Colossians and Philemon*, p. 138. In the LXX κράτος occurs some fifty times, the overwhelming majority of which are references to the power of God.

It is best to translate the phrase κατὰ τὸ κράτος τῆς δόξης αὐτοῦ as 'according to His glorious might', understanding the Greek as equivalent to the Hebrew phrase with a construct state. In this phrase Paul seems to have been using terms that were current in both Jewish and Christian liturgical formulations. He has pressed them into service in his petitionary prayer, not in any stereotyped manner, but with special reference to the Colossians' needs.

God's mighty power will strengthen the community 'for all endurance and longsuffering',[119] in the face of trials and opposition. Ὑπομονή, 'endurance',[120] signifies that kind of perseverance which enables one to hold the position already taken in battle against enemy attacks from without. By this 'endurance' the Colossian community will hold out and stand firm [121] in every (πᾶς) respect. Such endurance, however, does not derive from personal bravery or Stoical insensitivity but, as in the Old Testament and later Judaism, it is seen to spring from God who is its Source (cf. ὁ θεὸς τῆς ὑπομονῆς, Rom. 15:5—a wish-prayer). Thus He may be petitioned for it (as here, cf. 2 Thess. 3:5), or thanked when it is evident in the lives of believers (1 Thess. 1:3; cf. 2 Thess. 1:4). At the same time Christians are summoned to endurance and through it they prove their standing in the faith. With it they persevere through suffering (2 Cor. 1:6), steadily maintaining the certain hope of the fulfilment of the divine

---

Once in the New Testament κράτος is linked with the devil. At Heb. 2:14 he is said to have τὸ κράτος τοῦ θανάτου, i.e., death is subject to him. In all other passages κράτος refers to God's might. The context of Luke 1:51ff. stresses that power of God which none can withstand, and which is sovereign over all. In Colossians and Ephesians κράτος seems to denote the outer aspect of the divine strength (W. Michaelis, 'κράτος', *TDNT* 3, p. 908). The term is frequently used as the second element (or one of its members) in doxologies; 1 Tim. 6:16; 1 Peter 4:11; 5;11: Jude 25; Rev. 1:6; 5:13; cf. Deichgräber, *Gotteshymnus*, pp. 25-40, esp. p. 28.

[119] *Contra* Harder, *Paulus*, p. 204, who considers the Colossians are strengthened so as to give thanks.

[120] Ὑπομονή (which translates the Hebrew מִקְוֵה 'hope, confidence', and תִּקְוָה 'tense expectation, hope') and its cognate ὑπομένω can be directed to God and so mean to 'wait on Him', or, to the world connoting to 'endure, be steadfast'. The righteous in the Old Testament (particularly in the Psalter) are those who wait for the Lord (Pss. 37:9, 34; 25:3, etc.). Not only does Israel wait upon God, so that He can be called the 'hope of Israel', but also the individual looks expectantly to Him for personal help. Cf. F. Hauck, 'ὑπομένω', *TDNT* 4, pp. 581-588.

[121] It is interesting to note in the Lukan account of the parable of the sower, that those who receive the word aright καρποφοροῦσιν ἐν ὑ π ο μ ο ν ῇ, Luke 8:15.

promises (Rom. 8:25; 15:4). Such endurance can be exercised as the believer directs his attention towards the final day.[122]

Μακροθυμία [123] in both Old and New Testaments is used of the longsuffering of God and of His people. It is used to translate the Hebrew אֶרֶךְ אַפַּיִם, a significant reference being Exod. 34:6, 'The Lord, the Lord, a God merciful and gracious, slow to anger (אֶרֶךְ אַפַּיִם), and abounding in steadfast love and faithfulness', where God's glory is revealed to Moses. God's dealings with His people have given to this word, which was not very significant in secular Greek, a new and unexpectedly profound importance, so that the human attitude of μακροθυμία is now set in a new light. God's μακροθυμία to His people means they ought to act in a similar manner to others (cf. the parable of the wicked servant, Matt. 18:23-35, and 1 Thess. 5:14). Μακροθυμία is a fruit of the Spirit (Gal. 5:22), unable to be produced from the individual's own resources.

The apostle thus prayed that the believers at Colossae, empowered by God's glorious might, would demonstrate 'all patience and longsuffering' in the face of opposition, thereby showing that they had their hope set on Him.

Εὐχαριστοῦντες, v. 12, is the fourth and final participle linked with the infinitive περιπατῆσαι. It introduces the closing section of Paul's petitionary prayer report (vv. 12-14), though, as shown above, some have considered these words to be an introit to the hymn of vv. 15-20. Μετὰ χαρᾶς is to be taken with εὐχαριστοῦντες rather than the preceding words.[124] This preserves the balance of the three clauses ἐν παντὶ ἔργῳ ἀγαθῷ καρποφοροῦντες, ἐν πάσῃ δυνάμει δυναμούμενοι and μετὰ χαρᾶς εὐχαριστοῦντες,[125] and is favoured by

---

[122] Hamman, *Prière*, p. 302, comments: 'La même préoccupation se fait jour quand l'Apôtre prie pour l'ὑπομονή, qui désigne la persévérance, la patience, l'endurance, dans l'attente du dénouement final'.

[123] See J. Horst, 'μακροθυμία', *TDNT* 4, pp. 374-387. The word occurs with ὑπομονή occasionally in Christian literature: 2 Cor. 6:4, 6; 2 Tim. 3:10; James 5:10f.; 1 Clem. 64; Ign. Eph. 3:1.

[124] Most English versions and some commentators take μετὰ χαρᾶς with the preceding. The strongest reason for doing so is that elsewhere in the New Testament 'joy' is linked with suffering, e.g., Acts 5:41; James 1:2f.; 1 Peter 4:13. While this is a strong point in its favour, such an interpretation is not mandatory and because the other alternative seems to suit the context better it is preferable. Beare, *Colossians*, p. 158; Lohse, *Colossians and Philemon*, p. 32; and NEB mg link the prepositional phrase with 'giving thanks'.

[125] There may also be an example of word-play on χαρ-.

Phil. 1:4, μετὰ χαρᾶς τὴν δέησιν ποιούμενος. Εὐχαριστέω, of itself, need not imply rejoicing so the emphatic position of the words points to the writer's desire to accent this characteristic of their thanksgiving. Joyful thanksgiving was one object of Paul's petitionary prayer. This is the only instance in the Pauline corpus where thanksgiving plays such a role.[126]

The liturgical style of vv. 12-14 has already been noted. It is possible that the writer in his petitionary prayer report has selected terms and ideas that were current in early Christian worship. These ideas may well have been known in a baptismal setting. But the remembrance of being transferred from darkness to light, of receiving redemption and the forgiveness of sins would have been repeatedly the occasion for joyful thanksgiving. Some of the terms used may have been pre-Pauline but, if so, the apostle took them over and used them not only in his prayer report but also in his actual petitions for the Colossians. Even if the motifs were pre-Pauline their Old Testament and Jewish background is unmistakable, being correctly noted by many scholars.

The person to whom joyful thanksgiving is to be offered is 'the Father' (τῷ πατρί, v. 12),[127] and the grounds for such thanksgiving are expressed by means of a participial clause τῷ ἱκανώσαντι ὑμᾶς κτλ. (v. 12), and a relative sentence ὃς ἐρρύσατο κτλ. (v. 13). Both denote God's acts of salvation and deliverance in Christ, and have reference not only to the Colossian Christians but to other believers as well.[128] The aorist ἱκανώσαντι indicates that God had *already*

---

[126] (Though cf. 2 Cor. 1:11). It apparently occasioned difficulty at an early stage: P46 has καὶ ἅμα τῷ πατρί 'and giving thanks at the same time to the Father', while Codex B omits καί but retains ἅμα. With this reading εὐχαριστοῦντες would have to be construed with αἰτούμενοι (v. 9), thus referring to Paul and Timothy as the subjects of the verb. But these alternatives are incorrect, serving by an agreement in error, as G. Zuntz notes, *The Text of the Epistles* (London, 1953), p. 40, only to 'establish some close relationship between the papyrus and B'.

[127] Lohse, *Colossians and Philemon*, pp. 34f., correctly points out that apart from 1 QH 9:35, 'For Thou art a father to all (the sons) of Thy truth', God is not called Father in the Qumran literature. (In the introductory words of the Hodayoth He is always called 'Lord'). A glance at K. G. Kuhn's *Konkordanz zu den Qumrantexten* (Göttingen, 1960), p. 1, will show that אב is mostly used in the plural. In the Damascus Document 13:9 God is said to take pity כאב לבניו, but even this, which is a simile and not a direct statement, is a reference to Ps. 103:13; see C. Rabin, *The Zadokite Documents* (Oxford, ²1958), pp. 64f.

[128] There is no real doubt that ἡμᾶς is the object of ἐρρύσατο (v. 13), but the MS evidence is slightly in favour of ὑμᾶς at v. 12. In the latter case either reading makes good sense.

fitted or qualified the Colossians to share in the inheritance of His holy people. This verb, found on only one other occasion in the New Testament, at 2 Cor. 3:6, was used in the LXX. C. H. Dodd associated Job 31:2 (LXX) with these words of Col. 1:12, for ἱκανός was there a divine name, translating שדי ('the Almighty'). Dodd suggested that Paul's two uses of ἱκανόω had been influenced by the passage from Job.[129] The Almighty had qualified the Colossians, unworthy though they were, to share in the inheritance of His people.

Although the exact relationship of μερίς to κλῆρος is doubtful, the general sense of the phrase is clear.[130] We understand κλήρου as a partitive genitive, so that the phrase εἰς τὴν μερίδα τοῦ κλήρου means 'to have a share in the κλῆρος', i.e., the inheritance of God's people.[131] Τῶν ἁγίων, in this context, has occasioned some difficulty. Many commentators, understanding the present passage in the light of Eph. 1:18; Acts 20:32 and 26:18, and the 'holy ones' of Qumran (esp. 1 QS 11:7f., where the motifs of inheritance, lot and holy ones are found), consider τῶν ἁγίων refers to angels.[132] Certainly in the Old Testament 'holy ones' was used of angels (e.g., Deut. 33:3; Ps. 89:6). The Qumran community believed that God intended to unite the sect at the end of the age with the great company of His

---

[129] C. H. Dodd, *The Bible and the Greeks* (London, 1935), pp. 15f.; cf. Bruce, *Colossians*, p. 188; and Martin, *Colossians*, p. 38.

[130] Μερίς and κλῆρος are frequently side by side in the LXX, rendering the Hebrew חלק and גורל: Deut. 10:9; 12:12; 14:27, 29; 18:1; Josh. 19:9; Isa. 57:6; Jer. 13:25. Often κλῆρος, though never μερίς, stands for גורל, a term frequently found in the Qumran texts. According to the Scriptures of the Qumran community men may belong to 'the lot of Belial' or 'the lot of God' (see the discussion and references in A. R. C. Leaney, *The Rule of Qumran and Its Meaning* (London, 1966), p. 129; cf. Lohse, *Colossians and Philemon*, pp. 35f. Harder, *Paulus*, p. 102, draws attention to the use of חלק and גורל in the *Alenu* prayer within the context of election). Many commentators understand μερίς and κλῆρος as synonymous, referring to the allotted part. They thus treat the genitive κλήρου as appositional and translate 'the portion which consists in the lot'. The portion which belongs to the saints is situated in the kingdom of light.

[131] Moule, *Colossians and Philemon*, p. 55; and Bruce, *Colossians*, p. 188.

[132] H. Schlier, *Der Brief an die Epheser* (Düsseldorf, ⁶1968), p. 84; Lohmeyer, *Kolosser und Philemon*, p. 39; E. Käsemann, *Leib und Leib Christi* (Tübingen, 1933), pp. 142, 147; H. W. Kuhn, *Enderwartung und gegenwärtiges Heil* (Göttingen, 1966), p. 80; Deichgräber, *Gotteshymnus*, p. 79; and Lohse, *Colossians and Philemon*, p. 36. On the relevance of Qumran here, see Leaney, *Rule*, pp. 253f., and F. Mussner, 'Contributions made by Qumran to the understanding of the Epistle to the Ephesians', in *Paul and Qumran*, pp. 159-178, esp. p. 164.

angels. This idea of men and angels sharing a community is reflected in 1 Enoch 104:6; 2 Baruch 51:5, 10 and 12.[133]

However true this idea may be in the Qumran literature, the New Testament references mentioned above do not compel such an interpretation. In fact, the words attributed to Paul in Acts 26:18, κλῆρον ἐν τοῖς ἡγιασμένοις πίστει τῇ εἰς ἐμέ, can only refer to believers.[134] The supposed meeting of human and heavenly beings described in Heb. 12:22f., speaks of the arrival of the 'militant here in earth' in the *presence* of angels innumerable, but into the *membership* of the first-born in heaven (i.e., the whole communion of saints).[135]

Κλῆρος τῶν ἁγίων is thus understood as a reference to the inheritance allotted to God's people.[136] Ἐν τῷ φωτί is not taken with ἁγίων, as though referring either to the blessed dead who dwell in the light of God's presence or to angels, but with the whole phrase that precedes,[137] i.e., 'to share in the inheritance of the saints'. The point is that the inheritance for which the all-powerful Father had fitted them was in the realm of the light of the Age to Come.[138] Unlike Canaan it belonged to a spiritual dimension, unable to be ravaged by war, famine or the like. For the Colossian Christians who were Gentiles by birth this was good news indeed. They now had a share in God's inheritance with other believers, or to use the equivalent words of the thanksgiving report they had 'a hope laid up in heaven'.

The second ground for thanksgiving to the Father is expressed by the relative clause ὃς ἐρρύσατο [139] ἡμᾶς κτλ. Indeed it is probably more accurate to speak of vv. 13 and 14 as an exposition of v. 12.[140]

---

[133] Leaney, *Rule*, p. 254; cf. Wisdom 5:5, and for the references in the rabbinic literature, Str.-B. 3, p. 625.

[134] Schlier, *Epheser*, p. 84, omits the crucial words πίστει τῇ εἰς ἐμέ, while Lohse, *Colossians and Philemon*, p. 36, refers to the passage in support of the view that the 'holy ones' are angels. Deichgräber, *Gotteshymnus*, p. 80, however, rightly recognizes that Acts 26:18 has nothing to do with angels.

[135] F. F. Bruce, *The Epistle to the Hebrews* (London, 1964), pp. 372ff.

[136] So Dibelius, *An die Kolosser, Epheser, an Philemon*, p. 8; Hegermann, *loc. cit.*, p. 179; and most English-speaking commentators; cf. Percy, *Probleme*, p. 378, 'die für das Messiasreich Auserwählten'. Τῶν ἁγίων is taken as a possessive genitive.

[137] Lohse, *Colossians and Philemon*, p. 36; cf. Martin, *Colossians*, p. 38.

[138] A. Richardson, *An Introduction to the Theology of the New Testament* (London, 1958), p. 267.

[139] Norden, *Agnostos Theos*, pp. 202ff., and Harder, *Paulus*, p. 45, point out that in oriental hymnic style the finite verb stands at the beginning of the relative sentence.

[140] So C. H. Dodd, *New Testament Studies* (Manchester, 1953), p. 55.

Being fitted for God's inheritance in the realm of light meant that He had delivered them out of the realm of darkness, translated them into the kingdom of His beloved Son and given them redemption. The aorists ἐρρύσατο and μετέστησεν point to an eschatology that is truly realized, while the present ἔχομεν, a significant contrast, stresses the continued result of the redemption wrought in the past.

Deliverance from an alien power was an important theme in the Old Testament.[141] The Psalmists in particular loved to sing of Yahweh's past deliverances, both national and personal, and on the basis of these prayed to Him that He might deliver them from danger, sickness, death, enemies and hostile situations; cf. Pss. 33:18f.; 79:9; 86:13; etc. The influence of the Psalter on the later prayers of Judaism is quite marked. So in the *Tefillah* the sixth petition for the forgiveness of sins is followed by the words, 'Look upon our affliction and plead our cause, and redeem us speedily for Thy Name's sake'.[142]

Most of the New Testament instances of ῥύεσθαι are in prayer contexts. In the Synoptics, apart from the reference in Luke 1:74 (Zechariah's eulogy) and the mocking words of the Jewish leaders to Jesus on the cross that God would not answer His cry for deliverance (Matt. 27:43), the verb is only found in the Lord's Prayer (at Matt. 6:13 and Luke 11:4). All other New Testament occurrences (except 2 Peter 2:7, 9) appear in the Pauline corpus. Both the Lord's Prayer and the Psalter seem to have influenced the apostle.[143] In Paul's desperate cry of Rom. 7:24, 'Who shall deliver me from this body of death?', echoes of the latter source can be discerned.[144] Twice he requests others that they might intercede for his deliverance (Rom. 15:30f.; and 2 Thess. 3:2, where many commentators have detected the influence of the Lord's Prayer). In 2 Cor. 1:10, at the conclusion of his *berakah*, and immediately prior to his request for petitions on his behalf, the apostle mentioned that God had delivered him from a deadly peril. He was confident that the One on whom he

---

[141] Yahweh rescued His people from the hand of the Egyptians (Exod. 14:30; Judg. 6:9), from bondage (Exod. 6:6) and from all her enemies (Judg. 8:34). Note the other instances of ῥύομαι in the LXX, esp. the Psalter.

[142] Lohmeyer, *Prayer*, pp. 209f. For further examples see G. Dalman, *The Words of Jesus* (ET, Edinburgh, 1902), pp. 352f., and Harder, *Paulus*, pp. 102f. For Qumran parallels note 1 QH 2:35; 3:19; cf. Deichgräber, *Gotteshymnus*, pp. 80f., and Lohse, *Colossians and Philemon*, pp. 36f.

[143] So Orphal, *Paulusgebet*, pp. 8-11; Hamman, *Prière*, p. 328.

[144] On the 'prayer-sigh' of the Psalter see on Rom. 1:10.

had set his hope was able to deliver him again. In the introductory thanksgiving of 1 Thessalonians (1:10) Jesus was seen to be the deliverer from the coming wrath. The God who delivered Israel at the exodus and the Psalmists from their troubles, was the One to whom the early church prayed: 'Deliver (ῥῦσαι) us from the evil one' (Matt. 6:13), and gave thanks that 'he has delivered us from the dominion of darkness' (Col. 1:13).

The inheritance for which the Colossians had been fitted was in the realm of light, a complete contrast to the realm in which they once lived, ἡ ἐξουσία τοῦ σκότους.[145] Like a mighty king who was able to remove peoples from their ancestral homes and to transplant[146] them into another realm God had taken the Colossians from the *tyranny*[147] of darkness transferring them to the kingdom in which His beloved Son held sway.[148]

In the phrase τὴν βασιλείαν τοῦ υἱοῦ τῆς ἀγάπης αὐτοῦ we note one of the few New Testament references to the kingdom of Christ. Those commentators who consider Paul was referring to an interim period between the resurrection of Jesus and the final coming of the kingdom of God are probably right.[149] The apostle seems to have distinguished two aspects of the heavenly kingdom in the phrases 'kingdom of Christ' and 'kingdom of God'.[150] The heavenly kingdom in its present aspect was called the 'kingdom of Christ'. God had

---

[145] The most helpful passage for illuminating the phrase ἐκ τῆς ἐξουσίας τοῦ σκότους is Luke 22:52f., where Jesus referred to the supernatural forces marshalled against Him. Satan did have a brief hour of opportunity against Jesus, but the battle went decisively against him. In consequence of His victory at the Cross Jesus was now able to raid the tyranny of darkness and deliver from the Evil One those held captive; cf. Bruce, *Colossians*, p. 189.

[146] So Josephus (*Ant.* 9, 235) concerning Tiglath-pileser and the tribes of Transjordan, writes: μετέστησεν εἰς τὴν αὐτοῦ βασιλείαν. Μεθίστημι is used of transferring mountains in 1 Cor. 13:2.

[147] Chrysostom aptly notes that 'power' equals 'tyranny' here; so Lohse, *Colossians and Philemon*, p. 37.

[148] Ὁ υἱὸς τῆς ἀγάπης αὐτοῦ is best understood as a Hebraism, and is reminiscent of the divine voice at the baptism and transfiguration of Jesus; Mark 1:11; 9:7; 12:6, and parallels.

[149] E.g., O. Cullmann, *Christ and Time* (ET, London, ³1962), pp. 144ff., esp. p. 151; and G. Vos, *The Pauline Eschatology* (Grand Rapids, 1952), pp. 236ff., 258ff.

[150] Most of the references to the latter concern the final consummation (1 Cor. 6:9f.; 15:50; Gal. 5:21; 2 Tim. 4:1, 18), although some have a more general significance (e.g., Rom. 14:17; 1 Cor. 4:20; Col. 4:11).

already rescued the Colossian Christians from the power of darkness, and *already* transferred them to the kingdom of His Son.[151]

The relative of v. 14, ἐν ᾧ, refers to the Son, rather than the Father (cf. the ὅς-clause of v. 13), and opens the way for the introduction to the hymn of vv. 15-20, 'He (ὅς) is the image of the invisible God...' In the kingdom where God's Son held sway there was redemption (ἀπολύτρωσις). This was equated with, or at least in apposition to, the forgiveness of sins,[152] indicating 'very clearly how entirely moral and spiritual the conception of the kingdom of God or of Christ was for the disciples of Christ'.[153] Redemption was not simply the object of hope. It is here an existing reality, a present possession,[154] as often elsewhere in the Pauline writings, and is 'bound up strictly with the person of Jesus'.[155] God has made Him to be our redemption (1 Cor. 1:30).[156]

The associated expression, τὴν ἄφεσιν τῶν ἁμαρτιῶν, did not occur frequently in Paul's writings. It is a well-known fact that he referred to 'sin' in the singular on many occasions and that this use predominated over the plural. Here the apostle may have been using a traditional expression to describe the blessings of forgiveness given in Christ. The linking of this motif with redemption might well be due to the specific problem at Colossae, for it is possible that the false teachers like those of a later period to whom Irenaeus referred (*Heresies* i. 21, 2), distinguished between 'the remission of sins' as the

---

[151] Such a distinction in Pauline thought finds support in 1 Cor. 15:24-28 where Christ is said to reign until all enemies (incl. death) are totally subject to Him. He then hands over the kingdom to God and He Himself becomes subject to the Father.

[152] On the subject of redemption see B. B. Warfield, *The Person and Work of Christ* (Philadelphia, 1950), pp. 429ff.; F. Büchsel, 'λύω', *TDNT* 4, pp. 335ff.; L. Morris, *The Apostolic Preaching of the Cross* (London, 1955), pp. 9ff.; and D. Hill, *Greek Words and Hebrew Meanings* (Cambridge, 1967), pp. 49ff., esp. p. 74.

[153] Moule, *Colossians and Philemon*, p. 58.

[154] Büchsel, *TDNT* 4, p. 353. Reading ἔχομεν which has the strongest MS support, rather than ἔσχομεν—probably a scribal change to bring it into line with ἐρρύσατο and μετέστησεν of v. 13.

[155] Büchsel, *TDNT* 4, p. 354.

[156] The concept of redemption is first encountered in the Biblical data at the Exodus where God redeemed His people with a high hand and an outstretched arm. Yahweh was also seen to be the Kinsman-Redeemer of His people, a theme taken up and developed in Deutero-Isaiah. In recent times scholars have differed as to whether the idea of the payment of a price is to be seen in the metaphor. There are occasions where the idea of a ransom-price is not to the fore. In the present context it is not explicitly mentioned.

first stage received in baptism and 'redemption' as the final stage coming from the divine Christ.[157] It would be quite understandable why Paul would show that both were present realities experienced in God's Son.[158]

The language of thanksgiving now passes to that of a hymn. Many wide-spanning blessings have already been received by the Colossian Christians. The Father had acted decisively on their behalf, and this He had done in His Son. They should respond in joyful thanksgiving. It was to this end that the apostle interceded, for if they responded in such a manner it would show that they were walking worthily of the Lord, and prove that they were being filled with the knowledge of His will.

6. *General Conclusions*

From the introductory observations and the detailed exegesis we are now in a position to summarize our general conclusions about the introductory thanksgiving period of Col. 1:3-14 within the letter as a whole, and how the paragraph contributes to our understanding of Paul's thanksgivings and petitions.

Concerning the *function* of the thanksgiving period we note the following:

1. The *epistolary purpose* is clearly in evidence. Major themes, such as the universal spread of God's true word, the gospel (in contrast to the limited circle of the Colossian heresy), the Christian hope, true wisdom and knowledge with a resulting behaviour that pleases the Lord (in contrast to the falsely-called wisdom of the heretical teachers with its rigorous asceticism and show of humility), thanksgiving to the Father, deliverance from tyranny, etc., are introduced in the period. They are then expanded, in answer to the heresy, in the body of the letter. Stylistic qualities, e.g., liturgical phrases, grammatical features including cognate expressions, synonyms used side by side, and the dependent genitive, are foreshadowed in the passage. The degree of intimacy of the letter can also be observed here. Paul does not know this church personally, and thus does not

---

[157] Suggested by Bruce, *Colossians*, pp. 191f.

[158] Percy has pointed out that in a passage such as Col. 1:12ff., the phrase 'remission of sins' fits the liturgical language better than the distinctively Pauline terms 'justification', 'non-reckoning of trespasses', etc.; *Probleme*, pp. 85f.; Bruce, *Colossians*, pp. 191f.

write in the warm manner of the Philippian letter. The doubling up of expressions in vv. 6-9 suggests a certain awkwardness on the apostle's part. Here he commends, registers praise whenever he can (cf. καθὼς καὶ ἐν ὑμῖν of v. 6) and generally seeks to gain an entrance. There are similarities with Rom. 1:1ff., though in the Colossian passage there is no need to dwell at length on his apostleship.

2. The *didactic function* is more clearly to be seen here than in the corresponding passages of Philippians and Philemon. Important theological motifs occur in both the intercessory prayer and the thanksgiving, e.g., faith, love, hope, gospel, knowledge, His will, spiritual wisdom and understanding, power, His glorious might, the inheritance of the saints in the realm of light, the power of darkness, the kingdom of His beloved Son, redemption and the forgiveness of sins. It was the apostle's concern that these motifs be fully grasped by the recipients, and as we have already shown he expanded many of these in the body of the letter. In the light of the heresy, as it is able to be reconstructed from the letter, and Paul's declared intention to proclaim with all his energy the mystery of Christ 'warning every man and teaching every man in all wisdom, that we may present every man mature in Christ' (Col. 1:28), it is not surprising that the didactic function of the thanksgiving period is clearly in evidence.

3. At the same time Paul, by his actual prayers and the recording of them (even if these reports are summaries of the actual prayers offered to God) demonstrated his *pastoral concern* for the recipients. He desired that they might grow in spiritual knowledge so that they might combat the dangers facing them. Such wisdom could only come from above, and we may suggest that Paul recognized that apart from God's granting such insight his teaching and exhortation in the words which were to follow would be of no avail.

4. The *paraenetic function* has already been mentioned. Catechetical references to longsuffering (3:12), the putting on of love (3:14)—as well as its exercise by husbands (3:17, the *Haustafeln*)—the corporate giving of thanks to the Father (3:15ff.), walking in the tradition they had received (2:6) and so behaving wisely to those 'outside' (4:5) though not spelled out in detail, are nonetheless prefigured in the introductory passage.

Regarding Paul's *prayers of thanksgiving and petition* we observe:

1. The language of the prayers, as might be expected, has come from various sources. The primitive Christian triad of faith, love and hope, though probably not the apostle's creation, has been used by

him within the framework of his thanksgiving to God. But it is significant to observe that Paul has adapted, modified and developed the material. In the thanksgiving periods there is variation : e.g., one member of the triad is omitted (cf. Phm. 5), the order is reversed, other Christian graces such as work, labour and patience (1 Thess. 1:3) are linked with faith, love and hope, while in the Colossian passage the meaning and function of hope has changed. The parable of the sower was known to Paul and applied to his and Epaphras' ministry of the gospel as well as to the recipients themselves. If our suggestions concerning the *Sitz-im-Leben* of the parable (Mark 4:1ff.) are correct, then one may observe that Paul has adapted certain phrases to the Colossian situation, as well as expounded the meaning of 'bearing fruit' and 'increasing' in the immediate context. Traditional material has been developed (cf. his use of 'remission of sins' and his linking it with 'redemption') in the prayer reports and thus in the prayers that lie behind them.

Theological terms such as 'gospel', 'saints', 'knowledge', etc., and certain eschatological references, perhaps deriving from missionary preaching are also present in the Colossian thanksgiving period.[159]

The Old Testament and Jewish influence on both the terms of vv. 9-14 (e.g., knowledge, His will, wisdom and understanding, power, might, glory, patience, longsuffering, lot or inheritance, etc.) and their meanings is unmistakable, as the exegesis has shown. The apostle's mind, as evidenced by his theology and his prayers, was saturated in the Old Testament.

But one of the most striking features of the Colossian prayer is the liturgical language. Words and phrases can be observed in the passage, even though are they present in a somewhat modified form—since Paul was addressing a letter to his readers and not an actual prayer to God. Such phrases are 'God the Father of our Lord Jesus Christ', 'His will' (cf. 4:12, a prayer report), 'being strengthened with all power', 'according to His glorious might' and 'joyfully thanking the Father who has qualified us...' Some ideas show the influence of the Psalter. Others, such as 'God the Father of our Lord Jesus Christ' and phrases from vv. 12-14, have probably been derived from early Christian worship. Such a source is not unusual for it might be expected that Paul, in his private prayers, would use phrases which

---

[159] W. Bieder, 'Gebetswirklichkeit und Gebetsmöglichkeit bei Paulus', *TZ* 4 (1948), pp. 22-40, has noted the kerygmatic element in Pauline prayer.

he and other Christians uttered in their corporate worship to God. However, to acknowledge the presence of liturgical phrases, is not to suggest that the whole thanksgiving period, or even vv. 9-14, constitute *one* liturgical unit. Several facts militate against this. First, even though one can observe liturgical phrases, some are remarkably relevant to the major issues of the letter. Furthermore, it is difficult, if not impossible, to consider the digression of vv. 6-8, where personal references abound, as being part of one unified liturgical piece. And finally, if vv. 9-14 were to be understood as such a unit, one might have expected the whole to have been more stereotyped, rather than containing liturgical phrases here and there. The evidence leads us to say no more than that Paul used various liturgical phrases in his prayers for the *particular* needs of the Colossian Christians.

2. The inter-relationship of thanksgiving and petition is more marked in the Colossian prayer than anywhere else. The importance of thanksgiving in this letter has already been stressed. The petition of v. 9, grammatically and logically sprang out of the thanksgiving, as in all other examples of type Ia (so Schubert). In Colossians, however, there is an unusual emphasis on parallel terms in each component. Those who gave thanks were those who offered petition. The request for increased knowledge was based on a prior knowledge of God's grace. Further, one of the objects of Paul's petition was that the Colossians might give thanks to the Father for His benefits. But, this petition itself arose out of the antecedent thanksgiving.

3. There was a greater emphasis on knowledge in this intercessory prayer (note the appearance of ἐπίγνωσις on two occasions, σοφία and σύνεσις), than in any other of Paul's petitions (though cf. Eph. 1:17-19; 3:16-19). Yet in true Jewish fashion this was to lead to right conduct. A right response would mean the reception of further knowledge. Not to walk worthily of the Lord would mean there was no true knowledge at all in their midst.

4. The reasons for the Colossians' giving of thanks were spelled out in greater detail than those for the apostle's thanksgiving. Yet the two were not unrelated. The basis of Paul's thanks was the gospel, for from it had come hope, and this itself was the basis of their faith and love. The grounds for thanksgiving in vv. 12-14 were an inheritance, deliverance, redemption and the forgiveness of sins, i.e., blessings mediated to the Colossians through the gospel. The ultimate reason for thanks was God's activity in Christ brought through the gospel. This was similar to the reasons for the same

Christian activity of thanksgiving in Philippians and Philemon. And it is to be observed that both thanksgivings in Colossians were eschatologically oriented.

5. While acknowledging the wide-ranging background from which Paul had drawn for his prayers, and the epistolary, didactic and paraenetic function of his reports, one still needs to underline the point that Paul's prayers were related to the specific situation at Colossae, even though his knowledge of it was second-hand. His petitions were offered in the light of the understood needs. At the same time, his intercessions were not so tied to those needs that they failed to take account of wider issues such as Christian maturity and readiness for the final day. Paul's aim was to present 'every man mature in Christ' (1:28), and this aim was evidenced not only in his teaching and exhortation but in his intercessions as well.

PART TWO

INTRODUCTORY THANKSGIVINGS
OF THE SECOND CATEGORY :
THANKSGIVING PRAYERS ALONE

CHAPTER FOUR

THANKSGIVING FOR GOD'S GRACE GIVEN:
1 COR. 1:4-9

The thanksgiving passage of 1 Cor. 1:4-9 is the first to be examined in which petitionary prayer plays no part. Terms for such prayer (e.g., προσεύχομαι, μνείαν ποιοῦμαι, etc.), found in other thanksgiving periods, do not appear in this passage, while the clause commencing with ἵνα, or its equivalent, and expressing the content of the intercessory prayer, is not to be found. This does not indicate that the paragraph is incomplete, but rather that its pattern and structure are different from those previously examined. It belongs to the second category (type Ib according to Schubert), less frequently found [1] than type Ia, which begins with the customary εὐχαριστέω-phrase, is followed by a ὅτι-clause and sometimes by a result clause, introduced by ὥστε, that is subordinate to the ὅτι-clause.

An investigation of this passage, therefore, will not reveal anything about Paul's intercessory prayers for his converts in Corinth. Nevertheless, this passage repays careful study, for from it insights can be gained about Pauline thanksgiving for a church whose relations with the apostle were not always happy. It is also important to determine from vv. 4-9 whether the various functions of the thanksgiving periods—i.e., epistolary, pastoral, didactic and paraenetic—can be discerned.

Unlike the thanksgiving period of Colossians, there is no difficulty in determining the limits and therefore the extent of the passage in 1 Corinthians. Vv. 4-9 form a well-knit unit. The customary eschatological motif appears in the climax, vv. 7 and 8,[2] while a confirming climax in v. 9 rounds out the passage in a well-balanced conclusion. In v. 10, with the introduction of the formal phrase, παρακαλῶ δὲ ὑμᾶς, ἀδελφοί, διὰ τοῦ ὀνόματος τοῦ κυρίου κτλ., the body of the

---

[1] 2 Thess. 2:13f. is another example of the second category, type Ib, while there is a mixture in Rom. 1:8ff. Both types are found in 1 and 2 Thessalonians (see below, chaps. 5 and 6 for the special problems associated with the thanksgiving periods of these letters). On the suggestion that there is an intercessory prayer at vv. 8f., see p. 128.

[2] Noted by Schubert, *Form*, p. 4, and Sanders, *JBL* 81 (1962), p. 348.

letter[3] commences. In the section which extends from chaps. 1:10 to 4:21,[4] Paul initially raised the matter of groups within the Corinthian congregation before dealing with true and false wisdom and his apostolic ministry. The lines of demarcation of the passage are thus clearly drawn, as in the Philippian counterpart.

1. *Thanksgiving for God's Grace : V. 4*

The principal verb εὐχαριστέω[5] in this introductory thanksgiving, as in the examples of type Ia, dominates the entire paragraph. The central motif of vv. 4-9 is thanksgiving and although v. 9 is a new sentence, separate from the long sentence of vv. 4 to 7 (or 8), the certainty of which it speaks is based on God's previous activity on behalf of the Corinthians ('God is faithful by whom you *were called* into the fellowship of his Son')—an activity which was the ultimate ground of the apostle's praise and thanksgiving.

The object of the principal verb is again τῷ θεῷ (some manuscripts read τῷ θεῷ μου),[6] while the third unit of the period is the customary temporal adverb πάντοτε. This is to be associated with the principal

---

[3] The παρακαλέω-sentence, a distinct form of up to seven elements, isolated by Sanders, *loc. cit.*, p. 349, was used to introduce new material, to indicate when an argument took a new turn, or to change the subject under discussion. Although Mullins, *NovT* 7 (1964), pp. 44ff., is unwilling to follow Sanders' rigid lines, he agrees that since another form (i.e., παρακαλῶ δὲ ὑμᾶς...) follows the thanksgiving period, 'the termination of the Thanksgiving is thereby marked'. Bjerkelund, *Parakaló*, pp. 21, 44f., 47, 50, 57, 63, 109f., 116, 118ff., sees a close formal relationship between the thanksgiving paragraphs and the παρακαλέω-sentences, not only in the Pauline corpus, but also in the papyri letters and, on occasion, in official inscriptions.

[4] N. A. Dahl, 'Paul and the Church at Corinth according to 1 Corinthians 1:10-4:21', in *Christian History and Interpretation : Studies Presented to John Knox*, ed. W. R. Farmer *et al.* (Cambridge, 1967), pp. 313-335, esp. pp. 317-322, who expresses his indebtedness to Bjerkelund (see *Parakaló*, pp. 141-146, 154f.), considers chaps. 1-4 to be an 'apologetic section' in which Paul justifies his apostolic ministry.

[5] The first person singular, rather than the plural, is used. It is Paul alone who gave thanks for the Corinthians; cf. R. Baumann, *Mitte und Norm des Christlichen* (Münster, 1968), p. 31. If the Sosthenes mentioned in the greeting is the same person described in Acts 18:17 as a ruler of the Corinthian synagogue then he would hardly have given thanks along with Paul for the Corinthian congregation of which he had become a member. However, we cannot be certain of the identification.

[6] The MS evidence for θεῷ μοῦ (ℵ^a A C D G P Ψ vg syr^{p,h} cop^{sa,boh} arm with several of the Fathers) is stronger than that for θεῷ (ℵ* B eth Ephraem). However, the insertion of the personal pronoun may have been due to assimilation (cf. Rom. 1:8; Phil. 1:3; Phm. 4).

verb [7] for it expresses the frequency with which Paul offered his thanks, while the words περὶ ὑμῶν, the fourth unit of the paragraph, refer to the addressees about whom thanks are given. These four units are to be understood as in the passages previously examined.

The ground for Paul's thanksgiving to God is expressed by means of the causal phrase ἐπὶ [8] τῇ χάριτι τοῦ θεοῦ κτλ. [9]—the only instance of such a phrase in the thanksgiving passages of the second category. The reference to 'the grace of God' (which is specific) [10] does not describe God's attitude of loving favour and bounty towards man as such, though this is of course the basis; in this phrase the sense passes over to the effect produced.[11] It is, as C. K. Barrett states, the universal grace of God which 'encounters particular Christians as a divine gift, constituting their Christian life, and enabling them to

---

[7] Wobbe, *Charis*, p. 82, when discussing the difference between εὐχαριστέω and χάρις as used to express thanksgiving, notes : 'Charis bezeichnet das *einmalige* Danken, den Akt des Dankens, Eucharistia hat neben diesem Sinn noch den von *dankbarer Gesinnung*, Dankbarkeit'. In partial support of Wobbe's distinction within the thanksgiving periods the temporal adverb πάντοτε is used with εὐχαριστέω to express constant thanksgiving, not with χάρις τῷ θεῷ (or its equivalent).

[8] So most commentators, e.g., H. A. W. Meyer, *Critical and Exegetical Handbook to the Epistles to the Corinthians* 1 (ET, Edinburgh, 1877), p. 17; T. C. Edwards, *A Commentary on the First Epistle to the Corinthians* (London, 1885), p. 5; J. Weiss, *Der erste Korintherbrief* (Göttingen, ⁹1910), p. 6; J. E. McFadyen, *The Epistles to the Corinthians* (London, 1911), p. 16; F. W. Grosheide, *Commentary on the First Epistle to the Corinthians* (London, ²1954), p. 27; J. Héring, *The First Epistle of Saint Paul to the Corinthians* (ET, London, 1962), p. 2; C. K. Barrett, *The First Epistle to the Corinthians* (London, 1968), p. 35, where 'accusative' should be 'dative'; H. Conzelmann, *Der erste Brief an die Korinther* (Göttingen, ¹¹¹1969 = 1st edn. New Series), p. 39; as well as Winer, *Grammar*, p. 393; Schubert, *Form*, pp. 55, 60f.; AG, p. 328; Bl.-D., para. 235 (2); Zerwick, *Greek*, para. 126.

[9] See above, p. 43.

[10] Note the definite articles and the following words, 'which was given' (τῇ δοθείσῃ). Although Wobbe, *Charis*, p. 91 ('Gnade und Dank hängen eng zusammen'), and Hamman, *Prière*, pp. 293f., point to the relationship between grace and thanksgiving (i.e., that thanksgiving is the response to God's grace), 1 Cor. 1:4 is the only place in the introductory thanksgivings where the two are linked in a causal manner.

[11] R. St. J. Parry, *The First Epistle of Paul the Apostle to the Corinthians* (Cambridge, ²1926), p. 31; Grosheide, *1 Corinthians*, p. 27; G. P. Wetter, *Charis* (Leipzig, 1913), p. 101, following J. Weiss, *1 Korinther*, p. 6, prefers to understand χάρις in this context as 'die Hulderweisung Gottes' rather than 'der Affekt oder die Gesinnung Gottes', but Meyer, *Corinthians*, p. 17, observes that the grace of God is described 'more precisely in verse 5 according to its effects'; Bultmann, *Theology* 1, pp. 288ff., asserts that Paul neither describes God as gracious nor man as given grace(!). He simply speaks of the act of grace.

perform services they are called to render in the church and for the world'.[12]

J. Armitage Robinson, in an essay on χάρις and χαριτοῦν,[13] pointed out that 'grace' in the latter half of Acts was found in narratives which dealt with the extension of the gospel to Gentiles.[14] Although the introduction of the word into Christian vocabulary was not due to Paul, Armitage Robinson considered that this new and special use of it, connected with the apostle's missionary efforts, was because of his influence. In a review of the Pauline references to the term Armitage Robinson listed some which were '*In regard to himself*

---

[12] Barrett, *1 Corinthians*, p. 36. Χάρις had a variety of meanings in Greek, and even from early times could connote the essentially human qualities of gracefulness (i.e., grace of form), graciousness (grace of speech), favour or acceptance, and gratitude (i.e., the reciprocal feeling produced by a favour); Robinson, *Ephesians*, p. 221; E. de W. Burton, *A Critical and Exegetical Commentary on the Epistle to the Galatians* (Edinburgh, 1921), p. 423; J. Moffatt, *Grace in the New Testament* (London, 1931), pp. 21ff. In the LXX χάρις was used almost exclusively to render the Hebrew חן, while חסד was normally translated with ἔλεος. חן, like the Greek term in its Classical usage, signified 'gracefulness', 'elegance' (Prov. 22:11; 31:30), but more frequently 'favour' or 'approval' of men (Gen. 30:27; 39:21) and of God (Exod. 33:12f.; 2 Sam. 15:25), especially in the phrases 'to find favour' and 'to cause to obtain favour'.

In the New Testament the purely Greek significations of the word fell into the background because of its appropriation to Christian use. There is a linguistic difference between the usage of the LXX and that of the New Testament. Χάρις assumes the semantic fields of both חן and חסד, with an emphasis on the latter (so N. H. Snaith, *The Distinctive Ideas of the Old Testament* (London, 1944), p. 103; cf. J. A. Montgomery, 'Hebrew Ḥesed and Greek Charis', *HTR* 32 (1939), pp. 97f.). Ἔλεος is found relatively infrequently in the New Testament. Its place has been taken, to a large extent, by χάρις.

Although there is ample evidence to show that the word and the theological motifs connected with it were current coin outside the Pauline churches, it was the apostle to the Gentiles who most thoroughly developed the theme of grace (H. Conzelmann, *An Outline of the Theology of the New Testament* (ET, London, 1969), p. 213, correctly points out that Paul used χάρις in the singular; cf. his *TDNT* article (with W. Zimmerli), 'χαίρω, κτλ.', Vol. 9, pp. 359-415). Thus, Paul's message was the 'gospel of the grace of God' (Acts 20:24, contrast Gal. 1:6); it stood opposed to any idea of work or merit —indeed the idea of gift (free and unearned) was at the heart of this word (cf. Eph. 2:8f.). Grace, 'favour towards men contrary to their desert', was attributed to God in His relations with sinful men (Rom. 3:21-24; 5:15; etc.), and to Christ (Rom. 5:15; 1 Cor. 16:23) inasmuch as the gracious attitude to men by God was also that of Christ (2 Cor. 8:9; cf. Rom. 5:8); and it was the work of Jesus, especially His death, that manifested God's grace (Rom. 3:24; 5:2; Eph. 1:6f.). It was the basis of the whole work of salvation.

[13] *Ephesians*, pp. 221-228.

[14] See Nickle, *Collection*, pp. 135f., on Paul's frequent use of the term χάρις in his discussion of the collection.

(i.e., Paul) as proclaimer of the universal Gospel', e.g., Rom. 1:5; 15:15; Gal. 1:15f.; 2:7ff.; while others were '*In regard to the Gentile recipients* of the universal Gospel', e.g., 2 Cor. 6:1. Paul's use of χάρις was:

> '... dominated by the thought of the admission of the Gentiles to the privileges which had been peculiar to Israel. Grace was given to the Gentiles through his ministry: grace was given to him for his ministry to them... The Divine favour had included the Gentiles in the circle of privilege: the Divine favour had commissioned him to be its herald for the proclamation of that inclusion'.[15]

1 Cor. 1:4 was cited by Armitage Robinson as an instance of the second group, i.e., with reference to '*the Gentile recipients* of the universal Gospel', and with this judgement we concur. The point is further emphasized when we note that the expression ἡ χάρις ἡ δοθεῖσα frequently had reference to the ministry of the gospel to Gentiles, i.e., of Paul[16] as an apostle to them (so Rom. 12:3; 15:15f.; 1 Cor. 3:10; Gal. 2:9).

This leads us to make several observations about the thanksgiving passage. First, the word χάρις and its cognates appear no fewer than four times in the space of several short verses. Perhaps its presence in the wish-prayer of v. 3 is not particularly significant: 'Grace (χάρις) to you and peace...' The second word, the cognate εὐχαριστέω, appears, as we have seen, in the following verse. The third instance, God's grace shown towards the Corinthians, is the basis for the thanksgiving that is offered (ἐπὶ τῇ χάριτι τοῦ θεοῦ τῇ δοθείσῃ ὑμῖν ἐν Χριστῷ Ἰησοῦ, v. 4). In no other introductory thanksgiving is the grace of God found to be the basis or ground for the giving of thanks. Certainly God's activity, in the gospel, is frequently mentioned, e.g., Phil. 1:6; Col. 1:4ff.; cf. Phm. 5f. But nowhere else is it explicitly stated that the grace of God—and this a grace which is given (δοθείσῃ)—is the ground for offering thanks. The fourth instance of a cognate word is found in v. 7. The apostle was thankful to God

---

[15] *Ephesians*, p. 226.

[16] F. Baudraz, 'Grace' in *Vocabulary of the Bible*, ed. J.-J. von Allmen (ET, London, 1958), pp. 157-160, esp. p. 159, observes, 'Grace signifies also ministry, an activity in the service of God. Especially the apostolic ministry ("the grace which has been given to me...")'. L. Cerfaux, *The Christian in the Theology of St. Paul* (ET, London, 1967), pp. 89-102, esp. p. 98, notes that Paul used χάρις in a way that was deliberate and almost as a technical term for his apostolic ministry to Gentiles. Cf. Munck, *Paul*, pp. 36-68, esp. pp. 49ff., and F. Hahn, *Mission in the New Testament* (ET, London, 1965), pp. 97ff.

for the many abilities and endowments which the Corinthians possessed. However, significantly he styled them 'gifts' (ὥστε ὑμᾶς μὴ ὑστερεῖσθαι ἐν μηδενὶ χαρίσματι).

Secondly, one is struck by the frequent use, in the paragraph, of verbs in the passive voice. We have already noted the conjunction of τῇ δοθείσῃ [17] with ἐπὶ τῇ χάριτι τοῦ θεοῦ. The Corinthians apparently indicated to Paul either by letter (cf. 1 Cor. 7:1), or through representatives (16:7) that they had become rich (4:8) and this in every way (ἐν παντί). Paul was willing to acknowledge this, yea even to thank God for it, but in the report of his prayer offered to the Father he indicated that the Corinthians were not rich in and of themselves. They had been 'made rich' (ἐπλουτίσθητε, v. 5)—where the logical subject of the activity is God—and their wealth was in Christ Jesus (ἐν αὐτῷ, v. 5). The 'testimony to Christ', v. 6, when presented by the apostle, albeit 'in weakness and in much fear and trembling' (2:3), was nevertheless 'in demonstration of the Spirit and power' (2:4), so that it was received by the Corinthians. Paul, however, accented the fact that this testimony was 'confirmed' (ἐβεβαιώθη, v. 6) *by God* in their midst. Indeed, not only did the Corinthians not confirm the message (though they had undoubtedly received it, and in spite of their failures presented a contrast to their pagan neighbours), they could not establish themselves so as to be blameless at the parousia. This God (or perhaps Christ) would do for them perfectly (βεβαιώσει ὑμᾶς ἕως τέλους, v. 8). The fourth and final example of a verb in the passive voice occurs in v. 9. The Corinthians may rightly claim that they were in fellowship with God's Son, Jesus Christ, though the different groups within the congregation (1:10ff.), and their attitude to the Lord's Supper (10:16ff.)

---

[17] The aorist participle indicates 'an action antecedent in time to the action of the principal verb', Burton, *Moods*, para. 134. The aorist tenses do not signify that Paul was criticizing the present condition of the church (*contra* F. Godet, *Commentary on St. Paul's First Epistle to the Corinthians* (ET, Edinburgh, 1889), pp. 51f.; Edwards, *1 Corinthians*, p. 6; McFadyen, *Corinthians*, p. 17). Rather, the aorists point back to the original preaching and the Corinthians' admission to the privileges of the gospel. After all they still possess these spiritual gifts and they still await Christ's revealing (both tenses are present)—albeit somewhat haphazardly. Baumann, *Mitte*, p. 32 (cf. p. 44), following Dinkler (see reference below), pp. 177, 190, understands the aorist as pointing back 'auf die Taufe als jenen Akt hinzielen, durch den die Korinther an dieser "Gnade" Anteil erhielten'. Dunn, *Baptism*, pp. 116f., refers this and the other aorists in the paragraph to a 'conversion-initiation' experience in which the Spirit is at work.

might make one wonder. Nevertheless the apostle gladly acknowledged this relation to God's Son in his closing benediction. This relationship was due to God's faithfulness since He had called them (ἐκλήθητε) into such fellowship.

What then are we to make of this emphasis on grace and the amazing activity of God in the past? Some commentators and exegetes have considered that Paul was using irony [18] when he dictated the words of the thanksgiving passage. Now we readily admit that the apostle has used irony in his first letter to the Corinthians (notably at 4:8), and one ought not, *a priori*, to exclude it from chap. 1:4-9. But if God's grace and activity are important thrusts in the period, as we have suggested, then for Paul to have written in such a vein would have been at best 'bad taste', or, worst of all, to mock God's gracious work in calling to Himself from the notorious city of Corinth those who could be termed 'saints' (1:2). Further, the terms used are no stronger than those found in chap. 6:11, where, having told the Corinthians that adulterers, idolaters, thieves, etc., will not inherit God's kingdom, he commented (without any irony whatsoever): 'And such were some of you. But you were washed (ἀπελούσασθε), you were sanctified (ἡγιάσθητε), you were justified (ἐδικαιώθητε) in the name of the Lord Jesus Christ and in the Spirit of our God'. We note again that the aorists (and two passives) are used to point back, as do the aorists in the thanksgiving period, to the Corinthians' baptism and conversion.

But to speak of irony within the introductory thanksgiving is to misunderstand the nature of these passages. We grant that the periods have a literary purpose, i.e., to introduce one or more of the main themes of the letter, but this is not their sole function.[19]

---

[18] C. T. Craig, 'The First Epistle to the Corinthians', in *The Interpreter's Bible* 10, p. 18: 'A thanksgiving normally follows the salutation, and in this case it is at best slightly ironical'; cf. E.-B. Allo, *Saint Paul: Première Épître aux Corinthiens* (Paris, ²1956), p. 4. Irony in the introductory thanksgiving is explicitly rejected by Godet, *1 Corinthians*, p. 50; P. Bachmann, *Der erste Brief des Paulus an die Korinther* (Leipzig, 1905), p. 50; A. Robertson and A. Plummer, *A Critical and Exegetical Commentary on the First Epistle of St Paul to the Corinthians* (Edinburgh, ²1914), p. 5; J. Moffatt, *The First Epistle of Paul to the Corinthians* (London, 1938), p. 7; Conzelmann, *1 Korinther*, p. 41; and Baumann, *Mitte*, p. 36.

[19] See above, pp. 10-15, where it was considered that Schubert, *Form, passim*, had overstated the literary purpose of the passages, failing to take account of the paraenetic, didactic and pastoral aims. Also the thanksgiving reports were not mere literary devices. Behind them lay *actual* prayers of the apostle.

Further, it is admitted that we do not possess any actual prayers of thanksgiving of the apostle in these paragraphs. Paul reports his thanksgivings and intercessions, and although such reports may be summaries of his actual prayers to God, the salient points are spelled out, and correspond to what was actually offered to God.[20] To suppose that the apostle used irony in his actual prayers is incorrect. As Godet comments, it 'is excluded by the expression, "I thank (my) God" '.[21]

A more adequate explanation for such a thrust as God's gracious activity can be discovered from the situation that prompted the writing of the letter. The Corinthians had received many spectacular gifts from God. They were indeed rich and the apostle gladly acknowledged this as evidence of God's grace in their midst. No doubt the contrast which they presented to their neighbours in that city was most striking.[22] At the same time the Corinthians had forgotten that what they had received were 'gifts' (note the biting words of 4:7, 'What have you that you did not receive? If then you received it, why do you boast as if it were not a gift?'), sovereignly distributed by the Holy Spirit (12:4-11, esp. v. 11) and that their purpose was 'for the common good' (12:7), or that the church may be edified (14:5).

The Corinthians might abuse God's gifts but gifts from God they were nonetheless. In the thanksgiving period Paul thus set not only their gifts but also their whole Christian existence within the context of God's grace in a most emphatic way,[23] and so instructed the Corinthians where their true perspectives ought to lie.[24] At the same time Paul had given thanks to God along these lines. He might have

---

[20] Indeed we may add that the report echoed his actual thanksgiving, offered to God once more as he dictated his letter.

[21] *1 Corinthians*, p. 50.

[22] J. B. Lightfoot, *Notes on the Epistles of St Paul* (London, 1895), p. 148; H. L. Goudge, *The First Epistle to the Corinthians* (London, ⁵1926), pp. 3f.; W. G. H. Simon, *The First Epistle to the Corinthians* (London, 1959), p. 62, correctly comments: 'we must not underestimate the genuine spiritual attainments of the Corinthians'; while Jülicher, *Introduction*, p. 79, with reference to Paul's first visit to Corinth, states: 'his success was great beyond his expectations'.

[23] At the conclusion of his study on early Christian hymns, when discussing the theology of praise and thanksgiving, Deichgräber, *Gotteshymnus*, p. 201, aptly comments: 'Der Lobpreis der Gemeinde ist die *Antwort* auf Gottes Heilstat... der Lobpreis nie das erste Wort ist, sondern immer erst an zweiter Stelle kommt... nie die prima actio, sondern immer reactio, reactio auf das Heilshandeln Gottes in Schöpfung und Erlösung'. This is theologically correct of Paul's thanksgiving in the present passage.

[24] On the paraenetic and didactic function of this introductory thanksgiving, see below.

to admonish the Corinthians in the words which followed, but the grace of God given to them in Christ Jesus was worthy of praise and thanksgiving.

Thus the apostle wrote neither in irony nor with flattery.[25] He was truly thankful to God for 'grace given' to Gentiles in Christ Jesus [26] just as he was ever thankful for 'grace given' to himself as their apostle. He reported his thanksgiving no doubt to encourage the recipients (even though stern words were to follow), so that both the

---

[25] C. F. G. Heinrici, *Der erste Brief an die Korinther* (Göttingen, ⁸1896), p. 45, rightly rejected the idea of irony on the one hand, and that of meaningless praise or exaggeration on the other. Cf. H.-D. Wendland, *Die Briefe an die Korinther* (Göttingen, ¹⁰1965), p. 12; Héring, *1 Corinthians*, p. 3; and Goudge, *1 Corinthians*, p. 4, who considers Paul wrote in such a vein not only because he had actually prayed along these lines and thereby showed his care for them, but also since he desired to encourage them. At the same time he did not stimulate their pride by praising them directly. Rather, he thanked God for them.

[26] Two difficulties arise in interpreting ἐν Χριστῷ Ἰησοῦ: (1) Is the phrase to be linked with τῇ χάριτι ... τῇ δοθείσῃ or with ὑμῖν? And (2) How is ἐν Χριστῷ Ἰησοῦ to be understood? In answer to (1) Weiss, *1 Korinther*, pp. 6f., connected ἐν with χάριτι. Conzelmann, *1 Korinther*, p. 40, and *Theology*, p. 210, considered the prepositional phrase was linked with δοθείσῃ rather than with ὑμῖν. Cf. F. Büchsel, ' "In Christus" bei Paulus', *ZNW* 42 (1949), pp. 141-158, esp. p. 147; Kramer, *Christ*, pp. 142f. A. Oepke, 'ἐν', *TDNT* 2, p. 541, writes more generally: 'They (i.e., the ἐν Χριστῷ formulae) sometimes denote the objective basis of fellowship with God'; while A. Deissmann, *Die neutestamentliche Formel "In Christo Jesu"* (Marburg, 1892), p. 121; Parry, *1 Corinthians*, p. 31; and Allo, *1 Corinthiens*, p. 4, relate the phrase to ὑμῖν, thus emphasizing that it is to the Corinthians in their being as Christians that grace is given. The two interpretations 'grace given... in Christ Jesus' and 'you in Christ Jesus' are closely related, and it is doubtful whether Paul intended to exclude either one or the other. Furthermore, both emphases are retained in v. 5 (ἐπλουτίσθητε ἐν αὐτῷ), i.e., '*you* are in Him', and 'you are *enriched* in Him'. Concerning (2) F. Neugebauer, 'Das paulinische "In Christo" ', *NTS* 4 (1957-1958), pp. 124-138, has criticised Deissmann and others for concentrating their attention on the preposition ἐν for an understanding of the entire phrase. Similarly, Cerfaux, *Christian*, p. 358, rightly contends that the simple preposition cannot bear the weight of A. Wikenhauser's 'ontological mysticism' in *Pauline Mysticism* (ET, London, 1960). Greek writers used the preposition ἐν in a vague and indeterminate sense, like our word 'in'. Thus the context must decide the exact nuance of the phrase. Christ is understood as the medium through whom (Oepke, *TDNT* 2, pp. 541f.; Wobbe, *Charis*, pp. 24 and 42, following Chrysostom, ἐν = διά; Büchsel, *loc. cit.*, p. 147; and Héring, *1 Corinthians*, p. 2; consider ἐν to be instrumental), and the sphere in which the Corinthians received God's grace; see Lightfoot, *Notes*, p. 147. Neugebauer, *loc. cit.*, p. 131, considering 'Jesus' and 'Christ' to refer to the one who was crucified and who rose from the dead, and understanding ἐν to mean 'determined by...', paraphrases the formula as 'determined by the fact that Jesus Christ died and rose' (p. 131). This interesting suggestion is accepted by Kramer, *Christ*, p. 143.

thanksgiving and its report are evidence of the apostle's deep pastoral and apostolic concern for the addressees. An apt sub-title to this passage might be the Lukan words used of Barnabas in connection with the church at Antioch: 'When he came and saw the grace of God, he was glad' (Acts 11:23).

2. Riches in Christ : V. 5

In his important study on the structure and function of the introductory Pauline thanksgivings Paul Schubert pointed out that one of the distinguishing marks of the second category of passages (type Ib) was the presence of a *causal* ὅτι-clause.[27] In every instance of the second category, the mixed types (Rom. 1:8ff.; 1 Thess. 1:5) and, indeed, in one instance of the first category (Phil. 1:6) this causal clause was to be found. So, according to Schubert, the thanksgiving period of 1 Corinthians was no exception, and in the words of v. 5, ὅτι ἐν παντὶ ἐπλουτίσθητε ἐν αὐτῷ, a cause for Paul's thanksgiving to God was mentioned. However, in this instance the ὅτι-clause is not dependent on the verb of thanksgiving, indicating a second ground for thanks, but is rather an elucidation[28] of the preceding words, ἐπὶ τῇ χάριτι τοῦ θεοῦ κτλ. God's grace had been bestowed on the Corinthians in Christ. Thus they were rich in every way, and the presence of such wealth was a sign that grace had been given.

It has already been observed that in many of Paul's prayers the related concepts of 'fulness', 'riches' and 'abundance' appeared. The One to whom the apostle directed his petitionary prayers and thanksgivings gave liberally and generously (cf. Jas. 1:5).[29] Various

---

[27] *Form, passim.* Robinson, in *Apophoreta*, pp. 201f., disagrees with Schubert's view (p. 168) that the form of the Pauline thanksgiving passages springs from a 'specifically pagan Hellenistic, non-Jewish origin'. The ὅτι-clauses of the second category according to Robinson indicate 'eine formale Verbindung der paulinischen Danksagung, besonders des Typs Ib, mit jüdischen—besonders heterodox-jüdischen—und frühchristlichen Gebeten finden' (p. 202). See above, pp. 10f.

[28] The ὅτι is explicative. So many commentators including Bachmann, *1 Korinther*, p. 44, who correctly comments: 'fügt... der explikative Satz mit ὅτι einen mehr konkreten Zug an'; *per contra* Parry, *1 Corinthians*, p. 31; Héring, *1 Corinthians*, p. 3; and AG, p. 328 (although the entry under ὅτι, pp. 592f., appears to contradict that under εὐχαριστέω).

[29] See above, p. 84, with reference to Col. 1:9; and cf. Harder, *Paulus*, p. 209.

terms were used to describe this abundance, e.g., πληρόω and περισσεύω.³⁰ In the Corinthian letters the *wealth of the Christian life* was often expressed by the word πλοῦτος and its cognates. Elsewhere the apostle spoke of God's or Christ's wealth (Rom. 2:4; 9:23; 10:12; 11:33; Phil. 4:19).³¹ The recurrence of this theme in the Corinthian correspondence suggests that the Corinthians themselves had informed Paul, either by letter (cf. 1 Cor. 7:1) or verbally by messengers (16:7), about their riches.³² They certainly exaggerated the wealth which they possessed—note the irony of 4:8, 'Already you are filled! Already you have become rich (ἐπλουτήσατε)!'—failing to recognize the source (2 Cor. 8:9), its terms of reference (2 Cor. 4:7), that it had been brought by a mere poverty-stricken apostle (2 Cor. 6:10, ὡς πτωχοὶ πολλοὺς δὲ πλουτίζοντες), and that its possession ought to have resulted in a deep-seated compassion for others (2 Cor. 8:2, 7).³³ Paul did not doubt their reception of all kinds (ἐν παντί,³⁴ 1 Cor. 1:5) of riches. Their source, however, was God (note the passive ἐπλουτίσθητε) ³⁵ who had given this wealth to them in Christ Jesus (v. 5).

In the phrase which follows, ἐν παντὶ λόγῳ καὶ πάσῃ γνώσει, the character of the Corinthians' wealth is described more precisely: 'in speech and knowledge of every kind'.³⁶ Much has been made by

---

³⁰ Bachmann, *1 Korinther*, p. 44, rightly observes that Paul usually prefers περισσεύω (to describe abundance in the Christian life) to πλουτέω and its cognates.

³¹ Πλοῦτος of wealth in the Christian life is restricted to the Corinthian correspondence. (Though cf. 1 Tim. 6:17ff. where those who are *rich*, τοῖς πλουσίοις, are to be *rich* in good deeds, πλουτεῖν ἐν ἔργοις καλοῖς, having set their hope on God who *richly* supplies everything for their enjoyment, πάντα πλουσίως εἰς ἀπόλαυσιν). Cf. Parry, *1 Corinthians*, p. 32; Barrett, *1 Corinthians*, p. 36; Conzelmann, *1 Korinther*, p. 40. F. Hauck-W. Kasch, 'πλοῦτος', *TDNT* 6, pp. 328f., observe: 'Riches is for him (i.e., Paul) a term to denote the being of Christ, the work of God in Christ, and the eschatological situation of Christ's community'.

³² Barrett, *1 Corinthians*, p. 36, adds: 'That the information came from Corinth is suggested by the kinds of wealth listed'.

³³ Note Paul's injunction at 1 Cor. 7:31.

³⁴ 'In every way' ought not to be pressed, being defined and virtually limited by the words which follow, so Meyer, *Corinthians*, p. 17; G. G. Findlay, 'St. Paul's First Epistle to the Corinthians', in *The Expositor's Greek Testament* 2, ed. W. Robertson Nicoll (London, 1900), p. 760; Parry, *1 Corinthians*, p. 32; Grosheide, *1 Corinthians*, p. 27; Conzelmann, *1 Korinther*, p. 40. Turner, *Syntax*, p. 265, is inclined to view the ἐν-phrase as equivalent to a dative of reference. On the rhetorical use of πᾶς see Wendland, *Literaturformen*, p. 288.

³⁵ Note the discussion above, pp. 112f.

³⁶ On the use of πᾶς with abstract nouns, Deichgräber, *Gotteshymnus*, p. 74, with reference to Eph. 1:8, points out that this reminds one of the Hebrew כל with abstract

exegetes of the fact that we are not told the Corinthians were rich in faith,[37] love and hope; indeed, we learn from the two canonical letters to Corinth that they were seriously deficient in these graces, particularly in love (cf. chap. 13).[38] The kinds of wealth mentioned were those which made the strongest appeal to the Corinthians. Various suggestions have been made about these two gifts (which are kindred, being linked by one preposition, ἐν): e.g., λόγος is the lower, γνῶσις the higher knowledge (a distinction which has no real foundation); λόγος refers to the gift of tongues, γνῶσις to that of prophecy (but the restriction to special gifts is not a warranted conclusion from the context, see below); and λόγος is the teaching of the gospel as offered to the Corinthians, γνῶσις their hearty acceptance of it. The best solution, however, is to understand λόγος as the outward expression, γνῶσις the inward conviction and apprehension.[39] Not only were the Corinthians rich in their understanding of the truths of the gospel, but they were also gifted with the power of clearly enunciating these truths. *Speech* includes the gift of speaking in tongues (cf. 12:10, 28; 14:2) but as it is 'of every kind', it means that prophecy (14:1) and other kinds of Christian converse are included. These gifts were obviously spectacular but whether we should state categorically with Conzelmann that: 'Es handelt sich um übernatürliche Gaben, nicht um Überhöhung der natürlichen',[40] is doubtful. It seems more consistent to include both

---

substantives found in both the Old Testament and the Qumran texts; cf. K. G. Kuhn, 'The Epistle to the Ephesians in the light of the Qumran texts', in *Paul and Qumran*, p. 119, and *Konkordanz*, pp. 99f., 102f.

[37] *Contra* Filson, *History*, p. 250, who states that Paul thanked God 'for their gifts and Christian faith'.

[38] Some commentators point to the omission of faith, love and hope, adding, for example: 'Hier muss man zwischen den Zeilen lesen', so W. Bousset, 'Der erste Brief an die Korinther', in *Die Schriften des Neuen Testaments neu übersetzt und für die Gegenwart erklärt 2* (W. Bousset und W. Heitmüller) (Göttingen, ³1917), p. 78; cf. also Weiss, *1 Korinther*, p. 6; Craig, *1 Corinthians*, p. 19; and Héring, *1 Corinthians*, p. 3. But as Barrett, *1 Corinthians*, p. 40, points out Paul's thanksgiving was ultimately based on God's faithfulness. That he said nothing about the trust, love and faithfulness of the Corinthians was.'partly, but only partly, due to circumstances in Corinth'.

[39] Grosheide, *1 Corinthians*, p. 28; Barrett, *1 Corinthians*, pp. 36f.; Conzelmann, *1 Korinther*, p. 41. See also Lightfoot's excellent discussion in *Notes*, pp. 147f. 'Speech and knowledge' is an important motif in this letter, but it is not *the* theme as Wendland, *Korinther*, p. 12, believes.

[40] *1 Korinther*, p. 41.

'übernatürliche Gaben' and 'Überhöhung der natürlichen'.[41] One would expect γνῶσις, which refers to the apprehension of truths, to precede λόγος, which deals with their expression. But λόγος was probably mentioned first since it was the more spectacular of the two.[42] If this is the reason, then the apostle may have been quoting once more what the Corinthians had previously said.

This is the first occurrence of the term γνῶσις [43] in the New Testament. It recurs frequently in the Corinthian correspondence (at chaps. 8:1, 7, 10, 11; 12:8; 13:2, 8; 14:6; 2 Cor. 2:14; 4:6; 6:6; 8:7; 10:5; 11:6), as does the related theme 'wisdom' (σοφία, cf. 1:17, etc.).[44] Various shades of meaning appear in particular contexts, but the notion of the intellectual apprehension and application of Christian truth is constant. In spite of the danger of this gift leading to an exaggerated individualism which loses concern for one's neighbour (cf. 8:11), and that it was inferior to love, it was still a good thing and worthy of thanksgiving to God. In some ways it was remarkable that the apostle should give thanks for those gifts (among others, if the broader sense of λόγος and γνῶσις be accepted) which were misused in such a way as to create serious problems within the Corinthian congregation. Yet Paul knew their ultimate source and the potential they had for good and for building up [45] other members of the church.

The point which Dupont makes, viz., that the terminology (both λόγος and γνῶσις) is derived from the Old Testament with special reference to the prophetic background,[46] has much to commend it.

---

[41] So Wetter, *Charis*, ad loc., following W. Sanday and A. C. Headlam, *A Critical and Exegetical Commentary on the Epistle to the Romans* (Edinburgh, ⁵1902), p. 21, with special reference to the gifts of 1 Cor. 12-14.

[42] Parry, *1 Corinthians*, p. 32.

[43] The word γνῶσις in itself does not necessarily point to the religious phenomenon described as Gnosis (Barrett, *1 Corinthians*, p. 37; cf. Cerfaux, *Christian*, p. 247). The term was generally used in Greek in a non-technical sense and although some of the other instances of γνῶσις in the Corinthian letters *may* point to a specific set of ideas current at Corinth (whether we style it 'Gnosticism' or 'incipient gnosticism') there is no ground for understanding the term in such a manner in the present context.

[44] See the discussion on these twin themes by Barrett, *1 Corinthians*, pp. 6, 49ff., etc., and especially in his 'Christianity at Corinth', *BJRL* 46 (1964), pp. 269-297, particularly pp. 275-286, where he discusses the work of T. W. Manson, A. Schlatter, W. Schmithals and U. Wilckens.

[45] G. Bornkamm, *Early Christian Experience* (ET, London, 1969), pp. 161-169, deals with the motif of edification in worship with reference to the Corinthians' gifts.

[46] *Gnosis*, p. 234.

The Corinthians' gifts, judging from chaps. 12-14, were not wholly unlike those which some prophets of Israel possessed.

3. *A Testimony Confirmed : V. 6*

The words of v. 6, 'even as (καθώς) [47] the testimony to Christ was confirmed among you', explain the reason [48] for the richness of spiritual endowment the Corinthians possessed. That cause was a testimony centred on Christ. The genitive τοῦ Χριστοῦ could be subjective [49] indicating that in true preaching it is Christ Himself who speaks [50] (cf. Rom. 10:14, 17),[51] yet it is more likely in the present context to be objective,[52] a testimony centred on Christ crucified (cf. 1 Cor. 1:23, and 2:2). The words thus point back to the original preaching of the gospel by Paul which had been accepted by the Corinthians. Although the words about 'riches' and 'speech and wisdom of every kind' may have been used by the Corinthians and subsequently taken up by the apostle, he knew from his own experience of preaching the gospel to them, that rightly understood, their statements were correct. The testimony to Christ was the source

---

[47] *Καθώς* is found in the thanksgiving periods (of all types) at 2 Cor. 1:5; Eph. 1:4; Phil. 1:7; Col. 1:6 (twice), 7; 1 Thess. 1:5; 2:13; 2 Thess. 1:3 (and according to Schubert, *Form*, pp. 31, 46, it is elliptical in Rom. 1:13, 17). Schubert's statement that 'a very definite formal and functional significance within the thanksgiving pattern attaches to it' (p. 31), has been challenged by Percy, *Probleme*, pp. 244f.; and Lohse, *Colossians and Philemon*, p. 19, who consider its function is not uniform and that it appears frequently in other parts of Paul's letters anyway.

[48] *Καθώς* is to be translated 'just as' (= 'since'), for this suits the context best. So grammarians (Bl.-D., para. 453 (2); Turner, *Syntax*, p. 320; cf. Robertson, *Grammar*, pp. 968, 1382), and commentators in general (Meyer, *Corinthians*, p. 18; Edwards, *1 Corinthians*, p. 6; Allo, *1 Corinthiens*, p. 4; Héring, *1 Corinthians*, p. 3; Barrett, *1 Corinthians*, p. 37; Conzelmann, *1 Korinther*, p. 41; and see AG, p. 392). *Per contra* Godet, *1 Corinthians*, p. 53, who considers καθώς indicates a mode rather than a cause.

[49] The subjective genitive is used with μαρτύριον in 2 Cor. 1:12, and 2 Thess. 1:10, but the objective genitive is found at Acts 4:33; 1 Cor. 2:1; and 2 Tim. 1:8. Cf. H. Strathmann, 'μάρτυς', *TDNT* 4, p. 504.

[50] This point is well made by G. W. Bromiley, *Christian Ministry* (Grand Rapids, 1960), p. 17.

[51] See especially C. K. Barrett, *The Epistle to the Romans* (London, 1957), pp. 204f.; J. Murray, *The Epistle to the Romans* 2 (London, 1965), p. 58.

[52] So most commentators. V. H. Neufeld, *The Earliest Christian Confessions* (Leiden, 1963), p. 29, who understands the phrase as a 'testimony to Christ', translates μαρτύριον as 'inspired preaching' (p. 30).

of their wealth. The presence of these riches was evidence that God's grace had been given to them as Gentiles and this was cause indeed for thankful praise to God.

In this context μαρτύριον is synonymous with εὐαγγέλιον or κήρυγμα (cf. 1 Cor. 1:21; 2:4). It has been noted that εὐαγγέλιον was an important theological term, frequently found in the thanksgiving periods.[53] The word does not appear in this paragraph, but its synonym μαρτύριον does. Εὐαγγέλιον in several of the periods was seen to be a *nomen actionis*; in Colossians and Philippians it was almost personalized (note the verbs used in conjunction with it).[54] This is not the case with μαρτύριον in the present context. Unlike μαρτυρία, μαρτύριον does not refer to the process of giving testimony. Rather, it is an objective testimony which is primarily a means of proof.[55] And the presence of ἐβεβαιώθη in the immediate context 'confirms' this interpretation.

Adolf Deissmann's work on the papyri has shown how frequently βέβαιος and its cognates were used as technical terms to speak of guaranteeing legal contracts.[56] Thus in P. Petr. III. 74 (a) βεβαιώσω σοι = 'I shall give you a guarantee'.[57] Because of this background some scholars have been inclined to detect a legal sense in most of the New Testament occurrences of these terms. Schlier, for example, considers ἐβεβαιώθη in 1 Cor. 1:6 to refer to 'the testimony to Christ' being given legal force by the apostles in the Corinthian community.[58] But this is doubtful. First, it is certain that the confirmation had not been brought about by Paul and his colleagues. They may have been the instruments by which the testimony to Christ was presented;

---

[53] See the author's article, 'Thanksgiving and the Gospel in Paul', *NTS* 21 (1974-1975), pp. 144-155.

[54] See the discussion above, pp. 82, 25.

[55] Strathmann, *TDNT* 4, p. 502.

[56] *Studies*, pp. 104ff.; cf. MM, pp. 107ff.

[57] MM, p. 108.

[58] H. Schlier, 'βέβαιος', *TDNT* 1, p. 603. Moffatt, *1 Corinthians*, p. 7, and P. J. Du Plessis, *ΤΕΛΕΙΟΣ. The Idea of Perfection in the New Testament* (Kampen, 1959), p. 159, strongly emphasize the aspect of legal validity. The latter considers that, in the present context, 'the witness of Paul to Christ was borne, verified and established with the legal validity furnished by the χαρίσματα'. Conzelmann's criticism of Schlier ('der Wortlaut lädt nicht zu dieser engen Fassung ein', *1 Korinther*, p. 41) also applies to Moffatt and Du Plessis and is 'valid'. W. G. Kümmel in H. Lietzmann-W. G. Kümmel, *An die Korinther I. II* (Tübingen, ⁵1969), pp. 166f., considers the context of vv. 5, 7 and 8 argues against Schlier's interpretation.

but the confirmation was God's (cf. 2 Cor. 1:21). Secondly, it is not clear in the present context whether or not the legal overtones have been left behind. E. Dinkler [59] has pointed out that the word-group is found in Paul in *two* contexts : (1) in association with *soteriological ideas*, e.g., with 'gospel' (Phil. 1:7), 'promise' (Rom. 4:16; 15:8), 'the testimony to Christ' (this passage), and with eschatological concepts, such as 'hope' (2 Cor. 1:7) and 'the day of the Lord' (1 Cor. 1:8); and (2) in association with *legal motifs*, e.g., 'defence' (Phil. 1:7) and at 2 Cor. 1:22 where a legal term 'guarantee' is found. Van Unnik, in an earlier treatment of 2 Cor. 1:15-24,[60] considered the key to understanding that passage was in the Aramaic אמן-motif which lay behind key words of these verses : 'faithful' (v. 18), 'yes' (vv. 19 and 20), 'establishes' (v. 21) and 'faith' (v. 24). It is quite possible that Paul had this concept of 'faithfulness' in mind when he penned these words, but whether his Corinthian readers would have detected such a hidden theme based on Semitic roots is doubtful.[61] Van Unnik's comments about the אמן-motif may be relevant to v. 9 of our passage, but not to ἐβεβαιώθη of v. 6 or βεβαιώσει of v. 8.

We consider that although Schlier's comments about the legal connotation are incorrect, for he has understood the passage in a sense that is too literal, it is possible that Paul has taken a metaphor from the language of contracts and guarantees and pressed it into service in this thanksgiving passage underlining the point that God has indeed confirmed [62] the gospel in the Corinthians' experience.

---

[59] 'Die Taufterminologie in 2 Kor. i. 21f.', in *Neotestamentica et Patristica. Freundesgabe Oscar Cullmann*, ed. W. C. van Unnik (Leiden, 1962), pp. 173-191, esp. p. 179.

[60] 'Reisepläne und Amen-Sagen, Zusammenhang und Gedankenfolge in 2 Korinther 1:15-24', in *Studia Paulina in honorem J. de Zwaan*, ed. J. N. Sevenster and W. C. van Unnik (Haarlem, 1953), pp. 215-234.

[61] Note the criticisms of James Barr, *The Semantics of Biblical Language* (Oxford, 1961), pp. 167f., 170; and P. E. Hughes, *Paul's Second Epistle to the Corinthians* (London, 1962), p. 38.

[62] Some commentators consider that the confirmation was either attended by or even took the external form of miracles. E. Osty, *Les Épîtres de Saint Paul aux Corinthiens* (Paris, ³1959), p. 24, sees 'une allusion aux miracles et aux effusions de l'Esprit qui ont accompagné la prédication de Paul'; cf. Goudge, *1 Corinthians*, p. 4. Paul saw that all χαρίσματα came from God. If there were miracles attendant on his ministry, as seems to have been the case, he did not unduly emphasize them. The great miracle was that there should have been a church in Corinth at all!

4. *Awaiting the Parousia : V. 7*

The ὥστε-clause of v. 7, with the infinitive ὑστερεῖσθαι, was understood by some of the older commentators to point to a *contemplated* result [63] rather than to an actual one; in Classical Greek an actual result was expressed by ὥστε with the indicative. So in v. 7 it was considered Paul was referring to what might be looked for in the Corinthians as the result of the grace of God (v. 4) given to them in Christ. According to this view the apostle was giving thanks for what would follow in the Corinthians' lives, rather than for what had actually taken place (although Robertson and Plummer [64] added the rider that there was much in the Corinthians' spiritual condition already which corresponded to the contemplated result). However true such a distinction may have been in Classical Greek, in the New Testament examples of ὥστε with the infinitive far outweigh those with the indicative,[65] so that the infinitival construction serves for both potential and actual consequences. [66] In the present context Paul is referring to an *actual result*.[67] Ὑστερεῖσθαι is not to be translated 'lack' as though the Corinthians lacked no gift of grace, i.e., as Christians they have potentially at their disposal all that God gives to men (cf. Rom. 8:32), or that at the moment they possessed all the gifts of grace in full measure. (Μηδενὸς χαρίσματος would have been used if the apostle had intended to indicate no gift of grace was lacking in them). Instead, the verb—a passive rather than a middle [68]—indicates 'you *come short* in no gift of grace'.[69]

---

[63] So Findlay, *1 Corinthians*, p. 760; Robertson and Plummer, *1 Corinthians*, p. 6; Allo, *1 Corinthiens*, p. 4, considers the ὥστε with the infinitive to be 'final', pointing to the future. Against this see Conzelmann, *1 Korinther*, p. 41.

[64] *1 Corinthians*, p. 6.

[65] Ὥστε with the indicative is rare, being found only at John 3:16 and Gal. 2:13.

[66] An example of an *actual* result expressed by ὥστε with the infinitive is Acts 15:39. For a clear analysis of why the infinitival construction serves for both potential and actual consequences, see Burton, *Moods*, paras. 235f. Cf. Moule, *Idiom Book*, p. 141; Bl.-D., para. 391 (2); and Turner, *Syntax*, p. 136.

[67] Grosheide, *1 Corinthians*, p. 29; L. Morris, *The First Epistle of Paul to the Corinthians* (London, 1958), p. 37; Barrett, *1 Corinthians*, p. 38; Conzelmann, *1 Korinther*, p. 41.

[68] Those who take ὑστερεῖσθαι as a middle translate it 'feel yourselves inferior'. It thus implies not merely a want but a felt want, and as such is a deliberate suggestion of criticism. But against this, see above, p. 112.

[69] The prepositional phrase, which according to Meyer, *Corinthians*, p. 19, is

The word χάρισμα ('gift of grace') had no traditional usage. It did not occur in the LXX,[70] and its only vogue in religion appears to have been in Philo (where its occurrences, anyway, were few). Paul used the word in several senses, e.g., the gracious gift of rescue from mortal danger, 2 Cor. 1:11 (the concluding verse of an introductory eulogy); the power to be continent in matters of sex, either by marriage or celibacy, 1 Cor. 7:7; in a more general sense of 'spiritual gift', Rom. 1:11, another thanksgiving passage; as well as the gracious gift of redemption, Rom. 5:15f.; 6:23. In 1 Cor. 1:7 where χάρισμα is used for the first time in the letter the term is not to be restricted to special gifts (such as are described in 1 Cor. 12). It is used in a more general sense of 'spiritual endowment',[71] at the same time including the special gifts of the Spirit and pointing forward to them in the latter half of the epistle. By comparison with other churches the Corinthians did not lag behind in spiritual endowments. Such gifts as 'concrete actualization(s) of God's grace'[72] were the result of the testimony to Christ being confirmed in their experience,[73] and evidence that God's grace had been given to them. Although some of the troubles at Corinth were related to their special gifts, this was due not to a deficiency of gifts, but to a lack of proportion and balance in estimating and using them.[74] The presence of such endowments was a reason for Paul offering thanksgiving to God.

The customary eschatological climax of the introductory thanksgivings is, in this instance, introduced by the participial clause 'waiting for the revealing of our Lord Jesus Christ' (v. 7). The eschatological note is struck twice in this passage—the second instance is in v. 8, 'He will keep you firm to the end, without reproach on the Day of our Lord Jesus' (NEB). The former reference draws attention to their expectant waiting for the last day, the latter to their being

---

conceived after the analogy of the positive πλουτίζειν ἐν, denotes that in which one falls behind. Thus the Corinthians, in no gift of grace, are less rich than other churches.

[70] In the text of Ecclesiasticus 'it is merely a mistake for χάρις (vii.33) and χρῖσμα (xxxviii.30)', so Moffatt, *Grace*, p. 105; cf. Conzelmann, *TDNT* 9, p. 403.

[71] So, for example, J. Calvin, *The First Epistle of Paul to the Corinthians* (new translation and edition, Grand Rapids, 1960), p. 22; Moffatt, *Grace*, p. 107; Wobbe, *Charis*, pp. 41f.; *contra* Weiss, *1 Korinther*, p. 9.

[72] Barrett, *1 Corinthians*, p. 38; for further references see E. Schweizer, *Church Order in the New Testament* (ET, London, 1961), p. 99.

[73] The ὥστε-clause of v. 7 is dependent, not on the ὅτι-construction of v. 5, but on the καθώς-clause of v. 6.

[74] Barrett, *1 Corinthians*, p. 38.

preserved blameless at the Great Assize.[75] The repetition of this motif in the introductory thanksgivings is not strange in itself. Such repetition was observed in the Philippian and Colossian counterparts. However, in these latter instances the eschatological motif was conjoined with the actual thanksgiving on the one hand, and with the intercessory prayer on the other. There is no intercessory prayer in the passage under review—though some scholars have considered v. 8 to be such (see the exegesis below). Here both eschatological statements are linked with the thanksgiving. The Corinthians' waiting expectantly for the Lord Jesus to reveal Himself is not strictly and grammatically a second result of the testimony to Christ being confirmed in their midst, since one would have expected the infinitive $\dot{a}\pi\epsilon\kappa\delta\dot{\epsilon}\chi\epsilon\sigma\theta\alpha\iota$ to have been used. However, apart from their acceptance of Paul's testimony and their incorporation into Christ Jesus there would have been no waiting for His revealing. Logically the expectant waiting is dependent on the confirmation of the testimony, although the participle is used to describe the attendant circumstances [76] rather than the result. The Corinthians do not fall behind in spiritual gifts *as they await* the revelation of their Lord Jesus Christ.

The verb $\dot{a}\pi\epsilon\kappa\delta\dot{\epsilon}\chi o\mu\alpha\iota$, perhaps a coinage of the apostle, was used by him [77] to express 'expectation of the End', with the following objects: adoption, Rom. 8:23; the hope of righteousness, Gal. 5:5; and the revealing of the sons of God, Rom. 8:19. The clause in 1 Cor. 1:7 is almost another definition of a Christian,[78] and it is interesting to note that in other contexts the Holy Spirit is sometimes mentioned with this verb (cf. Rom. 8:23; Gal. 5:5). By stating that the Corinthians await the revelation of Christ the apostle writes generously, describing the congregation as a whole. Later he will deal with the errors of those who denied the resurrection of the dead (1 Cor. 15:12,

---

[75] 'The revealing of our Lord Jesus Christ', v. 7, is parallelled by 'the day of our Lord Jesus Christ', v. 8, and both refer to Christ's parousia which coincides with the day of judgement. So Bultmann, *Theology* 1, p. 275; W. D. Davies, *Paul and Rabbinic Judaism* (London, ²1955), p. 296; G. B. Caird, *Principalities and Powers* (Oxford, 1956), p. 87; Richardson, *Theology*, p. 54; and Lövestam, *Wakefulness*, pp. 46, 68; cf. D. Lührmann, *Das Offenbarungsverständnis bei Paulus und in paulinischen Gemeinden* (Neukirchen-Vluyn, 1965), p. 104.

[76] Rightly Grosheide, *1 Corinthians*, p. 30.

[77] MM, p. 56. See also W. Grundmann, '$\delta\dot{\epsilon}\chi o\mu\alpha\iota$', *TDNT* 2, p. 56.

[78] Meyer, *Corinthians*, *ad loc.*; Barrett, *1 Corinthians*, p. 39.

'how can *some of you* say that there is no resurrection of the dead ?'), and will indicate with biting irony that the Corinthians sometimes behaved as if the age to come were already consummated (note 4:8, '*Already* you are filled! *Already* you have become rich!'), as if the saints had already taken over the kingdom [79] (cf. Dan. 7:18). For the moment, however, those aspects worthy of thanksgiving are isolated.

5. *Preserved Blameless : V. 8*

In the thanksgiving period to the end of v. 7 the apostle had been dealing with and giving thanks for those actions of God in the past which had had repercussions up to the present. But with the words 'He will keep you firm ($\beta\epsilon\beta\alpha\iota\omega\sigma\epsilon\iota$) to the end' (NEB) of v. 8 Paul linked his thanksgiving with what might be expected in the future.[80] This does not mean that there was any less certainty or assurance for it is God (or Christ) [81] who is the subject of the action. His activity in the past had been witnessed; the effects were still observable in the present; Paul was thus confident for the future. This progression of thought in the introductory thanksgiving of 1 Corinthians is remarkably similar to that already examined in the Philippian counterpart. In the latter passage Paul was thankful to God for the Philippians' financial help (Phil. 1:3, cf. v. 5). This was an aspect of their active participation in the gospel that had begun when they were converted and had continued up to the time of Paul's writing to them. However, such generosity demonstrated by the Philippians was evidence that God had been at work in their midst, and He who had begun such a good work could be relied upon to complete it. Confidence and certainty for the future were based on the past action of God. In the present passage it is stated that the Corinthians were given God's grace (v. 4), enriched in every way (v. 5), and had a

---

[79] '$E\beta\alpha\sigma\iota\lambda\epsilon\upsilon\sigma\alpha\tau\epsilon$ probably points to eschatological fulfilment, so Barrett, *1 Corinthians*, p. 109; contra Lightfoot, *Notes, ad loc.*

[80] See O. Piper, 'Praise of God and Thanksgiving', *Interp* 8 (1954), p. 16. Grosheide, *1 Corinthians*, p. 32, thus considers there are two distinct parts in this thanksgiving. The first is 'a thanksgiving in the proper sense' since it deals with things present. The second part relates to what may be expected in the future, but it is no less a thanksgiving for that and is offered with full assurance. Grosheide adds that : 'Both parts together anticipate the thoughts which will be developed in the sequel. These opening verses form the basis for subsequent admonitions'.

[81] See below.

message confirmed in their midst (v. 6). The present results were that they did not fall behind in any gift as they awaited the revelation of the Lord Jesus. In the future they would be kept blameless on the day of Christ.

Most commentators consider the antecedent of the relative ὅς to be τοῦ κυρίου ἡμῶν Ἰησοῦ Χριστοῦ (v. 7),[82] since the only other possible antecedent θεός is said to be too distant. Further, a new subject ὁ θεός appears to be introduced in v. 9. Accordingly, Christ is said to be the subject of βεβαιώσει and καί indicates correspondence, i.e., 'on His part', answering to ἐβεβαιώθη (v. 6), and possibly to ἀπεκδεχομένους (v. 7). The close position of 'our Lord Jesus Christ' certainly favours its being the antecedent of 'who will keep firm', but in spite of this our preference is to regard ὁ θεός as the subject,[83] for the following reasons: first, as indicated above it is best to understand God as the logical subject of the passive verbs, i.e., God has given, enriched, etc. Thus it is not unreasonable to consider He is the subject of this keeping activity too. Indeed, the correspondence expressed by καί is clearer on this interpretation and means that as God had confirmed the *testimony* in them, so now He would confirm the *Corinthians* [84] themselves. Secondly, although ὅς immediately follows τοῦ κυρίου ἡμῶν Ἰησοῦ Χριστοῦ, v. 8 appears as a new sentence with ὅς equivalent to 'He' rather than 'who'; cf. the NEB rendering: 'He will keep you firm to the end'. Thirdly, if ὁ κύριος ἡμῶν Ἰησοῦς Χριστός were the antecedent one might have expected ἐν τῇ ἡμέρᾳ α ὐ τ ο ῦ at the conclusion of v. 8. However, this argument is weakened [85] by the fact that in the first nine verses of the letter

---

[82] So, for example, P. W. Schmiedel, 'Die Briefe an die Thessalonicher und an die Korinther', in *Hand-Commentar zum Neuen Testament* 2.1, ed. H. J. Holtzmann *et al.* (Freiburg-i.-Br., ²1892), p. 96. Robertson and Plummer, *1 Corinthians*, p. 7 (who compare the passage with 2 Cor. 1:21 but do not note that the subject of the latter is ὁ θεός); Barrett, *1 Corinthians*, p. 39; and Du Plessis, *Perfection*, p. 159, who states categorically: 'The subject implied by the verb is obviously Christ'.

[83] As do Bachmann, *1 Korinther*, p. 48; Grosheide, *1 Corinthians*, p. 31; van Unnik, *loc. cit.*, pp. 227f. (apparently); Hughes, *2 Corinthians*, p. 39; Conzelmann, *1 Korinther*, p. 42; and Baumann, *Mitte*, pp. 39f.

[84] Grosheide's distinction, *1 Corinthians*, p. 31, i.e., that βεβαιόω was used of 'doctrine' and of 'life' is not strictly correct. The verb was employed of the 'testimony' on the one hand and the 'Corinthians' on the other.

[85] A point which Grosheide fails to see, *1 Corinthians*, p. 31, but it is correctly noted by Robertson and Plummer, *1 Corinthians*, p. 7. The solemn repetition of the sacred name instead of the simple pronoun is quite in Paul's manner; chap. 5:3, 4 and 2 Cor. 1:5; cf. 2 Tim. 1:18.

there is a solemn repetition of the name of Christ, so that even if ὅς did point back to 'Ιησοῦς Χριστός Paul could still have repeated the name at the end of v. 8. Fourthly, the opening words of v. 9, πιστὸς ὁ θεός, do not necessarily indicate a new subject, for if the sentence is a concluding benediction of an *ad hoc* kind then one ought not to expect a precise grammatical link with the preceding words. Finally, one of the strongest reasons for considering that God is the subject of the activity is that in a similar passage of a letter written to the same church (2 Cor. 1:21) He is clearly, indeed emphatically (because of the position of θεός at the end of the clause, ὁ δὲ βεβαιῶν ἡμᾶς σὺν ὑμῖν ... θεός), the subject of the same verb βεβαιόω while the Corinthians are its direct objects.[86] Although these reasons are not conclusive, when taken together they are clearly very strong.

The future tense βεβαιώσει does not indicate that the apostle is expressing a strong wish,[87] or even offering an intercessory prayer (as Héring[88] would suppose). Instead 'Paulus spricht... eine Gewissheit aus, wie im Proömium des Phil. (1, 6)'.[89] As God had confirmed the testimony in them, so now He would confirm the Corinthians themselves. The legal metaphor which Paul found to be appropriate when writing of the testimony to Christ, was taken and used in a slightly different sense [90] of the addressees with another legal term

---

[86] In the Philippian counterpart God is the subject of both the initiating and completing actions, Phil. 1:6; cf. 1 Thess. 5:23f.; 2 Thess. 1:11; 2:13; Eph. 1:4; Rom. 16:25 and 1 Peter 1:10. However, in 1 Thess. 3:11 and 2 Thess. 2:16f. God and Christ together are the subjects of the strengthening, while in 1 Thess. 3:12; 2 Thess. 3:3-5 and Eph. 5:25-27 Christ alone is the subject.

[87] Wiles, *Function*, pp. 82f., and more fully in his *Prayers*, pp. 97-101, presents this as a possibility. Harder, *Paulus*, p. 70, is undecided, while C. W. F. Smith, 'Prayer', in *The Interpreter's Dictionary of the Bible* 3, ed. G. A. Buttrick (New York, 1962), p. 864, considers v. 8 expresses a 'purpose' of Paul's prayers, i.e., the hope and perseverance of God's people.

[88] *1 Corinthians*, p. 3; so also L. Mattern, *Das Verständnis des Gerichtes bei Paulus* (Zürich, 1966), pp. 202f.

[89] Conzelmann, *1 Korinther*, p. 42; Parry, *1 Corinthians*, p. 33, considers the statement to be 'at once a word of encouragement and a word of warning'. On the paraenetic function see below.

[90] This is more likely than Harder's view, *Paulus*, pp. 70, 108f., that Paul at this point was *strongly* influenced by the LXX Psalter. On the other hand, the examples from the papyri of βεβαιόω and its cognates, cited by MM, pp. 107f., do not compel us to interpret the phrase in chap. 1:8 of legal validity as Du Plessis, *Perfection*, p. 159, asserts. In the papyri the personal pronoun is the indirect object after βεβαιόω and therefore in the dative case, e.g., βεβαιώσω σοι. Du Plessis and others seem to have overlooked this.

ἀνέγκλητος. The application of a metaphor to both the gospel and its recipients was noted in the Colossian thanksgiving passage.[91] There it was said that the gospel was bearing fruit and growing in the whole world (Col. 1:6). In his intercessory prayer that followed Paul prayed that fruit-bearing and increasing might be characteristic of the Colossians themselves (v. 10). In the Colossian passage Paul *prayed* that the power of the gospel might characterize the believers' lives; here in 1 Corinthians he *asserted* boldly what God would do—confirm His people completely to the end (ἕως τέλους, v. 8).[92]

Ἀνέγκλητος denotes a person or thing against which there can be no ἔγκλημα and which is 'free from reproach', 'without stain'.[93] The word was common in everyday speech, as the papyri show, and three examples in the Pastorals (Titus 1:6, 7 of presbyters and 1 Tim. 3:10 of deacons) point to this general usage. The remaining two New Testament instances are found in Col. 1:22 and the present passage, and in both cases the situation of the last judgement is in view. Christians will stand ἀνέγκλητοι before God, not in the sense of morally perfect, but without blame, since they will be acquitted at the Great Assize (cf. Rom. 8:33).[94] Christ's righteousness has been given to them. Ἀνέγκλητος is synonymous but not coterminous with ἄμωμος (Col. 1:22) and ἀπρόσκοπος (Phil. 1:10); the former had a sacrificial background (particularly in the LXX), while the latter in the papyri meant 'free from hurt or harm', and when used with εἰλικρινής in Phil. 1:10 pointed to an all-round fitness and preparedness for the last day. The eschatological note, it was observed above, was struck in the thanksgiving periods. Closely conjoined with it was

---

[91] See above, pp. 89ff., and the author's article in *NTS* 21 (1974-1975), pp. 144-155.

[92] Ἕως τέλους, which is to be preferred to the τελείους of P⁴⁶ (Zuntz, *Text*, pp. 20, 285, considers there is not sufficient manuscript support for τελείους. Further, τελείους ἀνεγκλήτους is doubtful stylistically. The traditional reading ἕως τέλους makes good sense), has a temporal reference, i.e., 'bis zum Weltende', Conzelmann, *1 Korinther*, p. 42. However, since the meaning can pass from a temporal reference to one of degree it can also mean 'completely'. In the present context the two ideas fuse with a further temporal reference in the words 'on the day of our Lord Jesus Christ'. (Many exegetes recognize the two-fold idea in the phrase, ἕως τέλους, e.g., Parry, *1 Corinthians*, p. 33; Grosheide, *1 Corinthians*, p. 31; Barrett, *1 Corinthians*, p. 39. G. Delling, 'τέλος', *TDNT* 8, pp. 55f., notes that when τέλος is used with prepositional expressions (i.e., εἰς, ἕως, ἄχρι and μέχρι): 'The context must decide whether the expressions are to be taken temporally or quantitatively' (p. 56). Here he understands the phrase to mean 'wholly and utterly').

[93] W. Grundmann, 'ἀνέγκλητος', *TDNT* 1, pp. 356f. MM, pp. 40f.

[94] Barrett, *1 Corinthians*, p. 39.

the idea of readiness for the last day, a motif found in the Philippian passage, as well as in two other Pauline prayers, 1 Thess. 3:13 and 5:23.

Ἐν τῇ ἡμέρᾳ τοῦ κυρίου ἡμῶν Ἰησοῦ (Χριστοῦ),[95] is to be associated with ἀνεγκλήτους rather than with βεβαιώσει. The 'day of the Lord' was a common Old Testament phrase used to describe the day of judgement (note the *locus classicus* Amos 5:18ff.; cf. Joel 2:31). Later in this epistle the writer will again have cause to raise the subject of 'the day' with reference to judgement, particularly concerning the type of superstructure the Corinthians with their lives might erect on the foundation, Jesus Christ (1 Cor. 3:11). Inferior materials (wood, hay and stubble, 3:12) and shoddy workmanship could not be concealed, for 'the day' would show them up (3:13). In the passage under review the apostle made it clear that the 'blamelessness' of the Corinthians on the final day would be due to God's activity alone.[96] They were not able to make themselves irreproachable, a point which, if properly understood, ought to have had the effect of deflating their pride (cf. 1 Cor. 5:2).

6. *God is Faithful* : V. 9

The climax of the thanksgiving period with its reference to acquittal at the Great Assize has now been reached. The apostle rounds out the passage with a confirming climax, in words not unlike a concluding benediction.[97] The confident hope expressed in v. 8 rests upon the faithfulness of God through whom they have been called into fellowship with His Son (v. 9). Πιστὸς ὁ θεός, as well as its equivalents, according to Professor van Unnik reminds one of the benedictions after the *Haftarah* in the synagogue ('the faithful God who speaks and acts').[98] Similar expressions are found in the Old Testament where the faithfulness of God is stressed,[99] e.g., Deut. 7:9 and Isa. 49:7.

---

[95] B joins P46 in omitting Χριστοῦ. For a discussion of the whole phrase see Zuntz, *Text*, p. 184.

[96] Barrett, *1 Corinthians*, p. 39, considers that in describing the Christian's expectation of the last day 'Paul is stating the doctrine of justification by faith without the use of the technical terms he employs elsewhere'.

[97] Sanders, *loc. cit.*, p. 358, following J. M. Robinson, *loc. cit.*, pp. 201f. Schubert, *Form*, p. 31, considers it has 'confirmatory force'.

[98] *Loc. cit.*, p. 221. Cf. Sanders, *loc. cit.*, p. 358. The text is found in S. Singer, *The Authorised Daily Prayer Book* (London, 241956), p. 149.

[99] Cf. A. Weiser, 'πιστεύω' (OT), *TDNT* 6, p. 185. Harder, *Paulus*, pp. 106, 112, sees a clear reference to a Jewish background.

In the Pauline writings the formula πιστὸς ὁ θεός is by no means fixed. At 1 Thess. 5:24, the conclusion of a paraenetic section in which seven injunctions are followed by a wish-prayer that has reference to blamelessness at Christ's parousia, the apostle emphasized the faithfulness of the One who calls. The faithfulness of ὁ κύριος (rather than ὁ θεός) is referred to in 2 Thess. 3:3, while in the second half of our letter (1 Cor. 10:13) δέ is inserted (πιστὸς δὲ ὁ θεός) to point to a contrast with what has immediately preceded: πειρασμὸς ὑμᾶς οὐκ εἴληφεν εἰ μὴ ἀνθρώπινης. Thus, we note that although v. 9 of the introductory thanksgiving is in the position of and fulfils the function of a concluding benediction, and contains terms possibly used in early Christian worship,[100] the choice and meaning of these terms is determined by the immediate context and the situation which lay behind it. The phrase 'God is faithful' draws attention to the reliability of the One whose activity has been described so clearly and forcefully in the preceding verses. The certainty of the Corinthians being kept blameless at the final day rests with God. Unlike the other passages in Paul's letters where the phrase (or its equivalents) is used in conjunction with verbs in the present or future tenses,[101] in 1 Cor. 1:9 the verb ἐκλήθητε is an aorist pointing back to the time of the Corinthians' incorporation into God's Son. Even the choice of the verb καλέω is not without significance, since it takes up a theme that has already been accented in the address (κλητὸς ἀπόστολος, 1:1, and κλητοῖς ἁγίοις, 1:2), and which recurs in the body of the letter (cf. κλῆσις in 1:26, and chap. 7 where καλέω is used with reference to marriage). In the present context the Divine initiative is stressed.[102] Thus, this benediction or confirming climax of v. 9 is not stereotyped. It is rather an *ad hoc* formulation with some terms and phrases that may have been current in early (i.e., pre-Pauline) Christian worship but which have been pressed into service by the apostle to relate to the faithfulness of God and the needs of the Corinthians.

God's calling of the Corinthians was into fellowship (κοινωνία) [103]

---

[100] See Kramer, *Christ*, pp. 173ff.; and L. G. Champion, *Benedictions and Doxologies in the Epistles of Paul* (published privately, Oxford, 1934), p. 33, with reference to the language of 1 Cor. 1:9 as a reflection of Paul's public prayers.

[101] 1 Cor. 10:13; 2 Cor. 1:18; 1 Thess. 5:24; 2 Thess. 3:3.

[102] See D. Wiederkehr, *Die Theologie der Berufung in den Paulusbriefen* (Freiburg, Schweiz, 1963), pp. 114-117.

[103] Κοινωνία is constructed with the objective genitive of the person and refers to a participation in God's Son. It is the only such New Testament passage where this

with His Son. Such participation does not refer to the future alone, but 'exists now and extends to eternity'.[104] It is enjoyed in the present and is the basis of true Christian worship [105] and fellowship in prayer.[106] One corollary of the Corinthians' participation in God's Son is that they have been called into a community in which they are 'brethren' who stand under the Lordship of Christ (note the following words of v. 10). Had the Corinthians been aware of this high calling they might not have permitted groups within the community. Thus by choosing the significant term κοινωνία the apostle not only pointed to the 'participation' in God's Son as their present calling, but also indirectly prepared the way for the words which followed, i.e., that such a calling of God is inconsistent with division.

A word of explanation is needed in connection with the lengthy title given to Christ in v. 9. Commentators have pointed to the frequent repetition of the name of Jesus Christ (with some variations) in the opening verses of this letter.[107] Indeed the pronoun 'he' is found only once, while the solemn note, in the longer title, is struck nine times in as many verses. Then at the beginning of the next section the apostle repeated the full title as if he could not mention it too often. In v. 4 ἐν Χριστοῦ Ἰησοῦ was used with reference to the grace of God given to the Corinthians. It is, according to Kramer, one of the eleven passages in which the ἐν-formula was used to qualify the blessings of salvation.[108] At v. 6 mention was made about the 'testimony to Christ' while in vv. 7 and 8, statements about the parousia, the words 'Jesus Christ' were linked with 'our Lord'. It is considered by some that the resulting fuller christological designation

---

construction occurs, apart from references to the Holy Spirit (where πνεῦμα is neuter). This does not mean that to defend the objective genitive one must consider Paul thought of Christ as a 'thing' (as Campbell, *JBL* 51 (1932), p. 380, seems to do. He considers Paul spoke of the risen and glorified Christ in a 'curiously impersonal way'). Seesemann (*op. cit.*, pp. 15f., 47; cf. George, *Communion*, p. 175) has cited occasional parallels in secular literature to this objective genitive of a person, and the immediate context demands that we understand κοινωνία in this way, translating it 'participation'.

[104] Robertson and Plummer, *1 Corinthians*, p. 8; cf. Wendland, *Korinther*, p. 13. *Per contra* Cerfaux, *Christian*, p. 323; and Thüsing, *Per Christum*, p. 144.

[105] C. H. Dodd, *The Meaning of Paul for Today* (London, 1920), p. 131.

[106] Nielen, *Gebet*, p. 145.

[107] Robertson and Plummer, *1 Corinthians*, p. 8; Parry, *1 Corinthians*, p. 31.

[108] Cf. Kramer, *Christ*, p. 142, for further examples.

indicates liturgical usage,[109] since in some contexts shorter expressions which denote the parousia (like 'the day of the Lord', 'the parousia of the Lord', 'the revealing of the Lord'), or what will happen at the parousia, mean the same thing. In v. 9 Paul used the title Son of God in conjunction with the phrase 'Jesus Christ our Lord'. At 2 Cor. 1:18 and in our passage the title immediately follows on the phrase 'God is faithful' while in Rom. 1:9, another introductory thanksgiving, it follows 'God is my witness'. The emphasis in each of these passages is upon God, but it is clear that the title 'Son of God' signified for Paul that there was a close relationship between Jesus, the bearer of salvation, and God.

This last point helps to explain the repeated use of 'Jesus Christ' (or 'our Lord Jesus Christ') in the introductory thanksgiving. Although it may be possible to state with Kramer that the fuller christological designations indicate a liturgical usage, the heaping up of such phrases cannot be explained *solely* along these lines, for there are similar passages in the Pauline corpus (e.g., other thanksgiving periods) where such repetitions do not occur.[110] The fuller designations may have been derived from early Christian worship (although it is difficult to determine whether Paul had any hand in such combinations). Their use here is explained by the immediate context. Paul had stressed the divine initiative at almost every point in the passage. At the same time he made it clear that God's gracious activity was intimately bound up with His Son (note the same point in Col. 1:12-14 —the conclusion of that thanksgiving period), the historical Jesus who is yet Lord and Christ.[111] The Corinthians had received grace in Jesus Christ, been called into fellowship with Jesus Christ; and as they awaited the revelation of their Lord they had the confidence that they would ultimately stand blameless before Him.

---

[109] Kramer, *op. cit.*, p. 174. F. Hahn, *The Titles of Jesus in Christology* (ET, London, 1969), pp. 100, 126, considers the shorter designation too was determined by its liturgical use.

[110] Kramer has not given sufficient weight to the contextual argument.

[111] *Contra* Kramer, *op. cit.*, pp. 191f., who states that: 'In those parts of the letters which require a more ponderous style it is the fuller designation which is preferred, simply because it has greater weight itself'. This is so, he contends, where other designations are added to the title 'Son of God'. 'All these are relatively superficial combinations'!

7. *Conclusions*

In conclusion it is necessary to draw attention to the characteristics and function of this introductory thanksgiving, as well as to the contribution it makes to our understanding of Pauline prayers of thanksgiving as a whole.

The apostle Paul was truly thankful for the grace of God that had encountered the Corinthians. On that first visit to Corinth though he had arrived in 'weakness, in fear and in much trembling'—and though he preached to audiences that seemed unpromising—the success that attended his mission was beyond his expectations.[112] The Corinthian converts stood in contrast to their pagan neighbours. The apostle, therefore, did not write with irony or in flattery. Further, although Paul was somewhat guarded in his statements in this introductory thanksgiving so that it does not have the warmth or intimacy found in the Philippian counterpart, we reject Weiss' suggestion that Paul would not have included a thanksgiving period in this letter had it not been normal.[113] The omission from Galatians shows its presence was not mandatory.

Regarding the *function* of the passage we observe that the *epistolary* purpose is present,[114] though not as obviously as in the Colossian parallel. In his first letter to the Corinthians the apostle dealt with many subjects, some in answer to questions of conduct and the like which the Corinthians themselves had raised in a letter to him [115] (e.g., marriage, food sacrificed to idols, spiritual gifts and the collection), others that arose through information from Chloe's household (e.g., the groups within the church) while others were matters of doctrine and Paul's relationship as an apostle to them. Some of these themes, though not all, were touched upon in the introductory thanksgiving. He treated motifs such as God's grace, riches in the Christian life, spiritual gifts, the gospel, awaiting the

---

[112] Cf. Jülicher, *Introduction*, p. 79.

[113] *1 Korinther*, p. 6. Eschlimann, *Prière*, pp. 90f., is nearer the mark when he speaks of it as pointing to living prayer.

[114] See above, p. 108, with reference to Dahl's and Bjerkelund's arguments about the thanksgiving period's epistolary function in relation to chaps. 1:10-4:21.

[115] Note the use of περὶ δέ... at chaps. 7:1, 25; 8:1; 12:1; 16:1, probably indicating that Paul was answering the questions raised by the Corinthians. He also appears to have quoted the letter on occasions. See J. C. Hurd's brilliant reconstruction, *The Origin of 1 Corinthians* (London, 1965), and Barrett's wise qualifications, *1 Corinthians*, pp. 6ff.

parousia, blamelessness on that day, God's faithfulness, His calling and fellowship with His Son Jesus Christ. Other subjects, such as Paul's apostolic authority (or at least his rights as an apostle), the resurrection, fornication and litigation within the church, behaviour at the Lord's supper, etc., were not prefigured in the introductory thanksgiving, though they were sometimes related to other themes which did appear. It is difficult to isolate any single thought in which other motifs cohere. Dinkler [116] considers one can find the inner line only with difficulty—for him it is the *Christ-event*. This, however, does not tell us much and might be posited of all the Pauline letters and thanksgivings. Parry [117] noted that the conception of the person of the Lord Jesus gave unity and coherence to the epistle. But important though this may be, it does not take account of the stress on God's initiative in the passage. Heinrici [118] noting this point considered the grace of God to be the basic thought in the introductory thanksgiving, while Allo [119] pointed to the Corinthians' calling into union with Christ as the significant motif. The variety of answers given shows the difficulty of the task! It seems best to consider that Paul was dealing with a series of themes that were linked with God's gracious activity in the gospel by which men were called into a special relationship with His Son.[120] All the subjects in the letter were not treated, but the apostle had set the tone and laid the foundation for the instruction, exhortation and rebuke that would follow. The theme of 'fellowship' smacked against the idea of groups within the church, and the name of Christ stood over against party slogans. Spiritual gifts came through grace alone. God's keeping His people so as to be blameless at the parousia ought to have deflated Corinthian pride.

This leads us to consider the second function of the period—the *didactic* one. Evans considered that the paragraph (1:4-9) was not didactic but allusive, asserting that the fundamentals of Christianity are 'assumed rather than stated'. He added that it was clear from this paragraph that:

---

[116] E. Dinkler, 'First Letter to the Corinthians', in *Dictionary of the Bible*, rev. ed. by F. C. Grant and H. H. Rowley (Edinburgh, 1963), p. 177.

[117] *1 Corinthians*, pp. lix, 31.

[118] *1 Korinther*, p. 50.

[119] *1 Corinthiens*, p. xxxv.

[120] Baumann, *Mitte*, pp. 44f., has rightly pointed to the stress on God's initiating activity and the 'christozentrische Tendenz' of this paragraph. For a discussion on the 'apparent diffuseness of structure and theme' (p. 136), see Wiles, *Prayers*, pp. 136-140.

'... the doctrines of the divine Sonship of Christ, of His grace and spiritual gifts, of His second coming to judgement, and of the importance of the Church as the fellowship of the Son of God, had formed part of the teaching originally given by St. Paul to his converts'.[121]

It is admitted that in this passage the apostle recalled the Corinthians to the first preaching of the gospel in their city. Further, he did remind them of aspects of his teaching as originally given.[122] But the didactic motif is present both in the recall to truths already known and in the correction of emphasis which the Corinthians needed. It is likely that the Corinthians had been instructed in the 'grace of God', but either because of forgetfulness or a failure to draw the obvious conclusions they did not see that all their spiritual endowments stemmed from this source. The apostle thus instructed them, either by way of recall or correction of emphasis.

The *paraenetic* or exhortatory function of this introductory thanksgiving is not entirely absent. There is an indirect exhortation to continue waiting for the 'revelation of our Lord Jesus Christ',[123] and a need to be 'irreproachable' on that last day.[124] To Paul these matters were important. He therefore pointed them out in the present passage. It is to be noted that although the exhortatory function of the thanksgiving periods of type Ia is to be seen most clearly in the intercessory prayer reports [125] this function is not absent in 1 Cor. 1 where no such intercessory prayer occurs. This purpose is seen in vv. 7 and 8.[126]

Paul's *pastoral care* for his converts is also clearly demonstrated. By reporting his actual thanksgiving Paul showed his concern for them and his desire to build them up and encourage them in spite of the strong words that might follow. Indeed his 'ability' to give thanks to God for a congregation which had erred in so many ways was evidence of his deep pastoral care.

Concerning Paul's actual *prayer of thanksgiving* we note that the

---

[121] E. Evans, *The Epistles of Paul the Apostle to the Corinthians* (Oxford, 1930), p. 64.

[122] There are indications in the letter that Paul's original preaching consisted of an emphasis on Christ's death and resurrection; cf. chaps. 2:1-5; 15:1-11; see Bauman, *Mitte, passim*. Note C. F. D. Moule, *The Birth of the New Testament* (London, ²1966), pp. 125ff., concerning the instruction given at the founding of the churches.

[123] They were not to act as though the parousia had already arrived; cf. chap. 4:8.

[124] As shown above, p. 130, this ought to have had the effect of deflating Corinthian pride.

[125] N. A. Dahl and Wiles, *Function*, p. 14, consider the paraenetic thrust is found *only* in the intercessory prayer reports, and Schubert, *Form*, p. 89, seems to have held this view.

[126] Baumann, *Mitte*, pp. 38f., cf. p. 35, considers vv. 7 and 8 to be admonitions of the apostle, the former 'eine leise Mahnung', while the latter is 'stärker'.

language has come from various sources. Some phrases, such as those which refer to the Corinthians' gifts and speak of wealth in the Christian life, have probably been adopted from the Corinthian letter. There is evidence of liturgical terms and phrases—e.g., the benediction of v. 9, and in the fuller christological titles given to Christ—possibly drawn by the apostle from early Christian worship. The historical situation of Paul's first visit to Corinth has dictated some of the terms and ideas that have been chosen. Further, we observe once more the presence of theological terms in the thanksgiving period. 'Grace', which features in Phil. 1:7, plays a significant role in Paul's thanksgiving for the Corinthians. 'Testimony' stands as the equivalent of 'gospel' and functions in a similar way. Acceptance of the testimony (or gospel) points forward to a corresponding conformity in conduct. The second coming of Christ, with the various terms used to designate this event, such as 'the day of the Lord', 'the revealing of the Lord', features prominently in yet another introductory thanksgiving, firstly, with an emphasis on the waiting for it, and secondly, with reference to one's fitness for that day. 'Fellowship' or 'participation' appears again—this time within the context of the concluding benediction—with a more comprehensive meaning. It does not describe the 'contributions', 'generosity' or 'liberality' of the addressees (cf. Phil. 1:5; Phm. 6), but refers to the 'participation' in God's Son to which the Corinthians have been called. Although the apostle had used language and ideas from the above-mentioned sources he had adapted and modified them to suit the needs of the Corinthian church. Indeed, we may add that not only had Paul used such motifs in his thanksgiving report but in his actual thanksgiving to God as well. He thus demonstrated that although certain ideas featured in his prayers of thanksgiving with some regularity there was at the same time a remarkable degree of flexibility that pointed to a man with a deep pastoral concern for the particular needs of his converts.

Paul's thanksgiving was directed to God, based on His activity in His Son and looked forward to the future with a confidence based on God's faithfulness. In this thanksgiving there was no attention paid to the achievements of the Corinthians—and with good reason! The eschatological motif was accented but this was done within the context of God's faithfulness in completing what He had begun. If the Corinthians had read, marked, learned and inwardly digested the report of their apostle's thanksgiving, then many of their errors and problems might have been speedily put right.

PART THREE

MIXED CATEGORIES OF INTRODUCTORY
THANKSGIVINGS

CHAPTER FIVE

THE THREE-FOLD THANKSGIVING OF 1 THESS. 1:2ff.

The introductory thanksgiving of 1 Thessalonians, assuming the traditional order of the Thessalonian correspondence be correct, is the first extant thanksgiving passage of the apostle we possess. For although some would date the letter to the Galatians before the two canonical letters to the church at Thessalonica, the former contains no introductory thanksgiving. Instead, the opening salutation is followed by the biting words: 'I am astonished ($\theta\alpha\upsilon\mu\acute{\alpha}\zeta\omega$) that you are so quickly deserting him who called you in the grace of Christ and turning to a different gospel ($\epsilon\grave{\iota}s$ $\ddot{\epsilon}\tau\epsilon\rho o\nu$ $\epsilon\grave{\upsilon}\alpha\gamma\gamma\acute{\epsilon}\lambda\iota o\nu$)', (1:6).[1]

This first thanksgiving period has been subjected to closer detailed, though by no means exhaustive, study than those in the other letters of the apostle. Paul Schubert, in his structural analysis of the Pauline thanksgivings, pointed to the similarities and differences of basic structure of this thanksgiving period with those of the imprisonment letters.[2] What appeared to be three separate thanksgivings (i.e., 1:2-5; 2:13 and 3:9-13), were in fact one introductory thanksgiving in which the basic $\epsilon\grave{\upsilon}\chi\alpha\rho\iota\sigma\tau\acute{\epsilon}\omega$-formula was repeated twice, thus unifying the whole section, chaps. 1:2 to 3:13. Its purpose within the letter, according to Schubert, unlike the other thanksgiving periods which functioned as rather formal introductions to the bodies of their letters, was to *convey* rather than to introduce information. The 'thanksgiving itself constitutes the main body of 1 Thessalonians'.[3]

G. P. Wiles,[4] one of Schubert's students, followed the latter's

---

[1] It is probably without significance that the theme of the gospel ($\tau\grave{o}$ $\epsilon\grave{\upsilon}\alpha\gamma\gamma\acute{\epsilon}\lambda\iota o\nu$, vv. 6f.; $\epsilon\grave{\upsilon}\alpha\gamma\gamma\epsilon\lambda\acute{\iota}\zeta o\mu\alpha\iota$, vv. 8 (twice) and 9) is raised at the point where one would have expected a thanksgiving. Because the Galatians have departed from the gospel of Christ there can be no thanksgiving; instead, a curse is pronounced on anyone who brings another message (v. 8).

[2] *Form*, pp. 16f.

[3] *Ibid.*, p. 26.

[4] In his Yale dissertation of 1965, *The Function of Intercessory Prayer in Paul's Apostolic Ministry with Special Reference to the First Epistle to the Thessalonians*;

structural suggestions (as did C. J. Bjerkelund)[5] with reference to 1 Thessalonians. His primary interest, however, was to determine the function and importance of intercessory prayer in Paul's apostolic ministry. In the meantime, scholars such as K.-G. Eckart[6] and W. Schmithals,[7] noting the unusual nature of the two-fold (or three-fold) thanksgiving, considered the canonical letter to have been the result of piecing together two or more genuine epistles[8] to the Thessalonians. W. G. Kümmel[9] and C. J. Bjerkelund,[10] however, have rightly challenged such reconstructions considering them to have been improperly based, and there is now substantial agreement that 1 Thessalonians is a genuine, single Pauline letter.

It is our intention, in this chapter, to draw upon the researches of Schubert and Wiles for assistance in determining the function of the

---

subsequently modified and expanded as *Paul's Intercessory Prayers* (Cambridge, 1974), pp. 45ff., 175ff.

[5] *Parakalô*, pp. 125-135.

[6] K.-G. Eckart, 'Der zweite echte Brief des Apostels Paulus an die Thessalonicher', *ZThK* 58 (1961), pp. 30-44. According to Eckart, 1 Thess. 2:13-16 is not a reference to persecution at Thessalonica, but a general, non-Pauline address for recent converts. Chaps. 2:17-3:4 are the text of a letter of recommendation for Timothy, and together with chaps. 1:1-2:12 and 3:11-13 formed the first letter. Four to six weeks later, states Eckart, Paul, when in Athens after Timothy returned, wrote a second letter commencing with chap. 3:6-10 (a thanksgiving), and continuing with chaps. 4:13-5:11, 4:9-10a and 5:23-26, 28.

[7] W. Schmithals, 'Die Thessalonicherbriefe als Briefkompositionen', in *Zeit und Geschichte. Dankesgabe an Rudolf Bultmann zum 80. Geburtstag*, ed. E. Dinkler (Tübingen, 1964), pp. 295-315. Schmithals considers the correspondence to have comprised four letters, the last of which (Thess D) extended from chaps. 2:13-4:2.

[8] B. A. Pearson, '1 Thessalonians 2:13-16 : A Deutero-Pauline Interpolation', *HTR* 64 (1971), pp. 79-94, considers vv. 13-16 'do not belong to Paul's original letter at all, but represent a later interpolation into the text' (p. 91).

[9] 'Das literarische und geschichtliche Problem des ersten Thessalonicherbriefes', in *Neotestamentica et Patristica*, pp. 213-227. This was an examination and criticism of Eckart's hypothesis. Cf. also Kümmel, *Introduction*, p. 185.

[10] *Op. cit.*, pp. 125ff. Bjerkelund has shown that Schmithals' reconstruction breaks down under its own weight. In particular he has demonstrated that chap. 4:1f. (which contains a παρακαλέω-sentence) hangs closely with what follows. Bjerkelund, following Schubert's analysis of chaps. 1:2-3:13, pointed to the weaknesses of both Eckart and Schmithals' hypotheses in failing to note that the three thanksgivings are closely linked. For a different view of the structure of 1 Thessalonians, see K. Thieme, 'Die Struktur des Ersten Thessalonicher-Briefes', in *Abraham Unser Vater. Festschrift für O. Michel*, ed. O. Betz *et al.* (Leiden, 1963), pp. 450-458. Note the careful treatment in favour of the unity of the epistle by E. Best, *A Commentary on the First and Second Epistles to the Thessalonians* (London, 1972), pp. 30ff.

thanksgiving period within the context of the whole letter, and to give a detailed exegesis of the thanksgiving and petitionary prayer reports.

1. *Limits and Structure of the Period*

Of all Paul's introductory thanksgivings the extent and limits of the first extant one we possess are the most difficult to assess.[11] Further, the structures of the thanksgiving period(s) do not seem, initially at least, to be of any assistance in our search for the conclusion of the passage, for none of the three relevant sections, chaps. 1:2-5; 2:13 and 3:9-13, is a full and complete example of either first or second category (i.e., types Ia or Ib) of introductory thanksgiving.

Most commentators have recognized that thanksgiving permeates the opening sections of 1 Thessalonians. Some consider that the introduction, with this motif, extends to chap. 2:16;[12] while others, entitling the section 'Historical and Personal', or 'Narrative Portion', mark the conclusion at chap. 3:13.[13] Almost all treat the opening thanksgiving within the narrative portion as extending from vv. 2-10 of chap. 1, but this is doubtful.[14]

---

[11] Wiles, *Function*, has not added anything of significance to Schubert's research on the extent of this thanksgiving period. Sanders, *JBL* 81 (1962), pp. 355f., has modified the latter's conclusions to the extent of observing two thanksgivings, the first ending at chap. 1:10, and a second beginning at chap. 2:13 and extending to chap. 3:13. Sanders, like Pearson, *loc. cit.*, pp. 79-94, has not accounted for καὶ διὰ τοῦτο καὶ ἡμεῖς εὐχαριστοῦμεν of chap. 2:13 and its obvious links with the preceding. Bjerkelund, *Parakaló*, pp. 125ff., has rightly given more importance than Schubert did to chaps. 4 and 5, linking the introductory thanksgiving with the παρακαλέω-sentences of instruction and paraenesis that follow.

[12] E.g., Dibelius, *Thessalonicher*, p. 1; and O. Holtzmann in *Das Neue Testament* 2 (Giessen, 1926), p. 458.

[13] So most commentators: G. Milligan, *St. Paul's Epistles to the Thessalonians* (London, 1908), p. 5; A. Plummer, *A Commentary on St. Paul's First Epistle to the Thessalonians* (London, 1918), pp. xix and 5; and Lightfoot, *Notes*, p. 8. Cf. also E. von Dobschütz, *Die Thessalonicher-Briefe* (Göttingen, [7]1909), p. 27; J. E. Frame, *A Critical and Exegetical Commentary on the Epistles of St. Paul to the Thessalonians* (Edinburgh, 1912), p. 72; J. W. Bailey, 'The First and Second Epistles to the Thessalonians', in *The Interpreter's Bible* 11, p. 256; B. Rigaux, *Saint Paul. Les Épîtres aux Thessaloniciens* (Paris, 1956), p. 356; and A. Oepke, *Die kleineren Briefe des Apostels Paulus : Die Briefe an die Thessalonicher* (Göttingen, [10]1965), p. 160.

[14] It is not denied that chap. 1:2-10 is part of the thanksgiving period, but rather that vv. 6-10 belong to the actual thanksgiving report. Paul's reported thanksgiving seems to end with the words of v. 5, 'with full conviction'.

There are good reasons for considering that Paul's introductory thanksgiving stretches from chaps. 1:2 to 3:13. These three chapters are not, *in toto*, reports of Paul's actual thanksgivings or petitions. A large part of the section is taken up with personal and official details: so chaps. 1:6-2:12 are a recital of the initial gospel preaching in Thessalonica, the response of the Thessalonians and Paul's ministry among them; while chaps. 2:17-3:8 are a discussion of Timothy's recent visit to the city. We have already noted that in each of the introductory thanksgivings, especially in that of Romans, it was not unusual for Paul to include personal and official details in and around his thanksgiving or petitionary prayer reports. The relevant sections of chaps. 1:2 to 3:13 are not simply digressions but integral parts of the whole period. Schubert has argued this at length and we refer to his discussion.[15]

The structure of 1 Thess. 1:2ff. seems to indicate an example of the first category, i.e., type Ia. The principal verb, εὐχαριστοῦμεν, as the first unit of the period, dominates the passage. It is immediately followed by the personal object, τῷ θεῷ. The third and fourth elements, i.e., the temporal adverb πάντοτε and the pronominal phrase περὶ πάντων ὑμῶν, then appear, with the temporal participial clause (μνείαν ποιούμενοι) and the temporal phrase (ἐπὶ τῶν προσευχῶν ἡμῶν) following. The sixth unit is in evidence with two causal participial clauses, introduced by μνημονεύοντες ὑμῶν τοῦ ἔργου κτλ., and εἰδότες, ἀδελφοὶ ἠγαπημένοι, κτλ. The seventh element, however, breaks the sequence. In all other examples of the first category [16] the final clause, introduced by ἵνα, ὅπως, εἰς τό... or an equivalent, presents the intercessory prayer report. Here the final clause is introduced by ὅτι (a regular mark of the second category),[17] and is dependent on the participle εἰδότες. No intercessory prayer report is mentioned in the immediate context. Thus, the period is either, similar to that of Rom. 1 where at v. 9 μνείαν ὑμῶν ποιοῦμαι refers

---

[15] *Form*, pp. 17-27. One interesting feature Schubert has drawn attention to is Paul's use of γίνομαι (pp. 19f.) in chaps. 1:5-2:14. Nine occurrences derive from and are logically dependent on that in chap. 1:5, οἷοι ἐγενήθημεν ἐν ὑμῖν δι' ὑμᾶς. There is a progression of thought and an 'antithesis' between writer and addressees (five uses of γίνομαι refer to Paul, four to the Thessalonians) in the section, chaps. 1:2-2:14ff. —evidence of the apostle's epistolary style.

[16] Rom. 1:10, εἴ πως; Eph. 1:17, ἵνα; Phil. 1:9, ἵνα; Col. 1:9, ἵνα; 2 Thess. 1:11f., ἵνα ... ὅπως; Phm. 6, ὅπως.

[17] 1 Cor. 1:5; cf. Rom. 1:8; 2 Thess. 1:3; 2:13; Phil. 1:6.

to intercessions by Paul for the Christians of that city but in the words which follow no specific details of these intercessions are given; or, as is more likely, the content of these intercessions is not spelled out until the conclusion of the period is reached, namely at chap. 3:10, 'praying earnestly night and day that we may see you face to face and supply what is lacking in your faith'.

At chap. 2:13 we again encounter the typical terminology and structure of a Pauline thanksgiving. Indeed, four of the five elements of the second structure are present,[18] the only omission being the phrase περὶ ὑμῶν. Nevertheless, the thanksgiving is neither independent nor complete. Διὰ τοῦτο gathers its meaning from the preceding paragraph.[19] This leads to renewed thanksgiving on the apostle's part, while the emphatic καὶ ἡμεῖς εὐχαριστοῦμεν points back to εὐχαριστοῦμεν of chap. 1:2.

The second repetition of the basic thanksgiving construction at chap. 3:9ff., 'achieves a properly heightened climactic effect through its fuller language'.[20] The simple 'we give thanks to God' is replaced by the rhetorical question, 'For what thanksgiving can we render to God...?', while four phrases 'for you', 'for all the joy which we feel', 'for your sake' and 'before our God', modify the principal verb and its infinitive. All the syntactical units [21] of the first category are present, though their inter-relationship is slightly varied. Neither the first thanksgiving report (1:2-5) nor the second (2:13) is rounded out by a final clause denoting petitionary prayer, but this is emphatically the case in the third and last occurrence (3:9-13).[22] Thus, the final clause of chap. 3:10 is the climax of the whole period (chaps. 1:2 to 3:13), while the wish-prayer of vv. 11-13, with its *eschatological associations*, concludes the introductory thanksgiving. The latter gives expression in prayer form to the main thrust of the whole introductory thanksgiving, at the same time preparing the way for the

---

[18] I.e., the principal verb εὐχαριστοῦμεν, indirect object τῷ θεῷ, temporal adverb ἀδιαλείπτως, and the final ὅτι-clause.

[19] It also points forward to what follows. See below.

[20] Schubert, *Form*, p. 23.

[21] The temporal participle δεόμενοι is modified by the adverb of manner ὑπερεκπερισσοῦ (cf. 'making my prayer with joy (μετὰ χαρᾶς)', Phil. 1:4). In this case the temporal adverbial phrase is νυκτὸς καὶ ἡμέρας, which is not related to the verb of thanksgiving (as its syntactical equivalent is in the other periods), for the thanksgiving to God in 1 Thess. 3:9f. is punctiliar, not continual. Thus the thrust of 1 Thess. 3:10 is upon continual, fervent *petitionary* prayer.

[22] Schubert, *Form*, p. 22; cf. Wiles, *Function*, pp. 189, 216.

paraenetic half of the epistle which immediately follows.[23] The thanksgiving period of 1 Thessalonians thus contains elements of both the first and second categories and like its counterpart in Romans is an example of a mixed type.

In the exegetical section below it is our intention to give an exegesis of the thanksgiving and intercessory prayer reports, but not of the narrative portions.

2. *Thanksgiving for Work, Toil and Patience : Chap. 1:2-5*

Immediately after the salutation Paul reported his thanksgiving to God for the good news he had received about the Christians at Thessalonica. The principal verb, εὐχαριστοῦμεν, is used in the first person plural, not as an epistolary plural,[24] but because Paul included, with himself, Silvanus and Timothy [25] who had played a considerable part in the mission and were present at the time of writing. The plural (cf. 'we also thank' of 2:13 and 'we feel... praying' of 3:9f.) perhaps gives a glimpse of the corporate daily prayer life of the three missionaries, meeting together and thanking God for His goodness to the Thessalonians.

Such thanksgiving is for all the addressees—none are exempted if the πάντων be pressed [26]—and it occurs whenever Paul and his associates intercede for the recipients of the letter.

The *immediate* [27] ground for such regular thanksgiving is spelled out in the causal clause of v. 3, introduced by 'remembering' (μνημονεύοντες). Paul and his companions remember the Thessalonians' 'work of faith, labour of love and patience of hope'. In spite of the strong reasons for taking 'unceasing' (ἀδιαλείπτως) with 'making

---

[23] See below, p. 157.

[24] Although some take it in this sense, Roller, *Formular*, pp. 169ff., is opposed to admitting the presence of an epistolary plural in Paul's letters.

[25] So Best, *Thessalonians*, p. 66. On the use of the plural in 1 and 2 Thessalonians see Best, *ibid.*, pp. 26-29, and the literature cited there, especially Rigaux, *Thessaloniciens*, pp. 77-80.

[26] Wiles, *Prayers*, p. 180, suggests that Paul prays 'not only for his faithful supporters, but for the idle, faint-hearted, weak (5:14), and the ones who actually oppose him'. G. Wohlenberg, *Der erste und zweite Thessalonicherbrief* (Leipzig, 1903), p. 20, notes the alliteration in πάντοτε περὶ πάντων.

[27] So G. G. Findlay, *The Epistles of Paul the Apostle to the Thessalonians* (Cambridge, 1904), p. 19, who is followed by Frame, *Thessalonians*, p. 75. This suits the context best.

mention (*sc.* in our prayers)' (μνείαν ποιούμενοι), there appear to be weightier grounds for linking the adverb with what follows.[28] The faith and example of the recipients were constantly in the thoughts of the apostolic band, and were 'la source de sa continuelle action de grâces'.[29] If this suggestion (of ἀδιαλείπτως being attached to μνημονεύοντες) be correct, then the adverb's function is different from that found in the other periods. Thus it is noted again that although the apostle followed certain forms in his introductory thanksgivings, he did not do so on every occasion. Though many structural similarities have been observed, it is important to realize that *ultimately* for Paul material considerations were more important than formal ones.

Μνημονεύοντες followed by the simple genitive, rather than the preposition περί, means 'remembering'[30] and not 'mentioning (*sc.* you in our prayers)'. The genitives in the following phrases ὑμῶν τοῦ ἔργου τῆς πίστεως καὶ τοῦ κόπου τῆς ἀγάπης ... Χριστοῦ, v. 3, are rather bewildering. Of the various interpretations, the one which commends itself to us understands ὑμῶν [31] (placed first for emphasis) as a possessive genitive that is linked with each of the three nouns ἔργον, κόπος and ὑπομονή. Πίστεως, ἀγάπης and ἐλπίδος are subjective genitives,[32]

---

[28] On the grounds that ἀδιαλείπτως is normally conjoined with verbs of praying (cf. Rom. 1:9f., which for some is decisive), Wohlenberg, *Thessalonicher*, p. 20; Milligan, *Thessalonians*, p. 6; Rigaux, *Thessaloniciens*, p. 361; C. Masson, *Les Deux Épîtres de Saint Paul aux Thessaloniciens* (Paris, 1957), p. 18; and L. Morris, *The Epistles of Paul to the Thessalonians* (London, 1959), p. 50 : take ἀδιαλείπτως with μνείαν ποιούμενοι. On the other hand, G. Lünemann, *Critical and Exegetical Handbook to the Epistles of St. Paul to the Thessalonians* (ET, Edinburgh, 1880), p. 21; W. Bornemann, *Die Thessalonicherbriefe* (Göttingen, [5,6]1894), p. 54; Findlay, *Thessalonians*, p. 19; von Dobschütz, *Thessalonicher*, pp. 64f.; Frame, *Thessalonians*, p. 75; Holtzmann, *Das Neue Testament* 2, p. 458; and Bailey, *Thessalonians*, pp. 257f., consider the position of the words favours taking ἀδιαλείπτως with μνημονεύοντες, as the majority of Greek commentators seem to have done. Fortunately the general sense is clear, whatever line is taken.

[29] Rigaux, *Thessaloniciens*, p. 362.

[30] Lightfoot, *Notes*, p. 10; Findlay, *Thessalonians*, p. 19; Milligan, *Thessalonians*, p. 6; Bl.-D., para. 175 and Turner, *Syntax*, p. 234. Other New Testament uses with the genitive in the sense of 'remember' are Luke 17:32; John 15:20; 16:4, 21; Acts 20:35; Gal. 2:10; Col. 4:18; Heb. 11:15; 13:7.

[31] Most commentators consider ὑμῶν is to be taken with all three phrases, and not simply with τοῦ ἔργου τῆς πίστεως; so, for example, Best, *Thessalonians*, p. 67.

[32] Milligan, *Thessalonians*, p. 6; von Dobschütz, *Thessalonicher*, p. 65; Frame, *Thessalonians*, p. 76; Morris, *Thessalonians*, p. 51; and Wiles, *Function*, p. 383. Although Lightfoot, *Notes*, p. 10, does not style the genitives as subjective, he indicates that they point to the source from which the work, labour and patience flow. A. L. Moore,

while τοῦ κυρίου is objective, qualifying ἐλπίδος alone.³³ The apostle's stress was laid, not on the faith alone, but on the work that sprang from faith; not on the love alone, but on the toilsome activity prompted by love; not on endurance alone, but on endurance that was inspired by hope in Christ.³⁴ This is the first use of the Christian triad faith-love-hope, and although it was probably not created by Paul,³⁵ in its present form it may well have been his coinage. Apart from ἔργον πίστεως in 2 Thess. 1:11 the above phrases are not found in the Greek Bible or the Apostolic Fathers.³⁶ In its present context the order is the most natural ('Faith rests on the past; love works in the present; hope looks to the future');³⁷ while hope has the prominent place one would expect in a letter devoted so largely to eschatological teaching.³⁸ It can be seen that the early Christian triad has been applied by the apostle to the Thessalonian situation, particularly when it is noted that the emphasis is on the practical results of faith, love and hope. Some scholars have detected an ascending scale

---

I and II Thessalonians (London, 1969), p. 25, does not differ greatly from this, though he calls the genitives 'descriptive', considering that they serve as strong adjectives. 'Paul means work prompted and characterized by faith...'. On the other hand, Findlay, *Thessalonians*, p. 20; and Bl.-D., para. 163 (cf. Plummer, *1 Thessalonians*, p. 8; and Moffatt, *Love*, p. 185), who consider the genitives to be subjective, put the stress on πίστεως, ἀγάπης and ἐλπίδος, while the Greek puts it on ἔργου, κόπου and ὑπομονῆς. H. Binder, *Der Glaube bei Paulus* (Berlin, 1968), p. 54, understands πίστεως as a genitive of quality. Ἔργον is, in the first instance, God's work.

³³ Many scholars interpret τοῦ κυρίου ἡμῶν Ἰησοῦ Χριστοῦ as applying to all three *Tugenden* of the Thessalonians. So, for example, Moore, *Thessalonians*, p. 26: 'for Paul faith, love and hope all spring from fellowship with Christ and have him as their object'. While it is true that the whole of the believer's life is lived in Christ, here Paul seems to be saying that the Christian hope is in Christ; so Morris, *Thessalonians*, p. 53; cf. A. Buttmann, *A Grammar of the New Testament Greek* (ET, Andover, 1873), p. 155; Lightfoot, *Notes*, p. 11; it is 'somewhat harsh to make these words depend on all three words πίστεως, ἀγάπης, ἐλπίδος'; and others. Ἔμπροσθεν τοῦ θεοῦ καὶ πατρὸς ἡμῶν presents the same difficulties of interpretation, and from most commentators the same response. The sentence could well have finished with ἐλπίδος, but in his characteristic manner Paul lengthens it by the addition of these two clauses; Milligan, *Thessalonians*, p. 7.

³⁴ Frame, *Thessalonians*, p. 76.

³⁵ See the discussion on p. 81.

³⁶ Frame, *Thessalonians*, p. 76. Ἡ ἐλπίς τῆς ὑπομονῆς is found at 4 Macc 17:4, but in that context the emphasis is on hope.

³⁷ Lightfoot, *Colossians and Philemon*, p. 132. Each of the results, however, is in the present.

³⁸ Milligan, *Thessalonians*, p. 6. For the same order of these results, cf. Rev. 2:2, τὰ ἔργα σου καὶ τὸν κόπον καὶ τὴν ὑπομονήν σου.

of fruits [39] in the triad, ἔργον — κόπος — ὑπομονή, the first referring to ordinary activity, the second to labour, toil or tiring and unpleasant work, while the last points to endurance under opposition or insult.

Τοῦ ἔργου τῆς πίστεως [40] is not to be restricted to any particular act of faith, as ἔργον is used quite generally.[41] The apostle gave thanks to God on account of the practical expression of the Christian faith of the recipients. If 1 Thessalonians was the first of Paul's canonical letters, then this was his first mention of πίστις, and its use here indicates he was far from approving some theoretical or sentimental faith. It is also interesting to note that ἔργον, with different meanings, and its cognate ἐργάζομαι appear frequently in the Thessalonian letters. Paul could give thanks for their 'work of faith', yet he strongly encouraged them to 'work with their hands' (1 Thess. 4:11).

Κόπος,[42] a word used in secular Greek of 'a beating, weariness (as though one had been beaten) and exertion', was the proper word for physical tiredness induced by work, exertion or heat. It denoted severe labour and, together with its cognate κοπιάω, was used in the New Testament of: (1) work in general, such as manual labour (2 Cor. 6:5; 11:27; Eph. 4:28); and (2) Christian work in and for the community. Under the latter heading κόπος could describe Paul's apostolic ministry (1 Thess. 2:9; 3:5; 2 Thess. 3:8; 2 Cor. 11:23; cf. κοπιάω 1 Cor. 4:12; 15:10; Gal. 4:11; Phil. 2:16; Col. 1:29) as well as the toil of Christians (1 Cor. 3:8; 15:58; 2 Cor. 10:15; cf. κοπιάω 1 Thess. 5:12; 1 Cor. 16:16; Rom. 16:6, 12 (twice)). It was one key term used of Paul's pastoral efforts and appears to have had some importance in the Thessalonian correspondence. In his thanks to God the apostle used the term of the recipients themselves. Their κόπος sprang from Christian love. Later in a paraenetic section he will urge these same recipients to respect τοὺς κοπιῶντας ἐν ὑμῖν (5:12). They were to do this ὑπερεκπερισσοῦ ἐν ἀγάπῃ, the basis being their leaders' ἔργον. Thus, again we encounter in an intro-

---

[39] Lightfoot, *Notes*, p. 10; E. J. Bicknell, *The First and Second Epistles to the Thessalonians* (London, 1932), p. 5; and W. Neil, *The Epistles of Paul to the Thessalonians* (London, 1950), p. 11.

[40] Frame, *Thessalonians*, p. 76: 'the activity that faith inspires'; Findlay, *Thessalonians*, p. 20: '*faith's work*', i.e., '*the offspring of faith*... (as) the aim and evidence of salvation'.

[41] So Milligan, *Thessalonians*, p. 6; Morris, *Thessalonians*, p. 51; cf. Findlay, *Thessalonians*, p. 20.

[42] See esp. F. Hauck, 'κόπος', *TDNT* 3, pp. 827-830; and Rigaux, *Thessaloniciens*, p. 363.

ductory thanksgiving a significant term used by Paul of his ministry; and once again a paraenetic thrust is prefigured in a thanksgiving report.

Both ὑπομονή and ἐλπίς appeared in the introductory thanksgiving of Colossians (1:11, 5) and their immediate significance in that context was discussed. Here the former springs out of the latter. Paul thanked God for their patience or steadfastness which was based on their hope in the Lord Jesus Christ. Ὑπομονή at Col. 1:11 was one subject of Paul's petitionary prayer, i.e., that the recipients might be strengthened 'for all patience (ὑπομονήν) and longsuffering'. Here it is one of the *immediate* grounds of Paul's thanksgiving. Ἐλπίς in Col. 1:5, unlike ἀγάπη and πίστις, was used objectively of the hope laid up in heaven. Here it is found with its more 'subjective' connotation. In both instances hope was an indirect ground of thanksgiving. Ἐλπίς and ὑπομονή appeared in both periods but with different meanings and functions. Ὑπομονή is not found again in 1 Thessalonians (it appears in the thanksgiving period of 2 Thess. 1:4; cf. 3:5), but the synonymous μακροθυμέω occurs in a paraenetic reference: 'Be patient (μακροθυμεῖτε) with all', 1 Thess, 5:14. Ἐλπίς is used again in a paragraph on eschatological teaching with reference to unbelievers, 'that you may not grieve as others do who have no hope (ἐλπίδα)', chap. 4:13; while in the context of an exhortation where the triad is repeated, believers are to put on for a helmet 'the hope (ἐλπίδα) of salvation', chap. 5:8. Hope in Christ, which is manifested in the presence of God, was part of the important eschatological teaching of this letter.

With the introduction of the causal participle εἰδότες Paul reported the *ultimate* ground [43] of his thanksgiving to God. The relationship of this second causal participial clause to the immediate cause (μνημονεύοντες κτλ.) is similar to that of the causal clause of Phil. 1:6, πεποιθὼς αὐτὸ τοῦτο ὅτι ... and the causal phrase ἐπὶ τῇ κοινωνίᾳ ὑμῶν κτλ. (Phil. 1:5).[44] In both thanksgivings the ultimate basis (God's activity or prior action) appears at the end. Here Paul

---

[43] Rigaux, *ibid.*, p. 369, correctly observes that the three participles dependent on εὐχαριστέω are not in the same relation. Frame, *Thessalonians*, p. 77, and Neil, *Thessalonians*, p. 13, judge εἰδότες to refer to the 'ultimate' basis of Paul's thanksgiving; Findlay, *Thessalonians*, p. 21, calls it 'the deeper ground'; Wiles, *Function*, p. 403, considers the participle to be causal, but does not relate it to the preceding. *Contra* Lightfoot, *Notes*, p. 12, 'giving the reason, whereas the previous participles explain the circumstances of εὐχαριστοῦμεν'.

[44] See pp. 25f.

has focussed his attention upon the 'achievements' of the Thessalonians; or, more accurately, upon those aspects of their behaviour and conduct he had observed when in their city. Yet even these were not simply human accomplishments; they sprang from faith, love and hope—divine gifts. Εἰδότες, to be translated 'having come to know', conveys the writers' assured knowledge of the Thessalonians' election.

Ἐκλογή, [45] 'election', is not found in the canonical books of the LXX, and indeed occurs only seven times in the New Testament, five of which are in the Pauline corpus. The term was used of God's election in the history of the patriarchs (Rom. 9:11), and of His choosing a remnant from Israel (Rom. 11:5). In this term the stress is on the free decision of God. Some scholars have agreed with Lightfoot that ἐκλογή was 'never used in the New Testament in the sense of election to final salvation',[46] but others,[47] on the basis of Rom. 11:5, 7, 28, consider such a view is difficult to maintain. In the immediate context of 1 Thess. 1:4 Paul undertakes no explanation of what election is, but it does seem that anything less than the Thessalonians' election to salvation (this is not to be understood in a narrow sense since the τέλος of election, i.e., conformity to Christ's likeness, is also in view) as the ultimate ground for Paul's thanksgiving is inadequate. The Thessalonians seem to have been familiar with the concept; it evidently formed part of the original preaching. It is interesting to note that Paul could speak with certainty [48] of the Thessalonians' election; though materially this is no different from speaking positively of God's completing what He had begun in the Philippians' midst (Phil. 1:6). In each case Paul was writing to a community in which God had been at work.

The apostolic band knew of the Thessalonians' election *because* (ὅτι) [49] 'our gospel (εὐαγγέλιον) came to you not only in word, but

---

[45] See G. Schrenk, 'ἐκλογή', *TDNT* 4, pp. 176-181.

[46] *Notes*, p. 12. Cf. Rigaux, *Thessaloniciens*, p. 372. Neil, *Thessalonians*, p. 14, considers that here Paul has the 'practical issue... in his mind'. But it is not any practical side of election that is to the fore; rather, 'Paul claims to recognize the election of his converts in Thessalonica by their positive response to the gospel', Moore, *Thessalonians*, p. 26. Election itself is not defined here.

[47] Notably Morris, *Thessalonians*, p. 55.

[48] Morris, *ibid.*; Moore, *Thessalonians*, p. 26. Schrenk, *TDNT* 4, p. 179, thinks ἠγαπημένοι ὑπὸ τοῦ θεοῦ is 'an interpretation of election', while the following ὅτι-clause shows 'this ἐκλογή is manifested in the powerful operation of the Spirit in the community'.

[49] The causal understanding of ὅτι is difficult to resist in the present context, although

also in power and in the Holy Spirit and with full conviction' (1 Thess. 1:5). Once again in a thanksgiving report we note the significant theological term εὐαγγέλιον. Paul might well have written 'we came with the gospel' (cf. 2 Cor. 10:14), but here, by stating 'our [50] gospel came', he put the emphasis upon the activity of the message. The manner [51] of the gospel's coming to the Thessalonians is stated first negatively (οὐκ ... ἐν λόγῳ μόνον), then positively [52] (ἀλλὰ καὶ ἐν δυνάμει καὶ ἐν πνεύματι ἁγίῳ καὶ πληροφορίᾳ πολλῇ). Ἐν δυνάμει [53] does not refer so much to the outward signs of the presence of the Holy Spirit,[54] as to the sense the preachers themselves had that their message was striking home. They preached with an assurance [55]

Lightfoot, *Notes*, p. 12; Milligan, *Thessalonians*, p. 8; and Best, *Thessalonians*, p. 73, consider it to be explicative, referring to the circumstances or manner of their election. See Rigaux's discussion, *Thessaloniciens*, pp. 372f., and B. Henneken, *Verkündigung und Prophetie im 1 Thessalonicherbrief* (Stuttgart, 1969), pp. 28, 43. D. Coggan, *The Prayers of the New Testament* (London, 1967), p. 148, rather unusually, understands the clause to express Paul's third reason for thanksgiving.

[50] According to B. Gerhardsson, *Memory and Manuscript* (ET, Lund, 1961), p. 264, when Paul refers to 'my (our) gospel' the main point of the message is 'that the Gentiles, without circumcision and without being made subject to the Law of Moses, can now be incorporated into the people of God, and can obtain a share in salvation through faith in Christ's atonement alone'. F. F. Bruce comments in 'Paul and Jerusalem', *TynB* 19 (1968), pp. 3-25, esp. p. 18 : 'The gospel according to Paul had distinctive emphases... these... were bound up with Paul's Gentile apostolate and with the "mystery" which Paul had been specially commissioned to make known'; cf. R. N. Longenecker, 'Can We Reproduce the Exegesis of the New Testament ?', *TynB* 21 (1970), pp. 3-38, esp. p. 31. Friedrich's comment, *TDNT* 2, p. 733, that the personal pronoun indicates 'he as an apostle is entrusted with its declaration', though true is inadequate. In this context Best, *Thessalonians*, p. 74, understands 'our' as referring to the 'historical occasion' on which Paul offered the gospel to the Thessalonians. Note also Rom. 2:16; 16:25; 2 Cor. 4:3; 2 Thess. 2:14; also 1 Cor. 15:1; Gal. 1:11; 2:2; 2 Tim. 2:8.

[51] Thus Bornemann, *Thessalonicher*, p. 58 : 'Die Zusätze mit ἐν bezeichnen die Art und Weise, wie die apostolische Verkündigung sich vollzug'; while Moule, *Idiom Book*, p. 78, considers ἐν to be of '*accompaniment, attendant circumstances*'.

[52] Cf. chap. 2:4, 13.

[53] Power and gospel are not unrelated in the *corpus Paulinum*; see the *locus classicus* Rom. 1:16f.; and cf. 1 Cor. 1:18; 2:4. Note the Old Testament background where God's word is said to be powerful (Isa. 55:10f.; Jer. 23:29); cf. Henneken, *Verkündigung*, pp. 32f.

[54] So most commentators, although Bultmann, *Theology* 1, p. 161; Munck, *Paul*, p. 275; and Hamman, *Prière*, p. 284, understand it as a reference to supernatural signs.

[55] Πληροφορία refers to the conviction or confidence of Paul and his fellow-preachers. According to Delling, *TDNT* 6, p. 311, it is to be interpreted along the same lines as ἐν δυνάμει and ἐν πνεύματι ἁγίῳ. The three terms are juxtaposed and characterize Paul's first preaching.

brought by the Holy Spirit (ἐν [56] πνεύματι ἁγίῳ καὶ πληροφορίᾳ πολλῇ). Further evidence of its potency was to be seen in the eagerness and joyfulness with which the Thessalonians had believed (v. 6). Rigaux has pointed out that after γίνομαι, εἰς 'indique un mouvement, soit le changement d'un endroit à un autre, soit d'une situation à une autre'.[57] The subject of γίνομαι εἰς does not have to be personal, but in the present context εὐαγγέλιον may once again be personalized.[58] If so, then this use, together with the emphasis on the activity of the message, parallels the occurrences in Col. 1:5f. and those instances where the word is used as a *nomen actionis* in the thanksgiving periods (Phil. 1:7; cf. Rom. 1:9, etc.). It is also noted that the verb used of the message (ἐγενήθη) was also applied to the recipients (ἐγενήθητε, v. 6), as well as to the agents (ἐγενήθημεν, v. 5).[59] Those who welcomed the gospel became imitators, not only of the messengers but also and pre-eminently, of the author of the gospel (v. 6, 'And you became imitators of us and of the Lord'). This characteristic of the recipients conforming to the message or its source has been noted frequently in the introductory thanksgivings.[60]

The latter part of v. 5, 'you know what kind of men we proved to be among you for your sake', is a topic sentence the development of which follows in chap. 2:1-12. Meanwhile vv. 6-10 of chap. 1 are an intimate and personal discussion of the Thessalonians' example to other believers. For our purposes the thanksgiving report has ended, and is not renewed until chap. 2:13.

3. *Receiving God's Word aright : Chap. 2:13*

Paul now breaks out into renewed thanksgiving because the Thessalonians gladly received the apostolic message as the word of God. Διὰ τοῦτο ('because') is related to what precedes, either vv. 1-4, or, more likely, vv. 1-12. In Col. 1:9 where the second major section

---

[56] The one preposition ἐν (rather than the two-fold ἐν which is not widely attested) is used with the two nouns.

[57] *Thessaloniciens*, p. 374.

[58] Bicknell, *Thessalonians*, p. 6, correctly notes that the gospel, in this context, is regarded as a living force. Cf. Rigaux, *Thessaloniciens*, p. 373.

[59] There is a definite word-play on γίνομαι in 1 Thessalonians 1 and 2, the significance of which has been formally assessed by Schubert, *Form*, pp. 19f.

[60] See my treatment 'Thanksgiving and the Gospel in Paul', *NTS* 21 (1974-1975), pp. 144-155.

of that introductory thanksgiving commenced, a new beginning was made with διὰ τοῦτο καὶ ἡμεῖς, thus linking the petitions with the preceding thanksgiving. Here the διὰ τοῦτο points back to the ministry of the apostolic band, as well as looking forward to the thanksgiving and its basis. Καί emphasizes, not ἡμεῖς, but εὐχαριστοῦμεν [61] with particular reference to the previous occurrence in chap. 1:2, 'we give thanks again…'

The ground for this renewed thanksgiving is expressed by the causal ὅτι-clause [62] which follows: 'because when you received the word of God which you heard from us, you accepted it not as the word of men but as what it really is, the word of God'. Παραλαμβάνω and δέχομαι are synonyms meaning 'to accept, receive or welcome'. It is difficult to pin-point the distinction: perhaps the former accents the outward reception, the latter the inward welcome.[63] Certainly we are not to distinguish the time of reception and that of welcoming. As von Dobschütz makes clear the participle and the finite verb describe one and the same act.[64] The former verb is the equivalent of the Hebrew קבל, used in Judaism of receiving a tradition, and thus many scholars [65] have seen at 1 Thess. 2:13 a further reference in the Pauline material to a Christian tradition. So W. D. Davies [66] when attempting to determine the content of this tradition believes that in the present context it is to be identified with the gospel or apostolic message itself. Λόγον ἀκοῆς, the direct object of the

---

[61] Bl.-D., para. 442 (12). See Moule, *Colossians and Philemon*, p. 52, and *Idiom Book*, p. 167; and Lohse, *Colossians and Philemon*, p. 24, both of whom refer to 1 Thess. 2:13; cf. von Dobschütz, *Thessalonicher*, p. 103, and Dibelius, *Thessalonicher*, p. 10. Contra Lightfoot, *Notes*, p. 30, and others.

[62] Though G. Bornkamm, *Paul* (ET, London, 1971), p. 164, suggests that the right reception of the word 'constitutes the reason for *and* forms the subject matter of Paul's thanksgiving' (our italics).

[63] Henneken, *Verkündigung*, p. 54, considers that: 'Das zweite Verbum spezifiziert das erste'.

[64] *Thessalonicher*, p. 104.

[65] Apart from some commentators, e.g., Rigaux, *Thessaloniciens*, pp. 438f., other scholars such as Gerhardsson, *Memory*, pp. 265, 290f., 295f.; W. D. Davies, *The Setting of the Sermon on the Mount* (Cambridge, 1964), pp. 341-366, esp. p. 354; and Cerfaux, *Christian*, p. 144, consider that in the present context the reference is to receiving material in a more or less fixed form. Contra K. Wegenast, *Das Verständnis der Tradition bei Paulus und in den Deuteropaulinen* (Neukirchen-Vluyn, 1962), pp. 49f., who thinks that the verb 'receive' is not employed as a technical term here even though it is so used elsewhere in Paul.

[66] *Setting*, p. 354.

participle παραλαβόντες, has been interpreted in various ways—sometimes ἀκοή has been understood in an active sense of 'hearing',[67] at other times as 'message or tradition' (with a passive connotation).[68] The general sense is not affected either way.[69] Although the message may have come through Paul and his companions (παρ' ἡμῶν), its ultimate source was God.[70] And the Thessalonians accepted the word preached as the word of God.[71] Here Paul is expanding the thought of chap. 1:6. Such an acceptance was cause indeed for thanksgiving to God, particularly as the same word [72] of God continued to work in their midst.

We observe in this sentence of the thanksgiving report that although the term εὐαγγέλιον does not appear the synonymous λόγος θεοῦ does. At chap. 1:5 the gospel is said to have come in power to the Thessalonians. Here it is stated that they welcomed the message as God's word. Now their continued Christian existence is said to be dependent on it.

Vv. 14-16 complete the immediate section of the letter. Having accepted the tradition handed on by Paul the Thessalonian Christians, through God's activity, became imitators [73] of the Christian Palestinian communities which constituted the primitive church, and which suffered at the hands of their fellow-countrymen. With biting words (unparalleled in Paul's writings), about the opposition of the Jews, the apostle concludes the paragraph.

---

[67] Lightfoot, *Notes*, p. 30, 'word of hearing'; Frame, *Thessalonians*, p. 107, 'the word which you heard'. In this active sense see Matt. 13:13; Acts 28:26.

[68] Bornemann, *Thessalonicher*, p. 100; Milligan, *Thessalonians*, p. 28; G. Kittel, 'ἀκοή', *TDNT* 1, p. 221; AG, p. 30; Gerhardsson, *Memory*, p. 265; Cerfaux, *Christian*, p. 144; R. Schippers, 'The pre-synoptic tradition in 1 Thessalonians ii 13-16', *NovT* 8 (1966), pp. 223-234, esp. p. 224, who takes ἀκοή in a passive sense of 'tradition', considers that in vv. 14-16 Paul is 'creatively handling a pre-synoptic tradition'.

[69] Rigaux, *Thessaloniciens*, p. 439. Davies, *Setting*, p. 354, who conjoins λόγον with τοῦ θεοῦ and understands ἀκοή in an active sense ('the word of God which you heard from us'), still discerns the aspect of tradition in the passage.

[70] Note the emphatic position of τοῦ θεοῦ.

[71] See Bornkamm's essay, 'God's Word and Man's Word in the New Testament', in *Experience*, pp. 1-13.

[72] Ὅς refers to λόγος, not θεός. So most commentators.

[73] See D. M. Stanley's treatment, ' "Become imitators of me" : The Pauline Conception of Apostolic Tradition', *Biblica* 40 (1959), pp. 859-877; and Cerfaux, *Christian*, pp. 314f. Paul urged this imitation on those communities which he had founded because of the special relationship between himself and them. They had accepted his gospel.

4. *Thanksgiving, Petition and a Wish-Prayer : Chap. 3:9-13*

Vv. 9ff. conclude the long introductory thanksgiving of 1 Thessalonians by means of a rhetorical question and a wish-prayer. Timothy returned from Thessalonica (v. 6) with the news that the converts had not only stood firm, but had also gone on in the faith. This acted like a tonic to Paul, for he had been somewhat depressed at the turn of events immediately after his own departure from Thessalonica. The converts were under sore persecution from the Jews, and well might Paul be concerned about their continuing in the faith. Joy prompted the question: 'For what thanksgiving can we render...?' The answer implied that adequate thanksgiving [74] was impossible.

In vv. 6-9 there is a mounting tone of joy.[75] This joyful progression crowns the whole period. It was the ground for Paul's thanksgiving ('for [76] all the joy which we feel for your sake', v. 9). Τίνα ... εὐχαριστίαν δυνάμεθα ... ἀνταποδοῦναι functions as did εὐχαριστοῦμεν at chaps. 1:2 and 2:13, but its meaning is somewhat different. The latter, together with the temporal adverbs πάντοτε or ἀδιαλείπτως, signify regular thanksgiving. The phrase in question is *punctiliar and particular*,[77] denoting Paul's immediate reaction to Timothy's good news. The intercessory prayer introduced by δεόμενοι is continual (νυκτὸς καὶ ἡμέρας) as well as fervent (ὑπερεκπερισσοῦ),[78] and thus only partly dependent on Timothy's report (cf. 1:2). Ἀνταποδοῦναι probably conveys the idea of a recompense which is both due and sufficient, the point being, in the present context, that adequate thanksgiving cannot be offered. 'In all the joy' echoes and corresponds

---

[74] Dibelius, *Thessalonicher*, pp. 15f., considering thanksgiving to be an *oratio infusa* wrought by the Spirit of God (cf. Rom. 8:26), suggested that the more thanksgiving was offered, the more God's glory was increased. Boobyer, "*Thanksgiving*", pursued this line of inquiry in his research conducted under Dibelius' supervision. Note the discussion above, p. 5.

[75] Noted by von Dobschütz, *Thessalonicher*, p. 145, and followed by Wiles, *Function*, p. 219; cf. Bultmann's discussion on this eschatological joy; *Theology* 1, pp. 339f.

[76] Here ἐπί with the dative case indicates the basis for thanksgiving; cf. 1 Cor. 1:4; Phil. 1:3, 5.

[77] Instead of εὐχαριστοῦμεν πάντοτε Paul used εὐχαριστίαν δυνάμεθα ... ἀνταποδοῦναι. No temporal adverb expressing continuity modifies the verb of thanksgiving. Wiles, *Function*, p. 245, suggests the thanksgiving is contingent on the ἐάν-clause and the νῦν ζῶμεν of v. 8.

[78] Lit. 'super-abundantly'. An 'almost extravagant intensive', according to Findlay, *Thessalonians*, p. 73. This double compound is found only at Dan. 3:22 outside the Pauline corpus (cf. 1 Thess. 5:13; Eph. 3:20).

to 'in all our affliction and tribulation' of v. 7, indicating the contrast Paul draws between his own troubles and the joy he experiences because of the Thessalonians' standing firm in the faith. Πᾶς points to the intensity of the joy rather than to its totality,[79] while χαρᾷ ᾗ [80] χαίρομεν is simply a substitute for χαρᾷ χαίρομεν, a not uncommon Hebraism.[81] Although the ground for Paul's joy is the Thessalonians (ὑμεῖς is used ten times in vv. 6-10), and in particular their constancy in persecution, his thanks are directed to God (τῷ θεῷ), and his joy said to be in God's presence (ἔμπροσθεν τοῦ θεοῦ ἡμῶν). The latter phrase excludes any notion of personal success or fleshly satisfaction on Paul's part. Thus the apostle, with a deep sense of gratitude,[82] turns consciously to God to render thanksgiving for that which makes him rejoice.

The rhetorical question, begun in v. 9, continues by referring to Paul's constant prayer, and thus introduces the wish-prayer of vv. 11-13. Although v. 10 is linked with the preceding there is a movement of thought. From the salutation to chap. 3:9 the apostle has dealt with what has already taken place among the Thessalonians. That is, issues of the past and present have been at the centre of Paul's thanksgiving.[83] V. 10, as a petitionary prayer report, and the exhortations and instructions that follow, point forward to the future. Von Dobschütz and others are therefore correct when they observe that the movement from v. 9 to v. 10 marks a major turning-point in the whole letter.[84]

The temporal phrase 'night and day' (νυκτὸς καὶ ἡμέρας) [85] is

---

[79] Von Dobschütz, *Thessalonicher*, p. 145; Rigaux, *Thessaloniciens*, p. 482; Wiles, *Function*, p. 236; and Best, *Thessalonians*, p. 144.

[80] *Ἡ could be an attraction of the relative (for ἥν); cf. Matt. 2:10.

[81] So representing the Hebrew construction with the infinitive absolute; cf. John 3:29. Such a cognate usage is not unknown in Greek, particularly in poetry.

[82] R. J. Ledogar, *Acknowledgment. Praise-Verbs in the Early Greek Anaphora* (Rome, 1968), p. 126, considers that the notion of gratitude, which is often present when εὐχαριστέω and εὐχαριστία are used, is especially clear in the present context.

[83] Phil. 1:6 is a notable example of thanksgiving offered for certain issues which still lie in the future; cf. 1 Cor. 1:7.

[84] *Thessalonicher*, p. 146; Wiles, *Function*, p. 241, and *Prayers*, p. 53.

[85] Like other adverbs of manner νυκτὸς καὶ ἡμέρας is not to be pressed literally (see above, pp. 21f.). It referred to continual prayer, i.e., at least to the keeping of regular hours of prayer. On special occasions, however, with a recognition of the spiritual warfare involved, prayer might be offered well into the night; cf. Harder, *Paulus*, pp. 20ff., with reference to 1 Cor. 7:5. Lövestam, *Wakefulness*, pp. 64ff., interprets this idea of praying day and night within the context of the 'spiritual wakefulness' motif

linked with 'praying' (δεόμενοι) rather than with the verb of thanksgiving. It signifies regular intercession for the addressees, and picks up the words 'mentioning you in our prayers' of chap. 1:2, introducing the final clause and the content of the intercessory prayer. There is not a causal link between 'praying' (δεόμενοι) and 'rejoicing' (χαίρομεν), as though Paul's intercessions were occasioned *only* by his joy.[86] Rather, the attachment is a loose one,[87] in the nature of an association of ideas.

Εἰς τό with the infinitive after a verb of petition is equivalent to ἵνα plus the subjunctive, and expresses the content of Paul's requests.[88] The immediate desire of the apostle is to see the Thessalonians in person. There is, however, another closely related [89] purpose in mind: that is, making good (καταρτίσαι) the deficiencies of their faith. Paul's converts, through this petitionary prayer report, are assured of the genuineness of his longing to see them and of his pastoral concern for their spiritual growth. Furthermore, they may be confident that their imperfections are not serious. It is interesting to observe that although the apostle rejoiced over their steadfastness, as a true pastor he was under no illusions about their deficiencies which still needed to be remedied. Also, it is not without importance that Paul considered petitionary prayer to be a significant weapon in achieving these pastoral aims.

Καταρτίζω originally 'to fit, join together' (of nets at Mark 1:19), was used in the New Testament by Paul and the author of Hebrews in the general sense of 'prepare' or 'perfect' anything for its full use.[90] Harder [91] drew attention to the fact that this verb in the LXX,

---

in which the Christian is to be vigilant, avoiding the darkness of this world. Nightly wakefulness (in a literal sense) in prayer to God was a practice familiar to the pious in the Old Testament (e.g., Pss. 42:9; 63:7; 77:3; 119:55, 62, 148). In later Judaism nightly studies of the Scriptures and prayer take place (cf. 1 QS 6:6-8).

[86] The petitionary prayer, the content of which is reported in v. 10, has already been introduced at chap. 1:2, prior to any mention of joy on the apostle's part.

[87] Lightfoot, *Notes*, p. 47; Frame, *Thessalonians*, p. 135; and Dibelius, *Thessalonicher*, p. 16.

[88] See p. 30. Cf. Burton, *Moods*, para. 412.

[89] The two infinitives are introduced by the one preposition εἰς and the single article τό.

[90] Rom. 9:22; 1 Cor. 1:10; Gal. 6:1; Heb. 10:5; see Milligan, *Thessalonians*, p. 42; and for the papyri references, MM, p. 332.

[91] *Paulus*, p. 70. Here καταρτίσαι is an active infinitive with Paul (and his associates) as the logical subject of the activity. The emphasis is thus on the agents of this perfecting work, not the source.

particularly in the Psalter, was used of God's creative act. In the immediate context the further thought of supplying what was lacking is suggested by ὑστερήματα. The latter word connoted a 'need, want or deficiency', in contrast to abundance—such is its meaning in the LXX [92]—as well as a 'lack or shortcoming', i.e., a defect which must be removed for the attainment of perfection. The latter use fits the present context, while the plural indicates more than one thing needed rectification.[93] We are not told specifically in this prayer report what τὰ ὑστερήματα τῆς πίστεως were, but we may suppose with some degree of certainty that the petitions of the wish-prayer: 'may the Lord make you increase and abound in love' (v. 12), and 'that he may establish your hearts unblamable in holiness' (v. 13), point to the most important aspects. This supposition is strengthened when we observe that the instructions and paraenesis which follow are intimately linked with these themes.

The conclusion of the thanksgiving period is reached with the wish-prayer (sometimes termed 'benediction')[94] of vv. 11-13.[95] Having reported his constant thanksgiving and earnest intercessory prayer for his readers, he turned to the more direct form (third person and the optative mood)[96] of a wish-prayer. It is closely linked with the preceding passage and has been regarded as the central intercessory wish-prayer in the epistle.[97] Such prayers are not otherwise found in the thanksgiving periods of Paul's letters, but appear in the salutations of the letters and at the conclusion of paraenetic passages.

---

[92] Judg. 18:10; 19:19; Ps. 34:9 (LXX 33:10); cf. AG, p. 857. For a history of exegesis of this term, with special reference to Col. 1:24, see J. Kremer, *Was an den Leiden Christi noch mangelt* (Bonn, 1956).

[93] Morris, *Thessalonians*, pp. 109f.; Bultmann, *Theology* 1, p. 324, 'lacks of faith'.

[94] Especially by Champion, *Benedictions*, and more recently by R. Jewett, 'The Form and Function of the Homiletic Benediction', *ATR* 51 (1969), pp. 18-34. There is little scholarly agreement as to how these prayers should be styled.

[95] Juncker, *Gebet*, p. 17, in his seminal study of 1905 had isolated this *Gebetswunsch* and noted some of its salient features. Note the recent careful treatment by Wiles, in his *Prayers*, pp. 52-63.

[96] Strictly speaking, in direct speech we would expect the second person to be used of God, and the third person of the addressees. According to the evidence from the Psalter, Psalms of Solomon, Talmud, etc., it is but a short step from σὺ δὲ αὐτὸς εἶ (= אתה הוא) Ps. 102 (101):28; or σὺ αὐτὸς βασιλεὺς ἡμῶν (= אתה הוא מלכנו) Ps. Sol. 17:1, to the use of the third person in prayers addressed to God; cf. Harder, *Paulus*, pp. 25f., who considers these wish-prayers to be the nearest thing to actual prayers of the apostle which we possess.

[97] Wiles, *Function*, p. 189.

The wish-prayers of 1 Thessalonians emphasize the well-being of the converts in their new life in Christ and their general readiness for the parousia. In the present context v. 11 repeats the ideas of v. 10a, δεόμενοι εἰς τὸ ἰδεῖν ὑμῶν τὸ πρόσωπον, while vv. 12 and 13 expand and develop v. 10b, καταρτίσαι τὰ ὑστερήματα τῆς πίστεως ὑμῶν. Paul had reported his constant and fervent intercessory prayer for the Thessalonians. Now, along similar lines, he offers a prayer to God for them.

L. G. Champion made a form-critical study of the 'benedictions' and doxologies in Paul's letters, and he concluded that their immediate origin was in Christian services of worship.[98] The majority of the fixed phrases found in these passages do not occur elsewhere in Paul's letters, but belonged to a general religious vocabulary already in existence. These wish-prayers and doxologies were often complete in themselves, and could be separated from their context without losing the sense of the latter. At the same time 'the motive for the selection of the particular phrases used is often found in the context'.[99] The variety among these wish-prayers and doxologies shows that they 'did not exist in any absolutely fixed forms. They arise out of the personal use of well-known phrases'.[100]

However true many of Champion's observations may be, vv. 11-13 are more closely integrated with their immediate context than he is willing to admit.[101] Not only do the two petitions of this wish-prayer spring out of the preceding, but also the themes have wider links with chaps. 2:17-3:10, i.e., Paul's desire to visit them (2:17) and their need for strengthening (3:2f.). Further, the passage gives expression to the main thrusts of the whole thanksgiving period (1:2 to 3:10). At the same time with its emphasis on brotherly love (cf. 4:9-12), holiness (cf. 4:3-8), and the parousia (cf. 4:13 to 5:11), the prayer

---

[98] *Benedictions*, esp. pp. 14ff. Champion surveyed a broad background in the world of the Old Testament, the synagogue and Judaism, as well as that of the Mandaeans and the Greeks, particularly with reference to forms of invocation, pp. 45-90. Champion had taken a cue from E. Lohmeyer's study, *ZNW* 26 (1927), pp. 158-173. Lohmeyer considered the introductory greetings were derived from early Christian worship. (For a criticism of this view see G. Friedrich, 'Lohmeyers These über das paulinische Briefpräskript kritisch beleuchtet', *TLZ* 81 (1956), cols. 343-346; and W. Schenk, *Der Segen im Neuen Testament* (Berlin, 1967), pp. 88-92).

[99] Champion, *Benedictions*, p. 24.

[100] *Ibid.*, p. 25.

[101] See his brief discussion of this passage on pp. 33f.

provides a basis for the instruction and paraenesis to follow.[102] Vv. 11-13 thus serve as an important bridge passage, summing up Paul's pastoral and apostolic concerns for the Thessalonians.

R. Jewett, on the basis of a form-critical examination of the 'benedictions' (but not the doxologies),[103] has suggested that the original setting of these prayers was the sermon. Passages such as 1 Thess. 3:11, 12-13 (cf. 1 Thess. 5:23; 2 Thess. 2:16f.; 3:5, 16; Rom. 15:5-6, 13; Heb. 13:20-21), according to him, adhered to a fairly rigid pattern while the content was quite flexible. Jewett, who classified the units as 'homiletic benedictions', considered they were used to climax and summarize the preceding arguments in their letters and thus opened up the way for what followed.

Because Jewett's thesis takes more account, than did Champion's, of the immediate context of the units it has much more to commend it. Nevertheless, it is difficult to prove.

Paul began his prayer, which concentrated on the central needs of the readers,[104] with an introductory δέ (αὐτὸς δὲ ὁ θεός), as he did on several other occasions.[105] At this point he was following the practice of ancient prayer in general, and of Judaism in particular.[106] It is unnecessary to seek a contrast with either the immediately preceding words (v. 10), since the prayer report 'that we may see you face to face' is resumed in what follows. But this particle may stand in contrast to the remoter words, ἐνέκοψεν ἡμᾶς ὁ Σατανᾶς (2:18).[107] However, the real point is that God Himself [108] will remove

---

[102] Frame, *Thessalonians*, p. 136; Wiles, *Function*, p. 216; and von Dobschütz, *Thessalonicher*, p. 154.

[103] *ATR* 51 (1969), pp. 18-34. A further treatment of the background and form of the intercessory wish-prayers is found in Wiles, *Prayers*, pp. 22-44.

[104] At the same time the prayer is a spontaneous expression of his inner feelings; Nielen, *Gebet*, p. 166.

[105] 1 Thess. 5:23; 2 Thess. 2:16; cf. Rom. 15:5, 13, 33; and 2 Thess. 3:5.

[106] See Harder, *Paulus*, pp. 26, 63f. In the Psalter references he lists the δέ in σὺ δέ is adversative, contrasting Yahweh with the psalmists' enemies, or His eternity with the psalmists' transitoriness. However, as Jewett, *loc. cit.*, pp. 22f., following others, has pointed out δέ need not always have an adversative sense. It can be used as a simple connective, and obviously in each case the context must decide.

[107] It is not clear whether an antithesis between God's activity and Satan's is in mind. Greeven, *Gebet*, p. 165, thinks there is.

[108] Αὐτός is emphatic, pointing to the direct agency of God that is needed in the present circumstances; cf. Milligan, *Thessalonians*, p. 43; Plummer, *1 Thessalonians*, p. 52.

any hindrances. Κατευθύνω, found frequently in the LXX,[109] is used only three times in the New Testament, where it refers to God rightly directing the heart and ways of man. In 1 Thess. 3:11 the original meaning 'make straight', with a probable reference to the removal of obstacles,[110] is in Paul's mind as he prays. Κατευθύναι (an optative was used to express a wish)[111] is singular in spite of its plural subject 'our God and Father himself and our Lord Jesus'. This has no particular theological significance in itself, since in such constructions the verb commonly agrees with the nearer subject.[112] But it is important to note that Christ is associated with the Father in this activity of making straight the apostle's way.

V. 12 expresses the second object of the invocation: that the Lord might make the Thessalonians increase in love. Δέ here introduces a new point and is adversative as the immediate context and the position of ὑμᾶς show. Whether the apostolic band visits the Thessalonians or not,[113] Paul desires that the latter will not come short in love. This second petition, directed to the Lord alone,[114] has in view the 'deficiencies' of v. 10. Πλεονάζω and περισσεύω are synonyms meaning 'to increase or abound'. The latter verb was used three times more frequently in the New Testament than the former, being found in other Pauline prayers,[115] esp. Phil. 1:9. Here the use of both verbs is to give emphasis to what Paul is saying.[116] The increase is to be 'in love' which is then defined more precisely by the phrases 'to one another and to all men'. In Paul's intercessory prayer for the Philippians (1:9) the emphasis was on the source of the love, i.e., it was divine love. Here the accent is upon the objects of that love—their

---

[109] See esp. Ps. 40:2 (39:3) and 1 Chron. 29:18; 2 Chron. 12:14; 19:3 with reference to 2 Thess. 3:5. AG, p. 423.

[110] Because τὴν ὁδὸν ἡμῶν is added; it is absent in 2 Thess. 3:5.

[111] For a discussion on the use of the optative in wish-prayers cf. Wiles, *Prayers*, pp. 32ff.

[112] F. F. Bruce, '1 and 2 Thessalonians', in *The New Bible Commentary Revised*, ed. D. Guthrie *et al.* (London, ³1970), p. 1158.

[113] Milligan, *Thessalonians*, p. 43; and Frame, *Thessalonians*, p. 137. On the other hand, von Dobschütz, *Thessalonicher*, p. 149, supposes ὑμᾶς δέ 'steht in einfachen Gegensatz zu τὴν ὁδὸν ἡμῶν'.

[114] That is, to Christ. On the subject of prayer to Christ see pp. 205f. The invocation of Christ's name features more prominently in these wish-prayers.

[115] See pp. 31f.

[116] The two verbs form 'an extremely forceful redundancy, a pleonasm', Spicq, *Agape* 2, p. 110.

fellow Thessalonians and all men. Thus the exhortation to abound in brotherly love at chap. 4:9ff. is prefigured in Paul's wish-prayer. And once more in this letter the idea of imitation is presented, this time by the words 'as we do for you' (v. 12).

Εἰς τὸ στηρίξαι (v. 13) expresses the purpose [117] of their growth in love: that their hearts may be established so as to be blameless in holiness. The abundance of love that Paul asks to be granted them is in order to strengthen their hearts. The phrase 'strengthen the heart' comes from the Old Testament where it was used in various ways (e.g., of food sustaining the body, Judg. 19:5, 8; Ps. 104 (LXX 103):15; with reference to courage, Ps. 112 (111):8). In the light of chap. 3:2 (εἰς τὸ στηρίξαι ὑμᾶς) 'heart' probably stands here for the whole person, so that 'your hearts' is equal to 'you'.[118] 'When a man loves, his intellect, volition and feeling, i.e. the whole man, are all involved and so through love it is the whole person who is strengthened'.[119] The thought is similar to that expressed in the prayer report of Phil. 1:10, where believers are to be 'blameless' (ἀπρόσκοποι) on the day of Christ; or that of the introductory thanksgiving of 1 Cor. 1:8, where they are to be 'guiltless' (ἀνέγκλητοι) on the day of our Lord Jesus (cf. 1 Thess. 5:23, another wish-prayer, and Col. 1:22). Ἄμεμπτος means 'unblamable'—and that before God. The notion of holiness appears in the phrase ἐν ἁγιωσύνῃ. This last word, as distinguished from ἁγιασμός which accents the process of sanctification, points rather to the resulting state. In the LXX ἁγιωσύνη was used only of God Himself.[120] In the New Testament it is applied to men only here and at 2 Cor. 7:1. The Thessalonians belong to God (they are called ἅγιοι); they are set apart for His service; and Paul prays that this fact may be fully realized among them.

The eschatological note is struck firmly at the conclusion of the intercessory prayer (ἔμπροσθεν τοῦ θεοῦ seems to be more emphatic than ἐνώπιον τοῦ θεοῦ, and has the idea of (blamelessness before)

---

[117] So among others von Dobschütz, *Thessalonicher*, p. 150: εἰς τό 'kann es nicht den Inhalt der Bitte nennen, sondern muss final sein... die Festigung des Herzens tritt als Ziel zu der Liebesmehrung'. (Cf. εἰς τό in Rom. 15:13, another wish-prayer). *Contra* Wiles, *Prayers*, p. 61, who takes this as the third petition of the wish-prayer.

[118] Best, *Thessalonians*, pp. 150f. On the Pauline use of καρδία, see W. D. Stacey, *The Pauline View of Man* (London, 1956), pp. 194-197; Cerfaux, *Christian*, p. 304; and Jewett, *Terms*, pp. 305-333, esp. pp. 315ff.

[119] Best, *Thessalonians*, p. 151.

[120] Pss. 30:4 (29:5); 96(95):6; 97(96):12; 145(144):5 and 2 Macc. 3:12. Note the preponderance of references in the psalms.

the tribunal of God). The parousia reference with its full christological title (suggesting it was culled from a liturgical source) is again encountered: ἐν τῇ παρουσίᾳ τοῦ κυρίου ἡμῶν Ἰησοῦ.[121] The final words, μετὰ πάντων τῶν ἁγίων αὐτοῦ, refer to those bright beings who will make up Christ's train, whether they be angels or saints who have gone before.[122] Paul's wish-prayer thus concerns the stability of the Thessalonians; it looks to a blamelessness in holiness before God that is set within the context of the ultimate event, Christ's parousia in all its glory.

5. Conclusions

The unusual length (forty-three verses out of a total eighty-nine) of this introductory thanksgiving has been noted. It is not only the first of the apostle's thanksgiving periods but also the longest, and serves to present the main themes rather than introduce them. At the same time the passage is more closely related to the παρακαλέω-sentences that follow,[123] than Schubert thought. The whole period does not consist entirely of thanksgiving and petitionary prayer reports, but contains lengthy personal sections which remind the recipients of Paul's previous relations with them. Thanksgiving to God permeates the section, as the apostle picks up and repeats this motif (cf. 2:13 and 3:9). At the conclusion of the thanksgiving report (3:9f.) a watershed in the epistle is reached, as the apostle passes from the past and present into the future of the intercessory prayer report (v. 10), and with it the themes that follow. This thanksgiving period is the only one to contain the more direct speech of a wish-prayer, and it crowns the passage with an eschatological climax, at the same time briefly summing up the pastoral concerns of Paul for the Thessalonians. The wish-prayer also prepares the way for what

---

[121] See pp. 132f.

[122] The reference is founded on Zech. 14:5, 'The Lord my God will come and all his holy ones (ἅγιοι) with him' (LXX). However, this description is based on earlier theophanic vocabulary of the Old Testament (e.g., Deut. 33:2; Ps. 68:17), and primarily refers to attendant angels. 'Holy ones' is found in the Qumran literature with reference to angels; cf. Deichgräber, *Gotteshymnus*, p. 79. Normally in Paul ἅγιοι refers to men (see pp. 95f.) but it is possible that this is an exception to the apostle's general usage. For a full discussion see Rigaux, *Thessaloniciens*, pp. 491f., and Best, *Thessalonians*, pp. 152f.

[123] As Bjerkelund, *Parakalô*, pp. 125ff., has demonstrated.

follows. Prayer does not lie far beneath the surface in this letter and comes to expression from time to time.

The epistolary function of the thanksgiving period has been examined by Schubert and recognized above. At the same time the paraenetic and didactic functions of the period as a whole and of the thanksgiving and petitionary prayer reports in particular must not be overlooked. Closely allied to these we note Paul's strong pastoral and apostolic concern for the welfare of the readers. He earnestly desired to see them, not simply as an end in itself, but so as to remedy the deficiencies in their faith. By reporting his thanksgiving and intercessory prayers Paul intended to strengthen his ties with the Thessalonians. The didactic purpose appears in the emphasis given to themes such as εὐαγγέλιον (1:5; 2:2, 4, 8, 9; 3:2; = λόγος θεοῦ at 2:13; cf. 1:6 and 9f.), the triad of πίστις — ἀγάπη — ἐλπίς (1:3; 2:19; 4:13; 5:8), ἐκλογή (1:4), the idea of tradition and the associated motif of imitation (2:13 and 1:6; 2:14 and 3:12), a life lived ἔμπροσθεν τοῦ θεοῦ (1:3; 3:9, 13; cf. 2:19), and holiness in the light of Christ's parousia (3:13; 4:13-5:11). These topics, found not simply in the wish-prayer or intercessory prayer report as Wiles supposed, but also in the thanksgiving reports as well, were important to the apostle, and he is concerned that they be properly understood. Some of these themes are expanded in the letter. Others, such as ἐκλογή, he does not develop but simply reminds the addressees of his initial preaching in their city. The didactic purpose is served by recall to known truths and by exposition and elaboration of others. The paraenetic thrust of the prayer reports is also in evidence. The exercise of charity (esp. to the brethren, 4:9ff.) is prefigured (3:12), as are other motifs, e.g., the demonstration of patience (1:3 and 5:14), being clothed with the triad of faith-love-hope (1:3 and 5:8), setting an example in one's work (4:11), rejoicing under all circumstances (3:9 and 5:16), giving thanks ἐν παντί (5:18; cf. 1:2; 2:13; 3:9), and interceding for others (including Paul and his associates, cf. 5:17, 25).

The language of Paul's prayers, as noted with reference to other thanksgiving periods, has been mined from various quarries. Phrases found in the wish-prayer of chap. 3:11-13, may well have been used in early Christian worship. Indeed, some which can be parallelled in the LXX (particularly in the Psalter) may have appeared in the worship of ancient Israel. The primitive Christian triad, with an emphasis on the practical results of faith, love and hope, occurs for the first time in the writings of the apostle. Traditional material (e.g., παραλαμβάνω and ἀκοή; cf. μιμητής) appears in the prayer reports. Εὐαγγέλιον, key concepts such as λόγος θεοῦ and parousia references, which were no doubt linked with Paul's missionary preaching, are also to be noted. But it is important to recognize that the apostle has adapted this material to the situation and needs of the Thessalonians. Thus, the liturgical expressions of the wish-prayer sum up precisely the basic needs of these converts. The triad is linked with work-toil-patience. The recipients of Paul's gospel are to conform their lives to those of the missionaries; indeed, ultimately they are to be imitators 'of the Lord'. Parousia references are linked with Christian stability and blamelessness in holiness.

The immediate grounds for Paul's constant thanksgiving at chap. 1:2ff. were the 'achievements' of the Thessalonians, i.e., their work, toil and patience. The ultimate basis, however, of those who are 'brethren beloved by God' was their election, and the evidence of this was the freedom and power with which Paul and his associates preached (v. 5), as well as the way the Thessalonians welcomed the gospel as God's word (v. 6; 2:13). The ground for Paul's *particular* thanksgiving of chap. 3:9 was the joy [124] he experienced, albeit 'before our God', when he heard the good news from Timothy that the converts stood fast even amidst persecution.

Thanksgiving and petitionary prayer are close to the surface in this letter, and Paul was apt to break out into one or other at any moment. He viewed petitionary prayer, in particular, as one of the most important means by which his apostolic and pastoral ministry was effected; on the one hand, a pastoral visit, hitherto hindered by Satan's activities (2:18), might come about because of his petitions;[125] on the other hand, his deepest concerns and aspirations for the Thessalonians (viz. their demonstrating of Christian love, stability, holiness before God and a readiness for Christ's parousia) could be brought to God the Father and the Lord Jesus in intercessory prayer, not simply as an expression of psychological release on Paul's part, but because God the Father was able to answer such requests.

Thus both thanksgiving and petitionary prayer were related to the needs of the converts on the one hand, and to the ultimate and broadest concerns of the gospel on the other. Paul was both a pastor and a minister of that gospel and knew how to offer both kinds of prayer.

---

[124] At Phil. 1:4 Paul makes his petition μετὰ χαρᾶς, while in Col. 1:11f. he prays that the addressees may give thanks to the Father μετὰ χαρᾶς. Here joy is the immediate ground for his thanksgiving.

[125] Cf. Rom. 15:30f.; and Phm. 22.

CHAPTER SIX

THE TWO THANKSGIVINGS OF 2 THESS. 1:3ff. AND 2:13f.

1. *Links with the Introductory Thanksgiving of 1 Thessalonians*

The introductory thanksgivings of 2 Thessalonians have linguistic, stylistic and structural similarities with, as well as differences from, the thanksgiving period of 1 Thessalonians. Structurally speaking, the thanksgiving passage of chap. 1 is, like that of the first letter, an example of a mixed type. The principal verb (εὐχαριστεῖν ὀφείλομεν, 1:3; cf. 2:13) is followed by the customary personal object (τῷ θεῷ), temporal adverb (πάντοτε), pronominal object phrase (περὶ ὑμῶν), causal ὅτι-clause, and καθώς-clause. These elements are characteristic of the second category (type Ib). V. 11, however, commences with εἰς ὃ καὶ προσευχόμεθα, and exhibits something of the structure of the first category (type Ia), with its verb of intercessory prayer, and its final ἵνα-clause introducing the object of the petition. The εἰς ὃ καὶ προσευχόμεθα takes up the initial εὐχαριστεῖν ὀφείλομεν of v. 3 in a similar way to what was noted in Phil. 1:9 (καὶ τοῦτο προσεύχομαι) and Col. 1:9 (διὰ τοῦτο καὶ ἡμεῖς εὐχαριστοῦμεν).

The second occurrence of the first εὐχαριστέω-formula in 2 Thess. 2:13 is like that of the first letter at chap. 2:13, and is another example of the second category. Apart from the customary καθώς-clause it is a complete thanksgiving [1] with its principal verb (ἡμεῖς δὲ ὀφείλομεν εὐχαριστεῖν, 2:13), personal object (τῷ θεῷ), temporal adverb (πάντοτε), pronominal object phrase (περὶ ὑμῶν), and causal ὅτι-clause. The two letters are thus similar in that their thanksgiving periods are examples of a mixed type. Further, 1 and 2 Thessalonians are the only letters in the Pauline corpus which boast of more than one εὐχαριστέω-formula.[2]

The thanksgiving periods of the second letter have material and stylistic similarities with the introductory thanksgiving of 1 Thess-

---

[1] *Contra* Schubert, *Form*, pp. 29f.

[2] Ephesians contains an introductory eulogy (1:3ff.), and an introductory thanksgiving (1:15ff.).

alonians. The principal verb of the thanksgivings appears in the first person plural [3] (εὐχαριστεῖν ὀφείλομεν, 1:3; cf. 2:13), ἀδελφοί is used in these thanksgiving reports (1:3 and 2:13),[4] πίστις and ἀγάπη appear as important motifs (1:3f.),[5] as also does ὑπομονή (1:4),[6] persecutions appear as a backdrop to the Thessalonians' progress, and election as a ground for thanksgiving occurs in both letters (ὅτι εἴλατο ὑμᾶς ὁ θεός, 2:13; cf. 1 Thess. 1:4).[7]

At the same time significant structural differences can be observed. In 1 Thessalonians the basic thanksgiving formula is repeated twice (2:13 and 3:9), while there is only one repetition in the second letter. Further, it was shown above that in 1 Thessalonians there was simply *one* thanksgiving, extending over three chapters. In 2 Thessalonians the limits of the opening thanksgiving period are clearly defined, so that the passage extends from vv. 3-12. The words of chap. 2:13, ὑμεῖς δὲ ὀφείλομεν εὐχαριστεῖν κτλ., which are designed to recall the thanksgiving of chap. 1:3ff., nevertheless constitute a separate thanksgiving.[8] We can thus speak of the *thanksgivings* of 2 Thessalonians, anticipating that the first (1:3-12) has an epistolary, didactic and paraenetic function as well as giving evidence of Paul's pastoral concern, while the second is specifically related to the problematic passage about the man of lawlessness (chap. 2:1-12).[9] The opening thanksgiving period of 2 Thessalonians, like others in the Pauline corpus, functions as an introduction to the body of the letter, while its counterpart in 1 Thessalonians constitutes the main body of that letter.

Other independent features are as follows: the use of εὐχαριστεῖν ὀφείλομεν (1:3; cf. 2:13) instead of εὐχαριστοῦμεν; an unusual paren-

---

[3] See the discussion on εὐχαριστοῦμεν in Col. 1:3, p. 76, and in 1 Thess. 1:2, p. 146.

[4] But it appears in no other Pauline thanksgiving outside the Thessalonian correspondence.

[5] The third member of the triad, ἐλπίς does not feature as in the first letter.

[6] Ὑπομονή functions differently in the introductory eulogy of 2 Cor. 1:6 and the introductory thanksgiving of Col. 1:11.

[7] Election as the basis of praise is found in Eph. 1:4f., ἐξελέξατο ἡμᾶς ἐν αὐτῷ πρὸ καταβολῆς κόσμου ... προορίσας ἡμᾶς.

[8] None of the three thanksgiving elements in 1 Thess. (1:2ff.; 2:13; and 3:9ff.) is structurally complete. But both passages in the second letter (1:3ff. and 2:13f.) contain all the necessary structural units (1:3ff. is a mixed type; 2:13f. is an example of the second category). *Per contra* P. Richardson, *Israel in the Apostolic Church* (Cambridge, 1969), p. 102: '... it seems obvious that in *both* 1 and 2 Thess. there is only one thanksgiving period' (our italics). His reasons (p. 107) are not sufficient to establish the structural unity of 2 Thess. 1:3-3:5.

[9] See the conclusions below.

thetical καθώς-clause immediately after the principal clause; an emphasis on the extraordinary growth or progress as the basis for thanksgiving to God (1:3); a statement in language based on the LXX concerning God's righteous judgement upon those who are disobedient to the gospel (vv. 5-10); and a reference to boasting within the context of the thanksgiving report (1:4).

The question immediately arises : How are these similarities, on the one hand, and differences, on the other, to be accounted for? Many scholars, rejecting the Pauline authorship of 2 Thessalonians,[10] detect the hand of a later writer who has used 1 Thessalonians as his basis. But this does not explain adequately the independent features of the thanksgivings. An imitator would be likely to produce far more resemblances. It is not our intention to enter into this question of the authorship of 2 Thessalonians. But I see no compelling reasons to doubt the authenticity and traditional order of 2 Thessalonians, and therefore in this study the Pauline authorship, etc., is assumed.[11]

2. *Limits of the Periods*

As suggested above the limits of the first thanksgiving period are clearly demarcated. Vv. 3 and 4 of the first chapter constitute the thanksgiving report, concluding with the words 'in the afflictions which you are enduring'. According to Schubert,[12] v. 5 begins a new period and the first phrase, ἔνδειγμα τῆς δικαίας κρίσεως τοῦ θεοῦ, is its principal clause. An ellipsis is due to the omission of some phrase such as ὅ ἐστιν [13] (ἔνδειγμα κτλ.). The eschatological thrust extends from vv. 5-10, and at vv. 11 and 12 the intercessory prayer report

---

[10] The grounds for considering this letter non-Pauline are : (1) a different approach to the parousia. Here the second coming is considered to be less imminent than in the first letter, for certain signs (apostasy, the appearance and work of Antichrist, 2:1-12) must precede it, while in 1 Thess. 5:1-11 the Day of the Lord comes suddenly; (2) a change of tone. The second letter is said to be more formal and frigid than the first which breathes a warm atmosphere; (3) different addressees. 2 Thessalonians is thought to assume a greater knowledge of the Old Testament (cf. 1:6-10; 2:1-12), and therefore not primarily addressed to Gentiles; (4) the close similarities in language. Some have concluded that Paul would not have repeated himself in this way.

[11] On this whole question apart from the standard introductions, see Rigaux, *Thessaloniciens*, pp. 124ff.; *Letters*, pp. 100f., 108f.; and Best, *Thessalonians*, pp. 37ff.

[12] *Form*, p. 28.

[13] Schubert, *ibid.*; and Rigaux, *Thessaloniciens*, p. 619.

is to be found. The welfare of the Thessalonians is prayed for, and the writer expresses the content of the request by means of the customary ἵνα-clause. A telic ὅπως-clause (chosen for the sake of variety) follows and is subordinate to the ἵνα-clause. The climactic eschatological note, a mark of the conclusion of these periods,[14] is clearly sounded in v. 12, 'so that (ὅπως) the name of our Lord Jesus may be glorified (ἐνδοξασθῇ) [15] in you'.

That the end of the period has been reached is confirmed by the following words, 'Now we ask (ἐρωτῶμεν) you, brothers, in connection with the parousia of our Lord Jesus Christ' (2:1).[16] This new form, an equivalent of a παρακαλέω-sentence, according to Bjerkelund, 'bringt das Wichtigste des ganzen Briefes'.[17] With the words of chap. 2 the thanksgiving has been left behind and 'l'occasion principale et le but de la lettre se révèlent le plus clairement'.[18]

The second occurrence of the εὐχαριστέω-formula in 2 Thess. 2:13f. is designed to recall the words of chap. 1:3 (note the repetition of ὀφείλω). Yet it is set within the context of vv. 1-17, by way of contrast (ὑμεῖς δὲ ὀφείλομεν εὐχαριστεῖν) with the preceding (esp. vv. 11f.), so that the action of God, the mention of those concerned, the means employed, and the ultimate end to be achieved are set in two contrasting series.[19] *Contra* Sanders this second εὐχαριστέω-period does not end with the eschatological climax of chap. 3:5.[20] The eschatological note has been struck with the words, 'so that you may obtain the glory of our Lord Jesus Christ' (2:14). V. 15 is a paraenetic thrust ('stand firm and hold to the traditions') in which

---

[14] Noted in all passages except the introductory thanksgivings of Rom. 1:8ff. and Phm. 4ff.

[15] See below.

[16] Schubert, *Form*, p. 4; cf. Sanders, *JBL* 81 (1962), p. 349; Mullins, *NovT* 7 (1964), p. 46; Bjerkelund, *Parakalô*, pp. 137ff.

[17] *Ibid.*, p. 136. According to Bjerkelund (p. 138), 2 Thessalonians is similar to 1 Corinthians and Philemon in that the παρακαλέω-sentence appears early in the letter.

[18] Rigaux, *Thessaloniciens*, p. 72, quoted by Bjerkelund, *op. cit.*, p. 136.

[19] C. H. Giblin, *The Threat to Faith* (Rome, 1967), pp. 47f. He argues that the two sets of verses (11f. and 13f.) are better understood when 'taken together with what immediately precedes (vv. 9-10) than when a line of demarcation is drawn between v. 12 and v. 13' (p. 48). See below.

[20] *JBL* 81 (1962), p. 356. Giblin, *Threat*, p. 44, differs with Sanders. Many commentators, rather questionably, separate vv. 13-17 from chap. 2:1-12 and link them with chap. 3:1-5.

the consequences (ἄρα οὖν)²¹ of the preceding are drawn out. The wish-prayer of vv. 16f. which encapsules Paul's desire for the Thessalonians, like other wish-prayers in this correspondence, concludes the whole section (vv. 1-17). The limits of the thanksgiving period are set at the end of v. 14, and the meaning of this second passage is to be sought, not in relation to the words which follow—as so many commentators suppose—but with reference to the preceding statements.²²

3. *Thanksgiving for Remarkable Growth : Chap. 1:3-4*

The opening words of this introductory thanksgiving, εὐχαριστεῖν ὀφείλομεν, 'we *ought* to give thanks', are slightly different from those previously examined. Ὀφείλομεν points neither to formality of language, grudging praise, nor 'auf einen kühleren Ton'.²³ It indicates the apostle was personally indebted to God to give thanks for the Thessalonians. Whether or not in a communication subsequent to the first letter (either by letter or by word of mouth) the Thessalonians had indicated they were unworthy of the praise accorded them,²⁴ we cannot say. But Paul's words had not been too strong. They were entirely appropriate in the circumstances, for the addressees had truly progressed in their Christian faith and life. Καθὼς ἄξιόν ²⁵ ἐστιν is not a tautological repetition of ὀφείλομεν for the sake of emphasis. According to Aus both are liturgical phrases ²⁶ employed to express the necessity and propriety of thanking God. These together

---

²¹ The particle combination, ἄρα οὖν, is peculiar to Paul in the New Testament (appearing at Rom. 5:18; 7:3, 25; 8:12; 9:16, 18; 14:12, 19; Gal. 6:10; Eph. 2:19; 1 Thess. 5:6; 2 Thess. 2:15), and its purpose is 'to provide an emphatically inferential connective'; M. E. Thrall, *Greek Particles in the New Testament* (Leiden, 1962), pp. 10f.

²² See the exegesis below.

²³ Dibelius, *Thessalonicher*, p. 33; cf. Oepke, *Thessalonicher*, p. 180. But most commentators reject this notion.

²⁴ Frame, *Thessalonians*, pp. 221, *passim*. For a recent criticism of this see R. D. Aus, 'The Liturgical Background of the Necessity and Propriety of Giving Thanks according to 2 Thess 1:3', *JBL* 92 (1973), pp. 432-438.

²⁵ Ἄξιος generally means 'worthy', but in 1 Cor. 16:4 it has the same meaning as in this verse: 'appropriate in the circumstances'; Moore, *Thessalonians*, p. 91; cf. AG, p. 77.

²⁶ Aus, *loc. cit.* Von Dobschütz, *Thessalonicher*, p. 235, considers καθὼς ἄξιόν ἐστιν to be a liturgical phrase, as do Harder, *Paulus*, pp. 62f., and Deichgräber, *Gotteshymnus*, p. 50, on the basis of parallels in Josephus and Philo.

with the affectionate form of address, ἀδελφοί,[27] found only in the thanksgiving reports of the Thessalonian correspondence,[28] were particularly appropriate for converts suffering persecution.

The ground for Paul's thanksgiving is expressed by the causal ὅτι-clause, 'because your faith increased mightily (ὑπεραυξάνει), and the love you have... grows ever greater (πλεονάζει)' (NEB). Faith and love, as in the first letter, appeared as bases for the apostle's thanks to God. But here the stress is not so much on the outworking of faith [29] and love as on their abundant growth. Although 2 Thessalonians was probably written only a few months after the first letter, the Thessalonians had grown in an extraordinary measure in πίστις and ἀγάπη. Further, Paul had prayed specifically for these ends. The intercessory prayer report of 1 Thess. 3:10 was concerned with repairing τὰ ὑστερήματα τῆς πίστεως ὑμῶν, while the wish-prayer of v. 12 was 'may the Lord make you increase and abound (πλεονάσαι καὶ περισσεύσαι) in love'. (An exhortation in 1 Thess. 4:9f. was along similar lines). This is not to suggest that the apostle's intercession had been exactly or completely answered.[30] Paul's intercessory prayer report of 2 Thess. 1:11 was concerned with ἔργον πίστεως, and in this thanksgiving there is mention of love ἑνὸς ἑκάστου πάντων ὑμῶν εἰς ἀλλήλους, but not to those outside (note εἰς πάντας of 1 Thess. 3:12).[31] Nevertheless, the Thessalonians' remarkable progress in faith and love was the reason for the apostle's emphatic prayer of thanksgiving. Ὑπεραυξάνω, a *hapax legomenon* in the New Testament —Paul favours compounds with ὑπέρ [32]—points to the unusual, even

---

[27] Its presence tells against the suggestion of a 'cooler tone' in the thanksgiving period.

[28] Ἀδελφοί is found in the thanksgiving *periods* of Rom. 1:13 and 2 Cor. 1:8 when linked with Paul's passing on further information to the addressees, but it occurs only in the thanksgiving *reports* of 1 Thess. 1:2ff.; 2 Thess. 1:3ff.; 2:13f.

[29] As in the thanksgiving of 1 Thess. 1:3. Even so, from the intercessory prayer of 2 Thess. 1:11 it is clear that this outworking of faith was not complete.

[30] Some commentators suggest this, but since Paul's intercessions were regularly related to a continued growth until the last day, one ought not to speak of them being completely answered.

[31] Note the further wish-prayer of 2 Thess. 3:5, 'May the Lord direct your hearts to the love (ἀγάπη) of God'.

[32] Ὑπερβαίνω, 1 Thess. 4:6; ὑπερεντυγχάνω, Rom. 8:26; ὑπερνικάω, Rom. 8:37; ὑπερεκτείνω, 2 Cor. 10:14. Rigaux, *Thessaloniciens*, p. 613, sees a point in favour of the authenticity of this letter in the use of ὑπεραυξάνω; while A. Plummer, *A Commentary on St. Paul's Second Epistle to the Thessalonians* (London, 1918), p. 11, following Lünemann, observes in such compounds 'an involuntary expression of his overflowing feelings'.

unexpected, progress of the addressees' faith. The basic verb αὐξάνω,[33] from which the former is compounded, conveys the idea of a seed [34] which has grown in favourable conditions and borne fruit,[35] or of a child's body which grows and develops till it reaches adulthood.[36] The present tense, ὑπεραυξάνει, probably indicates the growth had continued up to the time of writing, while the use of πίστις in v. 4 suggests that this growth was in the context of persecution and affliction.[37]

Although one would expect πίστις to precede ἀγάπη,[38] the accent on faith in this letter is quite marked. The noun appears three times in thanksgiving reports (1:3, 4; 2:13), and once in a petitionary prayer report (1:11), while the verb is found twice within the thanksgiving period to describe those who believed Paul's testimony (1:10), and who will rejoice in Christ's presence at the parousia (v. 10). In the apocalyptic passage about the man of lawlessness those who did not *love* the truth believed a lie (2:11). They did not believe the truth (v. 12) and therefore will be condemned (κριθῶσιν). After his recent exegetical and theological examination of 2 Thessalonians 2, C. H. Giblin [39] entitled the passage: 'The Threat to Faith'. While not neglecting the motifs of love and sanctification, he considered the main theme of the introductory chapter of 2 Thessalonians (i.e., the thanksgiving period) to be 'the fulfilment of faith'.[40]

The apostle selected the verb πλεονάζω to describe the recipients' growth in love. If ὑπεραυξάνω points to 'une croissance organique, intérieure', then the second verb 'marque plutôt une augmentation extérieure'.[41] Although a compound verb ὑπερπλεονάζω was available,[42] Paul kept the simple form of the verb,[43] probably because he

---

[33] Αὐξάνω is used with πίστις at 2 Cor. 10:15.
[34] Matt. 6:28; 13:32; Mark 4:8; 1 Cor. 3:6, 7.
[35] 2 Cor. 9:10, and in an introductory thanksgiving of the gospel, Col. 1:6, and its recipients, v. 10.
[36] Luke 1:80; cf. Col. 2:19; 1 Peter 2:2.
[37] 'Ανέχομαι is used in the present tense too.
[38] The usual order is reversed in Phm. 5, because of Paul's desire to emphasize Philemon's love. It is on the basis of this love that Paul makes his request.
[39] *Threat*.
[40] *Ibid.*, p. 8.
[41] Rigaux, *Thessaloniciens*, p. 613.
[42] 1 Tim. 1:14 within a thanksgiving.
[43] On the idea of growth and increase in Paul's prayers see pp. 31f., 85, 89ff.

had already used it in the wish-prayer of 1 Thess. 3:12.[44] The stress on a diffusive rather than an organic growth is apt for ἀγάπη. The direction of the progress is stated explicitly: the love extends to the entire Christian community—πάντων ὑμῶν (cf. 1 Thess. 1:2) εἰς ἀλλήλους (cf. 1 Thess. 3:12).[45]

The ὥστε-clause of v. 4, with the infinitive ἐγκαυχᾶσθαι ('boast') points, not to the potential, but to the actual consequences.[46] Paul boasted[47] about the Thessalonians in the churches of God. This boasting included the note of thankful joy, but was not self-glorying as though the apostle was boasting in what he had done for the Thessalonian Christians. It was glorying in what God had done (εὐχαριστεῖν ὀφείλομεν τῷ θεῷ, v. 3), and an expression of confidence in the congregation who at that moment were suffering, v. 4. Αὐτοὺς ἡμᾶς is not used reflexively, but intensively,[48] to mark an emphatic contrast. No antithesis is distinctly stated, and thus it could be over against the Thessalonians (note ἐν ὑμῖν placed before ἐγκαυχᾶσθαι) who were faint-hearted and made no claims for themselves;[49] or else

---

[44] So Spicq, *Agape* 2, p. 121. Note his good discussion on this verse, pp. 119-122.

[45] NEB: 'the love you have, each for all and all for each'.

[46] See the discussion on ὥστε ὑμᾶς μὴ ὑστερεῖσθαι, 1 Cor. 1:7, p. 123.

[47] Ἐγκαυχάομαι (see R. Bultmann, 'καυχάομαι', *TDNT* 3, pp. 645-654) is a rare word found only four times in the LXX (Pss. 51:3; 73:4; 96:7 and 105:47) while this occurrence at 2 Thess. 1:4, is a *hapax legomenon* in the New Testament. The simple καυχάομαι and the cognate καύχημα and καύχησις are used in the Greek Bible much more frequently. (It is difficult to see any difference in meaning between the compound and simple verbs). In the Old Testament there are many proverbs against self-glorifying or boasting (1 Kings 20:11; Prov. 25:14; 27:1). It is not simply a casual fault, but the basic attitude of the foolish and ungodly man (Pss. 52:1; 74:4; 94:3), for in it one sees the man who stands on his own feet and does not depend on God. On the other hand, opposed to self-confident boasting there is true boasting which consists in humbling oneself before God (Jer. 9:23f.), who is the praise (καύχημα = תְּהִלָּה) of Israel (Deut. 10:21; cf. 1 QH 9:26-31). A regular element in such glorying in God is that of confidence, joy and thanksgiving. In the New Testament καυχάομαι and its cognates were used almost exclusively by Paul alone. The idea was that of the Jew whose basic attitude was one of self-confidence before God, convinced that his keeping of the Law would bring glory to himself. In Rom. 3:21-27 the apostle set boasting in contrast to faith. Abraham who walked by faith had no καύχημα before God (Rom. 4:1). Faith implies the surrender of all self-glorying. Paradoxically, Paul boasted in his apostolic work, and in the immediate context boasting is linked positively with faith!

[48] As αὐτὸς ἐγώ in Rom. 7:25 and 2 Cor. 10:1; so Robertson, *Grammar*, pp. 287, 687, 689; Bl.-D., para. 281; E. Stauffer, 'ἐγώ', *TDNT* 2, p. 356, and others.

[49] So Frame, *op. cit.*, p. 223. Bruce, *Thessalonians*, p. 1162, considers the boasting is 'not inconsistent with 1 Thess. 1:8, "we need not say anything"; even if there was no need, they would speak all the same'.

in contrast to the apostle's former silence [50] (cf. 1 Thess. 1:8, 'so that we need not say anything'). If the latter alternative be correct, then the point would be that the church at Thessalonica had displayed the qualities of faith, love and patience in such outstanding measure that even its founders could not forbear to utter its praises. Ἐν [51] ταῖς ἐκκλησίαις τοῦ θεοῦ indicates the place of boasting, and denotes: either (1) the churches in Corinth and the surrounding neighbourhood;[52] or (2) the Christian communities in Judea;[53] or (3) that there is no particular limit to any one region.[54] Whatever be the exact location the thrust is that the apostolic band had indicated to other congregations that a community in Paul's Gentile mission had shown faith and patience in suffering in a remarkable way. Ἐν ὑμῖν specifies the object of the boasting, while the subordinate[55] phrase, ὑπὲρ τῆς ὑπομονῆς ὑμῶν καὶ πίστεως, v. 4, designates the qualities about which Paul boasted, i.e., the endurance and faith in persecutions and afflictions that had been both numerous (πᾶσιν) and continuous (ἀνέχεσθε). The single article τῆς applies to both ὑπομονῆς and πίστεως indicating that the two ideas are closely linked.[56] Ὑπομονή, found in other Pauline thanksgiving reports (cf. ὑπομονὴ τῆς ἐλπίδος, 1 Thess. 1:3) is mentioned first, possibly because it is the fruit of πίστις, or else because it can be observed more easily than the latter. Here ὑπομονή 'takes on a more quietistic aspect'[57] (cf. ἀνέχομαι). Πίστις does not mean 'faithfulness', but retains the same meaning as in v. 3, 'faith'. It is man's reliance on God's faithfulness, even in

---

[50] Morris, *Thessalonians*, p. 196; and Moore, *Thessalonians*, p. 91.

[51] Ἐν after ἐγκαυχάομαι in this instance is locative, as in Ps. 74 (73):4, ἐνεκαυχήσαντο ... ἐν μέσῳ τῆς ἑορτῆς σου.

[52] Wohlenberg, *Thessalonicher*, p. 126; Findlay, *Thessalonians*, p. 141; Milligan, *Thessalonians*, p. 87; Dibelius, *Thessalonicher*, p. 35; and Moore, *Thessalonians*, p. 91.

[53] Cerfaux, *Church*, p. 109, gives three reasons for this view: 'The parallel with the first epistle, the allusion to persecutions and tribulations, and the fact that we are only here at the beginning of Paul's foundations, suggests that here again, the "churches of God" are the communities in Judaea'.

[54] So Morris, *Thessalonians*, p. 196. He does not understand the expression distributively as though Paul had told every church in existence about the Thessalonians; rather, this inclusive expression indicates his praise had been 'completely uninhibited'.

[55] The abundance of subordinate constructions in the sentence is typically Pauline.

[56] Though they are not a hendiadys, as J. Moffatt, 'The First and Second Epistles to the Thessalonians', in *The Expositor's Greek Testament* 4, ed. W. Robertson Nicoll (London, 1910), p. 44, suggests: 'a single conception = faith in its special aspect of patient endurance... faithful tenacity of purpose'.

[57] Hauck, *TDNT* 4, p. 587.

the midst of persecution, and has a distinctly forward-looking aspect in this context (cf. 1 Pet. 1:5, 7ff. and Heb. 11:1), in much the same way as does ἐλπίς.[58] Indeed both ὑπομονή and πίστις have eschatological overtones as the following words make plain. The prepositional phrase 'in all your persecutions and afflictions' states the circumstances [59] in which their endurance and faith were shown.

Διωγμός and θλῖψις [60] are synonyms signifying 'persecution and affliction', being found together at Matt. 13:21 and Mark 4:17. The former noun is used specifically of religious persecution, and normally refers to actual attacks inflicted by enemies of the gospel (Acts 8:1; 13:50; cf. 2 Macc. 12:23). θλῖψις is a more general word, and although it does not appear frequently in Classical Greek, it is used often in the LXX for the most varied forms of distress or oppression. θλῖψις predominantly denotes the oppression and affliction of the people of Israel, or of the righteous who represent Israel. In the Psalter the term is used of the constant hostility and persecution the righteous [61] suffer from God's enemies. There are many references to θλῖψις and θλίβω in the New Testament, especially in Paul.[62] Those who experienced affliction were members of the church, and particularly the apostles. This tribulation was not simply factual;[63] it was also necessary. Indeed to the congregation at Thessalonica the apostle could write about such persecution in the following way: 'for you know that this is our appointed lot', 1 Thess. 3:3 (NEB), cf. v. 4.[64] Such necessary afflictions of the church and the apostle [65] are regarded as the sufferings of Christ, which are not yet filled up (Col. 1:24). θλῖψις is inseparable from the Christian life in this world. It has an eschatological note to it (cf. 1 Cor. 7:26ff.), and in the present passage

---

[58] Cf. von Dobschütz, *Thessalonicher*, p. 239.

[59] Frame, *Thessalonians*, p. 225; and Rigaux, *Thessaloniciens*, p. 618.

[60] See H. Schlier, 'θλίβω', *TDNT* 3, pp. 139-148; and Rigaux, *Thessaloniciens*, p. 382.

[61] The righteous experience many afflictions (Ps. 34:19 (33:18)); they walk in the midst of them (Pss. 37 (36):39; 50 (49):15, etc.). But God is the One who hears their prayer and is able to deliver them out of affliction (Pss. 9:9 (10); 32 (31):7, etc.). For fuller references see Schlier, *op. cit.*, pp. 142f.

[62] Of the fifty-five occurrences of θλίβω and θλῖψις slightly more than half are in the Pauline corpus.

[63] Though of course it was this (cf. Acts 11:19; 2 Cor. 1:4ff.; Phil. 4:14).

[64] The theme of suffering as the lot of the Christian is not confined to Paul: cf. Mark 13:9-13; John 15:20ff.; Acts 14:22; 1 Peter 4:12-19.

[65] The sufferings of Paul as an apostle are treated in the chapter on the introductory eulogy of 2 Cor. 1.

occurs within the immediate context of the last judgement, vv. 5ff. The 'θλίψις which the Church undergoes in the last days has within it something of the affliction of the last judgement'.[66] Πᾶσιν shows that their troubles had been many,[67] while ἀνέχεσθε [68] indicates they had not ended with the expulsion of the missionaries. As Rigaux aptly puts it: 'Ce passage implique qu'il existe un état endémique de persécutions'.[69]

Under such circumstances the growth of the Thessalonians' faith and love, and the demonstration of their endurance were remarkable. It was indeed fitting that the apostle and his colleagues give thanks to God for these young converts in the Gentile mission. And the recording of such thanksgiving was designed to encourage and strengthen them.

4. *A Two-fold Intercession : Chap. 1:11-12*

In vv. 11 and 12, immediately after the statements concerning God's righteous judgement on those who do not obey the gospel (vv. 5-10), the apostle takes up his intercessory prayer report. Once again Paul closes a section of a letter with a prayer for his converts, and we can thus discern his desires and aims for them. Εἰς ὅ 'to which end' is attached to the preceding sentence.[70] Paul has announced the victory over the wicked and the glorifying of the saints. But the triumph of the last day and the holiness of believers (which is essential to their salvation) are not automatic. So with his eyes fixed on this consummation, and with the above aim in view

---

[66] Schlier, *op. cit.*, p. 146.

[67] Frame, *Thessalonians*, p. 225; and Morris, *Thessalonians*, p. 197.

[68] If the present tense be pressed, then the persecutions were still going on. Most commentators take it this way, although Bruce, *Thessalonians*, p. 1163, comments: 'The persecution of the Christians seems to have died down'.

[69] Rigaux, *Thessaloniciens*, p. 618.

[70] *Contra* Kerkhoff, *Gebet*, p. 50, who links it with ἐν τῇ ἡμέρᾳ ἐκείνῃ (v. 10), and Lightfoot, *Notes*, p. 105, who connects it directly with εἰς τὸ καταξιωθῆναι (v. 5). Most understand εἰς ὅ—the neuter tells against Kerkhoff's suggestion—as loosely attached to the preceding; Milligan, *Thessalonians*, p. 93; von Dobschütz, *Thessalonicher*, p. 253, 'Die Anknüpfung ist so lose wie möglich'; Frame, *Thessalonians*, p. 238; Rigaux, *Thessaloniciens*, p. 637; Morris, *Thessalonians*, p. 209; and Moore, *Thessalonians*, p. 97; cf. Robertson, *Grammar*, p. 714. The phrase denotes purpose ('with this in mind' (NEB); cf. Bornemann, *Thessalonicher*, p. 345, and others), but the idea of direction is not excluded; so Bruce, *Paraphrase*, p. 59, 'with our eyes fixed on this consummation'.

Paul intercedes for these Gentile converts. Καί is not reciprocal indicating 'we too as well as you pray',[71] but rather 'hebt die Korrespondenz von Fürbitte und Dankgebet':[72] 'we pray as well as render thanks'. Πάντοτε περὶ ὑμῶν indicates in much the same way as οὐ παυόμεθα ὑπὲρ ὑμῶν προσευχόμενοι of Col. 1:9, that intercessory prayer is offered with the same frequency and for the same persons as the thanksgiving.

a. *Worthy of their calling*

Ἵνα introduces the content,[73] not the purpose,[74] of Paul's prayer, and ὑμᾶς, placed first for emphasis, underlines the apostle's special concern for them. The intercessory prayer is addressed to ὁ θεὸς ἡμῶν [75] and has two petitions to it: (1) ὑμᾶς ἀξιώσῃ τῆς κλήσεως, and (2) πληρώσῃ πᾶσαν εὐδοκίαν κτλ. Κλῆσις, a verbal noun which does not occur in the LXX in the sense of 'calling' (possibly due to a statistical accident),[76] appears nine times (out of a total eleven occurrences in the New Testament) in the Pauline corpus, and usually denotes the decisive moment when God calls men out of darkness into His glorious light,[77] i.e., 'der Anfang des Christseins'.[78] But

---

[71] Frame, *Thessalonians*, p. 238, presses the point about the addressees' faintheartedness too far, when he adds that, anxious about their salvation, they were 'praying constantly that God would equip them with the Spirit whose presence guaranteed a blameless life and the acquittal at the last day. This prayer, Paul reciprocates'. The καί is not linked with the pronominal subject, but with the verb (see the discussion on Phil. 1:9; Col. 1:9; and 1 Thess. 2:13, above).

[72] Von Dobschütz, *Thessalonicher*, p. 254.

[73] Cf. each of the final clauses (the seventh element) of the first category (type Ia); von Dobschütz, *ibid*.

[74] As Zerwick, *Greek*, para. 406; Frame, *Thessalonians*, p. 239; Rigaux, *Thessaloniciens*, pp. 637f.; and Morris, *Thessalonians*, p. 209, suppose.

[75] Rigaux, *Thessaloniciens*, p. 639, 'Dans une prière le sens de l'intimité est préférable', i.e., ἡμῶν includes the writer *and* the addressees (p. 78). See his discussion on 'I and We', pp. 77-90.

[76] K. L. Schmidt, 'καλέω', *TDNT* 3, pp. 487-536, esp. p. 493.

[77] E.g., 1 Cor. 1:26; Eph. 4:1; also some instances of καλέω, e.g., Rom. 8:30; 1 Thess. 4:7. Cerfaux, *Church*, pp. 178ff., comments that in the epistles καλέω and κλῆσις usually refer to the calling of the Gentiles. The Pauline idea of vocation and calling had been prepared first in the Old Testament, and later in primitive Christianity. Cerfaux detects a 'definite curve' in Paul's use of these words. In the early stages (i.e., in the Thessalonian correspondence) where the goal of the calling is holiness, the abovementioned influences are more noticeable. Later, calling can be disconnected from the notion of holiness, becoming an absolute thing. On Paul's view of his own calling, see *Christian*, pp. 75ff.

here, God's calling, first effected through the missionaries' testimony (ἐπιστεύθη τὸ μαρτύριον ἡμῶν ἐφ' ὑμᾶς, v. 10), is seen in its culmination, 'der Eingang in das vollendete Reich Gottes'.[79] If ἀξιόω, like other οω-verbs derived from adjectives of ethical qualities, was used in its usual sense of 'account or deem (worthy)', then the apostle's request was not so much a prayer that the Thessalonians might grow in grace as time went on, but that they might have so grown in grace that at the last day they would be counted worthy of their Master.[80] But many exegetes take the verb to mean 'make worthy'.[81] According to this view, Paul's prayer emphasized the point that only God could fit them for His kingdom by making them worthy. Such an action would be completed on the last day, but the request also had reference to their present spiritual progress.[82] Since Paul's intercessory prayers for his converts normally included the idea of present growth our preference is to accept the second alternative, and to understand ἀξιόω in this context as to 'make worthy'.

b. *Right resolutions and actions*

The second petition, πληρώσῃ πᾶσαν εὐδοκίαν κτλ., deals with the same issue, but from a different viewpoint. The first request is concerned with God's action in relation to *His* calling of the Thessalonians. The second petition also refers to God's activity, but this time with reference to the *Thessalonians'* good resolve and work of faith. As in other Pauline prayers, so here the idea of fulness appears. In the Corinthian letters the wealth of the Christian life was often expressed by the word πλοῦτος and its cognate. Here πληρόω is used, but unlike the intercessory prayer reports of Phil. 1:11 and Col. 1:9 where the passive voice is used and it is *inferred* that God

---

[78] Oepke, *Thessalonicher*, p. 181.
[79] Oepke, *ibid*.
[80] Neil, *Thessalonians*, p. 152.
[81] Von Dobschütz, *Thessalonicher*, p. 225: 'nur in diesem Sinne ist es hier zu verstehen'; Dibelius, *Thessalonicher*, p. 36; W. Foerster, 'ἄξιος', *TDNT* 1, pp. 379f., esp. p. 380; Wiederkehr, *Berufung*, pp. 59f., 65; AG, pp. 77f., who point out that the passive of ἀξιόω = 'to make worthy', appears in Diog. 9:1; Bruce, *Paraphrase*, p. 59, and tentatively Moore, *Thessalonians*, p. 97, 'that God may account you worthy by making you worthy'—'although in fact the stress here may well fall on the latter idea'.
[82] The aorist πληρώσῃ not necessarily exclude this latter notion since the sense probably points to the fulfilment without reference to its progress; cf. Burton, *Moods*, para. 39 (b); Moule, *Idiom Book*, p. 13.

is the One who richly fills the Christians, in 2 Thess. 1:11 God is *explicitly* mentioned as the subject of the active verb. Further, πληρόω in this context means not 'to fill', but 'to bring to completion'.[83] The first impersonal object πᾶσαν εὐδοκίαν ἀγαθωσύνης is not entirely clear in meaning. Εὐδοκία,[84] which is not a classical word, and is almost completely restricted to Jewish and Christian literature, in the LXX renders the Hebrew רצון and usually refers to the good pleasure of God.[85] But, on some sixteen occasions רצון is used to describe a human emotion or action. The Rabbis employed רצון for the 'divine good pleasure' or the 'will of God'. Frequently they used the term in this sense without any express reference to God, and so many exegetes consider that Paul is here speaking of God's good pleasure[86] in a concise formula. The other New Testament uses of εὐδοκία and its cognate εὐδοκέω appear to point in the same direction. But there are stronger reasons, we believe, for taking εὐδοκία as referring to the Thessalonians.[87] First, the parallel expression ἔργον πίστεως, understood as in 1 Thess. 1:3, 'the work that springs from faith', is something which men perform, and so it is not unreasonable to treat πᾶσαν εὐδοκίαν ἀγαθωσύνης in the same way. Secondly, ἀγαθωσύνη, a fruit of the Spirit (Gal. 5:22), is used in the New Testament[88] of man's goodness, and so is best treated as referring to the Thessa-

---

[83] Delling, *TDNT* 6, p. 297. Moore, *Thessalonians*, p. 97, understands the verb as in Matt. 3:15 and Acts 12:15 as meaning 'to accomplish'.

[84] See G. Schrenk, 'εὐδοκέω', *TDNT* 2, pp. 738-751; and Rigaux, *Thessaloniciens*, pp. 639f.

[85] Of the fifty-six occurrences forty are predicated of the pleasure, grace or will of God; Schrenk, *op. cit.*, p. 743.

[86] I.e., God is being requested in prayer to work out His good pleasure in the Thessalonians' lives. Morris, *Thessalonians*, p. 210, admits there is nothing unlikely in such a sentiment, though he prefers the second interpretation. Von Dobschütz, *Thessalonicher*, p. 256; and Moore, *Thessalonians*, p. 97, interpret εὐδοκία as applying to God, as do Schrenk, *TDNT* 2, p. 746, and Delling, *TDNT* 6, p. 297. Schrenk's point about this interpretation being 'in keeping with the liturgical flavour of 2 Th. 1', is not only doubtful, but also irrelevant.

[87] With most commentators: e.g., Lightfoot, *Notes*, p. 106; Wohlenberg, *Thessalonicher*, p. 135; Findlay, *Thessalonians*, p. 155; Milligan, *Thessalonians*, p. 93, although his contention that we might have expected the article before εὐδοκία if God's good pleasure was intended, in the light of rabbinic parallels, is doubtful; Frame, *Thessalonians*, p. 240; Dibelius, *Thessalonicher*, p. 36; Rigaux, *Thessaloniciens*, pp. 639f.; Morris, *Thessalonians*, p. 210; Wiederkehr, *Berufung*, p. 62; Bruce, *Thessalonians*, p. 1162; and AG, p. 319. Cf. Rom. 10:1; Phil. 1:15.

[88] Rom. 15:14; Gal. 5:22; Eph. 5:9. On two occasions in the Old Testament (Neh. 9:25, 35) ἀγαθωσύνη is used of God's goodness.

lonians. Πίστεως in the phrase ἔργον πίστεως is a subjective genitive, but ἀγαθωσύνης could be subjective, 'a resolve proceeding from goodness', or, as is more likely, objective, 'a resolve to do good'. Paul's intercessory prayer then, was that God might fulfill in the Thessalonians every good resolve and every [89] work of faith—note the progression from will to deed. Nothing short of divine power could accomplish this, as the emphatic ἐν δυνάμει [90]—to be taken with πληρώσῃ—indicates.

c. *Purpose: the glory of Christ and His people*

In v. 12 ὅπως, used as a stylistic variant for ἵνα,[91] introduces the purpose of the apostle's prayer of v. 11, viz., that the Lord Jesus be glorified by His followers, and that they share in His glory. The theme of glory [92] is not unimportant in these verses.[93] At v. 9, in a quotation from Isaiah 2:10, 19, 21, within the context of judgement, δόξα is used of the Lord's glorious presence from which those who disobey the gospel will be excluded. In the following words (v. 10) the Lord Jesus at His coming is said to be glorified ἐν τοῖς ἁγίοις αὐτοῦ. The influence of the LXX [94] is clearly in evidence (cf. Ps. 89:7 (88:8), ὁ θεὸς ἐνδοξαζόμενος ἐν βουλῇ ἁγίων), though significantly, it is Christ rather than God who is glorified ἐν τῇ ἡμέρᾳ ἐκείνῃ. Finally, at v. 12, having drawn on Isaiah 66:5 (and possibly 24:15), the apostle referred to τὸ ὄνομα τοῦ κυρίου ἡμῶν Ἰησοῦ being glorified (ἐνδοξασθῇ) among the Thessalonians (ἐν ὑμῖν). Paul, in common with other New Testament writers, drew on the Old Testament for his understanding of glory.[95] Yet the δόξα θεοῦ is transferred by them all to

---

[89] Πᾶς applies to both nouns, 'good resolve' and 'work'.

[90] So most commentators. Frame, *Thessalonians*, p. 240, points out that the stress here is on the energy being God's, without whose aid neither the resolve nor the action could be accomplished; cf. Harder, *Paulus*, p. 74. K. Prümm, 'Das Dynamische als Grund-Aspekt der Heilsordnung in der Sicht des Apostels Paulus', in *Gregorianum* 42 (Rome, 1961), p. 679, rather unusually, joins ἐν δυνάμει with ἔργον πίστεως.

[91] Several commentators draw attention to this, as well as Robertson, *Grammar*, pp. 986f.; Bl.-D., para. 369 (4) and Turner, *Syntax*, p. 105; other examples are: John 11:57; 1 Cor. 1:29; 2 Cor. 8:14.

[92] G. von Rad and G. Kittel, 'δοκέω', *TDNT* 2, pp. 232-255; and Rigaux, *Thessaloniciens*, pp. 633f.

[93] Note also εἰς περιποίησιν δόξης in the second thanksgiving of the letter, chap. 2:14.

[94] Especially in the use of ἐνδοξάζομαι; Kittel, *TDNT* 2, p. 254.

[95] Kittel, *op. cit.*, pp. 247ff.; Rigaux, *Thessaloniciens*, p. 633. H. Schlier, 'Doxa bei Paulus als heilsgeschichtlicher Begriff', in *Studiorum Paulinorum Congressus* 1 (Rome,

Jesus. If God is described as ὁ θεὸς τῆς δόξης (Acts 7:2), then Jesus is ὁ κύριος τῆς δόξης (1 Cor. 2:8; Jas. 2:1). Glory is an eschatological entity, an essential quality of the final revelation. Believers participate in this glory. Thus, in the Old Testament such participation is called 'seeing' (Lev. 9:6, ὀφθήσεται), and it was experienced in some measure by Moses (Exod. 34:29f.). This vision is the supreme blessing (cf. ὄψεται τὴν δόξαν κυρίου, Isa. 35:2; and 66:18). In the New Testament believers participate in Christ's glory. They will have a share in His appearing ἐν δόξῃ (Col. 3:4). Christians are fellow-heirs and therefore συνδοξασθῶσιν (Rom. 8:17). Christ is their ἐλπίς τῆς δόξης (Col. 1:27). Δόξα is regularly used with reference to final glory, and in the context of 2 Thess. 1:12, contra von Dobschütz,[96] the accent is upon Christ's being glorified among the Thessalonians at the parousia.[97] Ἐνδοξάζομαι is found only in this passage of the New Testament, though it appears on occasions in the LXX [98] where it is synonymous with the simple verb. The problem here is to assess the significance of ἐν ὑμῖν. Ἐν can be : (1) instrumental (Isa. 49:3 (B) : cf. 5:16, δοξάζομαι ἐν); or (2) local (Ps. 89:7 (88:8), ἐνδοξαζόμενος ἐν βουλῇ ἁγίων). Although in the earlier instance of ἐνδοξάζομαι both the instrumental sense (i.e., as Christ appears His followers will worship Him, rendering Him the glory due), and the local (i.e., His holy ones are to be transformed into His likeness in His presence) may be understood; in the words of the intercessory prayer report, because of the following phrase (καὶ ὑμεῖς ἐν αὐτῷ), the local sense is preferred.[99]

In the Old Testament, far from being a mere label, a person's name [100] was of profound significance disclosing the essential character

---

1963), pp. 45-56, esp. p. 47, points out that Paul's indebtedness to the Old Testament is not simply limited to citing one or two LXX texts in which δόξα appears. Rather, 'für ihn sind... gewisse Grundzüge des Phänomenes der δόξα, wie es das AT erkannt hat, selbstverständliche Voraussetzung seines Denkens'.

[96] *Thessalonicher*, p. 257.

[97] Cf. Masson, *Thessaloniciens*, p. 91.

[98] Eg., Exod. 14:4, 17f., where God is glorified in His punishment of Pharaoh, and Isa. 49:3, where He is glorified in those who serve Him.

[99] See Moore's discussion, *Thessalonians*, pp. 96 and 98, as well as Rigaux's examination, *Thessaloniciens*, pp. 633f.

[100] On the subject of the 'name' see J. Pedersen, *Israel. Its Life and Culture. I-II* (ET, London, 1926), pp. 245-259; E. Jacob, *Theology of the Old Testament* (ET, London, 1958), pp. 82ff.; W. Heitmüller, *Im Namen Jesu* (Göttingen, 1903), together with H. Bietenhard, 'ὄνομα', *TDNT* 5, pp. 242-283, and the vast amount of literature cited there.

of the person. Where the name of God is mentioned it 'expresses the concrete connection between God and man, the personal relationship which declares itself in a specific approach of God...'[101]. Here the glorification of the name means the showing forth of the Lord Jesus as He really is. The character in which He will be glorified is 'Lord' (appropriate in this context where references to the parousia abound), and 'Jesus' (the earthly person who humbled Himself for men).

The ultimate end of the prayer is not simply that the name of the Lord Jesus be glorified among His followers. Καὶ ὑμεῖς ἐν αὐτῷ advances the thought further, even beyond v. 10. By virtue of their union with Christ,[102] Christians share in His glory (cf. John 17:10, 22). In a limited and partial sense this is a present reality. It will be completely true when Christ appears in glory at His return.[103] Thus Paul's prayer has as its ultimate aim the glory of Christ and His people. The graces already mentioned are so to be manifest in the Thessalonians that Christ's splendour will be reflected in their transformed lives, so bringing glory to Him. At the same time they will share His glory. This aim of the prayer is bound up with the parousia; yet it would be fulfilled only if the Lord's name were glorified in them day by day.[104] In the concluding words, κατὰ τὴν χάριν κτλ., the apostle acknowledged that the glorification[105] for which the prayer was made was in accordance with[106] God's[107] grace. If Milligan is right, then the preposition, in a derived sense, indicates not merely the norm but the source[108] of glorification. Either way the words are

---

[101] Bietenhard, *op. cit.*, p. 272.

[102] Taking ἐν αὐτῷ as referring to 'Him', rather than to 'it', i.e., the name: so most commentators; *per contra* Lünemann, *Thessalonians*, ad loc.; and Frame, *Thessalonians*, p. 241. The latter takes ἐν to signify the ground.

[103] Giblin, *Threat*, pp. 7f., considers the aorist passive of ἐνδοξάζω 'brings out the notion of God's Day as one of glorious fulfillment and final union'. He also points out that Paul does not pray that the persecutions might cease in the present.

[104] Bruce, *Thessalonians*, p. 1163.

[105] Κατὰ τὴν χάριν κτλ. relates to the ὅπως-clause of v. 12, not to the whole sentence; so Findlay, *Thessalonians*, p. 156; *per contra* Wetter, *Charis*, p. 53.

[106] So Findlay, *op. cit.*, p. 156; Frame *Thessalonians*, p. 242; and Morris, *Thessalonians*, p. 212; on the significance of κατά.

[107] Τοῦ θεοῦ ἡμῶν καὶ κυρίου Ἰησοῦ Χριστοῦ refers to both God and the Lord Jesus Christ, even though one might have expected τοῦ to precede κυρίου. *Contra* Turner, *Insights*, p. 16. See the discussion in Rigaux, *Thessaloniciens*, p. 643.

[108] *Thessalonians*, p. 94; cf. Moore, *Thessalonians*, p. 98; and Neil, *Thessalonians*, p. 154, who, with somewhat of a flourish, considers the 'foundation, source or motive power' to be expressed by κατά. Wobbe, *Charis*, p. 26, with reference to 2 Thess. 1:12

not a meaningless addition.[109] The Thessalonians were Gentile recipients of the universal gospel. One might well have expected the name of God to have been glorified in Israel (cf. Isa. 49:3). But here, Paul asserted that in them as Gentiles the name of the Lord Jesus was to be glorified.[110]

5. *Thanksgiving for God's Activity from all Eternity : Chap. 2:13f.*

In a strict sense the second appearance of the εὐχαριστέω-formula does not indicate the presence of an *introductory* thanksgiving. It does not form part of the opening thanksgiving of chap. 1:3ff., nor does it have an epistolary function. However, it is included within the scope of our exegesis for the following reasons. First, ὀφείλομεν εὐχαριστεῖν (2:13) is a purposed repetition of the words in chap. 1:3. Secondly, the structural similarities between this and the other introductory thanksgivings are obvious. Here is an example of the second category (type Ib) of thanksgiving period. Thirdly, in spite of the differences there are structural similarities between the thanksgivings of 2 Thessalonians and those of the first letter.[111] Fourthly, although the passage does not have an epistolary function—at least in the sense of *introducing* basic themes of the letter—its presence is evidence of Paul's pastoral concern for the addressees and his desire to encourage them by instruction and teaching. Finally, the breadth and depth of this thanksgiving are quite remarkable. Denney's oft-quoted statement ('The thirteenth and fourteenth verses of this chapter are a system of theology in miniature. The Apostle's thanksgiving covers the whole work of salvation from the eternal choice of God to the obtaining of the glory of our Lord Jesus Christ in the world to come') [112] is apt. It is thus important to examine these verses in detail in order to throw light on the scope, bases, and occasion of Paul's prayers of thanksgiving.

---

states : 'Endzweck der Gnade Christi ist die Ehre Gottes und die Seligkeit der Menschen'. However true this may be it is doubtful exegesis of the phrase in question.

[109] As Dibelius, *Thessalonicher*, p. 36; and Holtzmann (*Das Neue Testament* 2, p. 458 : '... an Stelle der Herzlichkeit und Wärme und Wahrheit des ersten Briefes ist hier eine feierlich-liturgische Worthäufung ohne entsprechende Fülle der Gedanken') indicate.

[110] Robinson, *Ephesians*, p. 225.

[111] See above, pp. 167-169.

[112] J. Denney, *The Epistles to the Thessalonians* (London, 1892), p. 342. Rigaux, *Thessaloniciens*, p. 680, refers to the 'densité' of the theology of the passage.

Of the twelve instances of thanksgiving listed by Schubert [113] only 2 Thess. 2:13 begins with the particle δέ. It thus does not belong to the thanksgiving form, and a glance at the context indicates that the particle draws attention to the contrast [114] between vv. 11f. and vv. 13f. The action of God (πέμπει ... ὁ θεὸς ἐνέργειαν πλάνης, v. 11; εἵλατο ... ὁ θεὸς ἀπ' ἀρχῆς εἰς σωτηρίαν, v. 13), the persons concerned (αὐτοῖς, v. 11; ὑμᾶς, vv. 13f.), the means employed (ἐνέργειαν πλάνης, v. 11; διὰ τοῦ εὐαγγελίου ἡμῶν, v. 14), and the ultimate end to be achieved (ἵνα κριθῶσιν, v. 12; εἰς περιποίησιν δόξης, v. 14) are set in two contrasting series. Moore has pointed out that the 'contrast of sin and grace which Paul draws in Rom. 5:12-21 shows that parallelism has its limits'.[115] Here, too, a similar disproportion is to be seen. Unbelief is to be noted and understood as somehow involved in the purposes of God; but God's activity in saving and faith were, for the apostle, grounds for continual thanks. Although the word χαρά does not appear there is a real note of joy in the passage, and an atmosphere so different from the preceding.

As already pointed out ὀφείλομεν εὐχαριστεῖν is a studied repetition

---

[113] *Form*, pp. 54f. The instances are: Rom. 1:8ff.; 1 Cor. 1:4ff.; 2 Cor. 1:11; Eph. 1:15ff.; Phil. 1:3ff.; Col. 1:3ff.; 1 Thess. 1:2ff.; 2:13; 3:9ff.; 2 Thess. 1:3ff.; 2:13f.; and Phm. 4f.

[114] Because of the awkwardness of ἡμεῖς δέ some have thought that δέ was not adversative. So Frame, *Thessalonians*, p. 278, supposed the particle introduced a new point. A contrast between ἡμεῖς and the doomed of v. 10, he considered, would only have been pertinent if ἡμεῖς referred to the Thessalonians or all Christians. Bicknell, *Thessalonians*, p. 81, admitted the emphasis on ἡμεῖς was not clear and, like Frame, he thought the particle probably introduced a new point; similarly K. Prümm, *Diakonia Pneumatos I. Theologische Auslegung des zweiten Korintherbriefes* (Rome, 1967), p. 586. Moore, *Thessalonians*, p. 107, understood v. 13 as the beginning of a section but did recognize its close connection with vv. 11f. Bornemann, *Thessalonicher*, pp. 375f., rightly understood vv. 13f. as attached to the preceding, but then (p. 377) seemed somewhat embarrassed by the presence of ἡμεῖς δέ instead of 'but you': 'Trotz der Worte ἡμεῖς δέ werden nicht Paulus, Silvanus and Timotheus, sondern die Thessalonicher (περὶ ὑμῶν, ἀδελφοί) den in vv. 10-12 geschilderten Ungläubigen entgegengesetzt'. He has not explained why ἡμεῖς is emphatic. Giblin, *Threat*, pp. 42ff., has many penetrating insights, particularly in connection with the contrasts of vv. 11f. and 13f., but he has not accounted for ἡμεῖς if the adversative use of δέ is so plain. Plummer, *2 Thessalonians*, p. 74, and Lightfoot, *Notes*, p. 119 (cf. Bruce, *Paraphrase*, p. 61), have the best solution to the difficulty. Δέ is adversative, marking the contrast between what has been described and the writer's thankfulness for the convert's escape from such ruin. Ἡμεῖς is used since the interests of the writers are inseparably linked with those of the addressees.

[115] *Thessalonians*, p. 107.

of chap. 1:3. Paul wanted his readers to be in no doubt about his obligation to give thanks for them. We might have expected 'but you' (in contrast to what has preceded) instead of ἡμεῖς δέ. However, the interests of Paul and his colleagues were sufficiently identified with those of the converts to admit the language of the text.[116]

Immediately following the second (τῷ θεῷ), third (πάντοτε), and fourth (περὶ ὑμῶν) syntactical units, Paul used ἀδελφοί the affectionate term of address so frequently found in the Thessalonian correspondence. Significantly though, again in an introductory thanksgiving within the context of election,[117] ἠγαπημένοι ὑπὸ κυρίου is added (cf. 1 Thess. 1:4, where ἠγαπημένοι ὑπὸ θεοῦ is found near ἐκλογή). The expression appears in Deut. 33:12,[118] the blessing of Benjamin (and Paul was a Benjaminite !), where κύριος refers to Yahweh. Here Lord refers to Jesus,[119] and thus 'beloved of the Lord (Jesus)' is apt in a context where Antichrist's followers are being contrasted with Christ's beloved ones.[120]

The causal ὅτι-clause which follows mentions the grounds for thanksgiving, as Paul's mind ranges from everlasting to everlasting: from God's choice unto salvation before the foundation of the world, to the invitation given to the readers through the preaching of Paul's gospel, and to the consummation in the age to come, when the Thessalonians will acquire the glory which Christ possesses. There are few passages in the Pauline corpus, and none in the thanksgiving periods, where the breadth and depth of God's plan of salvation and its execution are so wonderfully compressed in so few words. Important theological motifs come tumbling out one after another, all within the context of a Pauline prayer. The unusually strong emphasis on God's activity (cf. the thanksgiving report of 1 Cor. 1:4-9 where God's gracious action in Christ is stressed),[121] rather than on any achievements [122] of the Thessalonians, is by way of contrast with

---

[116] Lightfoot, *Notes*, p. 119; see above.

[117] Most references to calling and election in the Thessalonian correspondence are in prayer contexts: 1 Thess. 1:4; 5:24; 2 Thess. 1:11; 2:13f.; cf. 1 Thess. 2:12; 4:7.

[118] Many commentators see an allusion to this text in Deuteronomy at 2 Thess. 2:13; so too E. Ellis, *Paul's Use of the Old Testament* (Edinburgh, 1957), p. 154.

[119] Otherwise ὁ θεός in the next clause would be superfluous.

[120] Moore, *Thessalonians*, p. 107; cf. Morris, *Thessalonians*, p. 237.

[121] For the reasons for this emphasis on grace and God's action in Christ see pp. 111ff.

[122] Πίστις is mentioned in 2 Thess. 2:13, but not in the sense of 'a human

the preceding verses where the mystery of lawlessness is at work. The report of the thanksgiving, then, would instruct and encourage the recipients.

Εἵλατο ὑμᾶς ὁ θεός speaks of the election of the Thessalonians from all eternity (ἀπ' ἀρχῆς). Αἱρέομαι,[123] a word that is frequent in profane Greek and in the LXX, is rare in the New Testament, being found on only two other occasions (Phil. 1:22 and Heb. 11:25)[124]. An excellent parallel to this verse is Deut. 26:18 : καὶ κύριος εἵλατό σε σήμερον γενέσθαι σε αὐτῷ λαὸν περιούσιον, where Israel is elected to be Yahweh's עַם סְגֻלָּה. Here in 2 Thess. 2:13 the election [125] of a congregation, predominantly composed of Gentiles, and within Paul's Gentile mission, is one important basis for the apostle's thanksgiving to God. Although there is good manuscript support for ἀπαρχήν [126] 'first-fruits' (suggesting as in James 1:18, 'die Erstlinge im Blick auf die nachher kommenden Heiden'),[127] our preference is for the other

---

achievement'. It is a habitual attitude springing from the sanctifying activity of the Holy Spirit. See the exegesis below.

[123] H. Schlier, 'αἱρέομαι', *TDNT* 1, pp. 180-185.

[124] In both instances there is the idea of choice or preference between two possibilities; Schlier, *op. cit.*, p. 180; and cf. Moore, *Thessalonians*, p. 107, with reference to 2 Thess. 2:13.

[125] No single word constantly expresses the idea of election, but the fundamental notion remains unchanged. The election terminology itself varies (e.g., ἐκλέγομαι, 1 Cor. 1:27; Eph. 1:4; cf. Jas. 2:5; προορίζω, Rom. 8:29f.; 1 Cor. 2:7; Eph., 1:5, 11; προγινώσκω, Rom. 8:29; 11:2; and words of more general meaning : τίθημι, 1 Thess. 5:9 ; καταξιόω, 2 Thess. 1:5), as do Paul's time expressions (e.g., πρὸ τῶν αἰώνων, 1 Cor. 2:7 ; πρὸ καταβολῆς κόσμου, Eph. 1:4; ἀπὸ τῶν αἰώνων, Eph. 3:9; Col. 1:26). Αἱρέομαι is not Paul's usual way of referring to God's election but he is possibly influenced by the contrast being drawn in this passage. On the subject see Rigaux, *Thessaloniciens*, pp. 682f.; Morris, *Thessalonians*, pp. 237f.; Moore, *Thessalonians*, p. 107; and Wiederkehr, *Berufung*, p. 68.

[126] B G[gr]P 33 81 and several other minicules, several Old Latin manuscripts; vg syr[h] cop[bo] Ambrose and some of the Fathers.

[127] W. Bieder, *Die Berufung im Neuen Testament* (Zürich, 1961), p. 40, accepts the reading ἀπαρχήν without any explanation (similarly W. Marxsen, *Introduction to the New Testament* (ET, Oxford, 1968), p. 38; cf. Richardson, *Israel*, p. 108). For Bieder election to be the firstfruits means : 'die Gemeinde ist eben dazu berufen, eine solche Anfängerschar zu sein, potenziell und aktiv missionarisch zu wirken... So zeigt auch die Korrespondenz an die Gemeinde zu Thessalonich wie sehr die Gemeinde des Paulus zur missionarischen Mitbeteiligung zusammen mit ihrem Pioneermissionar berufen worden ist' (pp. 40f.).

well-attested reading, ἀπ' ἀρχῆς [128] 'from the beginning'.[129] It does not denote the beginning of Paul's preaching at Thessalonica [130]—some addition like τοῦ εὐαγγελίου might be expected, cf. Phil. 4:15—but the eternity of God's choice (Eph. 1:4).

The purpose [131] of God's election is that the Thessalonians be saved (εἰς σωτηρίαν). Here as in many other Pauline references, σωτηρία connotes their final salvation [132] (cf. εἰς περιποίησιν δόξης, v. 14). But for the moment Paul leaves this aside and examines the process leading up to that goal, ἐν ἁγιασμῷ πνεύματος ... The eternal choice of God includes not only the salvation of the readers, but also the means [133] by which it is realised. Ἐν ἁγιασμῷ πνεύματος κτλ. is to be constructed with the whole phrase εἵλατο ... εἰς σωτηρίαν. The first words, ἐν ἁγιασμῷ πνεύματος, point to the operation [134] of the Holy Spirit, rather than to the sanctification of the believer's spirit.[135] In the earlier letter (4:3-8) Paul had explained that sanctification (ἁγιασμός, the process of sanctification, is used three times in these verses) was part [136] of God's will, and was made possible by the

---

[128] א D K Ψ 104 181 330 etc. syr^p cop^sa arm eth Ambrosiaster, Chrysostom and other Fathers.

[129] This latter reading is more likely since: (1) ἀπ' ἀρχῆς is not a typically Pauline expression, while ἀπαρχήν is; (2) while Paul employs the concept first-fruits on several occasions he does not otherwise connect it with election. On the other hand, election is regularly linked with some temporal expression; (3) Paul normally uses ἀπαρχή with a qualifying genitive (Rom. 8:23; 16:5; 1 Cor. 15:20; 16:15; but contrast Rom. 11:16; 1 Cor. 15:23); (4) if ἀπαρχήν be read then it could mean 'first' in contrast to others yet to come—which is a possible, though not entirely natural, way of expressing it—; or 'first' in Greece. But the Philippians were converted before the Thessalonians. See Frame, *Thessalonians*, pp. 280f.; Neil, *Thessalonians*, p. 181; Rigaux, *Thessaloniciens*, pp. 682, 683f.; Morris, *Thessalonians*, pp. 237f.; Moore, *Thessalonians*, p. 107; and Bruce, *Thessalonians*, p. 1164. Harnack, in line with his view of the destination of this letter, understood ἀπαρχή as indicating that Jewish believers were the 'firstfruits' of Paul's mission at Thessalonica.

[130] As Wohlenberg, *Thessalonicher*, p. 153, suggested.

[131] So Morris, *Thessalonians*, p. 238, comparing 1 Thess. 5:9, εἰς περιποίησιν σωτηρίας; and Moore, *Thessalonians*, pp. 107f. Cf. Oepke, *TDNT* 2, p. 428, 'εἰς denotes appointment'.

[132] Cf. Harder, *Paulus*, p. 114.

[133] So von Dobschütz, *Thessalonicher*, p. 299, and others who follow Chrysostom in understanding ἐν = διά.

[134] Πνεύματος is thus understood as a *genitivus auctoris*. So most commentators.

[135] I.e., regarding πνεύματος as an objective genitive.

[136] Perhaps the omission of the article indicates that what follows is not the whole of God's will; Moore, *Thessalonians*, p. 61.

Holy [137] Spirit (4:8). Further, he had indicated (5:23) that the whole [138] of man and not just his spirit was to be sanctified, so that all the Thessalonians might be presentable at the parousia of Christ (1 Thess. 3:13; 5:23). From 1 Thess. 4:7 it is implied that the process of sanctification has already begun and is to continue.[139] That the apostle should mention sanctification by the Spirit as an important means εἰς σωτηρίαν is not unusual in correspondence where the notion of holiness [140] is basic. According to Procksch, in the present context the emphasis does not fall on the character of the Spirit,[141] but 'on His operation, which consists in sanctification'.[142]

The second means by which ultimate salvation is attained, πίστει ἀληθείας (expressed under the same preposition ἐν), indicates that the human response is not overlooked. From vv. 10 and 12 it is clear that ἀλήθεια is not simply an ethical quality, but the truth of the gospel, bound up with the person of Jesus Christ. It is simplest to understand ἀληθείας as an objective genitive,[143] and the expression, which has been prompted possibly by way of contrast with ἃ μὴ πιστεύσαντες τῇ ἀληθείᾳ,[144] refers to the addressees' belief or faith in the truth of the gospel.[145] The order of these two phrases is somewhat surprising. Perhaps we are to understand that this faith in the truth of God can only follow upon the activity of the Spirit, and that the belief spoken of is not simply an initial act, but a continuing habit.[146]

---

[137] The stress is on τὸ ἅγιον and this is appropriate in the context.

[138] Τὸ πνεῦμα καὶ ἡ ψυχὴ καὶ τὸ σῶμα. Cf. Morris, *Thessalonians*, p. 238.

[139] Paul does not balance ἐπὶ ἀκαθαρσίᾳ (ἐπί = 'for the purpose of') with ἐπὶ ἁγιασμῷ. The preposition ἐν together with a noun which signifies the *process* of sanctification shows such a process has begun; Moore, *Thessalonians*, p. 65. Cf. Rigaux, *Thessaloniciens*, pp. 512f. See Morris, *Thessalonians*, p. 128 : ' "In" gives... the thought of atmosphere'.

[140] Ἅγιος : 1 Thess. 1:1, 5, 6; 3:13; 4:8; 5:26; 2 Thess. 1:10; ἁγιάζω : 1 Thess. 5:23; ἁγιασμός : 1 Thess. 4:3, 4, 7; 2 Thess. 2:13; ἁγιωσύνη : 1 Thess. 3:13.

[141] Notice that God, the Son and the Spirit appear in these verses.

[142] O. Procksch, 'ἅγιος', *TDNT* 1, p. 113.

[143] So among many commentators. *Per contra* Rigaux, *Thessaloniciens*, p. 685, 'la Vérité est agent d'adhésion'.

[144] Note the 'truth'/'falsehood' contrast in vv. 9-12.

[145] Although J. Murphy-O'Connor, 'Truth : Paul and Qumran', in *Paul and Qumran*, ed. J. Murphy-O'Connor (London, 1968), pp. 193f., considers 'truth' cannot be identified with 'gospel' in this context, since the former is a wider term than the latter. He believes that at this early stage 'truth' was not a term or revelation.

[146] Morris, *Thessalonians*, p. 238.

In v. 14 the apostle continued to describe the process of salvation up to the point of future glory, εἰς περιποίησιν δόξης. Εἰς ὅ, with most commentators, is to be taken with the whole of the previous expression εἰς σωτηρίαν ἐν ἁγιασμῷ πνεύματος καὶ πίστει ἀληθείας,[147] i.e., to the entire purpose of God, and not simply to salvation, or sanctification or faith. God's eternal purpose is historically manifested in His call (ἐκάλεσεν ὑμας; cf. καλέω in 1 Thess. 2:12; 4:7; 5:24, and κλῆσις in 2 Thess. 1:11), an invitation extended through the gospel which Paul and his associates preached (διὰ τοῦ εὐαγγελίου ἡμῶν;[148] cf. 1 Thess. 1:5, τὸ εὐαγγέλιον ἡμῶν ... ἐγενήθη εἰς ὑμᾶς). The aorist ἐκάλεσεν refers to the time when the Thessalonians had responded to the gospel. The thought is not unlike that of 1 Thess. 2:13 where these same people accepted the preaching of the missionaries as the word of God. In both cases the divine summons was heard and responded to in the proclamation of the good news. We note once more that εὐαγγέλιον appears as an important theological term within the context of a Pauline thanksgiving. Although it was not found in the thanksgiving or intercessory prayer *reports* of chap. 1, εὐαγγέλιον occurred in the section about judgement (vv. 5-10) where those who did not know God are described as 'those who do not obey the gospel (τὸ εὐαγγέλιον) of our Lord Jesus' (v. 8), while the Thessalonians, by contrast, accepted the apostolic *testimony* (τὸ μαρτύριον, v. 10). Thus both εὐαγγέλιον and μαρτύριον appeared in the first thanksgiving *period*. In 2 Thessalonians there is no reference to the recipients conforming their lives to the gospel (or its author). This the apostle had already made clear in the first letter to the church. Here he used εὐαγγέλιον on a broad canvas. God's call in history [149] came through the gospel, and an acceptance of it led to ultimate glory. Once more a Pauline thanksgiving is bound up with the gospel —this time with reference to God's call in that gospel.

The process described in these verses is similar to that which Paul mentioned in his letter to the church at Rome: οὓς δὲ προώρισεν, τούτους καὶ ἐκάλεσεν · καὶ οὓς ἐκάλεσεν, τούτους καὶ ἐδικαίωσεν · οὓς δὲ ἐδικαίωσεν, τούτους καὶ ἐδόξασεν (8:30). Here the stage of justification is omitted, and Paul proceeds immediately to the final

---

[147] Cf. Rigaux, *Thessaloniciens*, p. 685.

[148] On the significance of ἡμῶν, see the discussion on 1 Thess. 1:5.

[149] Milligan, *Thessalonians*, p. 107, notes that ἐκάλεσεν is 'the historical fulfilment of the Divine purpose expressed in εἴλατο'.

glory.[150] The εἰς is in apposition to εἰς ὅ[151] pointing to the final consummation of God's purpose. Περιποίησις, akin to περιποιέομαι, is used both actively and intransitively in the New Testament. The former is found in Heb. 10:39, while the intransitive use occurs at Eph. 1:14 and 1 Peter 2:9. Neither the noun nor the verb is used frequently in the Old or New Testaments,[152] and commentators differ on the sense and meaning of περιποίησις in the two Thessalonian references. However, we agree with Milligan and others[153] (*contra* Lightfoot and Selwyn)[154] that the active sense is best suited to the context and means 'acquiring, obtaining'. Δόξης is an objective genitive, as is σωτηρίας of 1 Thess. 5:9. Perhaps in this kind of context περιποίησις is a rather unusual word to have been selected,[155] but it has probably been chosen to stress the reality of the possession of this glory. The thought is not unlike that of chap. 1:12 where the ultimate aim of Paul's intercessory prayer report was the glory of Christ and His people.

The brief but wide-ranging thanksgiving of 2 Thess. 2 has ended. The apostle proceeded to an exhortation in which he urged the readers to stand firm and to hold fast to the traditions they had been taught (v. 15). We have noted that this thanksgiving does *not introduce* basic themes of the letter. It stands in contrast to what has preceded. However, a close examination reveals that each of the motifs of the thanksgiving has already been mentioned in the Thessalonian correspondence. So, links with the preceding thanksgiving are noted in the words ὀφείλομεν εὐχαριστεῖν τῷ θεῷ πάντοτε περὶ ὑμῶν. The affectionate term of address, ἀδελφοί, has been used frequently

---

[150] H. Kittel, *Die Herrlichkeit Gottes* (Giessen, 1934), p. 216, considers δόξα here retains, as in 1 Thess. 2:12, 'einen überschwenglichen eschatologischen Sinn'.

[151] Frame, *Thessalonians*, pp. 282f.; and Rigaux, *Thessaloniciens*, p. 685.

[152] See Robinson's discussion, *Ephesians*, pp. 148f.

[153] Milligan, *Thessalonians*, p. 69, on chap. 5:9; Abbott, *Ephesians and Colossians*, p. 24; Schlier, *Epheser*, p. 71; and AG, p. 656.

[154] Lightfoot, *Notes*, pp. 76, 121; Selwyn, *1 Peter*, p. 167; Robinson, *Ephesians*, p. 148, is not certain of its meaning here.

[155] Selwyn, *1 Peter*, p. 167, finds it difficult to accept the active sense, since the idea of the Christian's acquiring glory is without parallel in the New Testament. But such an expression might have been meaningful to those at Thessalonica who were in danger of becoming unduly down-hearted (cf. Morris, *Thessalonians*, p. 239). Further, περιποίησις is best understood in an active sense at chap. 5:9, with σωτηρίας as an objective genitive, and the thought there seems to be parallel with the present passage.

throughout the correspondence,[156] even in another thanksgiving report, while the appositional phrase 'beloved of the Lord', found in the context of election, has also appeared in that thanksgiving report (1 Thess. 1:4). The motif of election, although expressed by means of different terminology (perhaps αἱρέομαι is selected to indicate that over against those who refuse to love the truth, v. 10, and to whom God sends a strong delusion, v. 11, the converts are 'preferred'), has appeared in the first letter as the principal ground for apostolic thanksgiving. Σωτηρία as a future *Heilsgut* has already been employed in the context of the Lord's coming. So at 1 Thess. 5:8, and 9, first in combination with ἐλπίς, and then in contrast to ὀργή, σωτηρία obviously has an eschatological reference and means the final and complete salvation.[157] This is exactly its meaning in the thanksgiving of 2 Thess. 2:13. The importance of holiness in these letters has already been noted, as well as the activity of the Spirit in this domain.[158] Πίστις [159] has appeared at significant points in this letter, in thanksgiving and petitionary prayer reports, and especially in the central section of the letter where the man of lawlessness and his activities have been described. Faith in the truth of the gospel stands over against unbelief. The notion of God's calling [160] is another significant theme. God calls the Thessalonians to His kingdom and ultimate glory (δόξα), 1 Thess. 2:12; this call is not for uncleanness but 'in holiness' (4:7). God is faithful (πιστός) to complete what He has begun (5:24), and thus He may be petitioned to make the addressees worthy of their calling (1:11). As already noted, the gospel Paul preached fills an important role in these epistles, not least in the thanksgiving periods. It is described absolutely τὸ εὐαγγέλιον (1 Thess. 2:4); and with: τοῦ θεοῦ (2:2, 8, 9), τοῦ Χριστοῦ (3:2), and ἡμῶν (1:5 and 2 Thess. 2:14); while the verb εὐαγγελίζομαι is found at 1 Thess. 3:6; and synonyms such as λόγος (1 Thess. 1:6; τοῦ κυρίου, 1:8; τοῦ θεοῦ, 2:13), ἀκοή (2:13) and μαρτύριον (2 Thess. 1:10) also appear.

---

[156] According to Rigaux, *Thessaloniciens*, p. 371, the use of ἀδελφοί, as a term of address, frequently indicates the tone of a letter. In the Thessalonian correspondence it occurs twenty-one times: fourteen in the first letter (1:4; 2:1, 9, 14, 17; 3:7; 4:1, 10, 13; 5:1, 4, 12, 14, 25) and seven times in the second (1:3; 2:1, 13, 15; 3:1, 6, 13).

[157] Correctly noted by Lövestam, *Wakefulness*, p. 54, in his discussion of 1 Thess. 5:1-11 (pp. 45-58).

[158] See p. 189.

[159] See the discussion on faith in 2 Thessalonians, p. 173.

[160] Cf. Rigaux, *Thessaloniciens*, pp. 182f.

Περιποίησις, in an active sense and with reference to obtaining ultimate salvation (1 Thess. 5:9), has featured; while δόξα and its cognate ἐνδοξάζομαι [161] have been used of Christ's glory on the last day, and the readers' participation in it. Every term or idea in the thanksgiving report has at least one close parallel in the correspondence.[162] Paul's thanksgiving report is a full and compact statement of doctrine which seems to gather up a large part of the teaching of the two epistles.[163] The passage does not have an epistolary function (its place towards the end of the letter hardly permits this); but its didactic purpose is obvious, all the more so when it is observed in contrast to what has preceded. Whether Frame's contention about the recipients being faint-hearted be correct [164] or not, the passage still gives evidence of Paul's deep pastoral concern for them. And such a concern appears from the following words ἄρα οὖν, ἀδελφοί, στήκετε κτλ., and the wish-prayer of vv. 16f. There is no exhortatory function in the passage as such, but a right understanding of the truths contained in it will lead directly to conclusions of an ethical nature.

6. Conclusions

First, Paul's introductory thanksgiving in *2 Thess. 1* is evidence of his *pastoral concern* [165] for the addressees. Though they might consider themselves to be unworthy of the high praise accorded them in the first letter, Paul and his colleagues ought to thank God (εὐχαριστεῖν ὀφείλομεν, 1:3). It was entirely fitting (καθὼς ἄξιόν ἐστιν), since the recipients' faith and love had grown considerably. Indeed, Paul even

---

[161] Δόξα: 1 Thess. 2:12, 20; 2 Thess. 1:9; 2:14; contrast 1 Thess. 2:6; ἐνδοξάζομαι: 2 Thess. 1:10, 12; cf. δοξάζω: 3:1.

[162] But this does not mean that every theme in the letters is found in the thanksgiving. The 'day of the Lord', for example, is not mentioned as such (although εἰς περιποίησιν δόξης κτλ. points to the last day), perhaps because Paul had needed to correct the addressees' thinking on the subject.

[163] Selwyn, *1 Peter*, pp. 382ff., on the basis of parallels between 2 Thess. 2:13-17 and 1 Peter, sees the hand of the man associated with both letters—Silvanus.

[164] In general Frame's point *may be* correct, but he has pressed it in too many places in his exegesis of the letter. Further, we do not know whether or not a letter to this effect was sent by the Thessalonians to Paul.

[165] The reporting of his thanksgiving, as distinct from the prayer of thanksgiving itself, is usually proof of the apostle's deep concern for his converts. This pastoral care may show itself in different expressions and with different emphases, but care it was nevertheless.

boasted in other churches of the patience and faith they demonstrated in the midst of persecution (1:4). The same pastoral concern appears in his intercessory prayer report where he indicated he desired to see them be made worthy of God's high calling (1:11), at the same time fulfilling every good intention and deed which arose from their faith. Paul, with deep pastoral concern, looked forward to the day when Christ would be fully glorified in them, and they in Him (1:12).

Secondly, the *epistolary function* of the period can be discerned. The tone, language and style of the letter are set in these opening verses, not so much in the thanksgiving and intercessory prayer reports as in the 'digression' of vv. 5-10, where in eschatological language, some drawn from the LXX,[166] the apostle dealt with persecution, the judgement of God, Christ's revelation from heaven with His angels, etc. The scene is set for the second chapter, 'l'occasion principale et le but de la lettre',[167] where the enormities of the man of lawlessness and the events to precede the day of the Lord are treated. This introductory epistolary function of the passage has been underlined by Bjerkelund with reference to the linking of the εὐχαριστέω- and παρακαλέω-sentences. The teaching about faith in chap. 1 (in thanksgiving report, vv. 3f., digression, vv. 5-10, and intercessory prayer report, vv. 11f.) points to the 'Threat to Faith' in chap. 2.

The epistolary function, particularly with reference to faith, is related to the *didactic purpose* of the period. The continued growth of faith and love (1:3) are important, as is the constant exercise of patience in the midst of persecution (1:4). So Paul reminded them of these as he praised them. The Thessalonians' eschatological excitement had not abated—indeed, Paul's words in the first letter seem to have been misunderstood [168]—and so the subjects of God's judgement and the parousia are raised in the thanksgiving period, with the object of treating them in greater detail in chap. 2. Motifs such as God's calling, His power, Christ's being glorified in believers, their participation in His glory on the last day, and God's grace to Gentiles—some of which have been treated in other thanksgiving periods—find expression in the intercessory prayer report.

---

[166] Isa. 66:15; 2:10, 19, 21; Ps. 89:7 (88:8).

[167] Rigaux, *Thessaloniciens*, p. 72, quoted by Bjerkelund, *Parakalô*, p. 136.

[168] This seems to be the most reasonable explanation for the difference in emphasis between 1 Thess. 5 and 2 Thess. 2.

The *paraenetic function* of the passage is less clear than in the Philippian counterpart. Yet by praising the Thessalonians for their faith and love, and by boasting of their patience Paul was indirectly encouraging them to continue along these lines (1:3f.). From the petitionary prayer report it can be seen that the apostle wanted the recipients to walk worthily of their calling (1:11); further, he desired to see their good intentions translated into action, and their actions performed by God's power (1:11). In these words there seems to be a hint about those who refused to work for their living—the word ἐργάζομαι, akin to ἔργον of 1:11, appears no fewer than four times (3:8, 10, 11, 12) in one paragraph on the subject of idleness. If Paul's petition (1:11) is answered, then their 'work which springs from faith' will be performed powerfully (ἐν δυνάμει) by God's help (πληρώσῃ).

Concerning Paul's *actual prayers* we note a close link between thanksgiving and intercession. The opening words of chap. 1:11, εἰς ὃ καὶ προσευχόμεθα point back to εὐχαριστεῖν ὀφείλομεν (1:3). A similar syntactical device, as found in Phil. 1:9 and Col. 1:9, was used to indicate that logically and syntactically the petition was based on the preceding thanksgiving. Both *Fürdank* and *Fürbitte* were offered for these Gentile converts. At the same time, the apostle's thanksgiving of 2 Thess. 1:3f. was based on his prayers of 1 Thess. 3:10 and 12. In the former reference, v. 10, he asked for the repair of τὰ ὑστερήματα τῆς πίστεως, and now he gave thanks because ὑπεραυξάνει ἡ πίστις ὑμῶν, v. 3; in the latter, the wish-prayer of v. 12, his request was ὑμᾶς δὲ ὁ κύριος π λ ε ο ν ά σ α ι καὶ περισσεῦσαι τῇ ἀγάπῃ ε ἰ ς ἀ λ λ ή λ ο υ ς καὶ εἰς πάντας, and his present thanksgiving is because π λ ε ο ν ά ζ ε ι ἡ ἀγάπη ἑνὸς ἑκάστου πάντων ὑμῶν ε ἰ ς ἀ λ λ ή λ ο υ ς v. 3.

Pauline prayers of thanksgiving and petition are concerned with the believers' progress. Although Paul gave thanks to God because of the Thessalonians' ἔργον πίστεως (1 Thess. 1:3), he did not think that such work which sprang from faith was complete or perfect. The same phrase is found in his intercessory prayer (2 Thess. 1:11) that God might bring this to completion (πληρώσῃ) with His power (ἐν δυνάμει). Further, the particular emphasis of our introductory thanksgiving is on the remarkable growth of the Thessalonians in persecution. Paul had already given thanks for their 'work of faith' and 'labour of love' (1 Thess. 1:3). But here the faith 'grows exceedingly' (ὑπεραυξάνει, 2 Thess. 1:3), and their love 'abounds' (πλεονάζει).

This concern for progress, found in other introductory thanksgivings, but stressed in the present context, can also be seen in the frequent occurrence of verbs such as πληρόω (here at 1:11) and περισσεύω, used either of the believers themselves,[169] the graces which are to abound in them,[170] or of God who will bring to completion His work in them.[171] At the same time parousia references in the Pauline petitions point in the same direction. An aorist subjunctive, ἐνδοξασθῇ (1:12), refers to the final and complete glorification of the Lord Jesus in their midst. Paul might be thankful for the wonderful progress the Thessalonians have made; but he will only be satisfied at the parousia when their sanctification would be brought to completion.

The grounds for Paul's thanksgiving in chap. 1 were the faith and love of the addressees; the bases of the second thanksgiving (2:13f.) are not unrelated, for here too faith (in God's truth) is mentioned. But the great stress of the latter passage is God's work from everlasting to everlasting : His election from eternity to final salvation.

It has been shown previously that Paul's thanksgivings and petitionary prayers were related to the needs of the addressees, at the same time bound up with the concerns of the gospel, Christian maturity, the parousia, etc.[172] This two-fold thrust is particularly clear in the wish-prayer of 1 Thess. 3:11-13, where Paul's desires for the Thessalonians were expressed, and in the thanksgiving of 2 Thess. 2:13f., where the apostle declared what God had been and was doing on behalf of the recipients.

---

[169] Phil. 1:11 and Col. 1:9.
[170] Phil. 1:9 and Phm. 6.
[171] Cf. Phil. 1:6.
[172] This two-fold emphasis on present needs and eschatological direction is not unlike the thrusts of the *Tefillah* or the Lord's Prayer. So Kuhn, *Achtzehngebet*, p. 40, with reference to these two prayers comments : 'Beide Gebete, Achtzehngebet wie Vaterunser, zeigen eine Zweiteilung : die eine Hälfte Bitten, die sich auf die Situation des Frommen jetzt und hier in der Welt beziehen, die andere Hälfte eschatologische Bitten'. If there is any difference with Paul it is that one petition of his may be directed to both needs. However, in most of the intercessory prayers within the thanksgiving periods, the whole prayer is made up of several petitions (cf. Col. 1:9ff.; 1 Thess. 3:10-13). So the two-fold thrust is remarkably similar.

CHAPTER SEVEN

THANKSGIVING FOR A CHURCH UNKNOWN TO PAUL: ROM. 1:8ff.

1. *General*

The introductory thanksgiving of Paul's letter to the Romans (1:8ff.) has formal and structural similarities with, as well as differences from, others in the Pauline corpus. At first sight the passage appears to be a clear example of the second category (type Ib), in which the causal ὅτι-clause, an important unit in this type, is found. On closer examination one notes the presence of a petitionary prayer report, with its characteristic temporal participial clause and temporal adverbial phrase,[1] as well as a final clause, commencing with εἴ πως which states the content of the petitionary prayer. The introductory thanksgiving of this letter is, thus, an instance of a mixed type.

The petitionary prayer of v. 10, however, differs from most others in the thanksgiving periods.[2] This brief request concerned the apostle himself.[3] It was not an intercessory prayer for the recipients of the letter, as were almost all other petitions in these introductory periods. We admit that Paul's prayer of v. 10, 'asking that somehow by God's will I may now at last succeed in coming to you', was intimately bound up with his apostolic ministry to Gentiles, and that his arrival in Rome was in order that the Christians of that metropolis might be strengthened by the reception of some spiritual gift (v. 11). But, the apostle himself was the subject of the prayer, not the Roman Christians. Although it is possible to consider that Paul, in the thanksgiving period, has made no reference whatsoever to petitionary prayer for the addressees, it is more likely that ἀδιαλείπτως μνείαν ὑμῶν ποιοῦμαι (v. 9) refers to intercessions (the contents of which are not specified), offered by the apostle for the Roman Christians.[4]

---

[1] Πάντοτε ἐπὶ τῶν προσευχῶν μου δεόμενος (v. 10). Cf. ἀδιαλείπτως μνείαν ὑμῶν ποιοῦμαι (v. 9), and see the exegesis below.

[2] Cf. 1 Thess. 3:10f.

[3] It is one of the few recorded personal petitions offered by Paul; cf. 2 Cor. 12:8; and 1 Thess. 3:10f., a prayer report and a wish-prayer relating to his travels.

[4] See the exegesis below.

Other similarities and differences may be noted. First, in our study of the Philippian and Colossian thanksgiving periods it was pointed out that Paul not only recorded his actual thanksgivings and petitions, but also digressed from time to time, noting personal details and the like (Phil. 1:7f.; Col. 1:6-8). Here, in Rom. 1:8ff., the personal element is prominent. Paul longed ($\epsilon\pi\iota\pi o\theta\epsilon\omega$ is used again; cf. Phil. 1:8) to meet the members of the Roman church so as to have fellowship with them and be the means by which they are strengthened (note the passive $\sigma\tau\eta\rho\iota\chi\theta\hat{\eta}\nu\alpha\iota$, v. 11). He had often tried to visit the church at Rome, but because of other responsibilities had been prevented from doing so. However, since preaching the gospel was in his blood (vv. 14f.), he was anxious to go to Rome and tell the good news to the people there. He might thus reap some spiritual harvest among them (v. 13). These personal details of the apostle which led on to vv. 16 and 17 (the theme of the letter), were not a digression (as the personal notes of the Philippian and Colossian counterparts were). They formed an integral part of the period. We therefore have before us an introductory thanksgiving in which a large section dealt with personal matters, while the actual thanksgiving and petition, by comparison, were short.

A second observation may be made, viz., that it is difficult to demarcate the extent of this thanksgiving passage. The problem of determining the limits of the Colossian period has already been discussed. There it was noted that the intercessory prayer of the apostle (1:9-14) passed into a hymn in praise of the cosmic Christ.[5] Here it is not the extent of the petitionary prayer which is at issue. This clearly ends with the words $\dot{\epsilon}\lambda\theta\epsilon\hat{\iota}\nu\ \pi\rho\dot{o}s\ \dot{\upsilon}\mu\hat{a}s$ of v. 10.[6] Rather, the point to be determined is how far beyond this the introductory thanksgiving extends.

Thirdly, although the epistolary function of the passage is clearly in evidence, and Paul's pastoral concern for the addressees can be observed, the didactic and paraenetic thrusts are not as clear as in, for example, Col. 1:3ff. The function of the introductory thanksgiving and its place in the letter were integrally related to Paul's purpose in writing to the Roman Christians, and his relations with them. The relevant aspects of this vexed problem will be treated later.

Fourthly, it has been noted in the preceding chapters that thanks-

---

[5] See above, pp. 71-75, esp. p. 75.
[6] Cf. Wiles, *Prayers*, pp. 163f.

giving and petitionary prayer were part and parcel of Paul's life as an apostle. Although the petitionary prayer of Rom. 1:10 is brief (in fact it is the shortest petition found in the thanksgiving periods),[7] it is abundantly clear, from the content and the circumstances which surrounded the apostle at the time of writing to the Romans, that Paul regarded petition as an important instrument for carrying out his apostolic ministry. Not only was it a means by which the various communities would grow in love and Christian maturity (a point made clear in Paul's intercessory prayers in the thanksgiving periods); it was a God-given instrument that might enable him to reach Rome, and so strengthen the Roman Christians, preach the gospel in their region, and use Rome as a base for future operations in the West.

The complement of Paul's prayer (that God may allow him to go to Rome) is found in chap. 15:30ff. The Roman Christians too can use this weapon of petition. They can participate in Paul's ministry by interceding for him (v. 30),[8] asking God that the Gentile collection for the saints at Jerusalem may be acceptable (v. 31), and that *by God's will* Paul may be brought safely to Rome (ἵνα ἐν χαρᾷ ἐλθὼν πρὸς ὑμᾶς διὰ θελήματος θεοῦ συναναπαύσωμαι ὑμῖν, v. 32).[9] If petitionary prayer was an important weapon in Paul's armoury, it is remarkable that so few scholars mention the subject (let alone assess its significance) when dealing with the nature, function and other aspects of Paul's ministry as an apostle.[10]

---

[7] It comprises a mere thirteen words (cf. 1 Thess. 3:10, and the discussion below), while that in Phm. 6 contains seventeen. Schneider, *loc. cit.*, p. 18, correctly draws attention to the brevity of Paul's prayers. The present petition is a clear example of this.

[8] V. C. Pfitzner, *Paul and the Agon Motif* (Leiden, 1967), pp. 120ff., when treating Rom. 15:30-32, considers 'συναγωνίζεσθαί μοι expresses participation in an Agon of Paul himself' (p. 121). He rejects the usual interpretation (cf. O. Michel, *Der Brief an die Römer* (Göttingen, [13]1966), p. 373, who is representative of the customary view), which understands prayer as the ἀγών or *Gebetskampf*, i.e., a wrestling with God (for the decisions of the future), into which others may be drawn. (Cf. Harder, *Paulus*, pp. 125f., who saw the background to such a prayer struggle in Jacob's 'Kampf um den Segen Gottes' (p. 126); Gen. 32:24ff.). Instead Pfitzner understands Paul's ἀγών as his struggle for the gospel. Συναγωνίζεσθαι simply means to assist or support another, and the Romans are encouraged to participate in Paul's missionary struggle by means of intercessory prayer. For Pfitzner, in Rom. 15:30 and Col. 4:12, etc., prayer itself is not the ἀγών.

[9] Paul's request was answered somewhat differently from what he expected.

[10] Scholars such as Greeven, *Gebet*, pp. 165ff., and Hamman, *Prière*, pp. 300ff., who have dealt with Pauline prayer, have pointed to its relationship with Paul's apostolic ministry, while recently Wiles, *Prayers*, has carefully examined the place

2. *Limits of the Passage*

In some of Paul's introductory thanksgivings there has been little difficulty in determining the limits, and therefore the extent, of the paragraphs. So in 1 Corinthians and Philippians, the presence of the climactic eschatological note, together with a confirming climax (or benediction) or concluding doxology, has pointed to the end of the period. Immediately following the climax of the period, the presence of a new epistolary form, introduced by παρακαλῶ δὲ ὑμᾶς ... or its equivalent, indicates the body of the letter has been reached.[11] But in the introductory thanksgiving of Romans, as in the Colossian counterpart, such distinguishing marks are either absent, or at best, difficult to interpret.

Even Lohmeyer, who was one of the few commentators that saw an eschatological note in the introductory thanksgiving of Philemon (since he interpreted εἰς Χριστόν of Phm. 6 in an 'eschatologische Richtung'),[12] was forced to admit that '... Röm verhüllt aus Gründen der brieflichen Situation diesen eschatologischen Blick'.[13] Schubert conceded that this note was 'wanting... in Romans',[14] although he observed the eschatological significance of terms, such as σωτηρία, εὐαγγέλιον and δικαιοσύνη τοῦ θεοῦ found in vv. 8-17.[15] This latter observation, and the comment that the passage deals with the eschatological importance of Paul's apostolic ministry to Gentiles, however true they might be, are of no value in determining an eschatological *climax* to the period. The passage *as a whole* (vv. 8-17)

---

and significance of petition in Paul's apostolic work. But apart from one or two older works (e.g., J. Warneck, *Paulus im Lichte der heutigen Heidenmission* (Berlin, ⁴1922), pp. 24-28; 'Die Heidenmission stellt der Christenheit grosse Ziele für ihr Gebetsleben' (p. 26), 'Man kann einer Gemeinde zu ihrer Belebung nichts Besseres geben als das Missionsgebet. Paulus wünscht persönliches Fürbittegebet mit *konkreten* Bitten, nicht Missionsgebet als Abstraktum' (p. 27); and F. Büchsel, *Der Geist Gottes im Neuen Testament* (Gütersloh, 1926), pp. 318-321, so : 'Die ganze Energie seiner Missionsarbeit lebt auch in seinem Gebet') those which deal with Paul's apostleship rarely touch on the subject of prayer, much less do they understand it as playing a significant role in his ministry.

[11] Observed by Sanders, *loc. cit.*, pp. 348-362; Mullins, *NovT* 5 (1962), pp. 46-54; *NovT* 7 (1964), pp. 44-50; and Bjerkelund, *Parakaló*, pp. 141ff., 174ff.

[12] *Kolosser und Philemon*, p. 179. Wickert, *loc. cit.*, p. 231, agreed with Lohmeyer in seeing an eschatological reference in εἰς Χριστόν (Phm. 6).

[13] Lohmeyer, *Philipper*, p. 13.

[14] *Form*, p. 5.

[15] *Ibid.*, p. 33.

is concerned with Paul's apostolic ministry, while the term εὐαγγέλιον, which according to Schubert has eschatological associations is found in v. 9 (immediately before the petitionary prayer, and not simply at its conclusion), as well as in v. 16, while the cognate εὐαγγελίζομαι occurs at the end of v. 15. The eschatological note, therefore, is of no help in setting the limits of the period.

A second criterion that might have been used, viz., the presence of a concluding *berakah* or doxology, does not apply in this case, as Sanders admits.[16] There is nothing that resembles either a *berakah* or a doxology in vv. 8-17. Although the petitionary prayer of v. 10, εἴ πως ἤδη ποτὲ εὐοδωθήσομαι κτλ., reflects the prayer-sigh of the Old Testament, and particularly the Psalter, it is doubtful whether the term 'liturgical' ought to be used to describe its language. Certainly the ideas it contains have nothing to do with doxologies and benedictions, and do not tell us anything about the conclusion of the passage.

Although some consider the thanksgiving period ends at v. 12,[17]

---

[16] *Loc. cit.*, pp. 359f. Sanders was following a suggestion of J. M. Robinson, *loc. cit.*, pp. 194-235.

[17] At v. 13, with the introduction of the words οὐ θέλω δὲ ὑμᾶς ἀγνοεῖν, ἀδελφοί, ὅτι..., an opening formula, or according to Mullins a Disclosure form, appears. (Mullins, *NovT* (1964), pp. 46ff.; Sanders, *loc. cit.*, p. 360. R. W. Funk, 'The Apostolic "Parousia" : Form and Significance', *Christian History and Interpretation* : *Studies Presented to John Knox*, ed. W. R. Farmer *et al.* (Cambridge, 1967), pp. 249-268, esp. p. 253, detects here an example of the parousia form denoting 'the presence of apostolic authority and power' (p. 249)).

Four elements constitute this and other instances of the Disclosure form. 1. θέλω; 2. a noetic verb used in the infinitive (e.g., γινώσκειν, εἰδέναι); 3. the person(s) addressed (always in the accusative case); 4. the information (frequently, though not invariably, by means of a ὅτι-clause). Sometimes the vocative of the addressees is used (cf. ἀδελφοί, v. 13).

Mullins lists nineteen papyri examples, as well as making reference to the New Testament instances, of this form. The elements in the latter 'follow a fairly regular but not a rigid order'. And as a general rule, 'when the Thanksgiving is followed by any recognizable element of another form (such as the Disclosure), the termination of the Thanksgiving is thereby marked' (p. 49). According to this general principle of Mullins, based on his comparative study, the introductory thanksgiving of Romans ends at v. 12. The passage thus extends from vv. 8-12.

This conclusion, however, is doubtful. First, his case would be stronger if vv. 11 and 12 constituted part of Paul's petitionary prayer report. Instead, the words tell us something of Paul's reasons for wishing to make the journey to Rome. It would probably be correct to say that Paul has prayed he might be used by God to impart some spiritual gift to the Romans. But the apostle does not state this. The prayer report ends with

we are forced to conclude that the paragraph extends from vv. 8-15 at least, and from vv. 8-17 if we include the words of the theme, found in vv. 16 and 17. The introductory thanksgiving of this letter thus contains a thanksgiving report (v. 8), a petitionary prayer report (vv. 9f.), and personal details about Paul's plans for the future (vv. 11-15). Vv. 16f. are a bridge passage leading from Paul's entire preoccupation with preaching the gospel to an exposition of that gospel.

It is not our intention to give a detailed exegesis of all the elements in this introductory thanksgiving. Rather, we shall restrict our exegetical comments to the reports of Paul's thanksgiving and petitionary prayer at the same time setting them within the context of the *personal details* of chap. 1:11-15 and chap. 15:14-33, the *purpose* of the epistle as a whole, and Paul's reasons for writing to the Christians at Rome.

3. *Thanksgiving for a Faith Proclaimed Far and Wide : V. 8*

The verb of thanksgiving (εὐχαριστέω) does not dominate the entire paragraph as in most other introductory passages. The apostle passes from thanksgiving to petitionary prayer, and on to personal details about his concern for the Christians at Rome and his desire to visit them. The thanksgiving sets the stage for what follows, but it does not govern the passage beyond v. 10. Strictly speaking, the first sentence of the period ends with the words 'in all the world', of v. 8. A fresh statement begins with 'For God is my witness', and it is followed by Paul's assurance that he remembered the Roman Christians in his prayers. The tie-up between thanksgiving and petition is not as close as in the parallel passage of Colossians,[18] and one detects

---

v. 10, and something of his longing to see them is mentioned in the words which follow. The strongest argument against Mullins' conclusion, however, is that vv. 13ff. are closely conjoined with the preceding. Admittedly, a new sentence commences with the Disclosure form, οὐ θέλω δὲ ὑμᾶς ἀγνοεῖν, ἀδελφοί κτλ., but it follows on directly from vv. 11 and 12, indicating how frequently in the past the apostle had tried to get to Rome and how he had been unsuccessful. In the latter half of v. 13, ἵνα τινὰ καρπὸν σχῶ κτλ., another reason (or perhaps an expansion of the first reason in v. 11, ἵνα τι μεταδῶ χάρισμα ὑμῖν πνευματικόν κτλ.) is given as to why Paul wished to go to Rome. If vv. 11 and 12 are to be included in the thanksgiving passage, then so ought vv. 13-15.

[18] See above, pp. 82-84.

here a certain awkwardness [19] on Paul's part as he writes to the believers of the capital, seeking to establish close relations with them.

The customary temporal adverb πάντοτε is not used in conjunction with εὐχαριστέω at Rom. 1:8.[20] Instead, the apostle commenced his thanksgiving report with the temporal note 'first of all' (πρῶτον μέν).[21] Having completed his long salutation of vv. 1-7 Paul wanted to begin by assuring his addressees that he gave thanks to his God for them. So the NEB paraphrases with : 'Let me begin by thanking my God'. Paul's report echoed his actual thanksgiving, and we may suppose that as he dictated his letter thanksgiving to God once again [22] welled up within him.[23]

To the object (τῷ θεῷ) of the principal verb Paul added the personal pronoun μου, thus stressing, as did the psalmists of old, the consciousness of a personal relation to Him.[24] The One thanked for

---

[19] Many commentators have observed Paul's awkwardness in the opening salutation, vv. 1-7.

[20] This is, therefore, an exception, though πάντοτε is employed to modify δεόμενος (v. 10), while the synonym ἀδιαλείπτως qualifies μνείαν ὑμῶν ποιοῦμαι of v. 9.

[21] According to H. A. W. Meyer, *Critical and Exegetical Handbook to the Epistle to the Romans* 1 (ET, Edinburgh, 1873), p. 56, πρῶτον μέν points to that which Paul, first of all, wants to write. J. Denney, 'St. Paul's Epistle to the Romans', in *The Expositor's Greek Testament* 2, ed. W. Robertson Nicoll (London, 1900), p. 587, puts it too strongly when he states : 'Nothing can take precedence of thanksgiving, when Paul thinks of the Romans...'; (cf. E. Kühl, *Der Brief des Paulus an die Römer* (Leipzig, 1913), p. 22, 'zuerst und vor allem').

[22] T. Zahn, *Der Brief des Paulus an die Römer* (Leipzig, 1/21910), p. 55, comments : 'er *eben jetzt*, da er seinem Schreiber diese Worte diktiert (16, 22), Gotte danksage'; (our italics). Michel, *Römer*, p. 46, makes the same point when he states : 'εὐχαριστῶ drückt den Akt des Dankgebetes selbst aus (nicht nur die dankbare Gesinnung), der aber nicht ein einmaliges Geschehnis der Vergangenheit bleibt, sondern sich in der Gegenwart immer wieder vollzieht (Präs.)'. Wobbe's distinction, *Charis*, p. 82, between *charis* as the 'Akt des Dankens', and *eucharistia* as 'dankbarer Gesinnung, Dankbarkeit' has, therefore, to be modified.

[23] The πρῶτον μέν is not followed by ἔπειτα δέ (Heb. 7:2) or ἔπειτα (Jas. 3:17), for the writer is carried away by his train of thought. Some commentators (e.g., F. Godet, *Commentary on St. Paul's Epistle to the Romans* 1 (ET, Edinburgh, 1890), p. 142, and B. Weiss, *Der Brief an die Römer* (Göttingen, 81891), p. 58) consider that the second idea the apostle had in mind is really found in v. 10, where he offered his prayer to God that he may be allowed soon to go to Rome. If this is the case, then Paul has not expressed it in a strictly logical form. Blass-Debrunner consider that 'the omission of δέ in some instances... is excusable or even good classical usage' (para. 447 (4)).

[24] The significance of this has been carefully assessed by Harder, *Paulus*, pp. 67f. Martin, *Worship*, p. 31, with reference to the prayers and praises of the early church, rightly comments : 'The use of the Psalter is important, as Christians instinctively,

the faith of the Romans is the God of the psalmists, known to Paul as Father.

Διὰ 'Ιησοῦ Χριστοῦ immediately follows. It is the only instance of such a formula in the introductory thanksgiving, although at Col. 1:3 the person to whom thanksgiving is offered, is described as τῷ θεῷ πατρὶ τοῦ κυρίου ἡμῶν 'Ιησοῦ Χριστοῦ. All commentators and exegetes are agreed that the phrase has reference to Christ as Mediator, but they differ considerably as to what this means. *Contra* A. Seeberg, A. Juncker and B. Weiss,[25] Christ is not the Mediator of the gift of grace (in this case, the faith of the Romans) for which Paul gives thanks. Instead, διὰ 'Ιησοῦ Χριστοῦ is conjoined with εὐχαριστέω, so that Christ is, in some sense, the Mediator of the thanksgiving.[26]

The διά-phrases (e.g., 'through our Lord Jesus Christ', 'through Jesus Christ our Lord', 'through Jesus Christ', 'through him'), occur frequently throughout the Pauline letters.[27] The oldest formula, according to Kramer, was 'through our Lord Jesus Christ', and it, together with the variants, 'through Jesus Christ our Lord' and 'through Jesus Christ', was associated in the first place with specific activities in the life of the church, such as 'exhorting the brethren', 'rejoicing in God', and 'giving thanks to God'.[28] Secondly, the formula was used to qualify the blessings of salvation, such as peace, salvation and victory.[29] At quite an early stage the διά-phrases were employed with reference to this second category, and came to be used increasingly in this way. 'Thus in the end the formula can describe God's operation, through Christ, in the saving events'.[30]

---

like their Lord (Luke xxiii, 46) turned to the Psalms of David for language in which to give vent to their deepest emotions'. In the present context see M.-J. Lagrange, *Saint Paul : Épître aux Romans* (Paris, 1916), p. 12.

[25] So A. Klawek, *Das Gebet zu Jesus* (Münster, 1921), p. 75.

[26] For Harder, *Paulus*, pp. 163ff., διὰ Χριστοῦ (or its equivalents) is one of the distinguishing marks of Christian prayer, especially thanksgiving.

[27] Kramer, *Christ*, p. 85, listed twenty-six διά-phrases linked with *Christ* in the Paulines, apart from other occurrences in the deutero-Paulines; cf. A. Schettler, *Die paulinische Formel 'Durch Christus'* (Tübingen, 1907), p. 9; and Thüsing, *Per Christum*, pp. 164ff., esp. pp. 174-183.

[28] E.g., Rom. 15:30 (cf. 1 Thess. 4:2); Rom. 5:11; 7:25.

[29] Rom. 5:1, 21; 1 Thess. 5:9; (poss. 1 Cor. 15:57).

[30] Kramer, *Christ*, p. 90. T. W. Manson, *On Paul and John* (London, 1963), p. 76, stated that διὰ Χριστοῦ indicated 'Christ (*sc.* is) the channel by whom God's grace and love flow to men'. By the expression 'Paul emphasizes that the whole business from beginning to end depends upon the work of Christ'.

According to Kramer the exhortation passages prove that there is no idea of any 'high priestly activity' on the part of the exalted Lord,[31] a view held by such exegetes as Sanday and Headlam, and Cullmann.[32] Others had rejected such an idea on the grounds that it was too precise,[33] or that Christ's acting as High Priest in *presenting* or *transmitting* each prayer to the Father ran counter to the idea that each Christian had direct access to God (Rom. 5:2).[34] Rather, prayer to God through Christ implied that worshippers might now approach the presence of the Father with confidence ($\pi\alpha\rho\rho\eta\sigma\iota\alpha$), because Christ's death had torn down the separating curtain which had excluded a direct approach.[35]

Although in the New Testament prayers were only occasionally addressed direct to Christ,[36] the formula 'through Jesus Christ'

---

[31] *Christ*, p. 88.

[32] Sanday and Headlam, *Romans*, p. 18, in their paraphrase render $\delta\iota\dot\alpha$ '$I\eta\sigma o\hat{v}$ $X\rho\iota\sigma\tau o\hat{v}$ as: 'through Him Who as High Priest presents all our prayers and praises'; while O. Cullmann, *The Christology of the New Testament* (ET, London, ²1963), p. 107, comments: 'to pray "in Jesus' name" shows that Christ continues his high priestly work after his ascension by bringing their (*sc.* the disciples') prayers before God in heaven. This is what is meant when Christians end their prayers with $\delta\iota\dot\alpha$ '$I\eta\sigma o\hat{v}$ $X\rho\iota\sigma\tau o\hat{v}$.'

[33] So J. Knox, 'The Epistle to the Romans', in *The Interpreter's Bible* 9, pp. 353-668, esp. p. 386; and Deichgräber, *Gotteshymnus*, p. 40. See also Marchel's criticism (*Abba*, p. 212) of A. Seeberg, *Die Anbetung des Herrn bei Paulus* (Dorpat, 1891), p. 25.

[34] Kuhl, *Römer*, p. 22.

[35] C. F. D. Moule, *Worship in the New Testament* (London, 1961), p. 71.

[36] *Ibid.*, p. 73. The question as to whether prayer was addressed directly to Christ cannot be answered in detail. Klawek, *Gebet*, has written an important monograph of 120 pages on the subject, and the discussion has continued since its publication (1921). At first sight it would appear that prayer was addressed to Christ, by Paul and other early Christians. Orphal, *Paulusgebet*, pp. 5, 147f., found 131 passages where prayer was addressed to God, and 83 directed to Christ. But we have already noted Orphal's methodological weaknesses, and his conclusions are therefore suspect. Harder, *Paulus*, p. 190 (cf. pp. 197ff.), states categorically: 'Die Frage also, ob Paulus eine Anbetung oder Anrufung des Herrn Jesus gekannt hat, musst bejaht werden', Delling, *Worship*, p. 117, is more cautious when he observes that the question cannot be answered by a simple yes or no. In the Pauline material the verbs $\pi\rho o\sigma\epsilon\acute{v}\chi o\mu\alpha\iota$, $\pi\rho o\sigma\kappa\upsilon\nu\acute{\epsilon}\omega$, $\lambda\alpha\tau\rho\epsilon\acute{v}\omega$ and the substantives $\delta\acute{\epsilon}\eta\sigma\iota\varsigma$, $\pi\rho o\sigma\epsilon\upsilon\chi\acute{\eta}$, and $\check{\epsilon}\nu\tau\epsilon\upsilon\xi\iota\varsigma$ are not used with reference to Christ. At 2 Cor. 12:8 the apostle selects $\pi\alpha\rho\alpha\kappa\alpha\lambda\acute{\epsilon}\omega$ which Greeven, *Gebet*, p. 160, considers is a synonym for prayer ('So ist 2 K. 12, 8 mit dem Verbum $\pi\alpha\rho\alpha\kappa\alpha\lambda\epsilon\hat{\iota}\nu$ offenbar ein anderes Wort vermieden, das nur auf das Gebet zu Gott passt; *de facto* bedeutet aber auch dieses $\pi\alpha\rho\alpha\kappa\alpha\lambda\epsilon\hat{\iota}\nu$ mit seinem Inhalt nichts anderes als ein Bittgebet'—*contra* Hamman, *Prière*, p. 270). 'Calling upon the name of Christ' probably does not indicate anything about community prayer to Christ (*contra* Nielen, *Gebet*, pp. 163f.), and may be: 'la confession de sa seigneurie, une invocation de sa médiation dans les sacrements,

figured in doxologies and thanksgivings as well as in early Christian greetings and expressions of good wishes. God's Amen to the prayers of believers (indeed to all His promises) is summed up in Christ and guaranteed by Him (2 Cor. 1:19f.). In the immediate context Paul addressed his thanksgiving to God through Christ the Mediator who had opened the way to the Father's presence. The Christians at Rome, therefore, might know that this thanksgiving was truly heard by Paul's God.

The addition of πάντων in the phrase, περὶ πάντων ὑμῶν (cf. Phil. 1:4; 1 Thess. 1:2), the fourth unit of the introductory thanksgiving, indicates a particular emphasis. Whether they be Jews or Gentiles,[37] they are included within the scope of his prayer. The circle for whom thanksgiving is offered is not limited to those who were personal acquaintances. Further, πάντων corresponds to πᾶσιν of the benediction or wish-prayer (the apostle wanted God's grace and peace to be upon all of God's beloved ones at Rome (v. 7)); and possibly to the words of v. 5 where the universality of Paul's commission is

---

les exorcismes... et la prière', Hamman, *Prière*, p. 271; cf. J. Jungmann, *The Place of Christ in Liturgical Prayer* (ET, London, 1965), p. 142. Von der Goltz, *Gebet*, p. 94, considers it is the same as prayer 'through Christ'. However, as Bieder, *TZ* 4 (1948), p. 37, points out, prayers in the name of Christ, can soon be addressed to 'the Lord'. (On the later, increasing calling on Christ in prayer, see Champion, *Benedictions*, pp. 110f.). Cf. Hamman, *Prière*, p. 271. Nevertheless, some requests, including some wish-prayers (2 Cor. 12:8; 2 Thess. 3:16; cf. 1 Cor. 16:22 : μαρανάθα which is a sigh of the waiting church—assuming we read the imperative μαρανα θα rather than the indicative—the fulfilment of which lay in the hands of God. (See, however, F. J. Dölger, *Sol Salutis*: *Gebet und Gesang im christlichen Altertum* (Münster, ²1925), pp. 198-219; and Barrett, *1 Corinthians*, pp. 396ff., and the literature cited)); and a thanksgiving (1 Tim. 1:12) are addressed to Christ (*contra* S. Lyonnet, 'Pauline Soteriology', in *Introduction to the New Testament*, ed. A. Robert and A. Feuillet (ET, New York, 1965), pp. 820-865, esp. p. 823: 'Paul's practice was to address his prayers to the Father'). The most satisfactory explanation is to note that *generally* prayers directed to Christ are marked by 'l'intimité... l'Apôtre s'adresse de préférence au Christ dans les affaires plus personnelles', Eschlimann, *Prière*, p. 140; on the whole subject see pp. 130-148. (So too Delling, *Worship*, pp. 119f.; Jungmann, *Place*, pp. 130f., 'Paul mentions that he turns at times to Christ in prayer... this is private prayer, to which he devotes himself on matters touching his vocation as an Apostle'). Hymns and praises (as distinct from *prayers*) were to be sung at one time to 'the Lord', at another to 'God' (Eph. 5:19; Col. 3:16) and Paul quotes texts (Eph. 5:14; cf. 1 Tim. 3:16) which belong to such hymns in praise of the Redeemer, just as they were used in the common assemblies.

[37] So J. Huby, *Saint Paul. Épître aux Romains* (Paris, ¹⁰1940), p. 54; cf. Murray, *Romans* 1, p. 19; Kühl, *Römer*, p. 21; and Michel, *Römer*, p. 46.

emphasized [38] (ἐλάβομεν χάριν καὶ ἀποστολὴν εἰς ὑπακοὴν πίστεως ἐν πᾶσιν τοῖς ἔθνεσιν).

The ground or basis of Paul's thanksgiving is expressed by the causal ὅτι-clause,[39] ὅτι ἡ πίστις ὑμῶν καταγγέλλεται ἐν ὅλῳ τῷ κόσμῳ, v. 8. This element, along with the preceding, demonstrates that the first part of the paragraph corresponds structurally to Schubert's second category. The faith of the Roman Christians was that basis for thanksgiving. Some commentators consider that ἡ πίστις ὑμῶν is practically equivalent to 'your Christianity' [40] or 'your acceptance of the kerygma'.[41] Others, such as C. K. Barrett, consider it would be pointless in a thanksgiving to refer to the faith which the Roman Christians held in common with all others. Thus, it must refer to the faith *as* the Romans hold it, that is 'the understanding, constancy and charity' with which they hold it.[42] One wonders, however, whether such a restriction is necessary. Paul might not have known a great deal about the quality of their faith.[43] He could give thanks for the love and faith of the Colossians in general, and Philemon in particular without specifically mentioning the quality of the faith, unless it be considered that the love which flowed from the faith pointed to its character.

At all events, the significant feature of the Romans' faith is that it was 'proclaimed far and wide', καταγγέλλεται ἐν ὅλῳ τῷ κόσμῳ, v. 8. These latter words are not to be understood as mere flattery on the one hand, or meaningless exaggeration on the other. Indeed,

---

[38] R. St. J. Parry, *The Epistle of Paul the Apostle to the Romans* (Cambridge, 1912), p. 37.

[39] See the discussion above about the causal ὅτι-clause in the introductory thanksgivings, pp. 7f.

[40] Sanday and Headlam, *Romans*, p. 19; cf. Denney, *Romans*, pp. 587f.; Lagrange, *Romains*, p. 12; K. Barth, *The Epistle to the Romans* (ET, London, 1933), p. 32; and Huby, *Romains*, p. 54.

[41] Bultmann, *TDNT* 6, pp. 212, 217.

[42] Barrett, *Romans*, p. 24; cf. O. Bardenhewer, *Der Römerbrief des heiligen Paulus* (Freiburg-i.-Br., 1926), p. 22. Against this idea Kühl, *Römer*, p. 23, comments: '... an eine sonderlich hervorragende Art, Kraft, und Betätigung ihres Glaubens ist dabei nicht gedacht'. Filson, *History*, p. 319, however, on the basis of Rom. 1:8, considers the church at Rome to have been strong.

[43] Although Guthrie, *Epistles*, p. 27, thinks Paul has probably received a fairly comprehensive account of the state of the church from Aquila and Priscilla and others of his associates who had had contact with it.

even the word 'hyperbole' [44] ought to be used with caution. Certainly Paul did not mean the whole world distributively, that is, every person under heaven, had heard of the faith of the Roman Christians. He had particularly in mind those places where Christianity had been established [45] (esp. cities and towns [46] where the gospel had been preached). The logical subjects of καταγγέλλω are believers,[47] and the words show that with the diffusion of the gospel throughout the known world went the report of the Roman believers' faith. Perhaps the phrase is also evidence of the sense of fellowship that existed between the various churches. For Paul, the mission strategist *par excellence*, the presence of a Christian congregation at the capital was not without significance,[48] not least because of the importance it might have in his own ministry further to the West.[49] The universal

---

[44] The term is employed by Meyer, *Romans* 1, p. 57; Godet, *Romans* 1, p. 142; Weiss, *Römer*, p. 58; Denney, *Romans*, p. 588; R. P. A. Viard, *Épître aux Romains* (Paris, 1948), p. 28; A. M. Hunter, *The Epistle to the Romans* (London, 1955), p. 27; F. J. Leenhardt, *The Epistle to the Romans* (ET, London, 1961), p. 42; and Str.-B. 3, p. 25. Parry, *Romans*, p. 37, considers it to be a 'not unnatural exaggeration' (cf. H. Lietzmann, *An die Römer* (Tübingen, ³1928), p. 27, a 'rhetorische Übertreibung', as is 1 Thess. 1:8). E. Schweizer, 'The Church as the Missionary Body of Christ', in *Neotestamentica* (Zürich, 1963), pp. 317-329, esp. p. 318, states that although the phrase in question may seem to be an exaggeration, it 'shows how the cosmic dimension is continually in the foreground when the proclamation of the gospel is in question'.

[45] F. F. Bruce, *The Epistle of Paul to the Romans* (London, 1963), p. 76. Deissmann, *Paul*, p. 56, considers the phrase has reference to 'the microcosmos of the Christian "world", not the great official world'. He refers to an inscription on a heathen epitaph, about the modesty of an Egyptian lady, Seratus, and her relations as being 'known in all the world' (κατὰ τὸν κόσμον λελάληται). Bultmann, *Theology* 1, p. 255, understands 1:8 to be synonymous with 16:19, 'your obedience is known to all'.

[46] Generally, Paul's activity was based on certain centres, e.g., Damascus, Tarsus, Antioch, Corinth, Ephesus, etc., rather than on a whole region. From these places the gospel was carried further afield by others; M. Dibelius and W. G. Kümmel, *Paul* (ET, London, 1953), pp. 68ff., and Hahn, *Mission*, p. 96.

[47] Correctly noted by Meyer, *Romans* 1, p. 57. The attitude of some unbelievers, at least, can be seen from Acts 28:22 : '... with regard to this sect we know that everywhere it is spoken against' (πανταχοῦ ἀντιλέγεται).

[48] Meyer, *Romans* 1, p. 57; Godet, *Romans* 1, p. 142; Weiss, *Römer*, p. 58; Zahn, *Römer*, p. 56; C. H. Dodd, *The Epistle of Paul to the Romans* (London, 1932), p. 34; A. Nygren, *Commentary on Romans* (ET, London, 1952), p. 60 : Paul is 'realistic enough to sense what it would mean for the Christian mission...'; Viard, *Romains*, p. 28; and Wiles, *Prayers*, pp. 188f.

[49] Leenhardt, *Romans*, pp. 42f., considers the expression is 'in part justified by the very situation of Rome... But the chief reason for this allusion is the apostle's plan of going to Spain'.

terminology of passages such as Col. 1:6, 23 and Rom. 10:18 is interpreted by Munck in accordance with his view of Paul's eschatological significance. He 'has been appointed by God to fill the key position in the last great drama of salvation'.[50] In 1 Thess. 1:8, as well as in the passage under review (both of which are introductory thanksgivings), the universal terminology is applied to the faith of the addressees, rather than to the gospel itself. The point is underlined when it is recognized that καταγγέλλω, a term which occurs only in Acts and Paul,[51] reflects directly the language of mission. It is a weighty term, otherwise used only of the gospel itself or some element [52] in it.

Thus once more it is to be noted in an introductory thanksgiving that mission terminology used of the message itself, or of some important element within it, is applied by the apostle to those brought within the scope of that mission. The only difference in the introductory thanksgiving of Romans is that concepts and ideas are not applied directly to the Christians themselves (as in Col. 1:10 and 1 Cor. 1:8), but to their faith (ἡ πίστις ὑμῶν). As the gospel had been proclaimed far and wide, so too had the Romans' faith. The accenting of such an element is perhaps not without point in a letter where the theme of faith is very important.[53] The language and ideas related to the ministry of the gospel (and now related to its recipients) were so significant for the apostle that they were used in his thanksgiving and petitionary prayer reports, thus indicating they had had an influence on his actual prayers to God. His thanksgivings and petitions for believers, known and unknown, were inextricably linked with, and in certain respects moulded by, the proclamation of the gospel, and were therefore connected with his calling as an apostle to the Gentiles.

On a broader canvas, any interpretation or assessment of Pauline prayers which fails to take account of this fundamental relationship must be regarded as seriously deficient. Ferdinand Hahn, in his

---

[50] Munck, *Paul*, p. 43; cf. Bruce, *Colossians*, p. 181.

[51] Noted by Parry, *Romans*, p. 37; and especially by J. Schniewind, 'καταγγέλλω', *TDNT* 1, pp. 70-72.

[52] So the gospel (1 Cor. 9:14), the mystery of God (1 Cor. 2:1), and the word of God (Acts 13:5; 17:13; cf. 15:36) are 'proclaimed' (καταγγέλλω), while sometimes Christ (Phil. 1:17f.), His death (1 Cor. 11:26) and resurrection (Acts 4:2), as well as the forgiveness of sins (Acts 13:38), were the significant elements in the apostolic announcement.

[53] Knox, *Romans*, p. 386. See below, p. 226.

important work, *Mission in the New Testament*, when dealing with Paul's conception of Mission (pp. 95-110), correctly noted that the apostle did not entertain a moment's doubt that the gospel must be preached in the whole world. 'His view of the mission is inseparable from his entire theological thought'.[54] Hahn proceeds to treat important motifs in the letter to the Romans (e.g., freedom, law, righteousness, election, the place of Jews and Gentiles in God's plan, the covenant, the collection, etc.) with reference to this theme. But apart from a passing reference to Rom. 15:30ff. on p. 109, he does not deal with the function and significance of Pauline prayer and thanksgiving in that mission.[55] One of the contentions in this study, based not only upon an exegesis of Rom. 1:8ff., but also from a comparative study of the other thanksgiving periods, is that the prayers of the apostle and the reciprocal intercessions of other believers were interwoven with Paul's anticipated fulfilment of his apostolic ministry of the gospel.[56]

4. *An Oath : the Guarantee of Thanksgiving and Intercession : V. 9*

With the words of v. 9, μάρτυς γάρ μού ἐστιν ὁ θεός, a sentence with an oath is introduced. Such oaths were used by Paul (2 Cor. 1:23; Phil. 1:8; 1 Thess. 2:5; cf. 2:10), and in them God is spoken of as a witness (μάρτυς) not in a judicial sense of witness to facts, but in a more general sense of His witnessing to the processes and motives in Paul's inner life, or the reasons for his behaviour under particular circumstances (e.g., why he had not paid a visit to a church when he had intended to do so), since no other factual witnesses could be produced to prove the truthfulness and authenticity of what he affirmed.[57] When Paul wrote to the Romans he was at a distance, and thus could not prove his loving concern for them. His thanks-

---

[54] *Mission*, p. 97.

[55] Deichgräber, *Gotteshymnus*, p. 210, notes the relationship between mission and the spread of the gospel on the one hand, and thanksgiving and intercessions on the other; while Hamman, *Prière*, pp. 300-302, esp. p. 300, correctly observes that behind the apparent multiplicity of thanksgivings and petitions lies the unifying factor of Paul's vocation as an apostle.

[56] Our conclusions concerning the close tie-up between prayer and Paul's apostolic ministry, although arrived at independently, are at one with those of Wiles, *Prayers*.

[57] Strathmann, *TDNT* 4, p. 491. Some examples of Old Testament oaths are: Josh. 22:27; 1 Sam. 12:5; Jer. 42:5.

giving to God for them did not stem simply from a conventional form,[58] but was evidence of his real interest in them. The One to whom he appealed as witness knew of his thanksgiving and ceaseless petition [59] on their behalf. Furthermore, although his failure to visit them might have been interpreted as a lack of interest in them, such was not the case. Rather, his failure to come was due to providential interference, a point Paul brings out later, at v. 13 and chap. 15:22-25.

Immediately following Paul's oath a statement about his rendering spiritual service in the proclamation of the gospel occurs: [60] ᾧ λατρεύω ἐν τῷ πνεύματί μου ἐν τῷ εὐαγγελίῳ κτλ. Λατρεύω,[61] akin to λάτρις, 'a hired servant', and λάτρον, 'hire', was applied in Classical Greek to the service of a higher power. In the LXX, where the word occurs approximately ninety times, it was used exclusively of religious service—either of the one true God, or of pagan deities.[62] This use is determinative of its New Testament occurrences [63] where the term has no reference to human relations much less to secular services. The ministry denoted by λατρεύω is always offered to God or to heathen gods.[64] On occasion in the New Testament it appears as a technical term for the ministry of prayer (e.g., the unwearying petition of Anna in the Temple, Luke 2:37; and the incessant supplication of Israel for the fulfilment of the promise, Acts 26:7; cf. Rev. 7:15; 22:3). Many commentators interpret the phrase λατρεύω ἐν τῷ πνεύματί μου in this specific sense of the ministry of prayer. Such a ministry [65] is considered to complement that of proclaiming the gospel (ἐν τῷ εὐαγγελίῳ τοῦ υἱοῦ αὐτοῦ).

---

[58] Eschlimann, *Prière*, p. 91, points out that Paul's thanksgivings are not simply formal, in spite of the solemnity of the expressions used.

[59] It is best to understand the oath as referring to *both* the thanksgiving of v. 8 (note the γάρ in v. 9), and the intercessions mentioned in the ὡς-clause of v. 9.

[60] A. Schlatter, *Gottes Gerechtigkeit* (Stuttgart, ⁴1965), p. 26, thinks that Paul has formed the relative sentences with Dan. 6:16 (ὁ θεός σου, ᾧ σὺ λατρεύεις ...) in mind.

[61] H. Strathmann, 'λατρεύω', *TDNT* 4, pp. 58-65.

[62] The apparent exceptions are Deut. 24:28 and Dan. 7:14; but cf. Strathmann, *op. cit.*, p. 60.

[63] In the letter to the Hebrews λατρεύω had particular reference to the sacrificial ministry of the Old Testament priests; Heb. 8:5; 9:9; 10:2; 13:10.

[64] Acts 7:42; Rom. 1:25.

[65] So Michel, *Römer*, p. 46, one of many commentators who interprets λατρεύω in this restricted sense, can write: 'Gebet und Verkündigung sind für ihn besondere Formen priesterlichen Dienstes (Rom. 15, 16)', while Strack-Billerbeck (Vol. 3, p. 26), who appealed to several Old Testament passages in support, as well as to the Sifre on Deut. 11:13, considered: 'Dienst im Herzen', to be 'Gebetsdienst'.

But λατρεύω is found in both the Pauline corpus and the other writings of the New Testament in a more general and figurative sense.[66] The comprehensive connotation of this verb, to describe the conduct of the righteous before God, is found first in Luke 1:74, of Zechariah. Luke employs the term in a similar manner to speak of Paul's serving the God of the fathers (Acts 24:14). In Phil. 3:3 λατρεύω is used in a comprehensive metaphorical sense to contrast Paul and other Christians, who are οἱ πνεύματι θεοῦ λατρεύοντες, with the Judaizers whose whole worship of God is in the flesh. The reference is not to be restricted to prayer but includes all that to which Christians are impelled by the Spirit. Rom. 1:9 has Paul's active religious service in mind. The apostle's service was rendered in the sphere of preaching the gospel of God's Son. This was the worship he offered to God. Ἐν τῷ πνεύματί μου has been interpreted by Schweizer and others as a reference to the Holy Spirit imparted to him.[67] But this is an unusual way [68] of stating such a fact. Would Paul have expressed this with the phrase in question? Strathmann,[69] who rejects any direct reference to the Holy Spirit, considers that λατρεύω oscillates in meaning in the present context. Two thoughts are present, according to him: Paul serves and worships God, actively in the proclamation of the message, and inwardly in intercession for the churches and for the progress of the gospel.

---

[66] Strathmann, *op. cit.*, p. 63. According to C. E. B. Cranfield, 'Divine and Human Action. The Biblical Concept of Worship', *Interp* 12 (1958), pp. 387-398, esp. p. 387, Rom. 1:9 (along with Luke 1:74; Phil. 3:3; and esp. Rom. 12:1) falls into the category which denotes 'the whole life of the community or of the individual viewed as service of God'. Indeed, this group is the most 'characteristic' for λατρεύω and λατρεία in the New Testament; cf. AG, p. 468. Schlatter, *Gerechtigkeit*, p. 26, rejects the idea of a reference to prayer.

[67] E. Schweizer, 'πνεῦμα', *TDNT* 6, p. 435; cf. 1 Cor. 14:14, where the personal pronoun μου is used; Rom. 12:11; 8:10f. See also Schweizer's *Neotestamentica*, pp. 197, 199; and O. Holtzmann, *Das Neue Testament: Der Römerbrief* 2 (Giessen, 1926), p. 620. Cerfaux's view (*Christian*, p. 307, that 'the seat of spiritual worship, prayer and the divine gift (referring to Rom. 1:9, 8:16; Gal. 6:18; resp.) is in the Christian's spirit, after this has been transformed by the action of the Holy Spirit'), though not unrelated to Schweizer's understanding, is clearly different in meaning. Cf. P. Seidensticker, *Lebendiges Opfer* (Münster, 1954), p. 227.

[68] By the addition of the personal pronoun, μου. The same difficulty is met at 1 Cor. 14:14.

[69] *TDNT* 4, p. 64, for a lengthy discussion of Rom. 1:9. S. Lyonnet, ' "Deus cui servio in spiritu meo" (Rom. 1:9)', *Verbum Domini* 41 (Rome, 1963), pp. 52-59, presents the unusual view that the sacrifice of the eucharist is not excluded from Paul's mind here.

Our preference, however, is to understand the phrase of Paul rendering spiritual service in the proclamation of the gospel. It is 'by using his spirit, in the field of activities proper to the spiritual side of his nature, that Paul renders God service'.[70] Ἐν τῷ πνεύματί μου may have been added in order to distinguish Paul's worship from what the heathen or Jews understood by λατρεία.[71] It was a similar πνευματικὴ or λογικὴ λατρεία which was required of all Christians as a response to the wonderful mercies of God (note the διὰ τῶν οἰκτιρμῶν τοῦ θεοῦ of chap. 12:1, which points back, not only to chap. 11:33-36, but to all the blessings of justification described in the preceding chapters).

The sphere [72] of Paul's service is described by the prepositional phrase ἐν τῷ εὐαγγελίῳ τοῦ υἱοῦ αὐτοῦ, v. 9. In the immediate context τὸ εὐαγγέλιον, as a *nomen actionis*, is equivalent to τὸ εὐαγγελίζεσθαι.[73] Τοῦ υἱοῦ αὐτοῦ, with many commentators, is to be understood as an objective genitive. The gospel in which Paul was engaged has God's Son as its subject. The objective genitive is to be interpreted in the light of v. 3 [74] of the salutation, taken by many to be part of a credal statement. Paul's calling as an apostle (κλητὸς ἀπόστολος, chap. 1:1) meant that he was set apart to preach the gospel (ἀφωρισμένος εἰς εὐαγγέλιον θεοῦ, v. 1). Formerly, he had served God as a Pharisee. But now in his new life he serves Him as an evangelist of His Son. Paul is indeed taken up with this task. He is not ashamed of the gospel, for in it God's power is at work leading believers to salvation (v. 16). In a statement that reflects the language of worship

---

[70] Barrett, *Romans*, p. 24. So also Sanday and Headlam, *Romans*, p. 20; Parry, *Romans*, p. 37; Schlatter, *Gerechtigkeit*, p. 26; and Huby, *Romains*, p. 55. P. Althaus (*Der Brief an die Römer* (Göttingen, [10]1965), p. 11, 'mit seinem ganzen Menschen, seiner ganzen Person als Christ'), Leenhardt (*Romans*, p. 43, 'the whole inner life of Paul'), Bultmann (*Theology* 1, p. 206, ' "with my spirit" ... emphasizes that Paul puts his whole person into the service of the gospel') and Hill (*Words*, p. 284), stress the point that Paul's service to God in the gospel is no partial involvement.

[71] Denney, *Romans*, p. 588; and A. Pallis, *To the Romans* (Oxford, 1920), p. 36. Cf. C. F. D. Moule, 'Sanctuary and Sacrifice in the Church of the New Testament', *JTS* N.S. 1 (1950), pp. 35 and 39, where spiritual = rejection of the external cultus; so too Schweizer, *TDNT* 6, p. 437.

[72] Meyer, *Romans* 1, p. 58; Parry, *Romans*, p. 38; Murray, *Romans* 1, p. 20; Pfitzner, *Paul*, p. 119.

[73] So most commentators incl. E. Molland, *Das paulinische Euangelion. Das Wort und die Sache* (Oslo, 1934), p. 52; contra J. Schniewind, *Die Begriffe Wort und Evangelium bei Paulus* (Bonn, 1910), p. 92.

[74] With Kühl, *Römer*, p. 23; and Michel, *Römer*, p. 47.

Paul describes himself as a minister of Christ (λειτουργὸς Χριστοῦ Ἰησοῦ, 15:16) who acts as a priest for the gospel of God (ἱερουργοῦντα τὸ εὐαγγέλιον τοῦ θεοῦ). His Gentile converts are the offering (ἡ προσφορά) which he presents to God. In v. 19 of this same chap. 15 Paul once again uses εὐαγγέλιον as a noun of agency to describe the mission in which he has been engaged. From Jerusalem (since it was the starting-point of the Christian movement as a whole) and round about as far as Illyricum he has 'completed the preaching of the gospel of Christ' (NEB). Since it was his practice to 'preach the gospel where Christ had not been named' (εὐαγγελίζεσθαι οὐχ ὅπου ὠνομάσθη Χριστός, 15:20), so as not to build upon another man's foundation, he himself laid the foundation and others built on it (1 Cor. 3:10). The references to the gospel in chap. 1:8-15 point forward to Paul's treatment of his missionary activity in chap. 15, with his plans to visit Rome and to use it as a base for future work in Spain. Indeed, the gospel, in its relation to God's righteousness, is the theme of the whole letter (1:16f.).

The apostle has introduced an oath to show that God knows *that* [75] he regularly remembers the Romans in his petitions. It has already been shown [76] that πάντοτε, in the context of prayer, did not refer to unceasing petition, or the like, but to prayer offered at frequent and regular intervals. The same may be demonstrated of ἀδιαλείπτως.[77] Here the two adverbs have been used synonymously, and so both do not apply to μνείαν ... ποιοῦμαι (v. 9). Ἀδιαλείπτως is linked with

---

[75] It is not easy to decide whether ὡς expresses the fact (i.e., = ὅτι, 'that'), or the manner (= 'how') of Paul's intercessions. Grammatically, either is possible. Lietzmann, *Römer*, p. 28, was the first in recent times to suggest that 'ὡς ist im Hellenistischen mit ὅτι identisch', and he was followed by Kühl, *Römer*, pp. 23f.; Lagrange, *Romains*, p. 13; and Huby, *Romains*, p. 55. On the other hand, Meyer, *Romans* 1, pp. 58f.; Denney, *Romans*, p. 588; and Parry, *Romans*, p. 38 (cf. NEB), understood ὡς to express manner or degree. Moulton, *Grammar*, p. 211, noted in 1906: 'The use of ὡς instead of ὅτι is limited'. But MM, p. 703 (written in 1930), gave examples of ὡς = ὅτι (item no. 6); and AG, p. 907, listed instances from the papyri, Philo, and Josephus in support of the claim that in Rom. 1:9; Phil. 1:8; and 1 Thess, 2:10, ὡς was equal to ὅτι (cf. Bl.-D., para. 396). Obviously, the context must decide the issue, and in our present passage it is best to understand Paul as assuring the Roman Christians *that* he prays for them (with AV, RSV, and Phillips), rather than that he is telling them the manner of his intercessions (i.e., 'how unceasingly' he prays).

[76] See above, pp. 21f.

[77] MM, p. 9, cite a first century B.C. inscription where ἀδιαλείπτως is used of a cough; i.e., it was intermittent but not continuous.

this clause, while πάντοτε is joined to δεόμενος (v. 10),[78] indicating that in his regular prayers (ἐπὶ τῶν προσευχῶν μου) Paul asked that God might allow him to visit Rome.

The introductory thanksgiving of Romans differs from others examined, for although Paul records that he offered intercessory prayer for the addressees, he does not spell out the content of those intercessions. One can only guess at the reason for such an omission. Perhaps it was because his petition to God to allow him to make the journey to Rome was uppermost in his mind, and since his prayer reports in this period are brief anyway, he has included only that which relates to the immediate needs. On the other hand, since this church was outside the sphere of his previous apostolic work, a statement of his prayer request for them might have been construed as an indirect criticism of certain aspects of their Christian experience. As such it would not help forge the links with this church of the capital. Whatever the reason, Paul has shown his concern by indicating he has regularly interceded for them over some period of time. We might expect the apostle would often pray for his own converts, but the words of v. 9 indicate that his intercessions extended beyond the immediate circle of personal acquaintance.[79]

---

[78] In this one clause πάντοτε and ἀδιαλείπτως would be tautologous. This has been observed by many commentators.

[79] G. Eichholz, 'Der ökumenische und missionarische Horizont der Kirche', *EvTh* 21 (1961), pp. 15-27, esp. p. 17, considers it is surprising that Paul should include all the members of the Roman church within the scope of his apostolic intercessions. The reason is that Paul's view of the church is world-wide. There is a strong bond between him and *all* Christians (p. 18). Paul's horizon is 'die *ganze* Christenheit auf Erden' (p. 20). Thus his thanksgivings and petitions for the Christians at Rome are 'nicht gelegentlich, sondern... unablässig' (*ibid.*). His solidarity with them is 'brüderlich'; therefore, distances do not matter (p. 24). In spite of Eichholz's many insights, he has not given sufficient attention to Paul's apostolic responsibilities. On pp. 24f., he mentions that Paul's reasons for wanting to go to Rome are due to brotherly ties, rather than apostolic ones. On the circle of Pauline intercession, see above, pp. 9f., 13, and also Eschlimann, *Prière*, pp. 78-80. Juncker, *Gebet*, p. 24, who rightly understood Paul's intercessions as an expression of brotherly love, considered that the mention of them would strengthen the ties of fellowship between the apostle and the churches.

5. *A Psalmist's Prayer-Sigh : V. 10*

We now turn to an examination of Paul's petitionary prayer [80] report of v. 10. Εἴ πως introduces the petition which corresponds to the final clause of the first category of introductory thanksgivings. Of these final clauses ἵνα is the conjunction most frequently used, while εἴ πως occurs only in this passage.[81] The first four words, εἴ πως ἤδη ποτέ, are difficult to render in English, and might be translated literally 'if perhaps (now) at length on some occasion'.[82] According to Zerwick εἰ expresses 'an uncertain expectation associated with an effort to attain something'.[83] Ἤδη denotes the present or near future in relation to the process by which it has been reached (= 'now, after all this waiting'), while ποτέ makes the moment more

---

[80] Some commentators have understood πάντοτε ἐπὶ τῶν προσευχῶν μου δεόμενος κτλ. as a more precise definition of the preceding ἀδιαλείπτως μνείαν ὑμῶν ποιοῦμαι, partly on the grounds that δεόμενος introduces a prayer for a particular benefit, εἴ πως..., while μνείαν ὑμῶν ποιοῦμαι is a more general reference. But several points militate against such an exegesis. First, it is difficult to consider πάντοτε as being a more precise term than ἀδιαλείπτως. They appear as interchangeable synonyms in the Pauline corpus, and wherever ἀδιαλείπτως is selected in preference to πάντοτε it is usually for stylistic reasons. Secondly, although the intercessions offered by Paul for the Romans are not spelled out in detail, this does not mean that they were not specific (*contra* G. R. Cragg, 'The Epistle to the Romans : Exposition', in *The Interpreter's Bible* 9, p. 387). In other introductory thanksgivings of the first category where μνείαν (or δέησιν) ποιούμενος is used (i.e., Phil. 1:4, 9; Phm. 4ff., cf. Eph. 1:16f.) the specific request is mentioned in the following 'final' clause. But the strongest reason for rejecting the idea that πάντοτε ἐπὶ τῶν προσευχῶν μου δεόμενος is a more precise definition of the preceding stems from the actual petition itself. It is difficult, if not impossible to interpret the prayer-sigh of the apostle as an intercession for the Roman Christians. Certainly his projected visit to Rome will be for their benefit (as well as for his own), since he desires to impart to them some spiritual gift. His coming will mean that they, as well as he, will be encouraged and strengthened. No doubt he prayed to God along these lines. But the petitionary prayer of v. 10, however much it is related to the Romans, concerns Paul himself, and it is difficult to understand how it might be styled an intercession.

[81] Ὅπως is used at Phm. 6 as a synonym for ἵνα, while εἰς τό with the infinitive is found at 1 Thess. 3:10.

[82] So rendered by Meyer, *Romans* 1, p. 59; cf. Murray, *Romans* 1, p. 21; and O. Kuss, *Der Römerbrief* (Regensburg, ²1963), pp. 17f. The NEB has : 'that by his will I may, somehow or other, succeed at long last in coming to visit you'.

[83] *Greek*, para. 403. Greeven, *TDNT* 2, p. 41, comments correctly : 'A petition the fulfilment of which is particularly uncertain is presented in an εἰ-clause in Ac. 8:22 and R. 1:10'. Zerwick had made his comment with reference to 'virtual questions'. We can be more specific and state that εἴ πως introduces a reported question of a 'prayer-sigh'.

indefinite.[84] These words betray a note of uncertainty on Paul's part, perhaps even of impatience,[85] as he does not know the conditions in which his prayer will find an answer.

Both the form and the content of this prayer point unmistakably to an Old Testament background,[86] and especially that of the Psalter. At the same time, the petition needs to be understood against the contemporary 'prayer-crisis' of the ancient world. Paul's petition was a prayer in the form of a question, and was similar to the sighs of the Psalmists.[87] The *actual*, as opposed to the reported, petition might have been something like: 'How long, O Lord, will it be before I go to Rome?' (Cf. Acts 22:10 in the account of Paul's conversion: 'What shall I do, Lord?'). Another short prayer in the form of a question is found at the conclusion of Rom. 7: 'Wretched man (ταλαίπωρος) that I am! Who will deliver me (τίς με ῥύσεται) from this body of death?' (v. 24).[88] The form of these two cries suggests that Paul had drunk deeply from the wells of the Psalter. At the same time the content of his request was directly related to his own predicament of

---

[84] Sanday and Headlam, *Romans*, p. 20. ῎Ηδη ποτέ is used in a second century A.D. ostracon from Thebes as in Rom. 1:10; see Deissmann, *Light*, p. 200, n. 5. Cf. AG, pp. 344, 701 and 219.

[85] Leenhardt, *Romans*, pp. 43f.; Michel, *Römer*, p. 47; and Wiles, *Prayers*, pp. 191f.

[86] One of the first Biblical prayers for a safe and prosperous journey was the vow which Jacob made as he set out from Bethel to seek a wife in Paddan-aram (Gen. 28:20-22). N. B. Johnson, *Prayer in the Apocrypha and Pseudepigrapha* (Philadelphia, 1948), p. 12, rightly notes it would be 'surprising if among a nomadic people like the early Hebrews we should find no prayers for a safe journey'. Ezra, many years later, prayed for a safe return of the exiles from Babylon to Jerusalem (Ezra 8:21-23). This tradition continued in the intertestamental period; cf. Johnson, *op. cit.*, pp. 12f., and the references he cites: Tob. 4:19; 11:1; Jub. 12:21; 13:7, 15; cf. 22:27; Wisd. 14:3, 4; 19:1-12 with reference to God's guidance in the past. Johnson seems to err, however, when he states: 'the New Testament contains no explicit prayer for safe travel' (p. 13). Paul's request in Rom. 1:10 (cf. 1 Thess. 3:11) that his way might be prospered would seem to cover this notion. Cf. Harder, *Paulus*, pp. 31f.; and Schneider, *loc. cit.*, p. 14, who instances some Rabbinic statements about prayer and safe travel, e.g., b.Ber. 29b: '... when thou goest forth on a journey, seek counsel of thy Maker and go forth'.

[87] Such short prayer-sighs are found in Pss. 35(34):17: κύριε, πότε ἐπόψῃ; 42:2 (41:3): πότε ἥξω καὶ ὀφθήσομαι τῷ προσώπῳ τοῦ θεοῦ, and 13(12):2: ἕως πότε, κύριε, ἐπιλήσῃ μου εἰς τέλος; where the question is asked, and the verb (as in Rom. 1:10) is used in the future tense; cf. Harder, *ibid.*, p. 32.

[88] Some of the ideas contained in this may be parallelled in the Psalter: esp. ταλαίπωρος, which may point to the עָנִי of the Pss., and ῥύομαι (treated above, pp. 96ff.); cf. Harder, *ibid.*

wanting to go to Rome, and yet being unable to do so up to the point of writing.

The Old Testament background to Paul's petition appears again with the verb εὐοδωθήσομαι.[89] Εὐοδόω occurs in the New Testament only at Rom. 1:10; 1 Cor. 16:2; and 3 John 2 (twice), and is always in the passive—implying the divine action. The uncommonly rich usage in the LXX appears to have had its influence on these New Testament examples, for parallels may be found in the earlier source for each instance of the latter. Whether one opts for the literal meaning ('to have a good journey') or the figurative connotation ('to succeed') for εὐοδωθήσομαι does not matter, for the following infinitive [90] (as well as the context of Rom. 1:10) makes it clear that Paul has in mind the making of a successful journey to Rome. An equivalent statement, which occurs in another Pauline prayer, is ὁ θεός ... κατευθύναι τὴν ὁδὸν ἡμῶν πρὸς ὑμᾶς (1 Thess. 3:11). This expression too was common in the LXX.[91] In both prayers God (or Jesus) was the One who could bring the anticipated success.[92]

This final point is underlined by the phrase ἐν τῷ θελήματι τοῦ θεοῦ, v. 10. In these words the apostle made clear that the proposed visit to Rome was not being undertaken merely because of his own wishes, although he did desire it earnestly.[93] Elsewhere Paul indicated

---

[89] Although a correct formation, εὐοδόω is rare outside the Bible and was possibly not used at all prior to the LXX (see W. Michaelis, 'ὁδός', *TDNT* 5, pp. 42-114, esp. 'εὐοδόω', pp. 109-114, for the following statistics). There are appoximately seventy-five instances in the LXX, of which fifty have a Hebrew original. Behind forty-four of these are forms of צלח. Both meaning and construction vary greatly, and from a literal connotation of 'to have a good journey', it came to be used in a metaphorical sense of 'to succeed'. It is perhaps not without significance that in some forty instances God is directly or indirectly the One to whom true success is ascribed (Lagrange, *Romains*, p. 14 : 'Le passif dans εὐοδέω (*sic* !) indique déjà l'action divine...'. The passive is found thirty-eight times in the LXX; Michaelis, *op. cit.*, p. 111; cf. Lietzmann, *Römer*, p. 28).

[90] The infinitive ἐλθεῖν πρὸς ὑμᾶς suggests εὐοδωθήσομαι should be taken to mean 'I will succeed'. The construction is found with εὐοδόω in the LXX; Michaelis, *op. cit.*, pp. 111, 113; Bl.-D., para. 392 (3).

[91] E.g., Pss. 5:8; 119 (118):5; Prov. 4:26; 9:15; 13:13; 29:27; Ezek. 18:25.

[92] Michaelis, *ibid.* Cf. Schlatter, *Gerechtigkeit*, p. 28 : 'Er (*sc.* Paulus) kann aber nur dorthin kommen, wenn ihm von einem Beschluss Gottes der Weg gebahnt wird'.

[93] Knox, *Romans*, p. 387. But Knox is too definite when he states : 'he is coming because God... has now specifically directed him to proceed to Rome' (p. 388). This is not the meaning of the text, nor is it supported by chap. 15:30-32. Meyer, *Romans* 1, p. 59, is more accurate in stating that on God's will εὐοδωθήσομαι 'causally' depends; cf. Lagrange, *Romains*, p. 14.

that his calling to be an apostle of Christ Jesus was διὰ θελήματος θεοῦ.[94] His ministry was subjected to this commission, since God's will was the ultimate cause of his apostolic power, of the commencement and the continuation of his ministry. That calling as an apostle of Christ through the will of God had direct reference to the ministry of the gospel to Gentiles. Rome was the centre of the Gentile world, and a visit [95] to that place in order to preach the gospel or to use it as a base for further missionary expansion was not inconsistent with his general calling, as he indicates in v. 13 (cf. vv. 1 and 5). But the will of God was not simply to be understood against the general background of apostleship. It extended to details too, as the present context makes clear. These details [96] were set within the will of God as much as the general calling.[97]

Not only did Paul cry out that the God of the Psalmists might answer his petition. He asked the Roman Christians themselves to engage in a similar struggle [98] in their prayers (συναγωνίσασθαί μοι ἐν ταῖς προσευχαῖς ὑπὲρ ἐμοῦ, chap. 15:30) that through the will of God (διὰ θελήματος θεοῦ, v. 32) he might come to them with joy. It is perhaps not insignificant that although Paul was not certain of the specifics of God's will concerning a possible visit to Rome, he exhorted his fellow Christians to pray along these lines, yet adding the important proviso, 'by God's will'.

At first sight it might appear that by hedging around his request with the words 'if God wills', Paul has become a victim of the prayer-

---

[94] 1 Cor. 1:1; 2 Cor. 1:1; Col. 1:1; cf. Eph. 1:1; 2 Tim. 1:1; and Rom. 1:1; as well as the strong words of Gal. 1:1; cf. v. 15 of the same chapter.

[95] Greeven, *Gebet*, p. 165, sets Paul's journeys in the framework of his general missionary work, and sees the latter 'in einen eschatologischen Zusammenhang'.

[96] Not only details which concern Paul, but also those which relate to his fellow-workers (1 Cor. 16:12). Regarding the apostle, Sanday and Headlam, *Romans*, p. 21, observe: 'all his movements are in the hands of God'. Cf. Michel, *Römer*, p. 47: 'Alle Reise- und Zukunftspläne stehen unter diesem theologischen Vorbehalt und dieser Formel des Gehorsams... Pls ist... nicht Herr über sich selbst und seine Pläne'; and Str.-B. 3, p. 758.

[97] On the many particular decisions as to spheres of work, departures, routes, etc., which had to be made against the general backdrop of God's will in calling Paul to the divine office of apostleship to the Gentiles, see J. A. Allan, 'The Will of God. III. In Paul', *ExT* 72 (1960-1961), pp. 142-145.

[98] For Pfitzner's views concerning this 'Agon', see above, p. 199.

crisis of antiquity.[99] In the pagan world of Paul's day there were problems associated with prayer to the gods, e.g., how the gods were to be addressed. But other questions arose, so that as doubt and speculation intruded, prayer either moved to pure hymnic forms, or, if it was petition, it lost any freedom or spontaneity there might have been. The worshipper expressed his requests with great reserve, prefacing any desires with words such as: 'May it be found well-pleasing in your sight'. Because of the uncertainty of journeys in ancient times, frequent and intensive prayers were offered to the gods for safe travel. Yet these requests were accompanied with very little assurance on the part of the person praying, so in order to account for any unforseen circumstances, the rider $\dot{\epsilon}\grave{\alpha}\nu$ $\theta\epsilon o\grave{\iota}$ $\theta\acute{\epsilon}\lambda\omega\sigma\iota$ was added.[100]

In spite of its wonderful heritage, Judaism was not unaffected by the contemporary issues. Harder points out that elements in the prayers of the people of God in the inter-testamental period indicate a grappling with this crisis of unanswered prayer.

Paul, however, has not fallen a prey to this uncertainty manifest in the prayers of antiquity. A measure of similarity in language does not indicate that $\dot{\epsilon}\nu$ $\tau\hat{\omega}$ $\theta\epsilon\lambda\acute{\eta}\mu\alpha\tau\iota$ $\tau o\hat{\upsilon}$ $\theta\epsilon o\hat{\upsilon}$ (or its equivalent) meant the same to the ancient man as to Paul. Harder aptly comments: 'Auf eine direkte Übernahme antiken Gebetsgutes lässt diese Wendung bei Paulus aber nicht schliessen'.[101] To Paul God's will was not capricious, for it was through the will of God that he had been called to be an apostle. Such an action on God's part was evidence of his unsurpassing grace. Paul might therefore commend specific details of that apostolic calling (such as a journey to Rome) to God's will with true confidence.[102] It was his great desire to go to Rome and in spite of his uncertainty about the actual outcome and its details,

---

[99] Orphal, *Paulusgebet*, p. 8, understands this reference to God's will as an echo of the third petition of the Lord's Prayer. This is possible, but unlikely. A. Resch, *Der Paulinismus und die Logia Jesu* (Leipzig, 1904), who lists hundreds of parallels (he believes) between the Pauline material and the *logia Jesu*, makes no reference to the will of God in Rom. 1:10 or 15:32. On the subject of the prayer-crisis, see Harder, *Paulus*, pp. 130-162.

[100] Harder, *ibid.*, p. 120. Deissmann, *Studies*, p. 252, with reference to the phrase $\tau o\hat{\upsilon}$ $\theta\epsilon o\hat{\upsilon}$ $\theta\acute{\epsilon}\lambda o\nu\tau o\varsigma$ (or its equivalent), states that the Fayyûm Papyri show how widespread was its use. Furthermore, examples of the formulae are found in private letters. See also his *Light*, p. 181; MM, p. 286; and Michel, *Römer*, p. 47.

[101] *Op. cit.*, p. 120.

[102] Cf. Bieder, *loc. cit.*, p. 30.

like the Psalmists of old, Paul knew that the One to whom he addressed his petition gave generously to men (Ps. 37:4).

6. *Reasons for a Visit to Rome*

The words of v. 11, ἐπιποθῶ γὰρ ἰδεῖν ὑμᾶς κτλ., provide the reason or explanation for the constancy of the prayer referred to in vv. 9 and 10.[103] But the loose and imprecise construction of vv. 11ff. suggests a certain embarrassment on Paul's part, since his plans are not clear.

The first purpose of such a visit would be to 'impart some spiritual gift to strengthen' them. The apostle wanted their Christian character and life to be even stronger than it was.[104] Paul might be the instrument by which that strengthening takes place (τι μεταδῶ [105] χάρισμα ὑμῖν πνευματικόν, v. 11), but God [106] was the One who would perform the action (στηριχθῆναι).[107] As in the introductory thanksgiving of 1 Corinthians, so here the particular gift that Paul had in mind is not specified.[108] Indeed, the addition of τι indicates

---

[103] So Murray, *Romans* 1, p. 21; but Lietzmann, *Römer*, p. 28, considers: 'γάρ kaum noch begründend, sondern Weiterführung'. Lagrange, *Romains*, p. 14, states: 'γάρ spécialise la pensée'; cf. Kühl, *Römer*, p. 24.

[104] Although it is not stated in so many words, it is probable that the strengthening (note στηρίζω is used elsewhere in Pauline prayers) of the Roman Christians was one of Paul's intercessions; cf. 1 Thess. 3:10, where a visit by Paul is in order καταρτίσαι τὰ ὑστερήματα τῆς πίστεως ὑμῶν.

[105] It would have been tantamount to false modesty on Paul's part not to say that he would be the instrument in their being made stronger in faith; cf. Nygren, *Romans*, p. 61.

[106] So Meyer (*Romans* 1, p. 60, who considers the activity is wrought by the Spirit), T. W. Manson ('Romans', in *Peake's Commentary on the Bible*, ed. M. Black and H. H. Rowley (London, ²1962), p. 941) and Murray (*Romans* 1, p. 22, who suggests it would not have been un-Pauline for the apostle to have said 'he might establish them'; 1 Thess. 3:2; cf. Luke 22:32; Acts 18:23. But modesty and the reference to the Holy Spirit in this context probably dictated the use of the passive). Michel, *Römer*, p. 48, after examining the New Testament instances of στηρίζω, affirms: 'Wir haben es mit einem Bildwort zu tun, das die Paränese des Urchristentums bestimmt'. It is only natural that in some prayer contexts, where this paraenetic term is used, God's strengthening activity should be emphasized (Rom. 16:25; 2 Thess. 2:17; 3:3).

[107] Εἰς τὸ στηριχθῆναι expresses purpose.

[108] It has been suggested that tongues or prophecy (through the laying on of hands (!), so J. K. Parratt, 'Romans i. 11 and Galatians iii. 5—Pauline evidence for the Laying on of Hands ?', *ExT* 79 (1967-1968), pp. 151f.) may have been the gift Paul had in mind. Schenk, *Segen*, p. 50, indicates that the spiritual gift (=πλήρωμα εὐλογίας Χριστοῦ of

that he desired to impart whatever *spiritual* enrichment was needed.[109] If, as Hunter suggests, he included in the expression some of his insights into the gospel, we may judge that he imparted much of his gift in this letter.[110]

With real tact,[111] lest it be thought that the spiritual advantage would be all on one side, Paul hastens to add that he too would benefit from such a visit, since his faith would be encouraged by theirs. Εἰς τὸ στηριχθῆναι ὑμᾶς might have been mentioned appropriately in a letter to Corinth [112] where he was both an apostle (1 Cor. 9:2) and a father (1 Cor. 4:15), but it was less suitable when writing as a stranger to an established and well-known church (v. 8) in the capital. Hence the awkward but important addition of v. 12.

Paul's second [113] aim in visiting Rome is to engage in active missionary work in the area served by the Roman community (vv. 13-15). His duty as an apostle to Gentiles was one which recognized no barriers of race or culture.[114] The Roman church was

---

15:29, cf. Eph. 1:3, ἐν πάσῃ εὐλογίᾳ πνευματικῇ) 'ist das Pneuma'. But this is doubtful. The language of Rom. 15:29 is vague and probably meant to be no more specific than that of 1:11.

[109] Lightfoot, *Notes*, p. 248; Pallis, *Romans*, p. 37, who considers it is not a monetary gift; Barrett, *Romans*, p. 25, who thinks it is 'hardly profitable here to inquire what precise gift' Paul may have had in mind; Schweizer, *TDNT* 6, p. 437; Murray, *Romans* 1, p. 22; Leenhardt, *Romans*, p. 44; Schlatter, *Gerechtigkeit*, p. 28; and Michel, *Römer*, p. 48. *Contra* E. E. Ellis, ' "Spiritual" Gifts in the Pauline Community', *NTS* 20 (1973-1974), pp. 128-144, esp. pp. 129-131.

[110] Hunter, *Romans*, p. 27; Denney, *Romans*, p. 588, puts it more strongly: 'No doubt in substance, Paul imparts his spiritual gift through this epistle'. For he wanted to further the Romans' 'comprehension of the purpose of God in Jesus Christ'. Cf. Parry, *Romans*, p. 38; Kühl, *Römer*, p. 24; and G. Klein, 'Der Abfassungszweck des Römerbriefes', in *Rekonstruktion und Interpretation* (München, 1969), pp. 129-144, esp. p. 144, who asserts 'der Brief geradezu als ein vorweggenommener Akt jenes εὐαγγελίσασθαι erscheint, welches Paulus persönlich in Rom noch vor sich hat'.

[111] By means of the awkward τοῦτο δέ ἐστιν ('or rather what I wish is'), which is found only here in the New Testament. It does not have the same meaning as τοῦτ' ἔστιν ('that is to say', cf. 7:18), and introduces not an explanation but a complement (Leenhardt, *Romans*, p. 44), or a correction (Barrett, *Romans*, p. 25; Bruce, *Romans*, p. 76). According to Michel, *Römer*, p. 48, τοῦτο δέ ἐστιν 'will nicht nur στηριχθῆναι erläutern oder verbessern, sondern den in v. 11 geäusserten Gedanken umbilden und weiterführen'.

[112] Barrett, *ibid.*

[113] We agree with the view of T. W. Manson (*Romans*, pp. 941f.; cf. Zahn, *Römer*, p. 62, 'eine zweite Zweckangabe'; and Bruce, *Romans*, p. 75), that v. 13 expresses a second purpose for visiting Rome.

[114] In his essay 'Christ and the World in the Early Christian Message', *Experience*, pp. 14-28, Bornkamm states of Paul: 'His missionary course and goal are determined

not founded by him, but the regions which it served came within the scope of his apostolic commission. Although Paul had no thought of asserting his apostolic authority at Rome,[115] he looked forward to preaching the gospel in that city and making some converts there, as in the rest of the Gentile world (vv. 15, 13). He had often intended visiting them for this purpose ($\pi o \lambda \lambda \acute{a} \kappa \iota s$ [116] $\pi\rho o\epsilon\theta\acute{\epsilon}\mu\eta\nu$ $\grave{\epsilon}\lambda\theta\epsilon\hat{\iota}\nu$ $\pi\rho\grave{o}s$ $\acute{\upsilon}\mu\hat{a}s$, v. 13), but had been prevented from doing so.[117] It had not been God's will up to the point of writing that Paul should come. This should probably be understood to indicate that urgent tasks (themselves part of his God-given responsibilities) had kept him in the East (cf. 15:18f., 22f.).[118]

At first sight it appears difficult to reconcile these purposes for wanting to visit Rome with his statements in chap. 15, where Rome appears to be simply an intermediate station on the way to the new mission field in Spain. In the introductory thanksgiving an extended stay in Rome appears to be envisaged, while there is no mention of Spain.[119] Further, it is considered that Paul's desire 'to preach the gospel... in Rome' (1:15) runs counter to his practice of not evangelizing where 'Christ has already been named' (15:20). So Lietzmann considers the reasons for Paul's visit to Rome (1:11f.) to be unclear.[120] Knox admits there is no 'necessary contradiction' between chaps. 1 and 15, but only that Paul justified his coming to Roman territory in somewhat different terms,[121] while Munck believes most overlook

---

and guided by the faith and confession that Jesus Christ is Lord and the whole world belongs to him, the Lord' (p. 15).

[115] *Contra* A. Fridrichsen, *The Apostle and his Message* (Uppsala, 1947), p. 7, who considers the 'main motive' (!) of Romans is to assert Paul's apostolic authority at Rome; and *contra* Klein, *op. cit.*, p. 135.

[116] Bruce, *Romans*, p. 76, 'Of these earlier occasions when Paul had hoped or planned to visit Rome we have no independent information'. So too other commentators and Eichholz, *loc. cit.*, p. 22.

[117] $\dot{E}\kappa\omega\lambda\dot{\upsilon}\theta\eta\nu$, a passive used in true Semitic fashion, conceals a reference to God.

[118] Cf. Bornkamm, *Paul*, pp. 51f., 57.

[119] Though Leenhardt, *Romans*, p. 45, is probably right when, following a suggestion of H. Windisch, '$\beta\acute{a}\rho\beta a\rho o s$', *TDNT* 1, pp. 546-553, esp. p. 552, he comments that 'the mention of barbarians is certainly an allusion to Spain and the missionary plans of the apostle'.

[120] *Römer, ad loc.*

[121] *Romans*, p. 361. See also his more recent study, 'Romans 15:14-33 and Paul's Conception of his Apostolic Mision', *JBL* 83 (1964), pp. 1-11.

chap. 15 with its qualifications of the first strong expressions (i.e., in chap. 1:11ff.).[122]

But the differences are not as great as they seem. Certainly Paul wished to go to Spain, since he had completed his apostolic responsibilities in the East. A journey to Spain would afford him an opportunity of realizing his desire of visiting Rome [123] and of having fellowship with the Christians of that place whose faith was renowned. The preaching of the gospel drove Paul to scale great heights, and this he sets forth clearly in the thanksgiving period. The opening passage prepares the way for what follows, and for the moment there is no need to place in the foreground details of his future plans.[124] These follow when he treats more fully the subject of his having 'completed the preaching of the gospel of Christ from Jerusalem as far round as Illyricum' (15:19, NEB). He then mentions his desire to visit Spain, to use Rome as a base for that mission, and to gain the active participation [125] of the Roman Christians.

7. *The Function of the Paragraph*

It has been suggested that there is no contradiction between chaps. 1 and 15. Nor ought it be thought that the latter presents a serious modification of the plans, reasons, etc., mentioned in the former. The introductory thanksgiving of chap. 1:8ff. prepares the ground for what follows in chap. 15, where ideas are then repeated and expanded.

---

[122] *Paul*, pp. 297f. Further, Munck's view that the 'Gospel preaching of which Paul speaks in ch. 1 is no missionary preaching, but preaching for the strengthening of a church already there' (p. 298), does not seem to be supported by chap. 1:13ff. See the argument above.

[123] Bruce, *Romans*, p. 258.

[124] This point (which has been noted in other introductory thanksgivings) seems to have been overlooked by those who stress the differences between chaps. 1 and 15. The right balance, though, is put by Schlatter (*Gerechtigkeit*, p. 24, who understands the letter as arising out of Paul's plans, and only a brief word is needed at the beginning) and Michel (*Römer*, p. 45 : 'er nicht seine zukünftigen Arbeitspläne in den Vordergrund stellt, sondern die erhoffte Begegnung von Mensch zu Mensch, von Apostel zu Gemeinde'. Later (i.e., chap. 15:14-33) he will deal more fully with his travel plans).

[125] G. Schrenk, 'Der Römerbrief als Missionsdokument', in *Studien zu Paulus* (Zürich, 1954), pp. 81-106, esp. pp. 82, 84, stresses this point of participation (E. Trocmé, 'L'Épître aux Romains et la méthode missionnaire de l'apôtre Paul', *NTS* 7 (1960-1961), pp. 148-153). Paul 'denkt universal—im Völkern'. And thus : 'Die römische Gemeinde ist die Mitarbeiterin'. Paul prepares them for his visit by telling them concrete details, and asking for their intercessions.

Most scholars consider that in chap. 1:8-15 (or 17) Paul set forth the external occasion, and the immediate purpose of the epistle. Through the letter (and in particular these opening words) Paul endeavoured to gain rapport with the Christians at Rome, since he wanted to visit them and enlist their brotherly help in the execution of his plans to extend his operation further west. His immediate purpose, then, was to create interest in his Spanish mission. But if this is all that the apostle intended to do he could have written this much more briefly in the words of chaps. 1 and 15 alone. The theological character of the letter is not adequately accounted for if the journey to Spain was the only purpose in writing.[126] Various explanations have been given: F. C. Baur and his school considered the purpose to have been polemical, others said its aim was conciliatory (i.e., Paul was attempting to vindicate his Gentile commission by reconciling Jewish and Gentile elements).[127] The traditional view has been to see in the letter a full statement of Paul's doctrinal position. Thus Romans was understood more as a treatise than a letter, with little reference to the historical situation out of which it arose. But doctrines of the church,[128] cosmic reconciliation and developed eschatology do not find a place in Paul's *summa theologica*. Further, chaps. 9-11 cannot be understood apart from Paul's missionary experience, while the personal details of the introductory thanksgiving (together with v. 7) show the letter was written to the Roman community,[129] and must be taken into account when determining its purpose. Some consider the purpose was to sum up the fruits of Paul's past work.[130] His mind had been dwelling on many of these

---

[126] In spite of the stream of literature in recent years concerning Paul's purpose in writing Romans there has been no scholarly consensus. See the standard introductions and W. S. Campbell, 'Why Did Paul Write Romans ?', *ExT* 85 (1973-1974), pp. 264-269, together with the literature cited there.

[127] This view too, was based upon the presuppositions of the Tübingen school.

[128] For some suggestions as to why the designation ἐκκλησία is missing in the prescript and throughout the letter (except chap. 16) note E. A. Judge and G. S. R. Thomas, 'The Origin of the Church at Rome: A New Solution ?', *RThR* 25 (1966), pp. 81-94; and Campbell, *loc. cit.*, pp. 265f., 268f.

[129] See the commentaries for a discussion of the textual difficulties of chap. 1:7 and 15 (ἐν Ῥώμῃ).

[130] Sanday and Headlam, *Romans*, p. xlii. Munck, *Paul*, pp. 196ff., following a suggestion of T. W. Manson, *Studies*, pp. 225ff., regarded the letter as a prepared manifesto based on material from Paul's debates over the relation of Judaism and Christianity. Both Manson and Munck considered the letter tells us little about the condition of the Roman church.

themes and he had decided to commit them to writing when telling the Roman church about his coming visit. A development of this view is to understand the letter as a 'spiritual testament'[131] of the apostle, written because he was unsure of the results that would flow from his trip to Jerusalem with the collection. Others emphasize the point that Paul aimed to meet the immediate needs of the readers. It is beyond the scope of this present inquiry to determine *precisely* the aims Paul had in mind when he dictated his letter to the Romans. However, it is thought that any further light thrown on the function of the introductory thanksgiving of Romans may help in ascertaining more precisely the purpose of the letter.

A close examination of the terms and ideas appearing in the introductory passage will show that not a few important *theological* as well as *paraenetic* motifs which are found in the body of the letter have already been prefigured. What, at first sight, seem to have been incidental comments in the thanksgiving passage re-appear in 'weightier' sections of the letter, and we consider that insufficient attention has been paid to some of these themes.

Faith is mentioned in the thanksgiving Paul offers to the Father, and this motif recurs many times[132] in the course of the letter. It appears in the theme verses of the epistle (1:16f.), as well as in chap. 3:21ff. where the subject of righteousness and Christ's death is expounded. Abraham who walked by faith received the promise through faith. Πίστις is an important theological term in Romans, occurring forty times, while the cognate verb is found on twenty-one occasions.

The significance of εὐαγγέλιον has already been noted. Not only is this motif important in the thanksgiving passage, but also in the body of the letter, suggesting that its use in the thanksgiving period prefigures the later occurrences. The gospel in which Paul served God, had at its centre 'His Son'. Kramer[133] had already pointed out that the title 'Son of God' was used by the apostle, pre-eminently to show that there was a very close relationship between Jesus as the bearer

---

[131] See esp. G. Bornkamm, 'The Letter to the Romans as Paul's Last Will and Testament', *ABR* 11 (1963), pp. 2-14.

[132] For detailed statistics on the language and style of Romans, see E. von Dobschütz, 'Zum Wortschatz und Stil des Römerbriefs', *ZNW* 33 (1934), pp. 51-66. On the theme of faith note H. W. Bartsch, 'The Concept of Faith in Paul's Letter to the Romans', *Biblical Research* 13 (Chicago, 1968), pp. 41-53.

[133] *Christ*, p. 184.

of salvation and the Father. This observation holds good for references to the Son in the body of the letter. So those who were God's enemies are reconciled to the Father by His Son's death (5:10). The Father sent the Son (8:3), did not spare His Son (8:32), but handed Him over for the sake of us all. Believers are predestined to be conformed to the Son's image (8:29). Such may be called 'sons of God' for they are led by the Spirit (8:14), and will participate in a future unveiling (8:19). Although there is no detailed exposition, the introductory thanksgiving of Romans mentions God's Son (cf. 1 Cor. 1:4ff.), and prepares the way for the important theological thrusts found in connection with this term.

The close relationship of the Son to the Father with reference to the blessings of salvation is seen when we examine some of the διά-phrases found in the letter. Thanksgiving is offered 'through Jesus Christ', for He has opened the way to the Father's presence (1:8; cf. 7:25, χάρις δὲ τῷ θεῷ διὰ Ἰησοῦ Χριστοῦ τοῦ κυρίου ἡμῶν). In the body of the letter διὰ Ἰησοῦ Χριστοῦ and its equivalents are used to indicate that εἰρήνη (5:1), προσαγωγή (5:2), σωτηρία (5:9), καταλλαγή (5:11) and victory (8:37) are mediated to us by Jesus Christ.

Other theological and paraenetic themes may be noted. Paul has prayed that by the will of God he might come to Rome (1:10). He encouraged the recipients of the letter to pray along similar lines (15:32). But they themselves, through obedience, may prove experimentally that the will of God is good, acceptable and perfect (12:2). Paul could refer to the spiritual χάρισμα he desired to impart to the Roman Christians (1:11). Later he will mention the χάρισμα of Christ, the federal head of the new humanity (5:15, 16; cf. 6:23), and of the different χαρίσματα graciously given to all believers (12:6). Κόσμος, found in the introductory thanksgiving of chap. 1:8, appears with a variety of meanings in the body of the letter. Paul's worship or service, in contrast to that of pagans, was ἐν τῷ πνεύματί μου. Indeed the latter have changed the truth of God for a lie, thus worshipping the creature rather than the Creator (ἐλάτρευσαν τῇ κτίσει παρὰ τὸν κτίσαντα, 1:25). But as Paul's worship was spiritual, and thus λογική,[134] so ought that of the Romans to be λογικὴ λατρεία. In

---

[134] See Leenhardt's good discussion on λογικός in Rom. 12:1, *Romans*, pp. 303f. Moule, *loc. cit.*, p. 34, states of λογικός and πνευματικός that they 'are not correlatives but virtual synonyms'. Λογικὴ λατρεία (Rom. 12:1) is used of the self-sacrifice by Christians of themselves, while in 1 Peter 2:5 similar sacrifices are called πνευματικαί.

Romans 1:10 Paul has used the word προσευχή; at chap. 12:12, in a paraenetic section he encourages the Romans τῇ προσευχῇ προσκαρτεροῦντες, while in the closing sections of the epistle he asks them to intercede for him (15:30ff.). In a didactic piece (8:26) the cognate προσεύχομαι is used to point to the Spirit's activity in prayer.

One final theme of the thanksgiving period ought to be mentioned: the notion of debt.[135] The apostle states: 'I am under obligation (ὀφειλέτης) both to the Greeks and to barbarians, both to the wise and to the foolish' (1:14). And it was because of this obligation or debt that Paul was eager to preach the gospel in Rome. In ordinary usage a sense of debt presupposes a gift from one person to another, and a knowledge and appreciation of that gift and its giver. In the present context neither did Paul know his creditors, nor had they given him anything. He had an apostolic responsibility for Gentiles, but chap. 1:14 speaks of indebtedness to them. Minear,[136] taking his cue from Schlatter, considers Paul accepted as a principle that 'a debt to Christ was immediately transmuted into a debt to those whom Christ wished to bring to salvation through them'.[137] Thus: 'Obligation to him who died produces obligation to those for whom he died'.[138] And the measure in which Paul was indebted to God for his calling, to that extent was he indebted to those Gentiles for whose sake God had called him.

The same understanding of debt underlies the use of ὀφειλέτης in chap. 8:12. Christians are not debtors to the flesh but to the Spirit who indwells them and seals them as Christ's possession. This debt determines their whole manner of living and existence. Diametrically opposed is the notion that God should be indebted to us (4:4, κατὰ ὀφείλημα). Paul's debt, like that of the Gentile believers to the saints in Jerusalem (15:27), is not unrelated to the notion of gratitude. Indeed it might be said, with Minear, that the apostle's sense of debt and his sense of gratitude are not only compatible, but almost identical. And his status as a debtor is related to missionary motivation.

---

[135] Dodd, *Meaning*, pp. 157f.; and P. S. Minear, 'Gratitude and Mission in the Epistle to the Romans', in *Basileia. Festschrift für W. Freytag* (Stuttgart, 1959), pp. 42-48, now reprinted in *The Obedience of Faith* (London, 1971), pp. 102-110. Page references are to the latter.

[136] *Obedience*, p. 104.

[137] Minear, *ibid*. Hahn, *Mission*, p. 99, agrees with this point.

[138] Minear, *ibid*.

We thus conclude this section by noting that Paul's words in the thanksgiving period prepare the way for his visit to Rome, and indicate his plans for a wider ministry to Gentiles. The importance of the gospel is stressed, and the thanksgiving leads to the key verses (1:16f.) of the letter. Terms and ideas of both a theological and paraenetic nature (some are only alluded to) occur first in the period and then within the body of the letter. The primary purpose or function of the period is thus epistolary. The paraenetic and didactic functions in a strict sense are absent and one may suppose that the reason for this is that Paul has had no previous relations with the church at Rome. However, the apostle in the body of the letter develops and expands many of the theological and paraenetic motifs mentioned in the introductory period.

Paul's apostolic concern shines through clearly in the passage under review. It is not motivated simply by a desire to use Rome as an intermediate station on his way to Spain, for the statements already examined in the detailed exegesis show that he had the well-being of these Christians at heart. The reports of these prayers helped, no doubt, to strengthen the ties of fellowship [139] with these Christians at the capital.

8. *Paul's Thanksgiving and Petitionary Prayer*

The thanksgiving and petitionary prayer in Rom. 1:8ff. are different from those previously examined in that they relate to a church which lay outside the scope of his previous apostolic activity. In his report the apostle has adapted and transformed the Greek epistolary style in such a way to show that his prayer was no perfunctory activity. Many of the ideas expressed in these prayers stem from an Old Testament background. Yet they are related to the situation in Rome (e.g., ἡ πίστις ὑμῶν καταγγέλλεται ἐν ὅλῳ τῷ κόσμῳ, 1:8) and the contemporary prayer-crisis of the pagan world. Although the apostle's prayer concerning his journey to Rome was in language not unlike prayers for safe travel of that period, there is a world of difference in the ideas that lay behind them.

Finally, it has been shown that prayer (particularly petitionary prayer) was an important weapon in Paul's apostolic armoury. In the

---

[139] Juncker, *op. cit.*, p. 24.

passage under review such petition had particular reference to his missionary movements, and (with 1 Thess. 3:10) is the only example of this in the introductory periods.

PART FOUR

AN INTRODUCTORY *BERAKAH*

CHAPTER EIGHT

THE INTRODUCTORY *BERAKAH* OF 2 COR. 1:3ff.

1. *A Berakah instead of a Thanksgiving*

In 2 Cor. 1:3ff., the most personal of Paul's introductory paragraphs in his letters,[1] the apostle opens with a *berakah* (εὐλογητὸς ὁ θεός) instead of a thanksgiving. Not only are the introductory words and their terms of reference dissimilar,[2] but the structure of the passage also is quite different from those in which the εὐχαριστέω-formula appears. Instead of a structure like that of the first or second (or mixed) category of thanksgiving period, Paul introduces the paragraph with a short christianized form [3] of the Jewish praise-giving or eulogy.

2 Cor. 1:3f. has formal similarities with Eph. 1:3ff. and 1 Peter 1:3ff., as well as significant differences.[4] Claus Westermann [5] has shown that

---

[1] This has been recognized by almost all commentators. Schubert, *Form*, p. 50, rather remarkably, comments that Paul, instead of beginning with the regular thanksgiving 'chose the more liturgical, *less personal* εὐλογία' (our italics). He has failed to distinguish the various kinds of *berakoth* (see the reference to Westermann's discussion, below), and his statement indicates he has not taken material considerations into account.

[2] Since Paul himself is included within its scope (ὁ παρακαλῶν ἡμᾶς, v. 4).

[3] Among commentators this is recognized by: A. H. Menzies, *The Second Epistle of the Apostle Paul to the Corinthians* (London, 1912), p. 4; H. Windisch, *Der zweite Korintherbrief* (Göttingen, ⁹1924), p. 37; J. Héring, *The Second Epistle of Saint Paul to the Corinthians* (ET, London, 1967), p. 2; Lietzmann-Kümmel, *Korinther*, p. 196; F. F. Bruce, *1 and 2 Corinthians* (London, 1971), p. 178; and C. K. Barrett, *The Second Epistle to the Corinthians* (London, 1973), p. 58.

[4] Each passage is an introductory eulogy, styled by N. A. Dahl, 'Adresse und Proömium des Epheserbriefes', *TZ* 7 (1951), p. 250, as a 'Briefeingangs-Eulogie' (cf. Deichgräber, *Gotteshymnus*, p. 64), in which the εὐλογητός-formula and the predicate, ὁ θεὸς καὶ πατὴρ τοῦ κυρίου ἡμῶν Ἰησοῦ Χριστοῦ, are common. But 2 Cor. 1:3f. differs from the other two in length and content; cf. Schenk, *Segen*, pp. 99ff. See below.

[5] C. Westermann, *The Praise of God in the Psalms* (ET, London, 1966), pp. 87-89; cf. J.-P. Audet, 'Esquisse historique du genre littéraire de la "Bénédiction" juive et de l'"Eucharistie" chrétienne', *RB* 65 (1958), pp. 371-399, esp. p. 376; J. M. Robinson, 'The Historicality of Biblical Language', in *The Old Testament and Christian Faith*, ed. B. W. Anderson (New York, 1963), pp. 124-158, esp. pp. 131 and 135; and Deichgräber, *Gotteshymnus*, p. 40.

in the Old Testament the earliest and simplest form of declarative praise [6] (such as the *berakah*) was a single sentence in which the recipient expressed his simple and joyous response to a definite act of God which had just been experienced. Its origin was not the cult. But in the second stage the *berakah* did not follow directly on God's actions, e.g., in 1 Kings 8:14f., 55f. it was reserved for the feast day, the great day of the dedication of the temple. The final stage of development can be seen in the eulogies that conclude the books of the Psalter.[7] In place of the very simple phraseology there now appears in the *baruk*-sentences (e.g., Ps. 72:18f.) a developed, liturgically full and solemn language. In the rabbinic literature there are many examples of this last kind.[8] But the earlier short form of eulogy was not lost.[9] The introductory *berakah* of 2 Cor. 1:3f. approximates more closely to the earlier type,[10] even though there are snatches of liturgical language contained in it. On the other hand, the longer *berakoth* of Eph. 1:3ff. and 1 Peter 1:3ff. conform more to the later eulogies.

The presence of an introductory *berakah* immediately raises several questions: Why should Paul begin this letter in such a manner? Do the *berakah* and the following words have an epistolary function? Can a paraenetic or didactic purpose be discerned within the passage? Are the personal references of chap. 1:3-11 evidence of the apostle's pastoral concern for the Corinthians? What is the significance of the reference to thanksgiving and petition in v. 11? And, in what ways does the paragraph contribute to our understanding of Pauline prayer? The answers to these and related questions will be attempted throughout and at the conclusion of the exegesis. For the moment we turn to:

---

[6] In both the historical books (e.g., Gen. 14:19f.; 1 Sam. 25:32, 39; 2 Sam. 18:28) and the psalter.

[7] Pss. 41:13; 72:18f.; 89:52; 106:48.

[8] Notably the *Tefillah*.

[9] According to Deichgräber, *Gotteshymnus*, p. 41 (who follows I. Elbogen, *Der jüdische Gottesdienst in seiner geschichtlichen Entwicklung* (Frankfurt, ²1924), p. 5), the rabbis distinguished between the short eulogy and the longer one. The latter were not only greater in length, but frequently repeated the ברוך-formula in the concluding line.

[10] G. Delling, 'Partizipiale Gottesprädikationen in den Briefen des Neuen Testaments', *ST* 17 (1963), pp. 1-59, esp. p. 13, correctly notes that 2 Cor. 1:3f. 'in einer spezielleren Situation des Lobpreisenden begründet ist'. Cf. 1 QH 5:20ff. where the particular ground is linked with more general bases.

2. The Limits of the Paragraph

Immediately following the εὐλογητός-formula Paul adds a threefold description of God as 'the God and Father of our Lord Jesus Christ', 'the Father of mercies' and 'God of all comfort', v. 3. The ground for giving praise is expressed by the clause 'who comforts us', while the purpose of the apostle's receiving this comfort is set forth by the words 'so that we may be able to comfort those who are in any affliction'. The *berakah* itself concludes with the words of v. 4, 'with the comfort with which we ourselves are comforted by God'. In v. 5, by means of a καθώς — οὕτως construction the apostle points out that the suffering experienced relates to τὰ παθήματα τοῦ Χριστοῦ while the comfort received in abundance is διὰ τοῦ Χριστοῦ. The following words indicate that Paul's suffering is related to the Corinthians' suffering on the one hand—for they are κοινωνοί ... τῶν παθημάτων—and their παράκλησις on the other.

The passage, however, does not end with the concluding remarks of v. 7. The words of v. 8, οὐ γὰρ θέλομεν ὑμᾶς ἀγνοεῖν κτλ.., in which Paul mentions his affliction in Asia as a particular instance of the sufferings of Christ, are closely conjoined (γάρ) with the preceding, and in spite of the presence of the new formula ought not to be separated from it.[11] Apparently the Corinthians were not ignorant of the character [12] of the affliction but rather of the terrible effects it had had on Paul. He had considered death to be the outcome of the θλίψις (ἐξαπορηθῆναι ἡμᾶς καὶ τοῦ ζῆν, v. 8; ἐν ἑαυτοῖς τὸ ἀπόκριμα τοῦ θανάτου ἐσχήκαμεν, v. 9); but instead 'the God who raises the dead' delivered him. The apostle anticipated further experiences of the same or a similar type, but he hoped that, with Corinthian co-operation by intercessory prayer, God would again deliver him.

---

[11] It therefore proves to be another exception to Mullins' general rule, *NovT* 7 (1964), p. 49. Sanders' points (*JBL* 81 (1962), pp. 360f. : (1) that v. 8 is a 'formula of injunction' (note Mullins' criticisms, *loc. cit.*, pp. 45ff.); (2) that 'Paul evidently concludes the theme of the eulogiac period in vs. 7'; and (3) that in vv. 8ff. Paul 'proceeds to the opening of the letter via an account of his own sufferings') are extremely doubtful. The only commentator, we have noted, who considers the body of the letter begins with v. 8 is P. Bachmann, *Der zweite Brief des Paulus an die Korinther* (Leipzig, 1/21909), p. 35 : 'so beginnt mit 1, 8, und nicht erst mit 1, 12 der eigentliche Sachinhalt des Briefes'. We do not deny that vv. 8-11 serve as a bridge passage. However, it is best to understand them as part of the introductory period.

[12] See the exegesis below.

Paul's introduction ends [13] with a reference to thanksgiving and petitionary prayer (v. 11), not as a report of two activities in which he was engaged, but in terms of a request for intercessions by the Corinthians, so that thanksgiving would be offered by many to God.

3. Praise for God's Comfort : Vv. 3-4

Εὐλογητός [14] renders the Hebrew ברוך (= 'blessed'), a term used frequently in the Old Testament [15] to introduce words of praise. On a few occasions men are called 'blessed',[16] but the large majority of Old Testament instances refer to Yahweh who has acted in the history of His people. All eight New Testament examples of εὐλογητός (five of which appear in the *corpus Paulinum*) [17] are used of God.[18] As distinct from doxologies ('beschreibenden Lob'),[19] the *berakah* with a following participle, relative clause or causal sentence belongs to Westermann's category of 'berichtenden Lobpreis'.[20]

---

[13] There are no parousia references in 2 Cor. 1:3-11, partly due, no doubt, to the fact that in the passage there is no intercessory prayer for the addressees. Eschatological overtones, however, are not entirely absent; cf. παράκλησις (discussed below), and the words of v. 9, ἐπὶ τῷ θεῷ τῷ ἐγείροντι τοὺς νεκρούς. But no eschatological note assists in determining the limits of the period.

[14] On the subject of blessing in the New Testament see : L. Brun, *Segen und Fluch im Urchristentum* (Oslo, 1932); F. Horst, 'Segen und Segenshandlungen in der Bibel', *EvTh* 7 (1947-1948), pp. 23-37; and 'Segen und Fluch' (II. AT), *RGG*³ 5, cols. 1649-1651; H. W. Beyer, 'εὐλογέω', *TDNT* 2, pp. 754-765; Schenk, *Segen*; and C. Westermann, *Der Segen in der Bibel und im Handeln der Kirche* (München, 1968); cf. Deichgräber, *Gotteshymnus*, pp. 30ff., 40-43, 64-78, and 87.

[15] The verb εὐλογέω occurs over four hundred times.

[16] Deut. 7:14; Ruth 2:20; 1 Sam. 15:13; 25:33; cf. Gen. 14:19.

[17] Rom. 1:25; 9:5; 2 Cor. 1:3; 11:31; Eph. 1:3; cf. Mark 14:61; Luke 1:68; 1 Peter 1:3. The stem εὐλογ—occurs sixty-eight times in the New Testament (εὐλογέω forty-four times and εὐλογία sixteen). To these may be added ἐνευλογέω (twice) and κατευλογέω (once); Schenk, *Segen*, pp. 33f.

[18] When men are called 'blessed' (as in the Gospels) εὐλογημένος is used.

[19] I.e., 'descriptive praise', Westermann, *Praise*, pp. 116ff. We distinguish between doxologies, in which δόξα or synonyms such as τιμή, κράτος, etc. appear, and eulogies (= *berakoth*) in which εὐλογητός occurs. A third category of praise sentence is the short thanksgiving (in German 'Charis-Sprüche'), occasionally found in the Pauline letters, whose basic form is χάρις τῷ θεῷ... (usually followed by the basis of the thanksgiving); Rom. 6:17; 7:25; 1 Cor. 15:57; 2 Cor. 2:14; 8:16; 9:15. At 1 Tim. 1:12 and 2 Tim. 1:3 its function is not unlike that of an introductory thanksgiving.

[20] I.e., 'declarative praise', *Praise*, pp. 81ff., esp. pp. 87-89. Deichgräber, *Gotteshymnus*, pp. 40-42, follows Westermann's distinctions.

Deichgräber is correct when he comments: 'die Eulogie die für das rabbinisch bestimmte Spätjudentum am meisten charakteristische Gebetsformel ist',[21] for there are many examples found in prayers such as the *Ahabah Rabbah*, the *Tefillah*, those at meals, as well as others recorded in the Tractate Berakoth of the Talmud. Because of these many occurrences, scholars have suggested that Paul had christianized a prayer from the synagogue liturgy. And this is no doubt correct. Whether the *berakah* as 'eine Briefeingangseulogie' is '*eine spezifisch christliche Sitte*' appears more difficult to determine.[22]

Does εὐλογητὸς ὁ θεός κτλ. in this context include the notion of thanksgiving (i.e., the outward giving of thanks as an expression of gratitude) as well as of praise? Are εὐχαριστέω and εὐλογέω synonymous? Von der Goltz[23] distinguished between these two terms and considered that the increasing use of the former and its cognates in Paul, due to the influence of Jesus, indicated there was a more personal element in the apostle's giving of thanks than had been known previously in the praises of Judaism.[24] Such a view, however, does not explain Paul's use of εὐλογητὸς ὁ θεός in the present context, and *contra* von der Goltz the notion of gratitude (as well as of praise) is present in this intensely personal paragraph. It is also hard to resist the conclusion that in Old Testament instances of personal deliverance those who praised God were, at the same time and in the act of praising, also expressing their gratitude to Yahweh.[25]

Westermann has drawn attention to the fact that the Old Testament did not have any separate term meaning 'to thank',[26] and he believed this showed there was no such *independent* concept. 'The expression of thanks to God is included in praise, *it is a way of praising*'.[27] However the non-use of terminology does not necessarily mean the

---

[21] *Ibid.*, pp. 41f.

[22] Deichgräber, *ibid.*, p. 64, considers there is no parallel to this New Testament use, for he rejects any appeal to 2 Chron. 2:11. For the opposite view see Dahl, *TZ* 7 (1951), pp. 250f.

[23] *Gebet*, pp. 104-112, 'Lobpreis und Dank'; cf. Wiles, *Function*, pp. 228f.

[24] Eschlimann, *Prière*, pp. 108f., erroneously we consider, makes this same point.

[25] Ledogar, *Acknowledgement*, p. 102, points out that Ps. 116:12, 'What shall I render to the Lord for all his bounty to me?' is an interrogatory way of saying 'I give thanks' (εὐχαριστέω).

[26] So also F. Buhl, 'Über Dankbarkeit im Alten Testament und die sprachlichen Ausdrücke dafür', *Festschrift für W. W. Graf von Baudissin* (Giessen, 1918), pp. 71-82.

[27] Westermann, *Praise*, pp. 25ff., esp. p. 27.

absence of the concept among such people.[28] Westermann and others (e.g., Audet) seemed to think that Hebrew was somehow richer for lacking such a word. Thanksgiving it was considered, an activity engaged in because of personal benefits received, was a descent from the lofty heights of praise. Now although our English word 'to thank' means to express gratitude to (a person for something) received,[29] and is therefore 'a special (and to some extent a man-regarding) expression' of praise, as Moule [30] puts it, Paul's use of εὐχαριστέω, in the thanksgiving periods at least, is broader than this. For in each of the introductory thanksgivings Paul used εὐχαριστέω with reference to graces [31] wrought in the lives of *others* [32] by God. The notion of gratitude is not lost,[33] but on the other hand the element of praise is present.[34] Further, the researches of Robinson and others [35] have shown that verbs such as εὐλογέω and εὐχαριστέω were used synonymously in the first century A.D., and the interchangeability

---

[28] Cf. McFarlane, *Motif*, p. 72; and Barr, *Semantics*, pp. 282ff., for the principle with reference to ἱερός, etc. Audet, in *Studia Evangelica* 1, p. 646, however, considers that in the spontaneous *berakah* admiration and joy predominate, while the notion of 'gratitude... is... secondary'. Still our basic point is not affected, viz. that the motif of gratitude need not be absent when a *berakah* is used.

[29] *The Concise Oxford Dictionary* (Oxford, ⁴1951), p. 1319.

[30] *Birth*, p. 19.

[31] There is often in a thanksgiving a word-play on χάρις or one of its cognates: 1 Cor. 1:4 (see the discussion above); 2 Cor. 1:11; cf. 2 Cor. 4:15; 1 Cor. 10:13.

[32] The only exception is Col. 1:12, εὐχαριστοῦντες τῷ πατρὶ τῷ ἱκανώσαντι ὑμᾶς κτλ. On this unusual reference see pp. 63, 93ff.

[33] Ledogar's concluding remarks about the praise vocabulary in the Hellenistic world are judicious: 'Εὐχαριστεῖν... does mean *to thank*, i.e.: to express outwardly the sentiment of gratitude... This meaning also differentiates it from the rest of the vocabulary of praise. Αἰνεῖν, ὑμνεῖν, εὐλογεῖν and the rest, may often be used to express gratitude, but they do not necessarily *imply* gratitude of themselves as does εὐχαριστεῖν', *Acknowledgement*, p. 98. And with reference to εὐχαριστέω in Paul he adds that he 'usually did have the notion of gratitude in mind' (p. 126, cf. p. 131).

[34] *Ibid.*, p. 131: 'Though... the verb εὐχαριστεῖν does not lose its fundamental significance as an expression of gratitude, this does not mean that it is completely uninfluenced by the rest of the Jewish-Greek praise vocabulary... the verb tends toward the same character of a public act of praise that is common to the more traditional vocabulary (i.e., εὐλογεῖν, etc.)'. According to Ledogar (pp. 131f.), rightly we believe, this is clearly in those passages (e.g., 2 Cor. 4:15; 9:11f.) where εὐχαριστέω and its cognate εὐχαριστία are linked with the glory of God. The corporate aspect of thanksgiving is also clear at 2 Cor. 1:11. Schenk, *Segen*, p. 100, also considers that the distinction between εὐχαριστέω and εὐλογητός ought not to be over-pressed.

[35] J. M. Robinson, in *Apophoreta*, pp. 194-235; also, for example, Audet, *loc. cit.*

of אודכה and ברוך אתה in the Qumran *Hodayoth* [36] seems to support this.

Obviously individual contexts must determine the precise nuance of each term. The notions of either 'thanking', 'being grateful', 'praising' or 'blessing' may predominate in any one instance. What we are concerned to point out is that the use of εὐχαριστέω does *not necessarily exclude* the idea of praise (be it public or private), while the appearance of the εὐλογητός-formula does not rule out any thought of personal gratitude, as the present context of 2 Cor. 1:3ff. makes plain.

Of far greater significance is the fact—unnoticed by almost all scholars [37]—that although either the εὐχαριστέω- or εὐλογητός-formulas could have been used of thanksgiving or praise to God for blessings *either* to others *or* for oneself, Paul, in the introductions of his letters, uses εὐχαριστέω consistently of *Fürdank* for God's work in the lives of the addressees, and εὐλογητός for blessings in which he himself participated. Whether we regard the ἡμᾶς of v. 4 as an epistolary plural or not this point is not affected. Either way the writer himself is included within the scope of God's blessing. The same is true of Eph. 1:3ff.[38] (whether the letter [39] is Pauline or not) and 1 Peter 1:3ff., where the εὐλογητός-formula is used of praise offered to God for blessings bestowed on the writers (and others). Apparently for Paul it seemed more fitting to use the term with a Greek background (εὐχαριστέω) when referring to graces, etc., given to others, particularly Gentiles; while the formula with a Jewish background (εὐλογητός κτλ.) was more apt when he himself [40] came within the circle of blessing.

---

[36] ברוך אתה (אדני) occurs seven times in 1 QH, while אודכה clearly begins ten hymns (cf. Kuhn, *Konkordanz*, pp. 38, 84), and is conjectured to have begun eight others. There does not seem to be any striking difference either in use or meaning; cf. Robinson, *loc. cit.*

[37] Schenk, *Segen*, pp. 99f., touches upon the point, but does not develop it.

[38] Ephesians is a good example of this distinction, for in chap. 1:15ff. the writer uses the εὐχαριστέω-formula for graces given to the readers. Note the contrast: εὐλογητὸς ὁ θεός ... εὐλογήσας ἡμᾶς, v. 3, and ἀκούσας τὴν καθ' ὑμᾶς πίστιν ... οὐ παύομαι εὐχαριστῶν ὑπὲρ ὑμῶν, vv. 15f.

[39] For an examination of the *berakah* and introductory thanksgiving of Eph. 1:3-19, see p. 3, n. 5.

[40] This does not explain why Paul opened his letter with an introductory *berakah* instead of a thanksgiving. See below.

Although the missing copula after εὐλογητός could be an optative or an imperative,[41] in the light of examples from the New Testament and other early Christian literature,[42] we should probably understand the missing word to be the indicative ἐστίν.[43] This accords well with the preference of the LXX translators.[44] So Delling sums up: 'the eulogy does not express a wish but describes a fact: blessed *is* God'.[45] Paul thus proclaims that God is the source of blessing.[46]

In the Old Testament the predicate was almost always[47] in the third person, though in later Judaism, as witnessed by the Qumran texts and the rabbinic literature,[48] the address ברוך אתה אדני in the second person is widely attested. Paul's three predicates ὁ θεὸς καὶ πατὴρ τοῦ κυρίου ἡμῶν Ἰησοῦ Χριστοῦ, etc., which are in apposition, are found in the third person. The distinctively Christian feature appears in the words καὶ πατὴρ τοῦ κυρίου ἡμῶν Ἰησοῦ Χριστοῦ.[49] The person to whom this praise is ascribed is the God of Israel who is now known to Paul as 'the Father of our Lord Jesus Christ'. The last title appears to have been a fixed phrase, known widely throughout

---

[41] I.e., εἴη or ἔστω. The optative, *vis-à-vis* the indicative, is preferred by B. Weiss, *Die paulinischen Briefe* (Leipzig, 1896), p. 236; Winer, *Grammar*, p. 74; Bachmann, *2 Korinther*, p. 25; J. E. Belser, *Der zweite Brief des Apostels Paulus an die Korinther* (Freiburg-i.-Br., 1910), p. 32; A. Plummer, *A Critical and Exegetical Commentary on the Second Epistle of St Paul to the Corinthians* (Edinburgh, 1915), p. 7; and Michel, *Römer*, pp. 223 and 228.

[42] Rom. 1:25; 2 Cor. 11:31; 1 Peter 4:11 (cf. Matt. 6:13, σοῦ ἐστιν ἡ βασιλεία in some MSS); Did. 9:4; 10:5; 1 Clem. 58:2; Apost. Const. 33:7; 34:1; 49:1.

[43] Lietzmann-Kümmel, *Korinther*, p. 196; Buttmann, *Grammar*, p. 137; Robertson, *Grammar*, p. 396; Bl.-D., para. 128(5); Turner, *Syntax*, pp. 296f.; and G. Kittel, *TDNT* 2, p. 248; Beyer, *TDNT* 2, p. 764; W. C. van Unnik, 'Dominus Vobiscum: the background of a liturgical formula', in *New Testament Essays*, ed. A. J. B. Higgins (Manchester, 1959), pp. 270-305, esp. p. 283; Schlier, *Epheser*, p. 43; Moule, *Worship*, p. 79, it signifies 'some element of confident affirmation'; E. J. Bickerman, 'Bénédiction et Prière', *RB* 69 (1962), pp. 523-532, esp. p. 527; Delling, *ST* 17 (1963), pp. 43f., 51; and Schenk, *Segen*, pp. 97, 99. E. Stauffer, *New Testament Theology* (ET, London, 1955), p. 243, refers to it as one of the 'formula-like affirmations about God'.

[44] For full details see Deichgräber, *Gotteshymnus*, pp. 30-32.

[45] *Worship*, p. 67.

[46] Cf. Ledogar, *Acknowledgement*, p. 86.

[47] The only exceptions are Ps. 119:12; 1 Chron. 29:10; and in blessing men: Deut. 28:3, 6.

[48] 1 QS 11:15; 1 QH 5:20; 10:14; 11:27, 29, 32; 16:8, etc., and the *berakoth* of the *Tefillah*.

[49] See the discussion of this phrase at Col. 1:3.

the Pauline churches of the Gentile mission, and even beyond (cf. 1 Peter 1:3).

The two predicates which immediately follow, ὁ πατὴρ τῶν οἰκτιρμῶν, and θεὸς πάσης παρακλήσεως, v. 3, are Semitisms and stand in a chiastic relationship (a b b a)[50] with the preceding (θεός ... πατήρ; πατήρ ... θεός). The former, ὁ πατὴρ τῶν οἰκτιρμῶν, corresponds to the Hebrew אב־הרחמים, which is not found in this form in the Old Testament.[51] However, the Old Testament influence is unmistakable[52] (from such texts as Ps. 103:13, 17; Isa. 51:12 and 66:13), even when we allow for Jeremias' caveats concerning the word πατήρ.[53] To date there has been no exact parallel found in the Qumran texts,[54] although the expression אל־הרחמים appears twice in the Hodayoth[55]—on both occasions as predicates in berakoth. האב הרחמן is used in the Ahabah Rabbah of the synagogue liturgy,[56] immediately before the Shema‘, but it is generally considered that the phrase is a later addition.[57] Nevertheless, the idea that God is merciful was well-known in Judaism,[58] for like Paul it was influenced by the many

---

[50] Noted by Windisch, 2 Korinther, p. 38; Delling, ST 17 (1963), p. 12; and Deichgräber, Gotteshymnus, p. 97.

[51] S. Holm-Nielsen, Hodayot. Psalms from Qumran (Aarhus, 1960), p. 178; Delling, ST 17 (1963), pp. 11f. Cf. Harder, Paulus, p. 65; Deichgräber, Gotteshymnus, pp. 93f.; and Jeremias, Prayers, pp. 26f.

[52] Where Yahweh is frequently said to be merciful (cf. Orphal, Paulusgebet, p. 55; and Harder, Paulus, pp. 44, 65).

[53] Prayers, esp. pp. 24ff.

[54] On the use of אב in the Qumran texts, see p. 94.

[55] 1 QH 10:14 and 11:29.

[56] In Singer, Prayer Book, p. 39.

[57] W. O. E. Oesterley, The Jewish Background of the Christian Liturgy (Oxford, 1925), pp. 48f., considers the words to be a later addition (as did L. Zunz, Die gottesdienstlichen Vorträge der Juden (Frankfurt, ²1892), pp. 382f., cited with approval by Jeremias, Prayers, p. 25); while C. W. Dugmore, The Influence of the Synagogue upon the Divine Office (Oxford, 1944), p. 77, thinks the whole of the Ahabah Rabbah 'was probably not known before the end of the second century A.D.' Cf. O. S. Rankin, 'The Extent of the Influence of the Synagogue Service upon Christian Worship', JJS 1 (1948-1949), pp. 27-32. For all the occurrences of אב־הרחמים see Jeremias, op. cit., p. 27. בעל־הרחמים occurs in b.Pes. 65, and κύριε τοῦ ἐλέους in Wisd. 9:1.

[58] R. Bultmann, 'οἰκτίρω', TDNT 5, pp. 159-161, esp. p. 161, is incorrect when he states that the 'designation (πατὴρ τῶν οἰκτιρμῶν) is a common one in Judaism'. But the notion that God was gracious and merciful (= רחום וחנון) appears frequently in post-canonical Jewish texts: Ecclus. 2:11; 15th Benediction of the Tefillah; 1 QH 16:16; the Hashkibenu; cf. James 5:11; 1 Clem. 60:1, which spring from a Jewish-Christian background.

statements to this effect in the Old Testament.⁵⁹ In the immediate context τῶν οἰκτιρμῶν ⁶⁰ has been understood as a *genitivus qualitativus* (= 'the compassionate Father'),⁶¹ or a *genitivus auctoris*,⁶² i.e., 'the Father from whom all compassion comes'. It is not necessary to choose between the two (even though the parallel expression θεὸς πάσης παρακλήσεως is an example of the latter genitive), since it is unlikely that Paul thought of the Father as being compassionate without showing it in particular acts (note the relevance to the present context). Both ideas ⁶³ are present, i.e., God is the compassionate Father, and He is the One from whom all compassion flows. It is just possible that the phrase was not composed by Paul for the occasion,⁶⁴ but even so it had particular relevance to him as he passed through the terrible θλίψις in Asia.

The third predicate,⁶⁵ θεὸς πάσης παρακλήσεως, v. 3, introduces us to the important motif of 'comfort'.⁶⁶ It is not without reason that 2 Cor. 1 has been called the greatest chapter in the New Testament on comfort, for in vv. 3-7 παρακαλέω and its cognate παράκλησις appear no fewer than ten times.⁶⁷ This word-group had a wealth of meanings in the Greek world of Paul's day, including 'to call someone to oneself', 'to beseech', 'to ask (sometimes in prayer)', 'to exhort', and 'to comfort'. According to Schmitz the last meaning is found on only a few occasions in ordinary Greek usage,⁶⁸ and even in these

---

⁵⁹ E.g., Exod. 34:6; 2 Chron. 30:9; Neh. 9:17, 31; Pss. 86:15; 103:8; 111:4; 145:8; Joel 2:13; Jonah 4:2.

⁶⁰ In both Old and New Testaments the noun (as a Semitism = רַחֲמִים, Bl.-D., para. 142) is used in the plural; cf. Bultmann, *TDNT* 5, pp. 160f.; and Windisch, *2 Korinther*, p. 38.

⁶¹ Meyer, *Corinthians* 2, p. 135; C. F. G. Heinrici, *Der zweite Brief an die Korinther* (Göttingen, ⁷1890), p. 14; F. V. Filson, 'The Second Epistle to the Corinthians', in *The Interpreter's Bible* 10, pp. 263-425, esp. p. 280.

⁶² Windisch, *2 Korinther*, p. 38; Lietzmann-Kümmel, *Korinther*, p. 99; Delling, *loc. cit.*, pp. 12f.

⁶³ Menzies, *2 Corinthians*, p. 5; Belser, *2 Korinther*, p. 33; cf. Plummer, *2 Corinthians*, p. 8.

⁶⁴ So Jeremias, *Prayers*, p. 27.

⁶⁵ Paul cannot be accused of multiplying titles in his addresses to God, as Gentiles and, on occasion, even Jews did (cf. 2 Macc. 1:23-29). Cf. Schneider, *Angelos* 4 (1932), p. 18; Harder, *Paulus*, pp. 66f., 130ff.

⁶⁶ See O. Schmitz-G. Stählin's fine article, 'παρακαλέω', *TDNT* 5, pp. 773-799; cf. A. Grabner-Haider, *Paraklese und Eschatologie bei Paulus* (Münster, 1968), pp. 47f.; and R. C. Tannehill, *Dying and Rising with Christ* (Berlin, 1967), pp. 90-98.

⁶⁷ Παρακαλέω : vv. 4 (three times), and 6; παράκλησις : vv. 3, 4, 5, 6 (twice) and 7.

⁶⁸ *TDNT* 5, pp. 776, 799. Instead the first three uses predominate.

instances the consolation is mostly at the level of exhortation or encouragement to those who sorrow. This is also true of the word-group in the LXX where there is no Hebrew original.[69] On the other hand, the use of παρακαλέω = 'to exhort' is common in the Greek and Hellenistic world, but is almost entirely absent from the translation Greek of the LXX.[70] In the New Testament it serves to denote missionary proclamation and as a kind of formula to introduce pastoral administration.[71] The meaning 'to comfort', 'comfort', 'consolation', though less common in the Greek world and Hellenistic Judaism, is more frequent in the translation Greek of the LXX where it is influenced by the Hebrew Old Testament.[72] Human comfort is spoken of in the Old Testament, where relatives, friends and those more distant are called upon to give it.[73] Ultimately, though, true consolation (παράκλησις ἀληθινή, Isa. 57:18) comes from God, while by comparison all else is vain (ματαία, Isa. 28:29).[74] Comforting is His proper work, for He turns earlier desolation into perfect consolation for individuals (esp. in the Psalter),[75] and the people of God (particularly in Deutero-Isaiah where God's great consoling promise to Israel appears: Isa. 40:1ff.).[76] In the time of salvation which draws near God Himself will console Zion. This comfort reaches man through mediators and

---

[69] *Op. cit.*, pp. 778f. In view of the wealth of meaning παρακαλέω has in 2 Macc. 'it is the more striking that in these portions of the LXX there is never the sense of divine or human consolation found in the LXX as a translation'.

[70] *Op. cit.*, pp. 776ff., 799.

[71] *Op. cit.*, pp. 794f. C. K. Barrett, 'The Holy Spirit in the Fourth Gospel', *JTS* N.S. 1 (1950), pp. 1-15, has suggested that in the early church the application of *paraklesis*, as exhortation, to the preaching arose out of the use of *paraklesis* as comfort. Cf. H. R. Boer, *Pentecost and Missions* (Grand Rapids, 1961), p. 106. For a separate study on the form and function of these παρακαλέω-sentences (with reference to thanksgiving) see Bjerkelund, *Parakalô*, esp. pp. 88ff., where he discusses Schmitz's comments. The omission of both the εὐχαριστέω- and the παρακαλέω-sentences from the translation Greek of the LXX makes clear 'dass die briefliche Funktion dieser Wörter ihren Ursprung nicht in hebräischem, sondern griechischen Sprachgebrauch hat' (p. 90).

[72] The majority of instances translate the Hebrew נחם, but other Hebrew words are originals of παρακαλέω.

[73] Job 2:11; cf. 2 Sam. 10:2. Visits were a customary means by which such consolation was given (Gen. 37:35; Job 42:11); such visits to offer sympathy were conventional in both East and West from earliest times. See Schmitz, *op. cit.*, pp. 788f., 782f. for examples.

[74] Cf. Zech. 10:2; Job 21:34. Apart from Yahweh man is without true comfort.

[75] Pss. 23:4; 71:21; 86:17; 94:19; 119.

[76] Isa. 54:11ff.; 51:3, 12. Cf. Boer, *Pentecost*, p. 106, who follows Barrett, *loc. cit.*

channels such as His word, Wisdom, the prophets, and particularly His Servant.[77] As might be expected God's consolation is an eschatological reality.

Judaism, like the Old Testament, extols God as the true Comforter, בעל נחמות.[78] But Palestinian and Hellenistic Judaism differ as to the means of divine comfort, the latter emphasizing the native hope God has sown in the human race,[79] while the former like the Old Testament accents the mediators of divine comfort. The Messiah, par excellence, mediates God's consolation. Indeed, נחמה in Palestine can be used as a comprehensive term for that eschatological reality, the Messianic salvation.[80] It embraced the whole hope of Israel, denoting in Palestinian Judaism nothing less than a 'resurrection'.[81]

In the New Testament παρακαλέω and its cognates were employed in a non-religious sense, but often the usage was determined in some way by the event of salvation, the coming of the Messiah. Thus the verb can refer to asking for help from Jesus,[82] or to exhortation that is 'in Christ' (Phil. 2:1), or 'by the name of our Lord Jesus Christ' (1 Cor. 1:10). At Rom. 12:1 such an exhortation is distinguished from a mere moral appeal by this reference back to the work of salvation as its presupposition and basis.

In the context of 2 Cor. 1 essentially and finally God is the Comforter. Not only is He called θεὸς πάσης παρακλήσεως,[83] for He continually comforts Paul (ὁ παρακαλῶν [84] ἡμᾶς) [85] 'in every affliction

---

[77] For references see Schmitz, *op. cit.*, p. 790.

[78] B. Ket. 8b; Harder, *Paulus*, p. 88; Schmitz, *op. cit.*, 792.

[79] E.g., Philo in *Praem.* 72.

[80] Str.-B. 2, p. 124: ' "Trost Israels" ist ein zus.fassender Ausdruck, der die Erfüllung der messian. Hoffnung bezeichnet'. For further references which show that 'comfort' is equivalent to the Messianic salvation itself, see pp. 124-126; cited by Tannehill, *Dying*, pp. 91f.

[81] The term παράκλησις is thus very appropriate in the context of 2 Cor. 1.

[82] So the centurion in Matt. 8:5, the elders of the Jews at Luke 7:4, the healed demoniac in Mark 5:18, etc., all ask for help. Schmitz, *op. cit.*, p. 794.

[83] I.e., He is the Source and Supplier of all comfort; Belser, *2 Korinther*, p. 33; Plummer, *2 Corinthians*, p. 9; Delling, *ST* 17 (1963), pp. 12f. On the use of πᾶς in this predicate Deichgräber, *Gotteshymnus*, p. 97, aptly comments: 'nicht eine Totalität im strengeren Sinne (exklusiv) zum Ausdruck bringen will, sondern lediglich etwas unbestimmt die Fülle bezeichnet'.

[84] This use of the participial predicate is also Semitic; Norden, *Agnostos Theos*, pp. 166ff., 201ff., and 380ff.; and for the relevance of recent material (Harder, *Paulus*, pp. 44ff.), especially that from Qumran, see Delling, *ST* 17 (1963), pp. 1ff., and Deichgräber, *Gotteshymnus*, p. 97. In this context ὁ παρακαλῶν expresses the cause for the

actually encountered' (ἐπὶ πάσῃ τῇ θλίψει ἡμῶν, v. 4),[86] but also any strengthening or encouragement experienced is said to derive from Him (ὑπὸ τοῦ θεοῦ, v. 4). Such consolation is intimately bound up with the Messiah (διὰ τοῦ Χριστου, v. 5), as are Paul's sufferings which are part of the Messianic woes (τὰ παθήματα τοῦ [87] Χριστοῦ, v. 5). Although the consoling help for Paul has been a past, and is now a present reality, it is integrally related to the future, for

---

apostle's eulogy to the 'Father of mercies and God of all comfort'; so too J. Calvin, *The Second Epistle of Paul the Apostle to the Corinthians and the Epistles to Timothy, Titus and Philemon* (a new translation and edition, Grand Rapids, 1964), p. 8.

[85] At first sight there seems to be doubt about the exact scope of the plural. Plummer, *2 Corinthians*, p. 9, rightly comments: 'It is unreasonable to suppose that St Paul always uses the 1st pers. plur. of himself in his Apostolic character, and the 1st pers. sing. when he speaks as a private individual'. However, he considers that here ἡμᾶς 'probably includes all missionaries, and perhaps indirectly all sufferers'. Roller, *Formular*, pp. 169-187, esp. p. 186, states: 'Die Beteiligung der Mitabsender ist also hier vollkommen', while others, with varying degrees of conviction, understand ἡμᾶς and the following first person plurals primarily, though not exclusively, of Paul; so Meyer, *Corinthians 2*, p. 136; Heinrici, *2 Korinther*, p. 15; Schmiedel, *Thessalonicher und Korinther*, p. 210; R. V. G. Tasker, *The Second Epistle of Paul to the Corinthians* (London, 1958), p. 41. However, because of the following words, vv. 5-7, and the undoubtedly personal references in vv. 8-11—where the apostle continues to use the first person plural—we agree with those exegetes who understand the reference to Paul alone. Whether a plural is epistolary or not can only be decided on contextual grounds, and here, we consider, the context is decisive; cf. H. L. Goudge, *The Second Epistle to the Corinthians* (London, 1927), p. 2; E.-B. Allo, *Saint Paul. Seconde Épitre aux Corinthiens* (Paris, ²1956), p. 8; Lietzmann-Kümmel, *Korinther*, p. 99; Bruce, *Corinthians*, p. 178.

[86] Although πᾶς with or without the article is used somewhat imprecisely in the New Testament, we agree with Blass-Debrunner, para. 275 (3), and other exegetes that, on contextual grounds, there is a deliberate distinction made in 2 Cor. 1:4 between ἐπὶ πάσῃ τῇ θλίψει ἡμῶν (= 'all tribulation actually encountered') and ἐν πάσῃ θλίψει (= 'in any which may be encountered'); so J. H. Bernard, 'The Second Epistle to the Corinthians', in *The Expositor's Greek Testament* 3, ed. W. Robertson Nicoll (London, 1903), pp. 1-119, esp. p. 38; Plummer, *2 Corinthians*, p. 10; Windisch, *2 Korinther*, p. 38; Robertson, *Grammar*, p. 772; Tasker, *2 Corinthians*, p. 41; and Turner, *Syntax*, p. 200, who, however, does not bring out the real distinction. *Contra* Prümm, *Diakonia Pneumatos* 1, p. 14, who is not sure there is any real difference in meaning.

[87] See esp. W. Michaelis, 'πάσχω', *TDNT* 5, pp. 904-939, esp. pp. 931-933, where this passage (and particularly the meaning of the genitive τοῦ Χριστοῦ) is discussed. Tannehill, *Dying*, p. 91, considers the phrase refers not only to the sufferings which derive from Christ (= genitive of source), and 'not only to the suffering which Paul suffers, but also to the suffering which Christ suffered. In his suffering Paul participates in the suffering and death of Christ'. Cf. Allo, *2 Corinthiens*, p. 9, 'le génitif est de sujet et d'objet tout à la fois'. On apostolic suffering in 2 Corinthians see E. Güttgemanns, *Der leidende Apostel und sein Herr* (Göttingen, 1966).

παράκλησις in this context has links with the consummation of God's saving purposes.[88] The difference between the New Testament writers (including Paul) and those of the Old Testament and Judaism is that in the former God's Messianic consolation is said to have dawned [89] (cf. Luke 2:25), and will finally be consummated. Thus in 2 Cor. 1:3-7 the apostle can refer to παράκλησις in the same prepositional phrase as σωτηρία, v. 6,[90] and in the context of ἐλπίς, v. 7.

The precise means by which Paul's being comforted took place —whether by calming or delivering, or both—is not stated in either the berakah or vv. 5-7. Only in vv. 8ff. does the apostle refer to a specific affliction, and there it is clear that his being delivered is central. At the same time we must not rule out the aspect of calming, so that the comforting possibly took place by words as well as by events. But here in the berakah Paul speaks of the larger fact of God's continual comfort in every trial, and this leads him on to state the purpose of such consolation: εἰς τὸ δύνασθαι ἡμᾶς παρακαλεῖν τοὺς ἐν πάσῃ θλίψει κτλ.[91]

This teleological affirmation draws attention to the notion of mediation already observed in the Old Testament and Palestinian Judaism. The consolation the Corinthians (or indeed any others) are to receive is God's, but it is mediated by His accredited apostle who is qualified to comfort (εἰς τὸ δύνασθαι ἡμᾶς παρακαλεῖν, v. 4) because he is 'der leidende Apostel'. He may not experience exactly the same θλίψεις as the Corinthians, but inasmuch as he has participated in τὰ παθήματα τοῦ Χριστοῦ and ἡ παράκλησις ... διὰ τοῦ Χριστοῦ he is fitted to comfort them in *any* tribulation they may pass through.

The short berakah of 2 Cor. 1:3f. has ended. Although Paul has passed through a severe θλίψις it is the motif of παράκλησις which

---

[88] According to Deichgräber, *Gotteshymnus*, p. 209, such experiences of God's help 'sind ja zumeist als Zeichen verstanden, in denen sich die Kräfte des neuen Äons bezeugen'.

[89] Barrett, *loc. cit.*, p. 13; Schmitz, *TDNT* 5, p. 798; Boer, *Pentecost*, p. 106; Tannehill, *Dying*, pp. 91f.

[90] Possibly σωτηρία is epexegetical of παράκλησις. Certainly it is not to be understood with Windisch, *2 Korinther*, p. 43, in a weakened sense.

[91] Εἰς τὸ δύνασθαι κτλ. ought to be understood as the purpose of Paul's sufferings, and not simply the result of them, though of course the latter notion is included; cf. Belser, *2 Korinther*, p. 34, 'nicht einfach = ὥστε, sondern den Zweck und Erfolg der trostung...'; Bernard, *2 Corinthians*, p. 38; Plummer, *2 Corinthians*, p. 10; Prümm, *Diakonia Pneumatos* 1, pp. 13f.; Lietzmann-Kümmel, *Korinther*, p. 196.

dominates his prayer of praise. The predicates by which God is described, especially θεὸς πάσης παρακλήσεως, are particularly appropriate to Paul's situation,[92] and set the tone, not only for the following words in the *berakah* and vv. 5-7, but also for chaps. 1-9 of the letter.

4. *Relationship of the* Berakah *to Vv. 5-7*

In v. 5,[93] through a ὅτι-clause Paul expands the ideas which conclude his *berakah*. Any θλίψις, v. 4, which Paul experiences, is seen as part of τὰ παθήματα τοῦ Χριστοῦ, and through a καθώς ... οὕτως construction these Messianic woes are linked with God's comfort which is mediated through His Messiah. The dual structure is continued in v. 6 (εἴτε ... εἴτε) where Paul develops the thought of v. 4 concerning the relation of the apostle to the Corinthian community. In this it is declared that the παράκλησις of the addressees derives first from the apostle's affliction and then from the comfort which he himself receives. In v. 7 these twin themes of comfort and affliction are continued, and in the subordinate clause (εἰδότες ὅτι κτλ.) the Corinthians are said to be (by means of the correlatives ὡς ... οὕτως) κοινωνοί of the sufferings and the comfort. Remarkably these sufferings (τῶν παθημάτων, v. 7; τῶν αὐτῶν παθημάτων, v. 6) are τὰ παθήματα τοῦ Χριστοῦ in which both the Corinthians and Paul share. They are not only sufferings which derive from Christ but are all of a part with the sufferings which Christ endured. There is probably the further notion of Christ continuing to suffer in His members, not least in Paul himself (cf. Phil. 3:10; Col. 1:24; and Acts 9:4).

Some commentators have asked how it is that the Corinthians could have experienced the same sufferings as Paul (v. 6), since they did not encounter any such affliction in Asia. But this is to miss the point, for Paul states that the addressees participate in the same Messianic woes,[94] but not in the same θλίψις. Paul suffers (καὶ ἡμεῖς πάσχομεν, v. 6) with them, but not in the same way. Indeed, the

---

[92] Paul has selected the predicates which best corresponded—he had no doubt many to choose from—with his own circumstances and those motifs he wished to set before the addressees. A good example of this is the wish-prayer of Rom. 15:5, where having noted that what was written formerly in the Scriptures (esp. Ps. 69:9) was for our ὑπομονή and παράκλησις, he addresses his request to ὁ θεὸς τῆς ὑπομονῆς καὶ τῆς παρακλήσεως.

[93] Cf. Tannehill, *Dying*, pp. 90ff.

[94] Schmitz, *TDNT* 5, p. 931.

careful distinction made in v. 4 (ἐπὶ πάσῃ τῇ θλίψει ἡμῶν ... ἐν πάσῃ θλίψει),[95] and the use of θλιβόμεθα with reference to Paul (vis-à-vis the Corinthians) in v. 6 indicates that their afflictions were, at that precise moment, different. The nature of the Corinthians' afflictions is not spelled out, but whatever they were they could be termed τὰ παθήματα τοῦ Χριστοῦ.

5. *The* Berakah *and Paul's Affliction in Asia*

Paul's ascription of praise in vv. 3f. concerns the 'Father of mercies and God of all comfort' who has continually comforted him in each θλίψις actually experienced. The purpose of such consolation is that he might be a mediator of God's παράκλησις to others (and particularly to the Corinthians) in their afflictions. In v. 8, by means of a 'Disclosure form' [96] (οὐ γὰρ θέλομεν ὑμᾶς ἀγνοεῖν κτλ.), Paul informs his addressees, not of the facts of his affliction in Asia,[97] but of its excruciating effects upon him. In this specific instance from his own recent experience of great trial and comfort Paul speaks of death and life [98] (vv. 9f.) rather than through the terms θλίψις, παθήματα and παράκλησις. It is probably that the new terminology is brought about by the extremity of the experience for Paul despaired of coming through it alive.

His θλίψις probably occurred after writing 1 Corinthians (otherwise it would have been mentioned in that epistle) [99] and since it happened 'in Asia' it was prior to his crossing from Troas to Macedonia (2 Cor. 2:12f.; 7:5). The general designation 'in Asia' suggests it was unnecessary for Paul to be precise about the locality, as this was already known to the Corinthians. The experience was a burden too heavy to be borne (καθ' ὑπερβολὴν ὑπὲρ δύναμιν ἐβαρήθημεν, v. 8), and was

---

[95] See above.

[96] Cf. Mullins, *NovT* 7 (1964), p. 48.

[97] The vagueness of the language suggests the Corinthians knew the facts of the affliction, while the following words indicate they did not realize its gravity; so Schmiedel, *Thessalonicher und Korinther*, p. 211; Bernard, *2 Corinthians*, p. 40; Menzies, *2 Corinthians*, p. 7; Plummer, *2 Corinthians*, pp. 15f.; R. H. Strachan, *The Second Epistle of Paul to the Corinthians* (London, 1935), p. 51; Filson, *2 Corinthians*, pp. 282f.; and Hughes, *2 Corinthians*, p. 16.

[98] The term 'resurrection' is not actually used; but see Tannehill, *Dying*, pp. 91ff.

[99] Some, e.g., A. Schlatter, *Paulus der Bote Jesu* (Stuttgart, ⁴1969), pp. 466f., identify the θλίψις in Asia with Paul's fighting beasts in Ephesus. See below.

so severe that Paul could see no possibility of survival (ἐξαπορηθῆναι [100] ἡμᾶς καὶ τοῦ ζῆν, v. 8). Indeed he had already received a death-sentence (τὸ ἀπόκριμα [101] τοῦ θανάτου, v. 9) and when he was snatched from the jaws of death he did not refer to it as from illness or violence but ἐκ τηλικούτων θανάτων, v. 10. Only the 'God who raises the dead' could have wrought such a miracle.

It is difficult to determine the precise character of this affliction in Asia.[102] Of the many conjectures two have greater claim than others : (1) that it was some severe persecution or deadly danger from without; or (2) that it was a severe malady that was recurrent or its effects were chronic. Fortunately a knowledge of its exact nature is not essential [103] for our understanding of Paul's *berakah*, his statements about prayer and thanksgiving in v. 11, or concerning the function of the whole period, i.e., vv. 3-11.

More significant is the point that although v. 8 alludes to an isolated event in the past, the following verses point to possible recurrences of the same or a similar θλίψις in the future. That it was an ever-present reality is suggested by : the two-fold ῥύσεται [104] (after ἐρρύσατο),

---

[100] The unusual ἐξαπορέομαι is found in the Greek Bible outside this passage only at Ps. 88:15 (LXX 87:16) and 2 Cor. 4:8. It may be significant that at the time of writing 2 Corinthians Paul can now state, in the context of apostolic suffering, ἀπορούμενοι ἀλλ' οὐκ ἐξαπορούμενοι (= 'bewildered, we are never at our wits' end', NEB). When passing through the θλίψις in Asia he possibly thought he was treading the path of the psalmist who offered a 'lament, unrelieved by a single ray of comfort or hope', A. Weiser, *The Psalms* (ET, London, 1962), p. 586.

[101] Deissmann, *Studies*, p. 257, states of this word, found as a technical term in the inscriptions, that 'an official decision is meant', e.g., the decisions of the Emperor Claudius; cf. T. Nägeli, *Der Wortschatz des Apostels Paulus* (Göttingen, 1905), p. 30; AG, p. 92. MM, p. 64, comment : 'Paul may be taken as meaning that he had made his distressed appeal to God, and kept in his own heart's archives the answer—"ἀποθάνη · τὸ δὲ ἀποθανεῖν κέρδος"', as we might reconstruct it'. Cf. C. J. Hemer, 'A Note on 2 Corinthians 1:9', *TynB* 23 (1972), pp. 103-107, who argues, *contra* Deissmann, that the term is not a judicial metaphor.

[102] For a careful examination of the evidence and proposed identifications of the θλίψις see M. J. Harris, *The Interpretation of 2 Corinthians 5:1-10, and Its Place in Pauline Eschatology* (unpublished Ph.D. thesis, University of Manchester, 1970), pp. 408-421. The language does suggest some terrible danger from without, but Harris, following Allo, Dodd and others, considers the most likely solution to be a reference to a severe malady and its effects.

[103] Bruce, *Corinthians*, p. 179, considers : 'If it was some external danger, the task of identifying it calls for speculation beyond the exegete's province'.

[104] Zuntz, *Text*, p. 197, would bracket the first καὶ ῥύσεται. But the point concerning Paul's expectation of future θλίψεις is not affected.

v. 10; the plural τηλικούτων θανάτων,[105] v. 10; the request for intercession in v. 11; and possibly the tense of ἐσχήκαμεν,[106] v. 9. Throughout this past experience Paul had learnt to repose his confidence (πεποιθότες ὦμεν) in the 'God who raises the dead' (ἐπὶ τῷ θεῷ τῷ ἐγείροντι [107] τοὺς νεκρούς, v. 9). This final phrase, an echo of the second benediction of the *Tefillah* (אתה מתים מחיה),[108] together with the periphrastic perfect tense of πείθω, suggests that this mighty deliverance was due, in some measure, to Paul's petitions to God.[109] If so, then we have a further point of contact with the *berakah* of vv. 3f. The predicates in both cases are directly linked with God's activity experienced in the past, and anticipated in the future. Further, if Tannehill's contention, that the death-resurrection and suffering (affliction)-comfort motifs are interlocking, be correct,[110] then these predicates (θεὸς πάσης παρακλήσεως, v. 3; τῷ θεῷ τῷ ἐγείροντι τοὺς νεκρούς, v. 9) are not simply parallel, but overlap in meaning. Paul's deliverance in Asia was a specific instance of God's comforting him ἐπὶ πάσῃ τῇ θλίψει ἡμῶν, v. 4.

6. *Intercession and Thanksgiving in V. 11*

The conclusion to this passage is remarkable. Formally, the marks of an introductory thanksgiving are in evidence.[111] Usually the principal εὐχαριστέω-clause forms the beginning of the thanksgiving

---

[105] According to Zuntz, *ibid.*, p. 104, 'The plural ("out of such tremendous, mortal dangers") bears the stamp of genuine Pauline diction; cf. *ib.* xi. 23 and vi. 4ff.; it could never have come about either by a scribe's slip or by intentional alteration. The singular clearly arose from the pedantic idea that no one could risk more than one death'.

[106] Scholars are divided as to whether ἐσχήκαμεν is to be given the full force of the perfect tense (e.g., Allo and others), or with Moulton it is to be understood as one of the 'genuinely aoristic perfects'; see Hughes' discussion, *2 Corinthians*, p. 19.

[107] Frequently the participle used with ἐγείρω is an aorist, and thus 'ganz spezifisch auf das Heilsgeschehen in Christus bezogen', Delling, *ST* 17 (1963), p. 32; so Rom. 4:24; 8:11; 2 Cor. 4:14; Gal. 1:1; Col. 2:12; cf. 1 Peter 1:21.

[108] Str.-B. 3, p. 212; cf. E. Käsemann, *Perspectives on Paul* (ET, London, 1971), p. 90.

[109] Orphal, *Paulusgebet*, p. 89, calls such a request a 'Grabgebet'.

[110] *Dying*, pp. 91-93.

[111] The principal verb εὐχαριστέω appears, as do the pronominal object phrase (ὑπὲρ ἡμῶν), a temporal participial clause (συνυπουργούντων καὶ ὑμῶν) and an adverbial phrase denoting intercessory prayer (τῇ δεήσει), as well as the equivalent of a causal adverbial phrase (τὸ εἰς ἡμᾶς χάρισμα). See Schubert's discussion, *Form*, pp. 46-50; cf. Sanders, *JBL* 81 (1962), pp. 360f.; and Wiles, *Prayers*, pp. 271-276.

period and is later followed by a final clause. But here the εὐχαριστέω-clause concludes the period, and εὐχαριστηθῇ, a rare passive instead of an active, is the verb of the final clause. Instead of Paul being the one who gives thanks,[112] here it is the Corinthians (the logical subject of εὐχαριστηθῇ). Usually it is the addressees who are referred to in the pronominal object phrase; but here it is Paul (ὑπὲρ ἡμῶν).[113] Δέησις is used again of intercessory prayer, but this time it is the addressees who intercede for the writer, and not *vice versa*. In other examples of the first category of thanksgiving period the verbs of thanksgiving and petitionary prayer describe an activity Paul has been engaged in prior to writing the letter and which he continues up to the time of its dictation. At 2 Cor. 1:11 these particular actions of the *addressees* will take place after their reception of the letter.

Thus we note several structural elements of a thanksgiving period, only in reverse. Schubert refers to v. 11 as a 'strangely consistent structural inversion' of an introductory thanksgiving, inserted because Paul 'could not refrain from bringing the εὐχαριστῶ-clause into the proemium of II Corinthians'.[114]

V. 11 is a request of the apostle for intercessory prayer on his behalf by the Corinthians, and thus it parallels similar appeals in Rom. 15:30-32; Eph. 6:19; Phil. 1:19; Col. 4:3; 1 Thess. 5:25; 2 Thess. 3:1f.; and Phm. 22. The paraenetic function of Paul's prayers of thanksgiving and petition has already been noted, and this purpose is not absent from the present passage. However, we prefer to call this a request or an appeal for petition rather than an explicit example of paraenesis.[115] In some of the parallel passages cited above the appeal for intercessory prayer has sprung directly out of a paraenetic injunction,[116] and although it was closely linked with the latter, it was nevertheless distinct. This seems to suggest that although the churches of Paul's mission had a responsibility to intercede for others, they had a particular obligation (though Paul does not speak in terms

---

[112] Εὐχαριστέω, however, is still used of *Fürdank*; see above.

[113] The reference is still singular, i.e., to Paul alone; cf. Nielen, *Gebet*, p. 151, and note the discussion above.

[114] *Form*, p. 50.

[115] The injunctions to watch and pray usually occur in the latter half of the paraenesis; cf. Selwyn, *1 Peter*, pp. 365ff.; Davies, *Paul*, pp. 126f.; and G. B. Caird, *The Apostolic Age* (London, 1955), p. 111.

[116] Eph. 6:19 (cf. v. 18); Col. 4:3 (cf. v. 2); 1 Thess. 5:25 (cf. v. 17).

of obligations) to pray for the ministry of the one who had brought the gospel to them.

In v. 10, on the basis of his having been delivered ἐκ τηλικούτων θανάτων, Paul states that God will deliver him again, or at least he has set his hope on the One 'who raises the dead' καὶ ἔτι ῥύσεται. The addressees are encouraged to help in prayer. Συνυπουργούντων καὶ ὑμῶν, a genitive absolute construction, is loosely linked with καὶ ἔτι ῥύσεται,[117] rather than ἐρρύσατο. It is probably temporal (= 'while you help'),[118] rather than conditional (= 'provided you help') and refers to their assistance to Paul [119] in prayer. Τῇ δεήσει is an instrumental dative indicating the way in which the Corinthians will help, while δέησις has its customary meaning in the thanksgiving periods of petitionary prayer [120] for others (ὑπὲρ ἡμῶν = 'for Paul'), i.e., intercession. It is not stated explicitly to whom such prayer is directed, but from the nature of Paul's θλίψις and the use of the relative pronouns (ὅς ... εἰς ὅν) we may be safe in assuming it is τῷ θεῷ τῷ ἐγείροντι τοὺς νεκρούς, v. 9.

The latter half of v. 11 is difficult to unravel, as it is overloaded with several awkward adverbial phrases.[121] Fortunately the general sense is clear.[122] The basis of thanksgiving by the Corinthians for Paul

---

[117] Belser, *2 Korinther*, p. 41: 'das *Partic. Praesens* συνυπουργούντων teilt den futurischen Charakter des Hauptsatzes: Gott wird mich retten'; also Wendland, *Korinther*, p. 145.

[118] So Plummer, *2 Corinthians*, p. 20; *contra* Allo, *2 Corinthiens*, p. 13, 'pourvu que'; and Wiles, *Prayers*, p. 273.

[119] Meyer, *Corinthians* 2, p. 144; Heinrici, *2 Korinther*, p. 23; Bernard, *2 Corinthians*, p. 41; Windisch, *2 Korinther*, p. 49. This is better on the basis of the context, and the parallel passages (e.g., συναγωνίσασθαί μοι, Rom. 15:30), than understanding the Corinthians as helping God (Schlatter, *Paulus*, p. 468) or one another.

[120] *Contra* Lietzmann-Kümmel, *Korinther*, p. 197; and Wendland, *Korinther*, p. 145, 'sie wird durch ihre Danksagung mithelfen an der zukünftigen Rettung des Paulus'.

[121] Windisch, *2 Korinther*, p. 49, draws attention to a 'gewisse Symmetrie... dem ἐκ πολλῶν προσώπων entspricht διὰ πολλῶν, dem εἰς ἡμᾶς das ὑπὲρ ἡμῶν, vielleicht ist auch in χάρισμα ... εὐχαριστηθῇ ein Wortspiel beabsichtigt'.

[122] Ἵνα introduces a consecutive clause, i.e., that thanksgiving will be offered by many for God's χάρισμα to Paul. The unusual construction τὸ εἰς ἡμᾶς χάρισμα ... εὐχαριστηθῇ is not the passive rendering of εὐχαριστέω τι, as most (influenced by Lietzmann, *op. cit.*, p. 101) suppose, but of the ordinary active εὐχαριστέω ἐπί τινι (note Schubert's detailed discussion, *Form*, pp. 46-50). Two parallels to this construction appear in close proximity in Justin's Apology (65:5 and 66:2). The second passage introduces the logical subject through διά with the genitive, δἰ εὐχῆς λόγου τοῦ παρ' αὐτοῦ, as does Paul, διὰ πολλῶν (which is equivalent to ἐκ πολλῶν προσώπων). So Schubert, *Form*, p. 49, and some other commentators. But Plummer, *2 Corinthians*, pp. 21f.,

(note the repeated and emphatic ὑπὲρ ἡμῶν, v. 11) is God's gracious gift (χάρισμα) [123] to him. In this context this can only refer to the blessing of deliverance [124] from future danger. As such it will be in answer to the Corinthians' intercession. If many intercede, and see their prayers answered as Paul implies, then many will have cause to give thanks. Here thanksgiving is the end result [125] of the Corinthians' petitions and God's answer. But later in the same canonical letter Paul will tell the Corinthians that the increase of thanksgiving by many (διὰ τῶν πλειόνων τὴν εὐχαριστίαν, 4:15) increases εἰς τὴν δοξαν τόῦ θεοῦ.[126]

The thanksgiving envisaged will be *corporate* [127] as the Corinthians unitedly thank God for the answer to their petitions. Here the notions of thanksgiving and praise coalesce, but as noted above Paul selects the word with a Greek background, εὐχαριστέω, for the *Fürdank* of the Corinthians, while the synonym εὐλογητός, from a Jewish background, is reserved for praise to God for blessing in which Paul participates. As δέησις could connote petition either for oneself or for another (= 'intercession'), but is used in the thanksgiving periods

---

taking πρόσωπον in its original sense of 'face, countenance', suggests the expression points to 'many upturned faces, lighted up with thankfulness, as praises for this preservation rise up from their lips'. Others, e.g., Allo, *2 Corinthiens*, pp. 13f., and Tasker, *2 Corinthians*, p. 44, have followed this suggestion; *per contra* Hughes, *2 Corinthians*, pp. 23f.

[123] Akin to εὐχαριστέω.

[124] Most exegetes (and authors of monographs, e.g., Wetter, *Charis*, p. 27; and Wobbe, *Charis*, pp. 74, 91) have noted this. Some of them, linking συνυπουργούντων καὶ ὑμῶν κτλ. with v. 10a, ἐρρύσατο ἡμᾶς, consider that the thanksgiving is to be offered for Paul's *past* deliverance. Although our preference is to understand συνυπουργούντων κτλ. as joined to v. 11b, and therefore referring to any future deliverance, the point of the context is that Paul's previous escape from death's clutches was now an incentive for 'redoubled prayer' for Paul. As a result thanksgiving to God would increase for *any further blessing* given in answer to those petitions; cf. Bruce, *Corinthians*, p. 179; and Boobyer, "*Thanksgiving*", pp. 2, 80.

[125] It is interesting that the chief reason for Paul's request is not that he should be spared to preach the gospel, but that thanksgiving may rise to God from many; cf. Boobyer, *ibid.*, and Eschlimann, *Prière*, p. 97.

[126] Boobyer, *ibid.*, p. 80, considers that although there is no mention of God's glory at 2 Cor. 1:11, from a comparison with chaps. 4:15 and 9:11f., it can be seen it was not far from his mind. It does appear that chap. 1:11 prepares for the references which follow, though we do not agree with Boobyer's quasi-material understanding of δόξα that enables him to state : 'The thanksgiving of God's children gives Him greater power'.

[127] Cf. Ledogar, *Acknowledgement*, p. 132, and the discussion above about thanksgiving being 'public'.

almost exclusively with the latter connotation, so εὐχαριστέω [128] is applied to thanksgiving for a grace (χάρισμα) another has received —in this instance, Paul. And thus by being delivered Paul will be able to carry on his apostolic ministry to both the Corinthians and others.

The paragraph which Paul's *berakah* introduces has ended. It is the most personal of all Paul's introductions to his letters because in it is contained a heart-rending description of the excruciating effects of the θλίψις in Asia, and of God's wonderful deliverance from it. The short *berakah* of vv. 3 and 4, and the appeal for intercession with its resulting thanksgiving of v. 11 also show this individual emphasis. But a recognition of this thrust ought not to blind us to the fact that the passage has an epistolary, as well as didactic and hortatory function. 2 Cor 1:3-11 introduces a letter in which Paul's apostleship and his relations with the addressees had been in question. And the introductory paragraph prepares the way for him to deal with these issues.

7. *Function of the Paragraph (1:3-11)*

a. *Epistolary*

It is important to observe that many of the terms occurring in this very personal introduction reappear, sometimes with slightly different nuances, in the *first nine chapters* of the letter: so words used of Paul's suffering and affliction recur (θλίβω : 4:8; 7:5; θλίψις : 2:4; 4:17; 6:4; 7:4; cf. 8:2, 13; βαρέω : 5:4; and the rare ἐξαπορέομαι : 4:8), as do those which speak of comfort (παράκλησις : 7:4, 7, 13; 8:4; cf. 8:17; παρακαλέω : 2:7; 5:20; 7:6 (twice), 7, 13; cf. 2:8; 6:1; 8:6; 9:5; 10:1; 12:8; 13:11). The themes of death and life reappear in different contexts (θάνατος : 2:16 (twice); 3:7; 4:11, 12; 7:10 (note the opposites : ζωή, πνεῦμα, σωτηρία); νέκρωσις : 4:10; ἀποθνῄσκω : 5:15 (four times); 6:9 (and the opposites : ζάω and ἐγείρω)), while the notions of abundance (περισσεύω : 3:9; 4:15; 8:2, 7 (twice); 9:8 (twice); 9:12), participation (κοινωνός : 8:23; κοινωνία : 6:14; and with a particular reference to the collection at 8:4 and 9:13) and thanksgiving (χάρις : 2:14;[129] εὐχαριστία : 4:15; 9:11, 12) are found

---

[128] Héring, *2 Corinthians*, p. 6, in order to obviate some of the difficulties of v. 11b, takes εὐχαριστέω as referring to 'request' as well as 'thanksgiving'.

[129] Other uses of χάρις occur at chaps. 4:15; 6:1; 8:1, 4, 6, 7, 9, 16, 19; 9:8, 14, 15.

in chaps. 1-9. To suggest that the language and stylistic features of the introductory period are similar to the rest of 2 Cor. 1-9 is not inconsistent with the evidence.

But not only do the same terms appear in these nine chapters. Important themes, using different words are taken up and expounded in the letter. The motif of consolation is an important one in 2 Cor. 1-9. Apostolic suffering for the community is described in chap. 1:3-7 under the terms πάθημα (θλίψις) and παράκλησις, while at chap. 4:10-12, the same issue is treated under the θάνατος-ζωή rubric (cf. 7:3). Further, in another important passage about apostolic suffering (6:4ff.), although θλίψις and several synonyms occur, παθήμα(-τα Χριστοῦ) does not appear. But this does not mean that his afflictions are not related to the sufferings of Christ (cf. 1:5f.). Chap. 5:1-10 has been regarded as a 'watershed' in Paul's eschatology, and the whole section chaps. 4:16-5:10 shows the influence of Paul's θλίψις in Asia.[130]

Several scholars have pointed out that (like the introductory period) 2 Corinthians is the most personal of Paul's letters,[131] and this seems correct. But one cannot separate Paul the man from Paul the apostle. 2 Corinthians is an apostolic writing [132] in which the apostolic ministry of Paul himself is a central theme. The apologetic character of the letter appears in this introduction, in the personal details of vv. 5-7 and 8-10, rather than in the *berakah* (vv. 3f.), or the request for intercession (v. 11). Paul is a true apostle because he suffers, participating in the sufferings of the Christ (1:5) as do the Corinthians (1:7, cf. vv. 6 and 5). He has not only received God's eschatological παράκλησις (διὰ τοῦ Χριστοῦ, 1:5), but by virtue of his suffering and comfort received can also mediate the divine consolation (life or salvation) to others. He has passed through a terrible experience (1:8-11) in the prosecution of his apostolic task. Thus, he is deserving of sympathy rather than censure. In chaps. 3:1-6:10 the greatness of the apostolic office comes into view.

But in the different tone of chaps. 10-13 Paul prepares for his visit

---

[130] See Harris, *Interpretation*. Per contra P. Hoffmann, *Die Toten in Christus* (Münster, ²1969), p. 328 : 'Gegen eine Überbewertung der Stelle in ihrem Einfluss auf 2 Kor 5 kann mit recht darauf verweisen werden'.

[131] E.g., E. Dinkler, 'Korintherbriefe', in *RGG*³ 4, cols., 17-24 esp. col. 21; and F. F. Bruce, *New Testament History* (London, 1969), p. 316, 'in the warmth of his emotion (*sc.*, his joy at Titus' news) he lays bare his heart more than anywhere else in his writings'.

[132] Cf. Dinkler, *loc. cit.*, col. 21.

to Corinth, confronting his adversaries with strong words, as well as the community which tolerates them.

Although the introductory period prefigures several important themes of the letter, as well as reflecting the tone and language of chaps. 1-9, it does not throw any light on the letter's unity.[133] All that the evidence will permit us to say is that the introductory *berakah* passage prefigures themes and ideas running through the remainder of chaps. 1-9. The problem of the last four chapters cannot be answered by reference to our introductory period.

b. *Didactic*

The didactic function of the passage is most clearly set forth in the purpose clause of v. 4, εἰς τὸ δύνασθαι ἡμᾶς παρακαλεῖν κτλ., and the elaboration of the twin themes παθήματα and παράκλησις with reference to the apostle on the one hand and the Corinthians on the other, in the ὅτι-clause of v. 5 and the words which follow. The Corinthians have not only been called into κοινωνία τοῦ υἱοῦ αὐτοῦ Ἰησοῦ Χριστοῦ—as the thanksgiving period in the first letter (1 Cor. 1:9) states—but they are also κοινωνοί with Paul in suffering and consolation (1:7). Knowing that they suffer together and that Paul passes through θλίψεις for their παράκλησις and σωτηρία they ought to realize that he possesses the marks of a true apostle.

c. *Hortatory*

In a strict sense a general paraenetic function is not present in 2 Cor. 1:3-11, but, as has been noted above, v. 11 constitutes an appeal by the apostle for the help of the Corinthians in intercessory prayer. If he is to pass through another such terrible experience then they can be identified with him in this petitionary activity. And as the God who raises the dead answers their prayers so the resulting corporate thanksgiving will redound to His glory (cf. 4:15).

At the conclusion of several letters in the *corpus Paulinum* similar appeals spring directly out of a piece of paraenesis that deals with

---

[133] The tone, language and themes of chap. 1:3-11 do not point forward to chaps. 10-13. These final chapters might have been appended by the apostle later. But such a statement would need to be substantiated on other grounds, for the epistolary function of our passage can neither affirm nor deny it. Further, it is beyond the scope of this work to enter into the question of chaps. 6:14-7:1, and its place in the epistle, or the relationship of chap. 8 to chap 9.

petitionary prayer. In the present context, however, the request of the apostle arises out of a vivid description of his θλίψις in Asia.

Then why did Paul begin this letter with a *berakah* instead of a thanksgiving? The following suggestions may be relevant: first, the apostle had already given thanks to God for the Corinthian community's graces (1 Cor. 1:4-9), and unlike the Thessalonians (who are praised in a *second* letter) they do not seem to have progressed, to any marked degree, in faith, love and so on.[134] Secondly, the deeply personal experience of the affliction in Asia, God's deliverance and His continual comfort had had a profound effect on Paul. It was quite natural that Paul as a converted Jew should mention this by means of an Old Testament *berakah* in his introduction to the Corinthian community. Thirdly, the *berakah* and the words which follow were well suited as an introduction to this intensely personal letter, for in it Paul could introduce themes and ideas to be elaborated later on. By opening his heart to them he shows that the terrible experience led to their being recipients of God's eschatological παράκλησις by means of his suffering and comfort.

8. *Praise, Petition and Thanksgiving*

The Old Testament and Jewish influence on Paul's *berakah* is obvious, extending to syntax, style and language as well as to concepts and ideas. At the same time Paul prays as a Christian [135] so that an addition, καὶ πατὴρ τοῦ κυρίου ἡμῶν ᾽Ιησοῦ Χριστοῦ (v. 3), and a different perspective on God's παράκλησις, which is mediated διὰ τοῦ Χριστοῦ (v. 5), are significant.

Paul's prayers of thanksgiving and petition in other thanksgiving periods, while bound up with the gospel, Christian graces, the parousia and maturity in Christ, were nevertheless related to the known needs of the readers. Here it is the *circumstances of the apostle*,[136] God's gracious consolation given in deep distress and the resulting blessing to others that are at the heart of the *berakah*.

---

[134] This is the basic reason for Paul's thanksgiving in 2 Thess. 1:3ff.; see above, pp. 171ff.

[135] This is developed at length by Harder, *Paulus*, pp. 163ff.

[136] Ideas such as gospel, the parousia, the Christian triad, patience, etc., found in the thanksgiving periods are absent from this passage.

In other introductory periods a close bond of fellowship between converts and apostle in thanksgiving and petition appears, as Paul offers thanks and intercedes for his readers. At 2 Cor. 1:11 that bond [137] exists, as *the Corinthians*, having Paul's needs clearly presented to them, pray for his deliverance. As their requests are granted and Paul is enabled to carry on his apostolic labours so thanksgiving will be offered. Thus the point noted in other sections of this work, viz., that prayer was an important means by which Paul's ministry was fulfilled, is true in the present context where others pray for him. Although the Corinthians' intercessions will help effect a future deliverance for him, it is to the result of corporate thanksgiving by many and therefore the glory of God that he ultimately looks.[138]

---

[137] Cf. E. R. Bernard, 'Prayer', in *A Dictionary of the Bible*, ed. J. Hastings (New York, 1902), pp. 38-45; Orphal, *Paulusgebet*, p. 133.

[138] With reference to chap. 4:15 Windisch, *2 Korinther*, p. 151, comments: 'der letzte Zweck dieser Tätigkeit, die Verherrlichung Gottes (*sc.* ist)'.

CHAPTER NINE

CONCLUSIONS

It is time to draw together the threads of our study and to summarize the conclusions. The purpose of this research, primarily an exegetical study, has been two-fold : (1) to determine the place, importance and function of the introductory thanksgiving *passages* within the Pauline letters they introduce; and (2) to examine the *prayers* found within these passages, particularly the thanksgivings and intercessions, with the aim of assessing their significance, frequency, the grounds for thanksgiving, the objects of Paul's intercessions, etc.

1. *Varied Nature of the Letters*

If Ephesians be included within the count,[1] then the introductory periods of nine letters from the hand of the apostle Paul have been examined. These nine are different from one another, and the diversity is reflected in the introductory thanksgivings. Thus Philemon is a private letter addressed to a colleague of Paul. The thanksgiving period is short, relatively simple in form, and more closely related to the introductory thanksgivings of ancient private letters, as evidenced in the papyri, than other periods in the *corpus Paulinum*. 1 and 2 Thessalonians, 1 and 2 Corinthians and Philippians were all written to churches well-known to the apostle; but it is in the Philippian period (1:3-11), where the longest of Paul's actual thanksgivings occurs, that the apostle clearly displays the intensity of his feeling and his deep longing for the addressees. In 1 Thessalonians we find the first extant Pauline thanksgiving passage. Thanksgiving permeates the first half of the letter (1:2-3:13) in a three-fold period which does not introduce information (as do all other introductory thanksgivings) so much as present it. The period constitutes the main body of the

---

[1] For an examination of the introductory period of Ephesians, chap. 1:3-19, and the problems associated with it see Appendix B of my thesis, *Introductory Thanksgivings in the Letters of Paul* (Manchester University, 1971), pp. 170 103, and the forthcoming article, 'The *Berakah* and Introductory Thanksgiving of Eph. 1:3-19'.

letter. In 2 Thessalonians two thanksgiving passages occur (1:3ff.; 2:13f.): the first stresses the remarkable growth of a church which has already been praised for the outworking of its faith, love and hope (1 Thess. 1:3); while the second, showing a breadth and depth not found elsewhere, emphatically stresses God's activity in saving His people from everlasting to everlasting. The thanksgiving period of 1 Corinthians (1:4-9), though addressed to a church well-known to the apostle concerns addressees whose relations with Paul were not always happy. In this passage petitionary prayer plays no part, while the opening period of the second canonical letter contains a *berakah* (2 Cor. 1:3ff.) rather than a thanksgiving.

Romans and Colossians were written to churches unknown to the apostle (although individuals within these congregations had met him). The purposes of these two letters were different—a point that may be seen in the introductory periods. While the former is addressed to a church that lay outside the scope of Paul's previous apostolic activity, the latter concerns a congregation whose existence was brought into being through a member of Paul's apostolic band.

Ephesians is the least specific of the letters examined, giving the fewest details about the situation of the addressees. Some consider this can be accounted for along the lines of a circular letter hypothesis.

So the differences in the letters, the persons addressed and the conditions in which they found themselves are reflected within the various introductory periods. Two basic structural types, together with a third mixed category, were noted. The second category (type Ib) was thought to be somewhat less personal than the first (type Ia), although all thanksgiving periods indicated a measure of formality on the one hand, and intimacy between the writer and addressees on the other. The subject matter, in spite of many formal similarities, differed from thanksgiving to thanksgiving. Occasionally, the order of particular units was reversed (cf. $\dot{\alpha}\gamma\acute{\alpha}\pi\eta$ and $\pi\acute{\iota}\sigma\tau\iota\varsigma$ in Phm. 5)—thus indicating where the apostle's attention was especially directed. The differences are clearly seen in the final clause (or seventh syntactical unit) of the first category (where the apostle spelled out the content of his intercessory prayer report), and the $\H{o}\tau\iota$-clause of the second category (where the grounds for thanksgiving were enunciated), for it was in these units that both content and structure were determined by the situation which called forth the letters.

2. Extent of the Thanksgiving Periods

The extent of the introductory thanksgivings differed from letter to letter, and Paul does not seem to have demarcated clearly the periods on all occasions. Although the introductory passages of Philippians (1:3-11) and 1 Corinthians (1:4-9) were well-rounded, those of 1 Thessalonians (1:2ff.), Romans and Colossians were not clear-cut in their endings. The thanksgiving period of Rom. 1:8ff. passed, by means of a bridge passage (1:16f.), into the body of the letter and Paul's detailed theological argument, while that of Col. 1:3ff. moved almost imperceptibly into a hymnic piece in praise of the cosmic Christ (1:15-20). Schubert had pointed out that a heightened eschatological climax assisted in defining the limits of the periods. But this was of no use in determining the extent of the introductory thanksgivings of Romans and Philemon where no climactic eschatological note was struck.

Although further research since Schubert wrote has directed attention to disclosure and $\pi\alpha\rho\alpha\kappa\alpha\lambda\acute{\epsilon}\omega$-forms, as well as to possible doxological endings to the periods (indicating, according to Sanders, that the transition to the body of the letter from the introductory thanksgiving was 'more formally structured' that Schubert supposed), these further criteria, in the cases of 1 Thessalonians and Romans at least, were not decisive in indicating where the periods ended. All that the evidence will permit us to conclude is that on occasions Paul rounded-out his periods with clear-cut endings. At other times he did not.

In the introductory thanksgivings three general types of material are to be found: (a) thanksgiving reports; (b) petitionary prayer reports; and (c) personal and apostolic details in which the addressees' relationship to Paul is mentioned. It is important to realize that these periods do not simply contain thanksgiving and petitionary prayer reports. The longer passages, viz., 1 Thess. 1:2ff. and Romans 1:8ff., contain extensive sections in which relations between Paul and the recipients are treated. Our exegesis, however, has been restricted to the prayer reports.

3. Manifold Function of the Introductory Thanksgivings

The purpose or function of the periods within the letters they introduce has been noted at the conclusion of each exegetical section. The following observations by way of summary may be made:

1. With Schubert it is agreed that, in general, the introductory periods have an *epistolary function*, i.e., they introduce and present the main theme(s) of their letters. The εὐχαριστέω-period of 1 Thessalonians, instead of being a rather formal introduction to the letter, constituted its main body. Thus it conveyed rather than introduced information. The second thanksgiving passage of 2 Thessalonians (2:13f.), because of its position in the letter did not introduce any themes. Instead, standing in contrast to the immediately preceding passage about the man of lawlessness, it emphasized God's activity on behalf of His people and presented a summary of many key themes of the two Thessalonian letters. It is also to be noted that the introductory *berakoth* of 2 Cor. 1:3ff. and Eph. 1:3ff. had an epistolary purpose, the former prefiguring many themes in chaps. 1-9, the latter, described by Maurer as the 'Schlussel zum ganzen Briefe', presenting both theological and paraenetic motifs that occurred later in this general letter.

2. Paul's introductory thanksgivings, particularly the thanksgiving and petitionary prayer reports, are evidence of the apostle's deep *pastoral and apostolic concern* for the addressees. The thanksgiving period of Philemon demonstrates Paul's care for an individual who came within the sphere of his pastoral responsibility, while in Phil. 1:3ff. the warmth of feeling for a church which had brought him great joy is clearly present. Paul's care is shown in various ways in his petitions and thanksgivings. At 1 Cor. 1:4-9 his thanksgiving precedes strong and biting words. Yet the apostle is able to give thanks to God for grace given in Christ. The important wish-prayer of 1 Thess. 3:11ff., which concludes Paul's long thanksgiving period of 1 Thessalonians, points to needs in the lives of the converts. Although the apostle rejoiced over their steadfastness, as a true pastor he was under no illusions about their deficiencies which still needed to be remedied. Yet Paul's converts, through this petitionary prayer report, are assured on the one hand of his longing to see them and of his pastoral concern for their spiritual growth on the other. Further, they may be confident that their imperfections are not serious. In the more general letter 'to the Ephesians' and those to congregations he did not know personally (i.e., at Rome and Colossae) Paul's prayer reports are evidence of a more general apostolic concern for predominantly Gentile recipients.

3. With the possible exception of Rom. 1:8ff. (where, however, theological themes are certainly prefigured), Paul's thanksgiving

periods have a *didactic function*. This is especially clear in the prayer reports of Col. 1:3ff., where there is an obvious emphasis on truth, gospel, wisdom and knowledge, etc.; at 2 Thess. 2:13f., a magnificent statement, in contrast to what has gone before, on the vastness and wonder of God's plan of salvation; in the intercessory prayer report of Phil. 1:9ff.; and in the introductory *berakah* of Eph. 1:3ff., where the author praises God for the wide-ranging blessings in Christ. At 1 Cor. 1:4-9 and 1 Thess. 1:2ff. Paul's didactic purpose is furthered primarily, though not exclusively, by his recall to teaching previously given when the churches in these two cities were founded. It is to be noted further that the didactic intent is present not only in the petitionary prayer reports but in the thanksgiving reports as well.

4. The *paraenetic purpose* also features in several of the thanksgiving periods. It is particularly clear in the petitionary prayer report of Phil. 1:9-11, the wish-prayer of 1 Thess. 3:11-13 where a transition to the second half of the letter occurs, and both the *berakah* and the intercessory prayer of Eph. 1. The paraenetic thrust of 2 Thess. 1:3ff. is present though not as clearly as in Phil, 1:9ff., while no explicit paraenetic intent is found in Phm. 4ff. The inverted thanksgiving of 2 Cor. 1:11 contains a request or an appeal for intercession rather than an explicit example of paraenesis. But allowing for these exceptions it can be said that expressly or implicitly the intercessory prayer reports and, on occasion (cf. 1 Cor. 1:7f.), the thanksgiving reports have a paraenetic function.

Paul's introductory thanksgivings have a varied function : epistolary, didactic and paraenetic, and they provide evidence of his pastoral and/or apostolic concern for the addressees. In some cases one purpose may predominate while others recede into the background. But whatever the particular thrust of any passage, it is clear that Paul's introductory thanksgivings were not meaningless devices. Instead, they were integral parts of their letters, setting the tone and themes of what was to follow.

4. *Language*

The language of Paul's introductory thanksgivings, as might be expected, has been mined from various quarries. It has already been shown that the apostle, with reference to the general form and function of the introductory thanksgivings, was following a contemporary Greek espitolary convention. But Paul was no slavish imitator and a glance at the structures of these periods shows they are highly developed and sophisticated. In the exegesis of the thanksgiving and petitionary prayer reports it has been frequently shown that the apostle was influenced by the language of the Old Testament, particularly the Psalter. This is especially clear in Col. 1:3ff. and Eph. 1:3ff. where further links with the language of Qumran have been noted. The wish-prayer of 1 Thess. 3:11ff., and the 'prayer-sigh' of Rom. 1:10 are two random examples where the Old Testament background is unmistakable. Many other instances could be cited, and the detailed exegesis above has shown that the apostle was saturated in the language of the Old Testament. He frequently addressed his prayers to the God of the Psalmists, used predicates found in the Old Testament, and made request for similar 'spiritual goods' to those of the Psalter.

The second source of the reports and the prayers which lie behind them is early Christian worship. Stereotyped phrases (including full christological titles, e.g., 'God the Father of our Lord Jesus Christ', 'the day of our Lord Jesus Christ', etc.) such as 'God is faithful', 'through Jesus Christ', etc., terminology from Col. 1:12-14 and Eph. 1:3ff. which might have been used in a baptismal context, as well as phrases from the wish-prayer of 1 Thess. 3:11-13 were probably used in pre-Pauline Christian worship. If so they were taken over and applied to the particular situations of the addressees. The early Christian triad (faith-love-hope) has also been used and adapted in the thanksgiving and petitionary prayer reports.

Another important source of terms and motifs in these reports was the early apostolic preaching. Such ideas are present in every introductory thanksgiving, e.g., εὐαγγέλιον, μαρτύριον, ὁ λόγος τοῦ θεοῦ, χάρις, πιστεύω, δέχομαι, παραλαμβάνω (a word connected with receiving a tradition), καταγγέλλω, etc. And it is clear from 1 Cor. 1:4-9 and 1 Thess. 1:2ff.; 2:13, etc., that Paul's thanksgiving reports recall the apostle's first preaching and its effects in Corinth and Thessalonica.

Other points may be noted: parousia references abound in both kinds of prayer reports (Phil. 1:6, 10; 1 Cor. 1:7, 8, etc.); in the Captivity Epistles there is a stress on knowledge, particularly ἐπίγνωσις which is found in all four letters; terms such as θέλημα, κοινωνία, and οἱ ἅγιοι appear not infrequently in these passages; πᾶς is often employed in the introductory thanksgivings; while Paul has a particular liking for words such as περισσεύω, πληρόω, etc., which stress the notions of fulness or abundance. The God to whom the apostle directs his thanksgivings and petitions gives richly and abundantly. Finally, certain phrases and terms which refer to the Corinthians' gifts (ἐν παντὶ λόγῳ καὶ πάσῃ γνώσει, 1 Cor. 1:5) and which speak of wealth in the Christian life (πλοῦτος and its cognates) seem to have been adopted from the Corinthian situation, probably from the Corinthians' letter to Paul.

But whatever the source of Paul's language it has been demonstrated above that the apostle has used these phrases with a remarkable degree of flexibility, adapting and applying them to the epistolary situation. So, for example, κοινωνία appears in three periods. Its meaning and function differ in 1 Cor. 1:9 from its occurrences in two Captivity Epistles. The early Christian triad (faith-hope-love) often appears in these introductory periods. Sometimes the order is changed, or one element is dropped out, while on other occasions one or more units appear in the intercessory prayer report rather than in the thanksgiving. If the exegesis above be correct, then ideas concerning fruitfulness, etc. have been drawn from the parable of the sower, developed and applied to the Colossian situation (1:6, 10) with reference to the gospel on the one hand, and its recipients on the other.

Perhaps the most striking feature in these paragraphs is the consistent use of εὐαγγέλιον and its equivalents (μαρτύριον, ὁ λόγος τοῦ θεοῦ, etc.). No thanksgiving period omits a reference to the gospel (although the term does not appear in the highly personal *berakah* of 2 Cor. 1:3f.). Even the proem of Gal. 1:6ff. has several references to the subject, thus making clear why no thanksgiving has been offered for these churches. The Galatian Christians are in serious danger of departing from the gospel!

But not only does 'gospel' or its equivalent appear in these passages. Its use on several occasions is almost personalized. Εὐαγγέλιον is often employed as a *nomen actionis*, while on occasion its dynamic activity is stressed (cf. 1 Thess. 1:5). Finally it is noted that Paul often goes out of his way to indicate that the addressees who have received this gospel are to conform their lives (or to be conformed) to it. Thanksgiving and the gospel are inextricably linked.

5. *Prayers of Thanksgiving and Petition*

Within the apostle's thanksgivings and introductory eulogies the following kinds of prayers are encountered: (1) actual thanksgivings offered by Paul (sometimes in conjunction with his colleagues) for the addressees; (2) *berakoth* in which the writer praises God for blessings in which he himself participates; (3) petitionary prayers of the following kinds : (a) intercessions by Paul (and his associates) for the same addressees on whose behalf thanksgiving has been offered; (b) the more direct form of a wish-prayer (1 Thess. 3:11-13)—this is also an intercession for the addressees; and (c) petitionary prayers offered to God in connection with Paul's travel to Rome (Rom. 1:10—a 'prayer-sigh' as frequently found in the Psalter) and Thessalonica (1 Thess. 3:10, cf. v. 11); (4) a reported doxology (Phil. 1:11); (5) a confirming climax (1 Cor. 1:9—referred to by some as a benediction); and (6) a request by Paul for intercession by the Corinthians (2 Cor. 1:11). In this concluding summary we direct our attention to the thanksgivings and petitions.

a. *Paul's thanksgivings*

While acknowledging that Paul's introductory periods have a varied function (epistolary, didactic, etc.), it must not be forgotten that in these passages Paul informs the recipients of his *actual* thanksgivings and *actual* petitions. His prayers of thanksgiving are directed to the God of the Psalmists ($\tau\hat{\wp}$ $\theta\epsilon\hat{\wp}$ or $\tau\hat{\wp}$ $\theta\epsilon\hat{\wp}$ $\mu o \upsilon$), who is known to Paul as the Father of Jesus Christ. On most occasions Paul's thanksgivings are offered 'always' or 'unceasingly'. These references to continual thanksgiving do not point to lengthy periods of time in unbroken prayer, but rather indicate that Paul did not forget his addressees in his regular times of prayer (not 'zu jeder Zeit' but 'im jedem Gebet'). In Rom. 1:8, at the conclusion of his long salutation (vv. 1-7), the apostle wants to begin ($\pi\rho\hat{\omega}\tau o\nu$ $\mu\acute{\epsilon}\nu$) by assuring his addressees that he gives thanks to God for them. Even as he dictates his letter thanksgiving once more wells up within him. At 1 Thess. 3:9 Paul's thanksgiving is *punctiliar* and particular, denoting his immediate reaction to Timothy's good news that the converts had not only stood firm, but had gone on in the faith. Specifically it is the joy that is the ground for Paul's thanksgiving ($\epsilon\pi\grave{\iota}$ $\pi\acute{\alpha}\sigma\eta$ $\tau\hat{\eta}$ $\chi\alpha\rho\hat{\alpha}$ $\hat{\eta}$ $\chi\alpha\acute{\iota}\rho o\mu\epsilon\nu$ v. 9), as he turns in prayer to God with a deep sense of gratitude (v. 9).

As pointed out above those for whom Paul gives thanks to God are the addressees some well-known to him, some converted through the ministry of a colleague, while others (e.g., the Christians at Rome —apart from some individuals), had not met Paul or his associates.

On one occasion the apostle gives thanks for the love and faith of an individual, Philemon (v. 4).

The grounds for thanksgiving, which are expressed by a causal participial clause, causal adverbial phrase or ὅτι-clause, are manifold. Frequently the apostle employed, with variations, the early Christian triad to express the *immediate* basis for thanksgiving. Thus the outward expression of faith, love and hope (= work, toil, and patience) was the first ground of Paul's thanksgiving for the Thessalonians (1 Thess. 1:2f.) and the remarkable growth of their faith and love constituted one reason for thanksgiving in the second canonical letter to Thessalonica (2 Thess. 1:3). Faith and love were also the grounds for thanking God on behalf of Philemon (v. 5), the Colossian Christians (Col. 1:4), while a faith that was proclaimed far and wide constituted the basis for thanksgiving for the Roman church (Rom. 1:8; cf. Eph. 1:15).

At first sight it might appear that Paul was unduly stressing the *Leistungen* of the addressees, as though they sprang from their own inherent virtues. But on closer examination we note that often the prior activity of God is seen as the *ultimate* ground for thanksgiving. Thus at 1 Thess. 1:4, with the introduction of the causal participle εἰδότες, the Thessalonians' election is seen to be the final basis for thanksgiving. And Paul could speak with certainty of this election because of the manner of the gospel's coming to the Thessalonians, the eagerness and joyfulness with which they believed (1 Thess. 1:5f.; cf. 2:13), and the sense the preachers had that their message was striking home (1 Thess. 1:5). This same stress on God's action is found in the Philippian period where the longest thanksgiving occurs. Paul is thankful for the addressees' financial assistance in times past (Phil. 1:3), and their participation in the activity of the gospel from the first day until now (1:5). These godly actions, however, are evidence that the God who has begun a good work in them will bring it to completion on the day of Christ Jesus (1:6).

God's gracious activity in Christ is emphatically stressed in 1 Cor. 1:4ff. Although the Corinthian Christians are rich, possessing spectacular gifts, it is because God has enriched them (ἐπλουτίσθητε, v. 5) in Christ Jesus (ἐν αὐτῷ). The testimony to Christ was confirmed (ἐβεβαιώθη, v. 6) *by God* in their midst. Not only did the Corinthians not confirm the message (though they had undoubtedly received it, and in spite of their failures presented a contrast to their pagan neighbours), they could not establish themselves so as to be blameless at the parousia. This God would do for them perfectly. Grace and the amazing activity of God demonstrated in such wonderful ways are the grounds for this Pauline prayer of thanksgiving.

In two other passages God's actions on behalf of His people are causes for thanksgiving: Col. 1:12-14 and 2 Thess. 2:13f. The former has reference to God's fitting the Colossian Christians to share in the inheritance of God's people (v. 12), and this is then expounded in terms of deliverance from the realm of darkness, transference into a kingdom in which the Son holds sway, redemption and the forgiveness of sins (vv. 13f.). In the latter passage, where the action of God is contrasted with the immediately preceding words, the causal ὅτι-clause mentions the grounds for thanksgiving. God has chosen the Thessalonians to be saved. This eternal choice includes not only the final salvation of the readers, but also the various means by which it is realised (v. 13). The first points to the operation of the Holy Spirit, the second to the human response. God's purpose is historically manifested in His call (v. 14), an invitation extended through the gospel which Paul and his associates preach. The thanksgiving concludes with a reference to the final consummation of God's purpose —the obtaining by the Thessalonians of the glory which the Lord Jesus possesses. Thus while not neglecting the human response, the brief but wide-ranging thanksgiving of 2 Thess. 2:13f. presents the greatness of God's activity on behalf of His people. His actions are grounds for thanksgiving indeed.

This latter passage directs our attention to four other significant points about the grounds for Pauline thanksgiving: first, the bases of Paul's thanksgivings are inextricably linked with the gospel. Those in whose lives faith, love and hope appear show that they have welcomed the word of God, believed the gospel, been called through Paul's gospel, had the testimony to Christ confirmed in their midst, demonstrated their active participation in the gospel, or received a hope that is an integral element in the gospel, etc. Secondly, thanks are offered to God not simply for events that have taken place in the past, or for graces, etc., that may be observed in the present. Paul often gives thanks for what he expects in the future. This, however, does not indicate the thanksgiving is any less sure or certain (cf. Phil. 1:6; 1 Cor. 1:8). Thirdly, thanksgiving is not infrequently linked with the parousia. The two passages just cited point to such a connection, while 2 Thess. 2:13f. refers to salvation in a future sense, and the obtaining of glory in terms of a final possession. However, in all of these instances the eschatological references are not concerned with the end as such. The point underlined is the faithfulness of God in preserving His people blameless to the end. Fourthly, all of Paul's thanksgiving prayers in his introductory periods, with the exception of Col. 1:12, are *Fürdank*, i.e., they do not relate to blessings he has received (rather Paul uses the εὐλογητός-formula when he himself comes within the sphere of blessing). His thanksgivings are offered to God for graces, etc., received by the addressees, i.e., those in his Gentile mission who had formerly been 'separated from Christ, alienated from the commonwealth of Israel, and strangers to the covenants of promise, having no hope and without God in the world' (Eph. 2:12).

b. *Petitionary prayer*

Not all of Paul's thanksgiving periods contain petitionary prayers. However, such prayers are to be found in most passages, and with the exception of Rom. 1:10 and 1 Thess. 3:10f., they are intercessions for the addressees.

Following Schubert it has been pointed out that the seventh syntactical unit of the type Ia category of introductory thanksgiving, where the contents of the intercessory prayers are spelled out, showed greater flexibility of form than did the other units. This was due to the stronger influence of the epistolary situation. In other words, although the intercessory prayers are introduced by a ἵνα-clause (or its equivalent), the form varies considerably. Leaving aside the petitionary prayer of Rom. 1:10, the shortest intercession in these periods is the single request of Phm. 6 : 'I pray that your generosity, which arises from your faith may lead you effectively into a deeper understanding and experience of every blessing which belongs to us as fellow-members in the body of Christ'. The companion letter to the Colossians contains the longest intercessory prayer (1:9-14, 90 words). Paul's petition is for a sensitivity to God's will consisting in an understanding of what is spiritually important. The result will be conduct that is pleasing to the Lord, i.e., a harvest of good deeds and growth in understanding. The power that will enable them to act in such a way is derived from God's glorious might. At the same time they will give thanks to the Father for an eternal inheritance, deliverance from the power of darkness, and the forgiveness of sins.

The following observations are made with reference to Paul's intercessions : first, these prayers are closely linked with his thanksgivings. Grammatically the petitionary prayer reports are joined to the thanksgiving reports—on several occasions when other material has intervened Paul goes out of his way to stress this conjunction (cf. Phil. 1:9; Col. 1:9; 2 Thess. 1:11). A fresh syntactical beginning is made so as to join the petition to the thanksgiving. But as if this were not enough, in the Colossian period the writer picks up and uses terms in the petitionary prayer which are not grammatically necessary, but which have already appeared in the thanksgiving. Other correspondences may be noted. Those who intercede, i.e., Paul and on occasion his colleagues, are the same persons who have given thanks. If thanksgiving is offered regularly for the addressees, it is matched with regular intercession. Further, the confidence which Paul has in his addressees, and ultimately in God who has acted in their lives, leads him to ask God that their growth may continue. Because Paul is convinced He will bring to completion on the day of Christ that work begun in the Philippians (1:6), so Paul prays to God that they may be pure and blameless on the day of Christ (1:10).

Secondly, the manifold requests of the apostle are primarily concerned with the growth in Christian maturity of the addressees. This explains Paul's frequent use of terms that refer to fulness, abundance, etc. The apostle will not be satisfied with anything less than their full Christian maturity. So progress is looked for in their love, while the deficiencies of their faith are to be repaired (cf. 1 Thess. 3:10). As mature Christians they are to be stable in holiness, at the same time being discerning so that they may choose those things that are vital. To be mature means they will have tact, understanding, knowledge and spiritual wisdom, be enlightened so as to know the nature of the hope bound up with their calling, the riches of the glorious inheritance they possess, and the amazing power of God available to them as believers. In true Hebraic fashion Paul prays that the knowledge they receive will be demonstrated in a conduct that is pleasing to the Lord in all things (Phil. 1:9ff.; Col. 1:9ff.). He also prays that they may offer corporate thanksgiving to the Father (Col. 1:12ff.), for in this He is glorified (2 Cor. 1:11; cf. 4:15).

Thirdly, along with this strong emphasis in Paul's intercessions on day-by-day growth in Christian maturity there is an eschatological perspective focussed especially on the parousia. At 2 Thess. 1:11f. with his eyes fixed on the consummation, Paul prays that the addressees will be made worthy of God's kingdom. The purpose of this petition of v. 11 is that the Lord Jesus be glorified by His followers and that they share His glory (v. 12). In other petitionary prayers the notion of the believers' preparedness for the day of Christ is underlined. At Phil. 1:10 εἰς ἡμέραν Χριστοῦ does not simply denote a limitation of time. The ideas of preparation for the scrutiny of that great day and the ability to withstand its test are also in view. Further, although Paul in his petitions frequently refers to 'blamelessness', 'irreproachability', etc., at the parousia, he desires that his Gentile addressees not only be acquitted. He also prays that they may be filled with a crop of godly deeds and actions—the result of a right relationship with God (Phil. 1:11, καρπὸν δικαιοσύνης).

Fourthly, it has already been pointed out in some detail that the apostle's intercessions are particularly related to the epistolary situation, and the needs of the addressees as he understood them. Deficiencies or lacks in Christian character of the believers are prayed for, while in didactic and paraenetic sections of these epistles the same matters are touched upon. Paul has obviously interceded for his converts along the lines in which he later instructs and encourages them. However, his intercessions are not restricted to these necessities. The requests catch up the particular needs (e.g., Phil. 1:9ff.; Col. 1:9ff., etc.) within a broader framework—a point made clear by the comprehensive connotation of such terms as 'love', 'knowledge', etc. The apostle is concerned not simply about the deficiencies of the moment but the believers' full maturity in Christ, a life consistent with the gospel and a fitness and perfection for the last day.

For Paul both thanksgiving and petition were important. He and his addressees ought to give thanks to God, privately and corporately —indeed under all circumstances (1 Thess. 5:18)—for by it God would be glorified (2 Cor. 1:11; 4:15). Although our research has touched upon only some of Paul's petitions, sufficient have been examined to show that this Christian activity was a significant weapon in his apostolic armoury. On the one hand the all-round readiness of the believers for the parousia, their Christian growth, etc., could be furthered through his intercessions. On the other hand, a visit hitherto prevented by Satan's activities (1 Thess. 2:18) could be brought to pass by Paul's petitions. And Paul's addressees too could play a significant part in his ministry (2 Cor. 1:11) by using this weapon of intercession.

BIBLIOGRAPHY

A. DICTIONARIES, ENCYCLOPAEDIAS AND SOURCE BOOKS

Arndt, W. F. and Gingrich, F. W., edd., *A Greek-English Lexicon of the New Testament and Other Early Christian Literature* (ET, Cambridge, 1957).
Barrett, C. K., *The New Testament Background : Selected Documents* (London, 1956).
Blass, F. and Debrunner, A., *A Greek Grammar of the New Testament and Other Early Christian Literature*, ed. R. W. Funk (ET, Cambridge, 1961).
Buttrick, G. A., ed., *The Interpreter's Bible* (New York, 1951-1957).
Charles, R. H., ed., *The Apocrypha and Pseudepigrapha of the Old Testament* (Oxford, 1913).
Galling, K., ed., *Die Religion in Geschichte und Gegenwart* (Tübingen, ³1956-1965).
Hatch, E. and Redpath, H. A., *A Concordance to the Septuagint and the Other Greek Versions of the Old Testament* (Oxford, 1897-1906).
Kittel, G. and Friedrich, G., edd., *Theological Dictionary of the New Testament* (ET of *Theologisches Wörterbuch zum Neuen Testament*, trans. and ed. by G. W. Bromiley, 1964-1974).
Kuhn, K. G., ed., *Konkordanz zu den Qumrantexten* (Göttingen, 1960).
Liddell, H. G., Scott, R. and Jones, H. S., ed., *A Greek-English Lexicon* (Oxford, ⁹1940).
Lohse, E., ed., *Die Texte aus Qumran. Hebräisch und deutsch* (München, 1964).
Metzger, B. M., ed., *Index to Periodical Literature on the Apostle Paul* (Leiden, 1960).
Morgenthaler, R., *Statistik des Neutestamentlichen Wortschatzes* (Zürich, 1958).
Moulton, W. F., and Geden, A. S., edd., *A Concordance to the Greek Testament* (Edinburgh, ⁴1963).
Moulton, J. H. and Milligan, G., edd., *The Vocabulary of the Greek Testament* (London, 1930).
Strack, H. L. and Billerbeck, P., edd., *Kommentar zum Neuen Testament aus Talmud und Midrasch*, Vols. 1-4 (München, 1922-1928).
Vermes, G., *The Dead Sea Scrolls in English* (London, 1962).

B. OTHER WORKS

Abbott, T. K., *A Critical and Exegetical Commentary on the Epistles to the Ephesians and to the Colossians* (Edinburgh, 1897).
Allan, J. A., 'The Will of God. III. In Paul', *ExT* 72 (1960-1961), pp. 142-145.
Allo, E.-B., *Saint Paul : Première Épître aux Corinthiens* (Paris, ²1956).
——, *Saint Paul : Seconde Épître aux Corinthiens* (Paris, ²1956).
Althaus, P., *Der Brief an die Römer* (Göttingen, ¹⁰1965).
Audet, J.-P., 'Esquisse historique du genre littéraire de la "Bénédiction" juive et de l'"Eucharistie" chrétienne', *RB* 65 (1958), pp. 371-399.
——, 'Literary Forms and Contents of a Normal Εὐχαριστία in the First Century', *Studia Evangelica* 1, ed. F. L. Cross *et al.* (Berlin, 1959), pp. 643-662.

Aus, R. D., 'The Liturgical Background of the Necessity and Propriety of Giving Thanks according to 2 Thes 1:3', *JBL* 92 (1973), pp. 432-438.
Bachmann, P., *Der erste Brief des Paulus an die Korinther* (Leipzig, 1905).
———, *Der zweite Brief des Paulus an die Korinther* (Leipzig, 1/21909).
Bailey, J. W., 'The First and Second Epistles to the Thessalonians', *The Interpreter's Bible* 11, pp. 243-339.
Bardenhewer, O., *Der Römerbrief des heiligen Paulus* (Freiburg-i.-Br., 1926).
Barr, J., *The Semantics of Biblical Language* (Oxford, 1961).
Barrett, C. K., 'Christianity at Corinth', *BJRL* 46 (1964), pp. 269-297.
———, *The Epistle to the Romans* (London, 1957).
———, *The First Epistle to the Corinthians* (London, 1968).
———, 'The Holy Spirit in the Fourth Gospel', *JTS* N.S. 1 (1950), pp. 1-15.
———, *The Second Epistle to the Corinthians* (London, 1973),
Barth, K., *The Epistle to the Philippians* (ET, London, 1962).
———, *The Epistle to the Romans* (ET, London, 1933).
Bartsch, H. W., 'The Concept of Faith in Paul's Letter to the Romans', *Biblical Research* 13 (Chicago, 1968), pp. 41-53.
Baudraz, F., 'Grace', *Vocabulary of the Bible*, ed. J.-J. von Allmen (ET, London, 1958), pp. 157-160.
Baumann, R., *Mitte und Norm des Christlichen* (Münster, 1968).
Beardslee, W. A., *Human Achievement and Divine Vocation in the Message of Paul* (London, 1961).
Beare, F. W., 'The Epistle to the Colossians', *The Interpreter's Bible* 11, pp. 131-241.
———, *The Epistle to the Philippians* (London, 1959).
Belser, J. E., *Der zweite Brief des Apostels Paulus an die Korinther* (Freiburg-i.-Br., 1910).
Benoit, P., *Les Épîtres de S. Paul : Aux Philippiens, à Philémon, aux Colossiens, aux Éphésiens* (Paris, 31959).
Bernard, E. R., 'Prayer', *A Dictionary of the Bible* 4, ed. J. Hastings (New York, 1902), pp. 38-45.
Bernard, J. H., 'The Second Epistle to the Corinthians', *The Expositor's Greek Testament* 3, ed. W. Robertson Nicoll (London, 1903), pp. 1-119.
Best, E., *A Commentary on the First and Second Epistles to the Thessalonians* (London, 1972).
Beyer, H. W., 'εὐλογέω', *TDNT* 2, pp. 754-765.
Bickerman, E. J., 'Bénédiction et Prière', *RB* 69 (1962), pp. 523-532.
Bicknell, E. J., *The First and Second Epistles to the Thessalonians* (London, 1932).
Bieder, W., *Die Berufung im Neuen Testament* (Zürich, 1961).
———, 'Gebetswirklichkeit und Gebetsmöglichkeit bei Paulus', *TZ* 4 (1948), pp. 22-40.
Bietenhard, H., 'ὄνομα', *TDNT* 5, pp. 242-283.
Binder, H., *Der Glaube bei Paulus* (Berlin, 1968).
Bjerkelund, C. J., *Parakalô* (Oslo, 1967).
Boer, H. R., *Pentecost and Missions* (Grand Rapids, 1961).
Boobyer, G. H., *"Thanksgiving" and the "Glory of God" in Paul* (Leipzig, 1929).
Bornemann, W., *Die Thessalonicherbriefe* (Göttingen, 5,61894).
Bornkamm, G., 'Das Bekenntnis im Hebräerbrief', *Studien zu Antike und Urchristentum* (München, 1959), pp. 188-203.
———, 'Die Hoffnung im Kolosserbrief—zugleich ein Beitrag zur Frage der Echtheit des Briefes', *TU* 77 (1961), pp. 56-64.

Bornkamm, G., *Early Christian Experience* (ET, London, 1969).
——, *Paul* (ET, London, 1971).
——, 'The Letter to the Romans as Paul's Last Will and Testament', *ABR* 11 (1963), pp. 2-14.
Bousset, W., 'Der erste Brief an die Korinther', *Die Schriften des Neuen Testaments neu übersetzt und für die Gegenwart erklärt* 2, ed. W. Bousset and W. Heitmüller (Göttingen, ³1917), pp. 74-167.
Bromiley, G. W., *Christian Ministry* (Grand Rapids, 1960).
Bruce, F. F., *An Expanded Paraphrase of the Epistles of Paul* (Exeter, 1965).
——, in E. K. Simpson-F. F. Bruce, *Commentary on the Epistles to the Ephesians and the Colossians* (London, 1957).
——, *New Testament History* (London, 1969).
——, *1 and 2 Corinthians* (London, 1971).
——, '1 and 2 Thessalonians', *The New Bible Commentary Revised*, ed. D. Guthrie et al. (London, ³1970), pp. 1154-1165.
——, 'Paul and Jerusalem', *TynB* 19 (1968), pp. 3-25.
——, 'St. Paul in Rome. 2. The Epistle to Philemon', *BJRL* 48 (1965), pp. 81-97.
——, 'St. Paul in Rome. 3. The Epistle to the Colossians', *BJRL* 48 (1966), pp. 268-285.
——, *The Epistle of Paul to the Romans* (London, 1963).
——, *The Epistle to the Hebrews* (London, 1964).
Brun, L., *Segen und Fluch im Urchristentum* (Oslo, 1932).
Büchsel, F., *Der Geist Gottes im Neuen Testament* (Gütersloh, 1926).
——, ' "In Christus" bei Paulus', *ZNW* 42 (1949), pp. 141-158.
——, 'εἰλικρινής', *TDNT* 2, pp. 397-398.
——, 'λύω' (in NT), *TDNT* 4, pp. 335-356.
Buhl, F., 'Über Dankbarkeit im Alten Testament und die sprachlichen Ausdrücke dafür', *Festschrift für W. W. Graf von Baudissin* (Giessen, 1918), pp. 71-82.
Bultmann, R., *Theology of the New Testament* 1 (ET, London, 1952).
——, 'γινώσκω', *TDNT* 1, pp. 689-719.
——, 'καυχάομαι', *TDNT* 3, pp. 645-654.
——, 'οἰκτίρω', *TDNT* 5, pp. 159-161.
——, 'πιστεύω' (in NT), *TDNT* 6, pp. 197-228.
Burnaby, J., 'Christian Prayer', *Soundings*, ed. A. R. Vidler (Cambridge, 1966), pp. 219-237.
Burton, E. de W., *A Critical and Exegetical Commentary on the Epistle to the Galatians* (Edinburgh, 1921).
——, *Syntax of the Moods and Tenses in New Testament Greek* (Edinburgh, ³1898).
Buttmann, A., *A Grammar of the New Testament Greek* (ET, Andover, 1873).
Caird, G. B., *Principalities and Powers* (Oxford, 1956).
——, *The Apostolic Age* (London, 1955).
Calvin, J., *The First Epistle of Paul to the Corinthians* (a new translation and edition, Grand Rapids, 1960).
——, *The Second Epistle of Paul the Apostle to the Corinthians and the Epistles to Timothy, Titus and Philemon* (a new translation and edition, Grand Rapids, 1964).
Campbell, J. Y., 'ΚΟΙΝΩΝΙΑ and its cognates in the New Testament', *JBL* 51 (1932), pp. 352-380.
Campbell, W. S., 'Why Did Paul Write Romans?', *ExT* 85 (1973-1974), pp. 264-269.
Carson, H. M., *The Epistles of Paul to the Colossians and Philemon* (London, 1960).

Cerfaux, L., *Christ in the Theology of St. Paul* (ET, London, 1959).
——, 'L'Apôtre en présence de Dieu', *Recueil Lucien Cerfaux* 2 (Gembloux, 1954), pp. 469-481.
——, *The Christian in the Theology of St. Paul* (ET, London, 1967).
Champion, L. G., *Benedictions and Doxologies in the Epistles of Paul* (published privately, Oxford, 1934).
Coggan, D., *The Prayers of the New Testament* (London, 1967).
Conzelmann, H., *An Outline of the Theology of the New Testament* (ET, London, 1969).
——, *Der erste Brief an die Korinther* (Göttingen, ¹¹1969 = 1st edn., New Series).
——, *Die kleineren Briefe des Apostels Paulus : Der Brief an die Kolosser* (Göttingen, ¹⁰1965).
—— (with W. Zimmerli), 'χαίρω', *TDNT* 9, pp. 359-415.
Coppens, J., ' "Mystery" in the theology of Saint Paul and its parallels at Qumran', *Paul and Qumran*, ed. J. Murphy-O'Connor (London, 1968), pp. 132-158.
Cragg, G. R., 'The Epistle to the Romans : Exposition', *The Interpreter's Bible* 9, pp. 353-668.
Craig, C. T., 'The First Epistle to the Corinthians', *The Interpreter's Bible* 10, pp. 1-262.
Cranfield, C. E. B., 'Divine and Human Action. The Biblical Concept of Worship', *Interp* 12 (1958), pp. 387-398.
Cullmann, O., *Christ and Time* (ET, London, ³1962).
——, *The Christology of the New Testament* (ET, London, ²1963).
Dahl, N. A., 'Adresse und Proömium des Epheserbriefes', *TZ* 7 (1951), pp. 241-264.
——, 'Anamnesis. Mémoire et Commémoration dans le Christianisme Primitif', *ST* 1 (1948), pp. 69-95.
——, 'Paul and the Church at Corinth according to 1 Corinthians 1:10-4:21', *Christian History and Interpretation : Studies Presented to John Knox*, ed. W. R. Farmer et al. (Cambridge, 1967), pp. 313-335.
Dalman, G., *The Words of Jesus* (ET, Edinburgh, 1902).
Daube, D., 'Participle and Imperative in 1 Peter', in E. G. Selwyn, *The First Epistle of St. Peter* (London, 1946), pp. 467-488.
——, *The New Testament and Rabbinic Judaism* (London, 1956).
Davies, W. D., *Paul and Rabbinic Judaism* (London, ²1955).
——, *The Setting of the Sermon on the Mount* (Cambridge, 1964).
Deichgräber, R., *Gotteshymnus und Christushymnus in der frühen Christenheit* (Göttingen, 1967).
Deissmann, A., *Bible Studies* (ET, Edinburgh, 1901).
——, *Die neutestamentliche Formel "In Christo Jesu"* (Marburg, 1892).
——, *Light from the Ancient East* (ET, London, ⁴1927).
——, *Paul* (ET, New York, ²1927).
Delay, E., 'À qui s'adresse la prière chrétienne ?', *RThPh* 37 (1949), pp. 189-201.
Delling, G., 'Partizipiale Gottesprädikationen in den Briefen des Neuen Testaments', *ST* 17 (1963), pp. 1-59.
——, *Worship in the New Testament* (ET, London, 1962).
——, 'αἰσθανόμαι', *TDNT* 1, pp. 187-188.
——, 'πληρόω', *TDNT* 6, pp. 283-311.
——, 'τέλος', *TDNT* 8, pp. 49-87.
Denney, J., 'St. Paul's Epistle to the Romans', *The Expositor's Greek Testament* 2, ed. W. Robertson Nicoll (London, 1900), pp. 555-725.

Denney, J., *The Epistles to the Thessalonians* (London, 1892).
Dewailly, L. M., 'La part prise à l'Évangile (Phil., I, 5)', *RB* 80 (1973), pp. 247-260.
Dibelius, M., *An die Kolosser, Epheser, an Philemon* (Tübingen, 3rd edn., revised by H. Greeven, 1953).
——, *An die Thessalonicher I. II. An die Philipper* (Tübingen, ³1937).
—— and Kümmel, W. G., *Paul* (ET, London, 1953).
Dietzel, A., 'Beten im Geist', *TZ* 13 (1957), pp. 12-32.
Dinkler, E., 'Die Taufterminologie in 2 Kor. i. 21f.', *Neotestamentica et Patristica. Freundesgabe Oscar Cullmann*, ed. W. C. van Unnik (Leiden, 1962), pp. 173-191.
——, 'Korintherbriefe', *RGG*³ 4, cols. 17-24.
——, 'First Letter to the Corinthians', *Dictionary of the Bible*, rev. ed. by F. C. Grant and H. H. Rowley (Edinburgh, 1963), pp. 177-180.
Dobschütz, E. von, *Die Thessalonicher-Briefe* (Göttingen, ⁷1909).
——, 'Zum Wortschatz und Stil des Römerbriefs', *ZNW* 33 (1934), pp. 51-66.
Dodd, C. H., *Colossians and Philemon* (London, 1929).
——, *New Testament Studies* (Manchester, 1953).
——, *The Bible and the Greeks* (London, 1935).
——, *The Epistle of Paul to the Romans* (London, 1932).
——, *The Meaning of Paul for Today* (London, 1920).
Dölger, F. J., *Sol Salutis : Gebet und Gesang im christlichen Altertum* (Münster, ²1925).
Doty, W. G., *Letters in Primitive Christianity* (Philadelphia, 1973).
Dugmore, C. W., *The Influence of the Synagogue upon the Divine Office* (Oxford, 1944).
Dunn, J. D. G., *Baptism in the Holy Spirit* (London, 1970).
Du Plessis, P. J., *ΤΕΛΕΙΟΣ. The Idea of Perfection in the New Testament* (Kampen, 1959).
Dupont, J., *Gnosis* (Paris, 1949).
Eckart, K.-G., 'Der zweite echte Brief des Apostels Paulus an die Thessalonicher', *ZThK* 58 (1961), pp. 30-44.
——, 'Exegetische Beobachtungen zu Kol. 1, 9-20', *ThViat* 7 (1959-1960), pp. 87-106.
Edwards, T. C., *A Commentary on the First Epistle to the Corinthians* (London, 1885).
Eichholz, G., 'Der ökumenische und missionarische Horizont der Kirche', *EvTh* 21 (1961), pp. 15-27.
Elbogen, I., *Der jüdische Gottesdienst in seiner geschichtlichen Entwicklung* (Frankfurt, ²1924).
Ellis, E. E., *Paul's Use of the Old Testament* (Edinburgh, 1957).
——, ' "Spiritual" Gifts in the Pauline Community', *NTS* 20 (1973-1974), pp. 128-144.
Eschlimann, J.-A., *La Prière dans saint Paul* (Lyon, 1934).
Esser, H. H., 'Εὐχαριστία', *Theologisches Begriffslexikon zum Neuen Testament* 1, ed. L. Coenen *et al.* (Wuppertal, 1967), pp. 171ff.
Evans, E., *The Epistles of Paul the Apostle to the Corinthians* (Oxford, 1930).
Ewald, P., *Der Brief des Paulus an die Philipper* (revised by G. Wohlenberg) (Leipzig, ⁴1923).
——, *Die Briefe des Paulus an die Epheser, Kolosser und Philemon* (Leipzig, 1905).
Exler, F. X. J., *The Form of the Ancient Greek Letter* (Washington, D.C., 1923).
Filson, F. V., *A New Testament History* (London, 1965).
——, 'Petition and Intercession', *Interp* 8 (1954), pp. 21-34.
——, 'The Second Epistle to the Corinthians', *The Interpreter's Bible* 10, pp. 263-425.
Findlay, G. G., 'St. Paul's First Epistle to the Corinthians', *The Expositor's Greek Testament* 2, ed. W. Robertson Nicoll (London, 1900), pp. 727-953.

Findlay, G. G., *The Epistles of Paul the Apostle to the Thessalonians* (Cambridge, 1904).
Fitzmyer, J. A., 'New Testament Epistles', *The Jerome Biblical Commentary*, ed. R. E. Brown *et al.* (London, 1968), pp. 223-226.
Foerster, W., 'ἄξιος', *TDNT* 1, pp. 379-380.
——, 'ἀρέσκω', *TDNT* 1, pp. 455-457.
Frame, J. E., *A Critical and Exegetical Commentary on the Epistles of St. Paul to the Thessalonians* (Edinburgh, 1912).
Fridrichsen, A., *The Apostle and his Message* (Uppsala, 1947).
Friedrich, G., *Die kleineren Briefe des Apostels Paulus : Der Brief an die Philipper* (Göttingen, [10]1965).
——, *Die kleineren Briefe des Apostels Paulus : Der Brief an Philemon* (Göttingen, [10]1965).
——, 'Lohmeyers These über das paulinische Briefpräskript kritisch beleuchtet', *TLZ* 81 (1956), cols. 343-346.
——, 'εὐαγγέλιον', *TDNT* 2, pp. 707-737.
Funk, R. W., 'The Apostolic "Parousia": Form and Significance', *Christian History and Interpretation: Studies Presented to John Knox*, ed. W. R. Farmer *et al.* (Cambridge, 1967), pp. 249-268.
Furnish, V. P., *Theology and Ethics in Paul* (Nashville, 1968).
Gabathuler, H. J., *Jesus Christus : Haupt der Kirche—Haupt der Welt* (Zürich, 1965).
George, A. R., *Communion with God in the New Testament* (London, 1953).
Gerhardsson, B., *Memory and Manuscript* (ET, Lund, 1961).
Giblin, C. H., *The Threat to Faith* (Rome, 1967).
Gnilka, J., *Der Philipperbrief* (Freiburg-i-.Br., 1968).
Godet, F., *Commentary on St. Paul's Epistle to the Romans* 1 (ET, Edinburgh, 1890).
——, *Commentary on St. Paul's First Epistle to the Corinthians* (ET, Edinburgh, 1889).
Goltz, E. von der, *Das Gebet in der ältesten Christenheit* (Leipzig, 1901).
Goudge, H. L., *The First Epistle to the Corinthians* (London, [5]1926).
——, *The Second Epistle to the Corinthians* (London, 1927).
Grabner-Haider, A., *Paraklese und Eschatologie bei Paulus* (Münster, 1968).
Greeven, H., *Gebet und Eschatologie im Neuen Testament* (Gütersloh, 1931).
——, 'Prüfung der Thesen von J. Knox zum Philemonbrief', *TLZ* 79 (1954), cols. 373-378.
——, 'δέομαι', *TDNT* 2, pp. 40-42.
—— (with J. Herrmann), 'εὔχομαι', *TDNT* 2, pp. 775-808.
Grosheide, F. W., *Commentary on the First Epistle to the Corinthians* (London, [2]1954).
Grundmann, W., 'ἀνέγκλητος', *TDNT* 1, pp. 356-357.
——, 'δέχομαι', *TDNT* 2, pp. 50-59.
Güttgemanns, E., *Der leidende Apostel und sein Herr* (Göttingen, 1966).
Guthrie, D., *New Testament Introduction. The Pauline Epistles* (London, 1961).
Hahn, F., *Der urchristliche Gottesdienst* (Stuttgart, 1970).
——, *Mission in the New Testament* (ET, London, 1965).
——, *The Titles of Jesus in Christology* (ET, London, 1969).
Hamman, A., *La Prière. I. Le Nouveau Testament* (Tournai, 1959).
Harder, G., *Paulus und das Gebet* (Gütersloh, 1936).
Harnack, A. von, Review article of E. Loening's *Die Gemeindeverfassung des Urchristenthums* (Halle, 1889), in *TLZ* 14 (1889), cols. 417-429.

Harris, M. J., *The Interpretation of 2 Corinthians 5:1-10, and Its Place in Pauline Eschatology* (unpublished Ph.D. thesis, University of Manchester, 1970).
Harrison, P. N., 'Onesimus and Philemon', *ATR* 32 (1950), pp. 268-294.
Hauck, F., 'κοινός', *TDNT* 3, pp. 789-809.
——, 'κόπος', *TDNT* 3, pp. 827-830.
——, 'ὑπομένω', *TDNT* 4, pp. 581-588.
—— and Kasch, W., 'πλοῦτος', *TDNT* 6, pp. 318-332.
Haupt, E., *Die Gefangenschaftsbriefe* (Göttingen, ⁷1902).
Hegermann, H., 'Die Vorstellung vom Schöpfungsmittler im hellenistischen Judentum und Urchristentum', *TU* 82 (1961), pp. 88-157.
Heiler, F., *Prayer* (ET, London, ²1933).
Heinrici, C. F. G., *Der erste Brief an die Korinther* (Göttingen, ⁸1896).
——, *Der zweite Brief an die Korinther* (Göttingen, ⁷1890).
Heitmüller, W., *Im Namen Jesu* (Göttingen, 1903).
Hemer, C. J., 'A Note on 2 Corinthians 1:9', *TynB* 23 (1972), pp. 103-107.
Henneken, B., *Verkündigung und Prophetie im 1 Thessalonicherbrief* (Stuttgart, 1969).
Héring, J., *The First Epistle of Saint Paul to the Corinthians* (ET, London, 1962).
——, *The Second Epistle of Saint Paul to the Corinthians* (ET, London, 1967).
Hill, D., *Greek Words and Hebrew Meanings* (Cambridge, 1967).
Hoffmann, P., *Die Toten in Christus* (Münster, ²1969).
Holm-Nielsen, G., *Hodayot. Psalms from Qumran* (Aarhus, 1960).
Holtzmann, O., *Das Neue Testament: Der Römerbrief* 2 (Giessen, 1926), pp. 618-678.
Horst, F., 'Segen und Fluch' (II. AT), *RGG*³ 5, cols. 1649-1651.
——, 'Segen und Segenshandlungen in der Bibel', *EvTh* 7 (1947-1948), pp. 23-37.
Horst, J., 'μακροθυμία', *TDNT* 4, pp. 374-387.
Hort, F. J. A. and Murray, J. O. F., 'Εὐχαριστία — εὐχαριστεῖν', *JTS* 3 (1902), pp. 594-598.
Huby, J., *Saint Paul. Épître aux Romains* (Paris, ¹⁰1940).
Hughes, P. E., *Paul's Second Epistle to the Corinthians* (London, 1962).
Hunter, A. M., *Paul and his Predecessors* (London, ²1961).
——, *The Epistle to the Romans* (London, 1955).
Hurd, J. C., *The Origin of 1 Corinthians* (London, 1965).
Jacob, E., *Theology of the Old Testament* (ET, London, 1958).
Jeremias, J., 'Chiasmus in den Paulusbriefen', *ZNW* 49 (1958), pp. 145-156.
——, *The Prayers of Jesus* (ET, London, 1967).
Jewett, R., *Paul's Anthropological Terms* (Leiden, 1971).
——, 'The Epistolary Thanksgiving and the Integrity of Philippians', *NovT* 12 (1970), pp. 40-53.
——, 'The Form and Function of the Homiletic Benediction', *ATR* 51 (1969), pp. 18-34.
Johnson, N. B., *Prayer in the Apocrypha and Pseudepigrapha* (Philadelphia, 1948).
Judge, E. A. and Thomas, G. S. R., 'The Origin of the Church at Rome: A New Solution?', *RThR* 25 (1966), pp. 81-94.
Jülicher, A., *An Introduction to the New Testament* (ET, London, 1904).
Juncker, A., *Das Gebet bei Paulus* (Berlin, 1905).
Jungmann, J., *The Place of Christ in Liturgical Prayer* (ET, London, 1965).
Käsemann, E., 'A Primitive Christian Baptismal Liturgy', *Essays on New Testament Themes* (ET, London, 1964), pp. 149-168.
——, *Leib und Leib Christi* (Tübingen, 1933).

Käsemann, E., *New Testament Questions of Today* (ET, London, 1969).
——, *Perspectives on Paul* (ET, London, 1971).
Kerkhoff, R., *Das unablässige Gebet* (München, 1954).
Kittel, G., 'ἀκοή', *TDNT* 1, pp. 221-222.
—— (with von Rad, G.), 'δοκέω', *TDNT* 2, pp. 232-255.
Kittel, H., *Die Herrlichkeit Gottes* (Giessen, 1934).
Klawek, A., *Das Gebet zu Jesus* (Münster, 1921).
Klein, G., 'Der Abfassungszweck des Römerbriefes', *Rekonstruktion und Interpretation* (München, 1969), pp. 129-144.
Knox, J., *Philemon among the Letters of Paul* (London, ²1960).
——, 'Romans 15:14-33 and Paul's Conception of his Apostolic Mission', *JBL* (1964), pp. 1-11.
——, 'The Epistle to the Romans', *The Interpreter's Bible* 9, pp. 353-668.
Koch, E. W., 'A Cameo of Koinonia. The Letter to Philemon', *Interp* 17 (1963), pp. 183-187.
Koskenniemi, H., *Studien zur Idee und Phraseologie des griechischen Briefes bis 400 n. Christus* (Helsinki, 1956).
Kramer, W., *Christ, Lord, Son of God* (ET, London, 1966).
Kremer, J., *Was an den Leiden Christi noch mangelt* (Bonn, 1956).
Kühl, E., *Der Brief des Paulus an die Römer* (Leipzig, 1913).
Kümmel, W. G., 'Das literarische und geschichtliche Problem des ersten Thessalonicherbriefes', *Neotestamentica et Patristica. Freundesgabe Oscar Cullmann*, ed. W. C. van Unnik (Leiden, 1962), pp. 213-227.
——, *Introduction to the New Testament* (ET, London, 1966).
Kuhn, H. W., *Enderwartung und gegenwärtiges Heil* (Göttingen, 1966).
Kuhn, K. G., *Achtzehngebet und Vaterunser und der Reim* (Göttingen, 1950).
——, 'The Epistle to the Ephesians in the light of the Qumran texts, *Paul and Qumran*, ed. J. Murphy-O'Connor (London, 1968), pp. 115-131.
Kuss, O., *Der Römerbrief* (Regensburg, ²1963).
Lähnemann, J., *Der Kolosserbrief. Komposition, Situation und Argumentation* (Gütersloh, 1971).
Lagrange, M.-J., *Saint Paul : Épître aux Romains* (Paris, 1916).
Leaney, A. R. C., *The Rule of Qumran and Its Meaning* (London, 1966).
Ledogar, R. J., *Acknowledgment. Praise-Verbs in the Early Greek Anaphora* (Rome, 1968).
Leenhardt, F. J., *The Epistle to the Romans* (ET, London, 1961).
Leipoldt, J., *Der Gottesdienst der ältesten Kirche. jüdische? griechisch? christlich?* (Leipzig, 1937).
Levertoff, P. P., 'Synagogue Worship in the First Century', *Liturgy and Worship*, ed. W. K. Lowther Clarke (London, 1932), pp. 60-77.
Lietzmann, H., *An die Römer* (Tübingen, ³1928).
—— and Kümmel, W. G., *An die Korinther I. II* (Tübingen, ⁵1969).
Lightfoot, J. B., *Notes on the Epistles of St Paul* (London, 1895).
——, *Saint Paul's Epistle to the Philippians* (London, ³1873).
——, *Saint Paul's Epistles to the Colossians and to Philemon* (London, ⁹1890).
Lövestam, E., *Spiritual Wakefulness in the New Testament* (Lund, 1963).
Lofthouse, W. F., 'I and We in the Pauline Letters', *ExT* 64 (1952-1953), pp. 241-245.
——, 'Singular and Plural in St. Paul's Letters', *ExT* 58 (1946-1947), pp. 179-182.

Lohmeyer, E., *Die Briefe an die Philipper, an die Kolosser und an Philemon* (Göttingen, ¹³1964; 9th edn. onwards revised by W. Schmauch, 1953).
——, 'Probleme paulinischer Theologie. I. Briefliche Grussüberschriften', *ZNW* 26 (1927), pp. 158-173.
——, *The Lord's Prayer* (ET, London, 1965).
Lohse, E., 'Christologie und Ethik im Kolosserbrief', *Apophoreta*: *Festschrift für Ernst Haenchen*, ed. W. Eltester and F. H. Kettler (Berlin, 1964), pp. 156-168.
——, *Colossians and Philemon* (ET, Philadelphia, 1971).
Longenecker, R. N., 'Can We Reproduce the Exegesis of the New Testament?', *TynB* 21 (1970), pp. 3-38.
Lührmann, D., *Das Offenbarungsverständnis bei Paulus und in paulinischen Gemeinden* (Neukirchen-Vluyn, 1965).
Lünemann, G., *Critical and Exegetical Handbook to the Epistles of St. Paul to the Thessalonians* (ET, Edinburgh, 1880).
Lund, N. W., *Chiasmus in the New Testament* (London, 1942).
Lyonnet, S., ' "Deus cui servio in spiritu meo" (Rom. 1:9)', *Verbum Domini* 41 (Rome, 1963), pp. 52-59.
——, 'Pauline Soteriology', *Introduction to the New Testament*, ed. A. Robert and A. Feuillet (ET, New York, 1965), pp. 820-865.
McFadyen, J. E., *The Epistles to the Corinthians* (London, 1911).
McFarlane, D. J., *The Motif of Thanksgiving in the New Testament* (unpublished M.Th. thesis, St. Andrews University, 1966).
Manson, T. W., *On Paul and John* (London, 1963).
——, 'Romans', *Peake's Commentary on the Bible*, ed. M. Black and H. H. Rowley (London, ²1962), pp. 940-953.
Marchel, W., *Abba. Père! La Prière du Christ et des Chrétiens* (Rome, ²1971).
Martin, R. P., *Colossians: The Church's Lord and the Christian's Liberty* (Exeter, 1972).
——, *The Epistle of Paul to the Philippians* (London, 1959).
——, *Worship in the Early Church* (London, 1964).
Marxsen, W., *Introduction to the New Testament* (ET, Oxford, 1968).
Masson, C., *L'Épître de Saint Paul aux Colossiens* (Paris, 1950).
——, *Les Deux Épîtres de Saint Paul aux Thessaloniciens* (Paris, 1957).
Mattern, L., *Das Verständnis des Gerichtes bei Paulus* (Zürich, 1966).
Menzies, A. H., *The Second Epistle of the Apostle Paul to the Corinthians* (London, 1912).
Meyer, H. A. W., *Critical and Exegetical Handbook to the Epistle to the Romans* 1 (ET, Edinburgh, 1873).
——, *Critical and Exegetical Handbook to the Epistles to the Corinthians* 1, 2 (ET Edinburgh, 1877, 1879).
Michael, J. H., *The Epistle of Paul to the Philippians* (London, 1928).
Michaelis, W., *Der Brief des Paulus an die Philipper* (Leipzig, 1935).
——, 'κράτος', *TDNT* 3, pp. 905-910.
——, 'ὁδός', *TDNT* 5, pp. 42-114.
——, 'πάσχω', *TDNT* 5, pp. 904-939.
Michel, O., *Der Brief an die Römer* (Göttingen, ¹³1966).
Milligan, G., *St. Paul's Epistles to the Thessalonians* (London, 1908).
Minear, P. S., 'Gratitude and Mission in the Epistle to the Romans', *Basileia. Festschrift für W. Freytag* (Stuttgart, 1959), pp. 42-48, now reprinted in *The Obedience of Faith* (London, 1971), pp. 102-110.

Moffatt, J., *Grace in the New Testament* (London, 1931).
——, *Love in the New Testament* (London, 1929).
——, 'The First and Second Epistles to the Thessalonians', *The Expositor's Greek Testament* 4, ed. W. Robertson Nicoll (London, 1910), pp. 1-54.
——, *The First Epistle of Paul to the Corinthians* (London, 1938).
Molland, E., *Das paulinische Evangelion. Das Wort und die Sache* (Oslo, 1934).
Montgomery, J. A., 'Hebrew Ḥesed and Greek Charis', *HTR* 32 (1939), pp. 97-98.
Moore, A. L., *I and II Thessalonians* (London, 1969).
Morris, L., *The Apostolic Preaching of the Cross* (London, 1955).
——, *The Epistles of Paul to the Thessalonians* (London, 1959).
——, *The First Epistle of Paul to the Corinthians* (London, 1958).
——, 'Καὶ ἅπαξ καὶ δίς', *NovT* 1 (1956), pp. 205-208.
Moule, C. F. D., *An Idiom Book of New Testament Greek* (Cambridge, 1953).
——, 'Sanctuary and Sacrifice in the Church of the New Testament', *JTS* N.S. 1 (1950), pp. 29-41.
——, *The Birth of the New Testament* (London, ²1966).
——, *The Epistles of Paul the Apostle to the Colossians and to Philemon* (Cambridge, 1957).
——, *Worship in the New Testament* (London, 1961).
Moulton, J. H., *A Grammar of New Testament Greek*. Vol. 3, *Syntax* (Edinburgh, 1963).
Müller, J., *The Epistles of Paul to the Philippians and to Philemon* (London, 1955).
Mullins, T. Y., 'Ascription as a Literary Form', *NTS* 19 (1972-1973), pp. 194-205.
——, 'Disclosure. A Literary Form in the New Testament', *NovT* 7 (1964), pp. 44-50.
——, 'Petition as a Literary Form', *NovT* 5 (1962), pp. 46-54.
Munck, J., *Paul and the Salvation of Mankind* (ET, London, 1959).
Murphy-O'Connor, J., 'Truth : Paul and Qumran', *Paul and Qumran*, ed. J. Murphy-O'Connor (London, 1968), pp. 179-230.
Murray, J., *The Epistle to the Romans* 1, 2 (London, 1959, 1965).
Mussner, F., 'Contributions made by Qumran to the understanding of the Epistle to the Ephesians', *Paul and Qumran*, ed. J. Murphy-O'Connor (London, 1968), pp. 159-178.
Nägeli, T., *Der Wortschatz des Apostels Paulus* (Göttingen, 1905).
Neil, W., *The Epistles of Paul to the Thessalonians* (London, 1950).
Neufeld, V. H., *The Earliest Christian Confessions* (Leiden, 1963).
Neugebauer, F., 'Das paulinische "In Christo" ', *NTS* 4 (1957-1958), pp. 124-138.
Nickle, K. F., *The Collection* (London, 1966).
Nielen, J. M., *Gebet und Gottesdienst im Neuen Testament* (Freiburg-i.-Br., 1937).
Norden, E., *Agnostos Theos* (Stuttgart, 1956 = ⁴1923).
Nygren, A., *Commentary on Romans* (ET, London, 1952).
O'Brien, P. T., 'Thanksgiving and the Gospel in Paul', *NTS* 21 (1974-1975), pp. 144-155.
Oepke, A., *Die kleineren Briefe des Apostels Paulus : Die Briefe an die Thessalonicher* (Göttingen, ¹⁰1965).
——, 'εἰς', *TDNT* 2, pp. 420-434.
——, 'ἐν', *TDNT* 2, pp. 537-543.
Oesterley, W. O. E., *The Jewish Background of the Christian Liturgy* (Oxford, 1925).
Orphal, E., *Das Paulusgebet* (Gotha, 1933).
Osty, E., *Les Épîtres de Saint Paul aux Corinthiens* (Paris, ³1959).
Pallis, A., *To the Romans* (Oxford, 1920).

Parratt, J. K., 'Romans i. 11 and Galatians iii. 5—Pauline evidence for the Laying on of Hands?', *ExT* 79 (1967-1968), pp. 151-152.
Parry, R. St. J., *The Epistle of Paul the Apostle to the Romans* (Cambridge, 1912).
——, *The First Epistle of Paul the Apostle to the Corinthians* (Cambridge, ²1926).
Pearson, B. A., '1 Thessalonians 2:13-16 : A Deutero-Pauline Interpolation', *HTR* 64 (1971), pp. 79-94.
Pedersen, J., *Israel. Its Life and Culture. I-II* (ET, London, 1926).
Percy, E., *Die Probleme der Kolosser- und Epheserbrief* (Lund, 1946).
Pfitzner, V. C., *Paul and the Agon Motif* (Leiden, 1967).
Piper, O., 'Praise of God and Thanksgiving', *Interp* 8 (1954), pp. 3-20.
Plummer, A., *A Commentary on St. Paul's First Epistle to the Thessalonians* (London, 1918).
——, *A Commentary on St. Paul's Second Epistle to the Thessalonians* (London, 1918).
——, *A Critical and Exegetical Commentary on the Second Epistle of St. Paul to the Corinthians* (Edinburgh, 1915).
Pollard, T. E., 'The Integrity of Philippians', *NTS* 13 (1966-1967), pp. 57-66.
Preiss, T., *Life in Christ* (ET, London, 1957).
Procksch, O. (with Kuhn, K. G.), 'ἅγιος', *TDNT* 1, pp. 88-115.
Prümm, K., 'Das Dynamische als Grund-Aspekt der Heilsordnung in der Sicht des Apostels Paulus', *Gregorianum* 42 (Rome, 1961), pp. 643-700.
——, *Diakonia Pneumatos I. Theologische Auslegung des zweiten Korintherbriefes* (Rome, 1967).
Rabin, C., *The Zadokite Documents* (Oxford, ²1958).
Rad, G. von (with Kittel, G.), 'δοκέω', *TDNT* 2, pp. 232-255.
Rankin, O. S., 'The Extent of the Influence of the Synagogue Service upon Christian Worship', *JJS* 1 (1948-1949), pp. 27-32.
Reicke, B., 'Some reflections on worship in the New Testament', *New Testament Essays*, ed. A. J. B. Higgins (Manchester, 1959), pp. 194-209.
Resch, A., *Der Paulinismus und die Logia Jesu* (Leipzig, 1904).
Richardson, A., *An Introduction to the Theology of the New Testament* (London, 1958).
Richardson, P., *Israel in the Apostolic Church* (Cambridge, 1969).
Rigaux, B., *Saint Paul. Les Épîtres aux Thessaloniciens* (Paris, 1956).
——, *The Letters of St. Paul* (ET, Chicago, 1968).
Robertson, A. and Plummer, A., *A Critical and Exegetical Commentary on the First Epistle of St. Paul to the Corinthians* (Edinburgh, ²1914).
Robertson, A. T., *A Grammar of the Greek New Testament in the Light of Historical Research* (Nashville, ⁴1923).
——, 'Philemon and Onesimus : Master and Slave', *Exp* 8, 19 (1920), pp. 29-48.
Robinson, D. W. B., 'Who Were the "Saints"?', *RThR* 22 (1963), pp. 45-53.
Robinson, J. Armitage, *St Paul's Epistle to the Ephesians* (London, ²1909).
Robinson, J. M., 'Die Hodajot-Formel in Gebet und Hymnus des Frühchristentums', *Apophoreta : Festschrift für Ernst Haenchen*, ed. W. Eltester and F. H. Kettler (Berlin, 1964), pp. 194-235.
——, 'The Historicality of Biblical Language', *The Old Testament and Christian Faith*, ed. B. W. Anderson (New York, 1963), pp. 124-158.
Rohr, I., *Das Gebet im Neuen Testament* (Münster, 1924).
Roller, O., *Das Formular der paulinischen Briefe* (Stuttgart, 1933).
Sanday, W. and Headlam, A. C., *A Critical and Exegetical Commentary on the Epistle to the Romans* (Edinburgh, ⁵1902).

Sanders, J. T., *The New Testament Christological Hymns* (Cambridge, 1971).
——, 'The Transition from Opening Epistolary Thanksgiving to Body in the Letters of the Pauline Corpus', *JBL* 81 (1962), pp. 348-362.
Schenk, W., *Der Segen im Neuen Testament* (Berlin, 1967).
Schermann, T., 'Εὐχαριστία und εὐχαριστεῖν in ihrem Bedeutungswandel bis 200 n. Chr.', *Philologus. Zeitschrift für das klassische Altertum* 69 (Leipzig, 1910), pp. 375-410.
Schettler, A., *Die paulinische Formel 'Durch Christus'* (Tübingen, 1907).
Schippers, R., 'The pre-synoptic tradition in 1 Thessalonians ii 13-16', *NovT* 8 (1966), pp. 223-234.
Schlatter, A., *Die Briefe an die Galater, Epheser, Kolosser und Philemon* (Stuttgart, 1949).
——, *Gottes Gerechtigkeit* (Stuttgart, ⁴1965).
——, *Paulus der Bote Jesu* (Stuttgart, ⁴1969).
Schlier, H., *Der Brief an die Epheser* (Düsseldorf, ⁶1968).
——, 'Doxa bei Paulus als heilsgeschichtlicher Begriff', *Studiorum Paulinorum Congressus* 1 (Rome, 1963), pp. 45-56.
——, 'αἱρέομαι', *TDNT* 1, pp. 180-185.
——, 'βέβαιος', *TDNT* 1, pp. 600-603.
——, 'θλίβω', *TDNT* 3, pp. 139-148.
Schmidt, K. L., 'καλέω', *TDNT* 3, pp. 487-536.
Schmiedel, P. W., 'Die Briefe an die Thessalonicher und an die Korinther', *Hand-Commentar zum Neuen Testament* 2.1, ed. H. J. Holtzmann *et al.* (Freiburg-i.-Br., 1892), pp. 1-276.
Schmithals, W., 'Die Thessalonicherbriefe als Briefkompositionen', *Zeit und Geschichte. Dankesgabe an Rudolf Bultmann zum 80. Geburtstag*, ed. E. Dinkler (Tübingen, 1964), pp. 295-315.
Schmitz, O. and Stählin, G., 'παρακαλέω', *TDNT* 5, pp. 773-799.
Schneider, C., 'Paulus und das Gebet', *Angelos* 4 (Leipzig, 1932), pp. 11-28.
Schniewind, J., *Die Begriffe Wort und Evangelium bei Paulus* (Bonn, 1910).
——, 'καταγγέλλω', *TDNT* 1, pp. 70-72.
Schrenk, G., 'Der Römerbrief als Missionsdokument', *Studien zu Paulus* (Zürich, 1954), pp. 81-106.
——, 'δικαιοσύνη', *TDNT* 2, pp. 192-210.
——, 'εὐδοκέω', *TDNT* 2, pp. 738-751.
——, 'ἐκλογή', *TDNT* 4, pp. 176-181.
—— (with Quell, G.), 'πατήρ', *TDNT* 5, pp. 945-1014.
Schubert, P., *Form and Function of the Pauline Thanksgivings* (Berlin, 1939).
Schweizer, E., *Church Order in the New Testament* (ET, London, 1961).
——, *Der Gottesdienst im Neuen Testament* (Zürich, 1958).
——, 'The Church as the Missionary Body of Christ', *Neotestamentica* (Zürich, 1963), pp. 317-329.
——, 'πνεῦμα' (in NT), *TDNT* 6, pp. 396-451.
Seeberg, A., *Die Anbetung des Herrn bei Paulus* (Dorpat, 1891).
Seesemann, H., *Der Begriff ΚΟΙΝΩΝΙΑ im Neuen Testament* (Giessen, 1933).
Seidensticker, P., *Lebendiges Opfer* (Münster, 1954).
Selwyn, E. G., *The First Epistle of St. Peter* (London, 1946).
Simon, W. G. H., *The First Epistle to the Corinthians* (London, 1959).
Singer, S., ed., *The Authorised Daily Prayer Book* (London, ²⁴1956).

Smith, C. W. F., 'Prayer', *The Interpreter's Dictionary of the Bible* 3, ed. G. A. Buttrick (New York, 1962), pp. 857-867.
Snaith, N. H., *The Distinctive Ideas of the Old Testament* (London, 1944).
Spicq, C., *Agape in the New Testament* 2 (ET, St. Louis, 1965).
Stacey, W. D., *The Pauline View of Man* (London, 1956).
Stanley, D. M., ' "Become imitators of me" : The Pauline Conception of Apostolic Tradition', *Biblica* 40 (1959), pp. 859-877.
Stauffer, E., *New Testament Theology* (ET, London, 1955).
——, 'ἀγαπάω' (in NT), *TDNT* 1, pp. 35-55.
——, 'ἐγώ', *TDNT* 2, pp. 343-362.
——, 'θεός' (in NT), *TDNT* 3, pp. 100-119.
Strachan, R. H., *The Second Epistle of Paul to the Corinthians* (London, 1935).
Strathmann, H., 'λατρεύω', *TDNT* 4, pp. 58-65.
——, 'μάρτυς', *TDNT* 4, pp. 474-514.
Stuhlmacher, P., *Das paulinische Evangelium. I : Vorgeschichte* (Göttingen, 1968).
Suhl, A., 'Der Philemonbrief als Beispiel paulinischer Paränese', *Kairos* 15 (1973), pp. 267-279.
Sullivan, K., 'Epignōsis in the Epistles of St. Paul', *Studiorum Paulinorum Congressus* 2 (Rome, 1963), pp. 405-416.
Swain, L., 'Prayer and the Apostolate in Paul', *The Clergy Review* 51 (1966), pp. 458-465.
Tannehill, R. C., *Dying and Rising with Christ* (Berlin, 1967).
Tasker, R. V. G., *The Second Epistle of Paul to the Corinthians* (London, 1958).
Taylor, V., *Forgiveness and Reconciliation* (London, 1941).
Therrien, G., *Le discernement dans les écrits pauliniens* (Paris, 1973).
Thieme, K., 'Die Struktur des Ersten Thessalonicher-Briefes', *Abraham Unser Vater. Festschrift für O. Michel*, ed. O. Betz et al. (Leiden, 1963), pp. 450-458.
Thomson, J. G. S. S., 'Prayer', *The New Bible Dictionary*, ed. J. D. Douglas (London, 1962), pp. 1019-1023.
Thornton, L. S., *The Common Life in the Body of Christ* (London, n.d., ? 1942).
Thrall, M. E., *Greek Particles in the New Testament* (Leiden, 1962).
Thüsing, W., *Per Christum in Deum* (Münster, ²1969).
Trocmé, E., 'L'Épître aux Romains et la méthode missionaire de l'apôtre Paul', *NTS* 7 (1960-1961), pp. 148-153.
Turner, N., *Grammatical Insights into the New Testament* (Edinburgh, 1965).
——, *Syntax*. See Moulton, J. H.
Unnik, W. C. van, '*Dominus Vobiscum* : the background of a liturgical formula', *New Testament Essays*, ed. A. J. B. Higgins (Manchester, 1959), pp. 270-305.
——, 'Reisepläne und Amen-Sagen, Zusammenhang und Gedankenfolge in 2 Korinther 1:15-24', *Studia Paulina in honorem J. de Zwaan*, ed. J. N. Sevenster and W. C. van Unnik (Haarlem, 1953), pp. 215-234.
Viard, R. P. A., *Épître aux Romains* (Paris, 1948).
Vincent, M. R., *A Critical and Exegetical Commentary on the Epistles to the Philippians and to Philemon* (Edinburgh, 1897).
Vos, G., *The Pauline Eschatology* (Grand Rapids, 1952).
Warfield, B. B., *The Person and Work of Christ* (Philadelphia, 1950).
Warneck, J., *Paulus im Lichte der heutigen Heidenmission* (Berlin, ⁴1922).
Wegenast, K., *Das Verständnis der Tradition bei Paulus und in den Deuteropaulinen* (Neukirchen-Vluyn, 1962).

Weiser, A., *The Psalms* (ET, London, 1962).
——, 'πιστεύω' (in OT), *TDNT* 6, pp. 182-196.
Weiss, B., *Der Brief an die Römer* (Göttingen, [8]1891).
——, *Die paulinischen Brief* (Leipzig, 1896).
Weiss, J., *Der erste Korintherbrief* (Göttingen, [9]1910).
Wendland, H.-D., *Die Briefe an die Korinther* (Göttingen, [10]1965).
Wendland, P., *Die urchristliche Literaturformen* (Tübingen, [2/3]1912).
Westermann, C., *Der Segen in der Bibel und im Handeln der Kirche* (München, 1968).
——, *The Praise of God in the Psalms* (ET, London, 1966).
Wetter, G. P., *Charis* (Leipzig, 1913).
White, J. L., 'Introductory Formulae in the Body of the Pauline Letter', *JBL* 90 (1971), pp. 91-97.
Whiteley, D. E. H., *The Theology of St. Paul* (Oxford, 1964).
Wickert, U., 'Der Philemonbrief—Privatbrief oder apostolisches Schreiben?', *ZNW* 52 (1961), pp. 230-238.
Wiederkehr, D., *Die Theologie der Berufung in den Paulusbriefen* (Freiburg, Schweiz, 1963).
Wikenhauser, A., *Pauline Mysticism* (ET, London, 1960).
Wiles, G. P., *Paul's Intercessory Prayers* (Cambridge, 1974).
——, *The Function of Intercessory Prayer in Paul's Apostolic Ministry with Special Reference to the First Epistle to the Thessalonians* (unpublished Ph.D. thesis, Yale University, 1965).
Windisch, H., *Der zweite Korintherbrief* (Göttingen, [9]1924).
——, 'βάρβαρος', *TDNT* 1, pp. 546-553.
Winer, G. B., *A Grammar of the Idiom of the New Testament* (ET, Philadelphia, [7]1872).
Wobbe, J., *Der Charis-Gedanke bei Paulus* (Münster, 1932).
Wohlenberg, G., *Der erste und zweite Thessalonicherbrief* (Leipzig, 1903).
Zahn, T., *Der Brief des Paulus an die Römer* (Leipzig, [1/2]1910).
——, *Introduction to the New Testament* 1 (ET, Edinburgh, 1909).
——, in *Zeitschrift für kirchliche Wissenschaft und kirchliches Leben* 6 (Leipzig, 1885), pp. 185-202.
Zerwick, M., *Biblical Greek* (ET, Rome, 1963).
Ziesler, J. A., *The Meaning of Righteousness in Paul* (Cambridge, 1972).
Zuntz, G., *The Text of the Epistles* (London, 1953).
Zunz, L., *Die gottesdienstlichen Vorträge der Juden* (Frankfurt, [2]1892).

INDEX OF PASSAGES CITED

A. THE OLD TESTAMENT

Genesis
- 1 & 2 — 27
- 1:22 — 89
- 1:28 — 89
- 8:17 — 89
- 9:1 — 89
- 9:7 — 89
- 14:19f. — 234
- 14:19 — 236
- 28:20-22 — 217
- 30:27 — 110
- 32:24ff. — 199
- 37:35 — 243
- 39:21 — 110

Exodus
- 6:6 — 97
- 14:4, 17f. — 182
- 14:30 — 97
- 15:26 — 88
- 31:3 — 36, 86
- 33:12f. — 110
- 34:6 — 93, 242
- 34:29f. — 182
- 35:31 — 86
- 35:35 — 86

Leviticus
- 9:6 — 182
- 10:19 — 88

Deuteronomy
- 7:9 — 130
- 7:14 — 236
- 10:9 — 95
- 10:21 — 174
- 12:8 — 88
- 12:12 — 95
- 14:1f. — 77
- 14:27 — 95
- 14:29 — 95
- 18:1 — 95
- 24:28 — 211
- 26:18 — 187
- 28:3 — 240
- 28:6 — 240
- 32:6 — 77
- 33:2 — 164
- 33:3 — 95
- 33:12 — 186
- 34:9 — 86

Joshua
- 19:9 — 95
- 22:27 — 210

Judges
- 6:9 — 97
- 8:34 — 97
- 18:10 — 159
- 19:5, 8 — 163
- 19:19 — 159

Ruth
- 2:20 — 236

1 Samuel
- 12:5 — 210
- 15:13 — 236
- 25:32 — 234
- 25:33 — 236
- 25:39 — 234

2 Samuel
- 7:14 — 77
- 10:2 — 243
- 15:25 — 110
- 18:28 — 234
- 22:50 — 37

1 Kings
- 8:14f. — 234
- 8:55f. — 234
- 20:11 — 174

1 Chronicles
17:13	77
22:10	77
22:12	86
28:6	77
29:10	240
29:18	162

2 Chronicles
1:10f.	86
2:11	237
12:14	162
19:3	162
30:9	242

Ezra
8:21-23	217

Nehemiah
9:17	242
9:25	180
9:31	242
9:35	180

Job
2:11	243
12:13	86
21:34	243
31:2	95
42:11	243

Psalms
1:6	53
2:11	27
3:7	21
5:2	21
5:8	218
7:1	21
7:3	21
7:6	21
9:9	176
11:1	27
13:2	217
13:3	21
17:3	34
18:2, 6, 21, 28	21
21:13	37
22:1	78
23:4	243
25:2	27
25:3	92
26:2	34
30:4	163
32:7	176
33:18f.	97
34:9	159
34:19	176
35:17	217
35:28	37
37:4	221
37:9	92
37:34	92
37:39	176
40:2	162
41:13	37, 234
42:2	217
42:9	158
50:15	176
51:3	174
52:1	174
57:1	27
63:7	158
66:10	34
68:5	77
68:17	164
69:9	247
71:21	243
72:18f.	234
73:4	174
74:4	174, 175
77:3	158
78:22	79
79:9	97
80:14ff.	90
86:13	97
86:15	242
86:17	243
88:15	249
89:6	95
89:7	181, 182, 194
89:26	77
89:52	234
94:3	174
94:19	243
96:6	163
96:7	174
97:12	163

INDEX OF PASSAGES CITED

102:28	159	35:2	182
103:7	86	38:3	88
103:8	242	40:1ff.	243
103:13	94, 241	40:26, 28	27
103:17	241	41:4	27
104:15	163	41:20	27
105:47	174	42:5f.	27
106:48	234	42:5	27
111:4	242	43:1, 7, 15	27
112:8	163	44:1-6	27
116:12	237	44:6	27
118:8	27	45:7, 8, 12, 18	27
119	243	48:12	27
119:5	218	49:3	182, 184
119:12	240	49:7	130
119:55	158	51:3	243
119:62	158	51:12	241, 243
119:148	158	54:11ff.	243
125:1	27	54:16	27
143:10	86	55:10f.	152
145:5	163	57:6	95
145:8	242	57:18	243
		63:16	77
Proverbs		64:8	77
4:26	218	66:5	181
5:2	34	66:13	241
8:10	34	66:15	194
9:15	218	66:18	182
11:30	36		
13:13	218	Jeremiah	
14:7	34	3:4	77
15:7	34	3:16	89
21:3	88	3:19	77
22:11	110	9:7	34
25:14	174	9:23f.	174
27:1	174	11:20	34
27:21	34	12:6	79
29:27	218	13:25	95
29:48	88	23:3	89
31:30	110	23:29	152
		31:9	77
Isaiah		42:5	210
2:10, 19, 21	181, 194		
5:1-7	90	Ezekiel	
5:16	182	18:25	218
11:2	86		
24:15	181	Daniel	
28:29	243	1:17	86

3:22	156
3:42	91
6:16	211
7:14	211
7:18	126

Joel
2:13	242
2:31	130

Amos
5:18ff.	130
6:13	36

Jonah
4:2	242

Zechariah
10:2	243
14:5	164

Malachi
1:6	77
2:10	77

B. THE APOCRYPHA AND PSEUDEPIGRAPHA OF THE OLD TESTAMENT

Baruch
5:5	44

2 Baruch
51:5, 10, 12	96

Ecclesiasticus
2:11	241
7:33	124
38:30	124
39:6, 9f.	86

1 Enoch
104:6	96

Jubilees
12:21	217
13:7	217
13:15	217
22:27	217

1 Maccabees
12:11	21

2 Maccabees
1:11ff.	8
1:23-29	242
3:12	163
12:23	176
13:12	21

4 Maccabees
17:4	148

Prayer of Manasses
14	91

Psalms of Solomon
17:1	159

Tobit
4:19	217
11:1	217

Wisdom
5:5	96
9:1	241
14:3, 4	217
19:1-12	217

C. THE NEW TESTAMENT

Matthew
2:10	157
3:15	180
5-7	53

INDEX OF PASSAGES CITED

6:13	97, 98, 240
6:28	173
8:5	244
11:25ff.	78
13:13	155
13:21	176
13:32	173
18:23-35	93
19:21	89
27:43	97
27:46	78

Mark
1:11	98
1:19	158
4:1ff.	90, 102
4:1-9	89
4:8	173
4:13-20	89
4:17	176
5:18	244
9:7	98
11:24	84
12:6	98
13:9-13	176
14:36	78
14:61	236
15:34	78

Luke
1:51ff.	92
1:68	236
1:74	97, 212
1:80	173
2:37	211
7:4	244
8:15	92
11:4	97
14:19	34
15:17	32
17:32	147
22:32	221
22:52f.	98
23:46	204

John
3.10	123
3:29	157
7:4	89
11:57	181
15:20ff.	176
15:20	147
16:4	147
16:21	147
17:10	183
17:22	183

Acts
2:42	21
2:46	21
4:2	209
4:33	120
5:41	93
6:4	21
7:2	182
7:42	211
8:1	176
8:22	216
9:4	247
11:19	176
11:23	116
12:15	180
13:5	209
13:38	209
13:50	176
14:22	176
15:36	209
15:39	123
17:13	209
18:15	89
18:17	108
18:23	221
20:24	110
20:32	95
20:35	147
22:10	217
24:14	212
24:16	35
26:7	211
26:18	95, 96
28:22	208
28:26	155

Romans
1	223, 224, 225
1:1ff.	101

292 INDEX OF PASSAGES CITED

1:1-7	203, 266	3:22	80
1:1	213, 219	3:24	110
1:3	213	3:26	80
1:5	25, 111, 206f., 219	4:1	174
1:7	206, 225	4:4	228
1:8ff.	8, 107, 116, 170, 185, 197-230, 261, 262	4:16	122
		4:24	250
1:8-17	200, 201, 202, 225	5:1-5	30
1:8-15	202, 214, 225	5:1	204, 227
1:8-12	201	5:2	110, 205, 227
1:8	7, 9, 20, 21, 23, 62, 65, 76, 108, 144, 202-210, 211, 222, 227, 229, 266, 267	5:7	57
		5:8	110
		5:9	227
1:9f.	9, 202	5:10	227
1:9	21, 50, 133, 144f., 153, 197, 201, 203, 210-215, 221	5:11	204, 227
		5:12-21	185
		5:15f.	124, 227
1:10	21, 22, 43, 61, 97, 144, 197, 198, 199, 201, 202, 203, 215, 216-221, 227, 228, 264, 266, 269	5:15	110
		5:18	171
		5:21	204
		6:17	7, 9, 62, 236
1:11ff.	221, 224	6:23	124, 227
1:11-15	202	7:3	171
1:11f.	223	7:13	57
1:11	124, 197, 198, 201, 202, 221, 222, 227	7:18	222
		7:19	57
1:12	201, 202, 222	7:24	97, 217
1:13ff.	202, 224	7:25	7, 20, 62, 65, 171, 174, 204, 227, 236
1:13-15	202, 222		
1:13	120, 172, 198, 201, 202, 211, 219, 222, 223	8:3	227
		8:8	88
1:14f.	198	8:10f.	212
1:14	228	8:11	250
1:15	201, 223, 225	8:12	171, 228
1:16f.	152, 198, 202, 214, 226, 229, 261	8:14	227
		8:15f.	9
1:16	201, 202, 213	8:15	78
1:17	120, 202	8:16	212
1:21	62	8:17	182
1:22	89	8:19	125, 227
1:25	211, 227, 236, 240	8:23	125, 188
2:4	117	8:24f.	81
2:10	57	8:25	93
2:16	152	8:26f.	9
2:18	35	8:26	156, 172, 228
3:21ff.	226	8:29f.	187
3:21-27	174	8:29	187, 227
3:21-24	110	8:30	178, 190

8:32	123, 227	15:8	122
8:33	129	15:13	9, 32, 79, 161, 163
8:37	172, 227	15:14-33	202, 223, 224
9-11	225	15:14	85, 180
9:3	89	15:15f.	111
9:5	236	15:15	111
9:11	57, 151	15:16	211, 214
9:16	171	15:18f.	223
9:17	26	15:19	214, 224
9:18	171	15:20	214, 223
9:22	158	15:22-25	211
9:23	117	15:22f.	223
10:1	180	15:26	24
10:12	117	15:27	228
10:14	120	15:29	221f.
10:17	120	15:30ff.	199, 210, 228
10:18	209	15:30-32	9, 199, 218, 251
11:2	187	15:30f.	97, 166
11:5	151	15:30	199, 204, 219, 252
11:7	151	15:31	199
11:16	188	15:32	199, 219, 220, 227
11:28	151	15:33	161
11:33-36	213	16	225
11:33	117	16:4	62
12:1	212, 213, 227, 244	16:5	188
12:2	34, 57, 227	16:6	149
12:3	111	16:12	149
12:6	227	16:15	80
12:9	57	16:19	208
12:11	212	16:22	203
12:12	9, 21, 228	16:25	128, 152, 221
12:13	24		
12:21	57	1 Corinthians	
13:3	57	1-4	108
14:6	20, 62	1:1	131, 219
14:12	171	1:2	113, 131
14:16	57	1:3	111
14:17	98	1:4ff.	7, 83, 185, 227, 267
14:19	171	1:4-9	3, 107-137, 186, 257, 260, 261, 262, 263, 264
14:20f.	35		
15	214, 223, 224, 225	1:4-7(8)	108
15:1	88	1:4	9, 21, 26, 43, 62, 76, 108-116, 123, 126, 132, 156, 238
15:2	57, 88		
15:3	88		
15:4	93	1:5	112, 115, 116-120, 121, 124, 126, 144, 265, 267
15:5f.	9, 161		
15:5	92, 161, 247	1:6	112, 120-122, 124, 127, 132, 267
15:6	76		

INDEX OF PASSAGES CITED

1:7f.	263, 264	7:1	112, 117, 134
1:7	107, 111, 121, 123-126, 127, 132, 136, 157, 174	7:5	157
		7:7	124
1:8f.	27, 107	7:25	134
1:8	107, 112, 121, 122, 124, 125, 126-130, 132, 136, 163, 209, 268	7:26ff.	176
		7:31	117
		7:32	88
1:9	107, 108, 112, 122, 127, 128, 130-133, 137, 256, 265, 266	7:33	88
		7:34	88
		8:1	119, 134
1:10-4:21	108, 134	8:7	119
1:10ff.	112	8:10	119
1:10	107, 132, 158, 244	8:11	119
1:14	62	9:2	222
1:17	119	9:14	209
1:18	152	10:13	131, 238
1:21	121	10:16ff.	112
1:23	120	10:30	62
1:26	131, 178	10:32	35
1:27	187	10:33	88
1:29	181	11:24	62
1:30	68, 99	11:26	209
2:1-5	136	12-14	53, 119, 120
2:1	120, 209	12	124
2:2	120	12:1	134
2:3	112	12:4-11	114
2:4	112, 121, 152	12:7	114
2:7	187	12:8	119
2:8	182	12:10	118
3:6	173	12:11	114
3:7	173	12:28	118
3:8	149	13	118
3:10	111, 214	13:2	98, 119
3:11	130	13:8	119
3:12	130	13:13	30
3:13	130	14:1	118
4:7	114	14:2	118
4:8	112, 113, 117, 126, 136	14:5	114
4:12	149	14:6	119
4:15	222	14:14	212
4:20	98	14:16	62
5:2	130	14:17	62
5:3	127	14:18	62
5:4	127	15:1-11	136
5:8	35	15:1	152
6:9f.	98	15:10	149
6:11	113	15:12	125f.
7	131	15:20	188

INDEX OF PASSAGES CITED

15:23	188		185, 234, 236, 238, 249, 250-254, 255, 256, 258, 263, 266, 270, 271
15:24-28	99		
15:50	98		
15:57	7, 20, 62, 65, 204, 236	1:12	35, 120, 235
15:58	32, 149	1:15-24	122
16:1	134	1:18	122, 131, 133
16:2	218	1:19f.	206
16:4	171	1:19	122
16:7	112, 117	1:20	122
16:12	219	1:21f.	122
16:15	188	1:21	122, 127, 128
16:16	149	1:22	122
16:21	47	1:23	210
16:22	206	1:24	122
16:23	110	2:4	254
		2:7	254
2 Corinthians		2:8	254
1-9	247, 255, 256, 262	2:12f.	248
1	176, 242, 244	2:14	7, 9, 62, 119, 236, 254
1:1	219	2:16	254
1:3ff.	7, 233-258, 260, 262	2:17	35
1:3-11	7, 234, 236, 249, 254-257	3:1-6:10	255
		3:4	54
1:3-7	242, 246, 255	3:6	67, 95
1:3f.	233, 234, 236-247, 248, 250, 254, 255, 265	3:7	254
		3:9	254
1:3	74, 76, 235, 236, 241, 242, 250, 257	4:3	152
		4:6	119
1:4ff.	176	4:7	117
1:4	44, 76, 233, 235, 239, 242, 245, 246, 247, 248, 250, 256	4:8	249, 254
		4:10-12	255
		4:10	254
1:5-7	245, 246, 247-248, 255	4:11	254
1:5f.	255	4:12	254
1:5	120, 127, 242, 245, 247, 255, 256, 257	4:13	68
		4:14	250
1:6	56, 92, 168, 242, 246, 247, 248, 255	4:15	5, 9, 62, 238, 253, 254, 256, 258, 270, 271
1:7	122, 235, 242, 246, 247, 255, 256	4:16-5:10	255
		4:17	254
1:8ff.	235, 246	5	255
1:8-11	235, 245, 255	5:1-10	249, 255
1:8-10	255	5:4	254
1:8	172, 235, 248, 249	5:15	254
1:9f.	248	5:20	254
1:9	235, 236, 249, 250, 252	6:1	111, 254
1:10	97, 249f., 252, 253	6:4ff.	250, 255
1:11	5, 7, 9, 62, 63, 94, 124,	6:4	93, 254

6:5	149	12:21	21
6:6	93, 119	13:11	254
6:9	254		
6:10	117	Galatians	
6:14-7:1	256	1:1	219, 250
6:14	254	1:6ff.	265
7:1	163	1:6f.	141
7:3	255	1:6	110, 141
7:4	254	1:8	141
7:5	248, 254	1:9	141
7:6	254	1:10	88
7:7	254	1:11	152
7:10	254	1:15f.	111
7:13	254	1:15	219
8	256	2:2	151
8:1	254	2:7ff.	111
8:2	117, 254	2:9	111
8:4	24, 254	2:10	147
8:6	254	2:13	123
8:7	32, 117, 119, 254	2:16	80
8:9	110, 117, 254	2:20	80
8:13	254	3:3	26
8:14	181	3:5	221
8:16	7, 62, 236, 254	3:22	80
8:17	254	3:26	79
8:19	254	4:6	9, 78
8:23	254	4:11	149
9	256	5:5f.	30
9:5	254	5:5	81, 125
9:8	254	5:6	79
9:10	173	5:21	98
9:11f.	5, 62, 238, 253, 254	5:22	36, 93, 180
9:12	254	6:1	158
9:13	24, 254	6:10	57, 171
9:14	254	6:11	47
9:15	7, 9, 62, 236, 254	6:18	212
10-13	63, 255, 256		
10:1	174, 254	Ephesians	
10:2	89	1	263
10:5	119	1:1	219
10:14	152, 172	1:3ff.	7, 167, 233, 234, 239, 262, 263, 264
10:15	149, 173	1:3-19	3, 239, 259
11:6	119	1:3-12(14)	3
11:23	149, 250	1:3	76, 222, 236, 239
11:27	149	1:4f.	168
11:31	76, 236, 240	1:4	120, 128, 187, 188
12:8	197, 205, 206, 254	1:5	187
12:9	91		

INDEX OF PASSAGES CITED

1:6f.	110	1:3	12, 19, 20, 21, 22, 25, 38, 40, 41-46, 62, 76, 108, 126 156, 267
1:8	117		
1:11	187		
1:14	191	1:4-6	38
1:15ff.	7, 167, 185, 239	1:4	9, 19, 21, 22, 26, 31, 38, 50, 78, 94, 145, 166, 206, 216
1:15f.	3, 239		
1:15	9, 51, 79, 80, 267		
1:16f.	216	1:5	19, 22, 23, 25, 26, 38, 39, 40, 43, 46, 55, 56, 126, 137, 150, 156, 267
1:16	9, 21, 22, 43, 62		
1:17-19	3, 87, 103		
1:17	32, 56, 76, 85, 144	1:6	19, 22, 23, 25, 26, 27, 28, 38, 39, 40f., 51, 79, 111, 116, 128, 144, 150, 151, 157, 196, 264, 267, 268, 270
1:18f.	91		
1:18	79, 95		
1:19	91		
2:8f.	110		
2:12	269	1:7f.	19, 20, 29, 37, 38, 40, 198
2:19	171		
3:2	25	1:7	22, 24, 25, 39, 46, 120, 122, 137, 153
3:7	91		
3:8	25, 80	1:8	198, 210
3:9	187	1:9ff.	39, 263, 270, 271
3:16-19	87, 103	1:9-11	9, 14, 19, 20, 29-37, 40, 263
3:16	91		
3:18	80	1:9	22, 29, 31, 32, 33, 39, 54, 78, 83, 85, 144, 162, 167, 178, 195, 196, 216, 270
3:20	91, 156		
4:1	178		
4:2-5	30		
4:13	56	1:10f.	20
4:28	149	1:10	28, 35, 36, 37, 39, 129, 163, 264, 270, 271
5:4	62		
5:9	180	1:11	20, 35f., 37, 39, 89, 179, 196, 266, 271
5:14	206		
5:19	206	1:12f.	20, 39
5:20	21, 62	1:12	24, 39
5:25-27	128	1:14	27, 38
6:10	91	1:15-18	38
6:18	21, 80, 251	1:15	180
6:19	251	1:16	24, 39
6:22	26	1:17f.	209
		1:18	38
		1:19	25, 251
Philippians		1:22	39, 187
1:1	80	1:25	22, 27, 38
1:2	22	1:26	32
1:3ff.	7, 185, 262	1:27	24, 39
1:3-11	19-46, 259, 261	1:30	25
1:3-6	19, 20-28, 29, 37, 40	2:1ff.	30, 39
1:3f.	83	2:1-11	14

298   INDEX OF PASSAGES CITED

2:1	39, 244	1:3ff.	7, 63, 83, 185, 198, 261, 263, 264
2:2	38		
2:5	40	1:3-14	62-104
2:13	26	1:3-8	67, 71
2:14-16	14	1:3-5	75-82
2:15f.	39	1:3	21, 22, 50, 62, 63, 69, 76, 83, 168, 204, 240
2:16	28, 149		
2:17f.	38	1:4ff.	111
2:17	22	1:4f.	30, 79, 81
2:22	24, 39	1:4	9, 23, 51, 53, 69, 79, 81, 83, 267
2:24	27, 38		
2:28	38	1:5f.	153
2:29	38	1:5	26, 67, 68, 69, 70, 81, 150
3:1ff.	38		
3:1	38	1:6-9	101
3:2f.	38	1:6-8	81, 103, 198
3:3	27, 38, 212	1:6f.	90
3:4	27, 38	1:6	67, 68, 69, 70, 83, 85, 87, 89, 90, 101, 120, 129, 173, 209, 265
3:6ff.	39		
3:8	40		
3:9	80	1:7f.	51
3:10	39, 247	1:7	67, 69, 82, 120
3:13f.	40	1:8	68, 83, 87
3:18f.	38	1:9ff.	73, 79, 196, 270, 271
4:1ff.	30	1:9-20	73
4:1-3	14	1:9-14	69, 82-100, 102, 103, 198, 269
4:1	38, 39		
4:2ff.	39	1:9-12	73
4:3	24, 39	1:9-11	83
4:4	38	1:9f.	32, 56, 85
4:6	9, 61, 62	1:9	21, 63, 67, 68, 69, 82, 83, 84, 86, 89, 94, 116, 144, 153, 167, 178, 179, 195, 196, 270
4:8f.	14, 40		
4:9	38		
4:10-20	38, 45, 46		
4:10	38, 46	1:10	63, 67, 68, 69, 82, 83, 89, 90, 129, 173, 209, 265
4:11	89		
4:12	32		
4:14f.	25	1:11f.	166
4:14	39, 46, 176	1:11	63, 67, 69, 72, 74, 83, 89, 91, 150, 168
4:15	24, 39, 46, 188		
4:16	44	1:12ff.	66, 100, 270
4:17	39, 46	1:12-20	72, 73, 74, 75
4:18	32, 46	1:12-14	63, 72, 73, 74, 93, 94, 102, 103, 133, 264, 268
4:19	21, 91, 117		
4:21	22	1:12	9, 62, 64, 67, 68, 69, 72, 73, 74, 83, 89, 93, 94, 95, 96, 238, 268, 269
Colossians			
1:1	219	1:13-29	74

INDEX OF PASSAGES CITED

1:13f.	69, 73, 268	3:1-4	69, 81
1:13	67, 68, 74, 75, 94, 96, 98, 99	3:4	68, 69, 81, 182
		3:5-4:6	64
1:14	67, 71, 74f., 96, 99	3:5	64
1:15ff.	75	3:7	69
1:15-20	68, 71, 72, 73, 74, 83, 93, 99, 261	3:8	83
		3:10	69
1:15	72, 74f.	3:11	83
1:19	69	3:12-17	64
1:20	68, 71	3:12	64, 69, 101
1:21-2:3	71	3:14	69, 83, 101
1:21-23	71	3:15ff.	101
1:21	64, 66	3:15	62, 64, 69
1:22	69, 129, 163	3:16f.	83
1:23ff.	76	3:16	62, 64, 69, 206
1:23	69, 70, 71, 81, 209	3:17	20, 62, 65, 69, 77, 101
1:24	68, 69, 159, 176, 247	3:18	64
1:25	69	3:19	69
1:26f.	81	3:20	83
1:26	68, 69, 187	3:22	83
1:27	66, 68, 69, 70, 81, 182	4	69, 70
1:28	69, 83, 101, 104	4:2-6	64
1:29	56, 68, 69, 91, 149	4:2	21, 62, 64, 65, 69, 251
2:1f.	79	4:3	69, 251
2:1	76	4:5	69, 101
2:2f.	83	4:7ff.	64
2:2	56, 59, 68, 69, 70	4:7	67, 69, 83
2:3	69, 71	4:8	26
2:4	68	4:9	69, 83
2:5	69, 80	4:11	98
2:6ff.	71	4:12	22, 51, 69, 83, 84, 102, 199
2:6f.	64		
2:6	64, 69, 101	4:16	48
2:7	32, 62, 64, 69	4:17	48, 69
2:8	64, 87	4:18	47, 147
2:9f.	83		
2:9	69	1 Thessalonians	
2:10	69	1:1-2:12	142
2:11-15	69	1:1	189
2:11	68	1:2ff.	7, 8, 141-166, 168, 172, 185, 261, 263, 264
2:12	68, 69, 91, 250		
2:13	83	1:2-3:13	141, 142, 144, 145, 259
2:15	68	1:2-3:10	160
2:16	68	1:2-10	143
2:19	69, 83, 173	1:2-5	141, 143, 145, 146-153, 154
2:22	83		
2:23	69, 87	1:2f.	9, 267
3	69	1:2	21, 22, 43, 62, 76, 145,

299

	156, 158, 165, 168, 174, 206	2:19	165
		2:20	193
1:3ff.	14	3:2f.	160
1:3	23, 24, 30, 79, 92, 102, 146, 147, 165, 172, 175, 180, 195, 260	3:2	163, 165, 192, 221
		3:3	176
		3:5	149
1:4	151, 165, 168, 186, 192, 267	3:6-10	142, 157
		3:6-9	156
1:5-2:14ff.	144	3:6	156, 192
1:5-2:14	144	3:7	157, 192
1:5f.	26, 267	3:8	156
1:5	116, 120, 143, 144, 152, 153, 155, 165, 166, 189, 190, 192, 265, 267	3:9ff.	7, 145, 156, 168, 185
		3:9-13	141, 143, 145, 156-164
		3:9f.	145, 146, 164
1:6-2:12	144	3:9	43, 62, 76, 156, 157, 164, 165, 166, 168, 266
1:6-10	143, 153		
1:6	153, 155, 165, 166, 189, 192	3:10-13	196
		3:10f.	61, 197, 269
1:8	54, 174, 175, 192, 209	3:10	21, 145, 157, 158, 160, 161, 162, 164, 172, 195, 199, 216, 221, 230, 266, 270
1:9f.	165		
1:10	98, 143		
2:1-12	153		
2:1-4	153	3:11ff.	262, 264
2:1	192	3:11-13	2, 9, 142, 145, 157, 159, 160, 161, 165, 196, 263, 264, 266
2:2	165, 192		
2:4	88, 152, 165, 192		
2:5	210	3:11	128, 160, 161, 162, 217, 218, 266
2:6	193		
2:8	165, 192	3:12-13	161
2:9	149, 165, 192	3:12	30, 31, 32, 128, 159, 160, 162, 163, 165, 172, 174, 195
2:10	210, 214		
2:12	186, 190, 191, 192, 193		
2:13-4:2	142	3:13	80, 130, 143, 159, 160, 163, 165, 189
2:13-16	142, 155		
2:13	7, 9, 21, 62, 76, 120, 141, 143, 145, 146, 152, 153-155, 156, 164, 165, 166, 167, 168, 178, 185, 190, 192, 264, 267	4	143
		4:1f.	142
		4:1	88, 192
		4:2	204
		4:3-8	160, 188
		4:3	189
2:14-16	155	4:4	189
2:14	165, 192	4:6	172
2:15	88	4:7	178, 186, 189, 190, 192
2:16	143	4:8	189
2:17-3:10	160	4:9ff.	163, 165
2:17-3:8	144	4:9-12	160
2:17-3:4	142	4:9f.	32, 172
2:17	160, 192	4:9-10	142
2:18	161, 166, 271		

4:10	192
4:11	149, 165
4:13-5:11	142, 160, 165
4:13	150, 165, 192
5	143, 194
5:1-11	169, 192
5:1	192
5:4	192
5:6	171
5:8	30, 150, 165, 192
5:9	187, 188, 191, 192, 193, 204
5:12	149, 192
5:13	156
5:14	93, 146, 150, 165, 192
5:15	57
5:16	165
5:17	21, 165, 251
5:18	9, 62, 165, 271
5:23-26	142
5:23f.	128
5:23	130, 161, 163, 189
5:24	27, 131, 186, 190, 192
5:25	165, 192, 251
5:26	189
5:28	142

2 Thessalonians

1	180, 190, 193, 196
1:3ff.	8, 167-196, 257, 260, 263
1:3-3:5	168
1:3-12	168
1:3f.	168, 171-177, 194, 195
1:3	7, 9, 21, 23, 62, 76, 120, 144, 167, 168, 169, 170, 171, 173, 174, 184, 186, 192, 193, 194, 195, 267
1:4	92, 150, 168, 169, 173, 174, 175, 176, 194
1:5ff.	177
1:5-10	169, 177, 190, 194
1:6-10	169
1:5	169, 177, 187
1:8	190
1:9	181, 193
1:10	120, 173, 177, 179, 181, 183, 189, 190, 192, 193
1:11f.	144, 177-184, 194, 270
1:11	21, 83, 128, 148, 167, 169, 172, 173, 180, 181, 186, 190, 192, 194, 195, 196, 270
1:12	169, 170, 181, 182, 183f., 191, 193, 194, 196, 270
2	173, 191, 194
2:1-17	170, 171
2:1-12	168, 169
2:1	170, 192
2:9-12	189
2:9f.	170
2:10-12	185
2:10	185, 189, 192
2:11f.	170, 185
2:11	173, 185, 192
2:12	170, 173, 185, 189
2:13-17	170, 193
2:13f.	107, 168, 170, 172, 184-193, 196, 260, 262, 263, 268
2:13	7, 9, 21, 62, 76, 128, 144, 167, 168, 170, 173, 184, 185, 186, 187, 189, 192, 268
2:14	152, 170, 171, 181, 185, 188, 190, 192, 193, 268
2:15	170, 171, 191, 192
2:16f.	128, 161, 171, 193
2:16	79, 161
2:17	221
3:1-5	170
3:1f.	251
3:1	192, 193
3:2	97
3:3-5	128
3:3	131, 221
3:5	92, 150, 161, 162, 17,0 172
3:6	192
3:8	149, 195
3:10	195
3:11	195
3:12	195
3:13	192

3:16	161, 206	4-7	48
3:17	47	4-6	47-61
		4f.	50-54, 185
1 Timothy		4	21, 22, 43, 50f., 54, 62, 76, 78, 108, 267
1:12ff.	2, 7		
1:12	20, 62, 91, 206, 236	5f.	23, 26, 111
1:14	79, 173	5	9, 49, 50, 51, 52, 53, 56, 58, 79, 80, 102, 173, 260, 267
2:1	62		
2:4	56		
3:10	129	6	30, 32, 48, 49, 51, 54-58, 59, 60, 85, 137, 144, 196, 199, 200, 216, 269
3:13	79		
3:16	206		
4:3, 4	62	7	49, 50, 53, 56, 58
6:16	92	8ff.	49
6:17ff.	117	8	49
6:18	24	9	49, 53
		10	49
2 Timothy		12	49
1:1	219	19	47, 59
1:3ff.	2, 7	20	49
1:3	21, 62, 236	21	56
1:4	21	22	61, 166, 251
1:8	120	25	48
1:13	79		
1:18	127	**Hebrews**	
2:4	88	2:14	92
2:8	152	5:12	89
2:25	56	7:2	203
3:7	56	8:5	211
3:10	93	9:9	211
3:15	79	10:2	211
4:1	98	10:5	158
4:18	98	10:26	56
		10:39	191
Titus		11:1	176
1:1	56	11:4	89
1:6	129	11:15	147
1:7	129	11:25	187
		12:22f.	96
Philemon		13:7	147
1f.	48	13:10	211
1	48	13:16	24
2	48	13:20f.	161
3-6	58, 59		
3	48, 76	**James**	
4ff.	7, 170, 216, 263	1:2f.	93
4-22	48	1:5	116
4-24	47f.	1:18	187

INDEX OF PASSAGES CITED

2:1	182	2 Peter	
2:5	187	1:2	56
3:17	203	1:8	56
3:18	36	2:7, 9	97
5:10f.	93	2:20	56
5:11	241	3:1	35
1 Peter		3 John	
1:3ff.	233, 234, 239	2	218
1:3	76, 236, 241	5	51
1:5	176		
1:7ff.	176	Jude	
1:10	128	25	92
1:21	250		
2:2	173		
2:5	227	Revelation	
2:9	191	1:6	92
4:11	92, 240	2:2	148
4:12-19	176	5:13	92
4:13	93	7:15	211
5:11	92	22:3	211

D. THE DEAD SEA SCROLLS

Rule of the Community (1 QS)

1:8	88
3:15	86
3:21	88
4:3ff.	87
5:10	88
5:11	86
6:6-8	158
9:24	88
11:7f.	95
11:15f.	60
11:15	240
11:17f.	86

Formulary of Blessings (1 QSb)

4:25	37
5:25	87

Damascus Document (CD)

3:12	88
13:9	94

Psalms of Thanksgiving (1 QH)

2:35	97
3:19	97
4:27	86
5:20ff.	234
5:20	240
9:26-31	174
9:35	94
10:14	240, 241
11:27	240
11:29	240, 241
11:32	240
12:11f.	87
14:25	87
16:8	240
16:16	241

Commentary on Habakkuk (1 QHab)

11:1	86

E. RABBINIC LITERATURE

The Babylonian Talmud
  Berakoth
    29b   217
    32a   21

Kethubboth
  8b   244

Pesahim
  65   241

F. HELLENISTIC AUTHORS

Josephus
  Ant.
    I. 193   43
    IX. 235   98

Philo
  Cong.
    96   80

  Heres
    31   43
    174   80

  Mut.
    222f.   80

  Praem.
    72   244

  Spec.
    I. 67   43
    I. 283   43
    I. 284   43
    II. 185   43

G. WRITINGS OF THE EARLY CHURCH

Apostolic Constitutions
  33:7   240
  34:1   240
  49:1   240

1 Clement
  58:2   240
  60:1   241
  64   93

Didache
  9:4   240
  10:5   240

Epistle to Diognetus
  9:1   179

Hermas
  Simil.
    9:14:3   43

Ignatius
  Ephesians
    3:1   93

Irenaeus
  Heresies
    i, 21, 2   99

Justin Martyr
  Apology
    65:5   252
    66:2   252

INDEX OF AUTHORS

Abbott, T. K.   78, 80, 82, 86, 88, 191
Allan, J. A.   219
Allmen, J.-J. von   111
Allo, E.-B.   113, 115, 120, 123, 135, 245, 249, 250, 252, 253
Althaus, P.   213
Anderson, B. W.   233
Arndt, W. F.   26, 32, 34, 81, 88, 109, 116, 120, 155, 159, 162, 171, 179, 180, 191, 212, 214, 217, 249
Audet, J.-P.   10, 233, 238
Aus, R. D.   171
Bachmann, P.   113, 116, 117, 127, 235, 240
Bailey, J. W.   143, 147
Bardenhewer, O.   207
Barr, J.   122, 238
Barrett, C. K.   109f., 117, 118, 119, 120, 123, 124, 125, 126, 127, 129, 130, 134, 206, 207, 213, 222, 233, 243, 246
Barth, K.   29, 32, 34, 36, 207
Bartsch, H. W.   226
Baudissin, W. W. Graf von   237
Baudraz, F.   111
Baumann, R.   108, 112, 113, 127, 135, 136
Baur, F. C.   225
Beardslee, W. A.   60
Beare, F. W.   31, 35, 67, 79, 80, 84, 90, 93
Belser, J. E.   240, 242, 244, 246, 252
Benoit, P.   25
Bernard, E. R.   258
Bernard, J. H.   245, 246, 248, 252
Best, E.   142, 146, 147, 152, 157, 163, 164, 169
Betz, O.   142
Beyer, H. W.   236, 240
Bickerman, E. J.   240
Bicknell, E. J.   149, 153, 185
Bieder, W.   102, 187, 206, 220
Bietenhard, H.   182, 183
Billerbeck, P.   96, 208, 211, 219, 244, 250
Binder, H.   148
Bjerkelund, C. J.   10, 12, 20, 49, 71, 108, 134, 142, 143, 164, 170, 194, 200, 243

Black, M.   221
Blass, F.   23, 26, 32, 36, 42, 44, 52, 53, 76, 83, 86, 88, 89, 109, 120, 123, 147, 148, 154, 174, 181, 203, 214, 218, 240, 242, 245
Boer, H. R.   243, 246
Boobyer, G. H.   5, 62, 156, 253
Bornemann, W.   147, 152, 155, 177, 185
Bornkamm, G.   67, 72, 73, 74, 81, 119, 154, 155, 222f., 226
Bousset, W.   118
Bromiley, G. W.   120
Brown, R. E.   11
Bruce, F. F.   48, 52, 56, 57, 65, 66, 70, 71, 79, 81, 90, 91, 95, 96, 98, 100, 152, 162, 174, 177, 179, 180, 183, 185, 188, 208, 209, 222, 223, 224, 233, 245, 249, 253, 255
Brun, L.   236
Büchsel, F.   35, 99, 115, 200
Buhl, F.   237
Bultmann, R.   29, 33, 52, 57, 85, 109, 125, 142, 152, 156, 159, 174, 207, 208, 213, 241, 242
Burnaby, J.   61
Burton, E. de W.   28, 34, 110, 112, 123, 158, 179
Buttmann, A.   148, 240
Buttrick, G. A.   128
Caird, G. B.   125, 251
Calvin, J.   124, 245
Campbell, J. Y.   55, 132
Campbell, W. S.   225
Carson, H. M.   49, 52, 78
Cerfaux, L.   20, 85, 111, 115, 119, 132, 154, 155, 163, 175, 178, 212
Champion, L. G.   131, 159, 160f., 206
Coggan, D.   152
Conzelmann, H.   65, 67, 74f., 109, 110, 113, 115, 117, 118, 120, 121, 123, 124, 127, 128, 129
Coppens, J.   86
Cragg, G. R.   216

Craig, C. T.   113, 118
Cranfield, C. E. B.   212
Cross, F. L.   11
Cullmann, O.   98, 205
Dahl, N. A.   72, 74, 108, 134, 136, 233, 237
Dalman, G.   97
Daube, D.   73
Davies, W. D.   125, 154, 155, 251
Debrunner, A.   23, 26, 32, 36, 42, 44, 52, 53, 76, 83, 86, 88, 89, 109, 120, 123, 147, 148, 154, 174, 181, 203, 214, 218, 240, 242, 245
Deichgräber, R.   5, 74, 75, 92, 95, 96, 97, 114, 117f., 164, 171, 205, 210, 233, 234, 236, 237, 240, 241, 244, 246
Deissmann, A.   79, 88, 115, 121, 208, 217, 220, 249
Delay, A.   20
Delling, G.   11, 21, 34, 65, 84, 129, 152, 180, 205, 206, 234, 240, 241, 242, 244, 250
Denney, J.   184, 203, 207, 208, 213, 214, 222
Dewailly, L. M.   25
Dibelius, M.   24, 26, 48, 51, 52, 55, 70, 71, 86, 96, 143, 154, 156, 158, 171, 175, 179, 180, 184, 208
Dinkler, E.   112, 122, 135, 142, 255
Dobschütz, E. von   143, 147, 154, 156, 157, 161, 162, 163, 171, 176, 177, 178, 179, 180, 182, 188, 226
Dodd, C. H.   55, 57, 95, 96, 132, 208, 228, 249
Dölger, F. J.   206
Doty, W. G.   1, 10, 11, 47
Dugmore, C. W.   241
Dunn, J. D. G.   26, 75, 112
Du Plessis, P. J.   121, 127, 128
Dupont, J.   33, 119
Eckart, K.-G.   73, 142
Edwards, T. C.   109, 112, 120
Eichholz, G.   215, 223
Elbogen, I.   234
Ellis, E. E.   186, 222
Eltester, W.   10
Eschlimann, J.-A.   6, 62, 65, 134, 206, 211, 215, 237, 253

Evans, E.   135f.
Ewald, P.   36, 42, 80
Exler, F. X. J.   11
Farmer, W. R.   108, 201
Feuillet, A.   206
Filson, F. V.   56, 118, 207, 242, 248
Findlay, G. G.   117, 123, 146, 147, 148, 149, 150, 156, 175, 180, 183
Fitzmyer, J. A.   11
Foerster, W.   88, 179
Frame, J. E.   143, 146, 147, 148, 149, 150, 155, 158, 161, 162, 171, 174, 176, 177, 178, 180, 181, 183, 185, 188, 191, 193
Freytag, W.   228
Fridrichsen, A.   223
Friedrich, G.   23, 29, 48f., 52, 54f., 152, 160
Funk, R. W.   201
Furnish, V. P.   60
Gabathuler, H. J.   74, 75
George, A. R.   23, 56, 132
Gerhardsson, B.   152, 154, 155
Giblin, C. H.   170, 173, 183, 185
Gingrich, F. W.   26, 32, 34, 81, 88, 109, 116, 120, 155, 159, 162, 171, 179, 180, 191, 212, 214, 217, 249
Gnilka, J.   19, 25, 27, 29, 34, 36
Godet, F.   112, 113, 114, 120, 203, 208
Goltz, E. von der   4, 20, 22, 61, 206, 237
Goudge, H. L.   114, 115, 122, 245
Grabner-Haider, A.   242
Grant, F. C.   135
Greeven, H.   29f., 48, 51, 52, 65, 69, 161, 199, 205, 216, 219
Grosheide, F. W.   109, 117, 118, 123, 125, 126, 127, 129
Grundmann, W.   125, 129
Güttgemanns, E.   245
Guthrie, D.   69, 162, 207
Haenchen, E.   10, 73
Hahn, F.   73, 111, 133, 208, 209f., 228
Hamman, A.   9, 20, 62, 64, 93, 97, 109, 152, 199, 205, 206, 210
Harder, G.   6, 20, 21, 22, 60, 61, 72, 78, 86, 89, 91, 92, 95, 96, 97, 116, 128, 130, 157, 158, 159, 161, 171, 181, 188, 199, 203, 204, 205, 217, 220, 241, 242, 244, 257

INDEX OF AUTHORS

Harnack, A. von 42, 188
Harris, M. J. 249, 255
Harrison, P. N. 48, 56
Hastings, J. 258
Hauck, F. 23, 24, 55, 92, 117, 149, 175
Haupt, E. 26
Headlam, A. C. 119, 205, 207, 213, 217, 219, 225
Hegermann, H. 74, 96
Heinrici, C. F. G. 115, 135, 242, 245, 252
Heitmüller, W. 118, 182
Hemer, C. J. 249
Henneken, B. 152, 154
Héring, J. 109, 115, 116, 118, 120, 128, 233, 254
Higgins, A. J. B. 240
Hill, D. 99, 213
Hoffmann, P. 255
Holm-Nielsen, G. 241
Holtzmann, H. J. 127
Holtzmann, O. 143, 147, 184, 212
Horst, F. 236
Horst, J. 93
Huby, J. 206, 207, 213, 214
Hughes, P. E. 122, 127, 248, 250, 253
Hunter, A. M. 30, 81, 208, 222
Hurd, J. C. 134
Jacob, E. 182
Jeremias, J. 22, 52, 53, 77, 78, 241, 242
Jewett, R. 29, 37, 38, 45, 159, 161, 163
Johnson, N. B. 217
Judge, E. A. 225
Jülicher, A. 56, 114, 134
Juncker, A. 4f., 62, 159, 204, 215, 229
Jungmann, J. 206
Kasch, W. 117
Käsemann, E. 34, 72, 73, 74, 75, 95, 250
Kerkhoff, R. 21, 177
Kettler, F. H. 10
Kittel, G. 155, 181, 240
Kittel, H. 191
Klawek, A. 204, 205
Klein, G. 222, 223
Knox, J. 47f., 49, 51, 56, 58, 59, 108, 201, 205, 209, 218, 223
Koch, E. W. 55
Kramer, W. 28f., 52, 58, 76, 115, 131, 132f., 204, 205, 226

Kremer, J. 159
Kühl, E. 203, 205, 206, 207, 213, 214, 221, 222
Kümmel, W. G. 47, 48, 56, 68, 69, 81, 121, 142, 208, 233, 240, 242, 245, 246, 252
Kuhn, H. W. 95
Kuhn, K. G. 86, 94, 118, 196, 239
Kuss, O. 216
Lähnemann, J. 66
Lagrange, M.-J. 204, 207, 214, 218, 221
Leaney, A. R. C. 95, 96
Ledogar, R. J. 157, 237, 238, 240, 253
Leenhardt, F. J. 208, 213, 217, 222, 223, 227
Lietzmann, H. 121, 208, 214, 218, 221, 223, 233, 240, 242, 245, 246, 252
Lightfoot, J. B. 19, 21, 22, 24, 29, 30, 32, 42, 43f., 48, 51, 52, 53, 55, 57, 76, 85, 87f., 89, 90, 91, 114, 115, 118, 126, 143, 147, 148, 149, 150, 151, 152, 154, 155, 158, 177, 180, 185, 186, 191, 222
Loening, E. 42
Lövestam, E. 65, 125, 157f., 192
Lofthouse, W. F. 76
Lohmeyer, E. 5, 19, 22, 27, 29, 31, 33, 35, 36, 41, 49, 52, 53, 55, 56, 57, 65, 67, 68, 72, 74, 76, 77, 78, 84, 86, 88, 90, 95, 97, 160, 200
Lohse, E. 21, 30, 53f., 66, 67, 68, 71, 73, 76, 81, 83, 84, 86, 88, 89, 90, 93, 94, 95, 96, 97, 98, 120, 154
Longenecker, R. N. 152
Lührmann, D. 125
Lünemann, G. 147, 172, 183
Lund, N. W. 53
Lyonnet, S. 206, 212
McFadyen, J. E. 109, 112
McFarlane, D. J. 10-12, 238
Manson, T. W. 119, 204, 221, 222, 225
Marchel, W. 77, 205
Martin, R. P. 23, 29, 34, 37, 45, 64f., 74, 75, 89, 95, 96, 203f.
Marxsen, W. 187
Masson, C. 67, 84f., 147, 182
Mattern, L. 128
Maurer, C. 262
Menzies, A. H. 233, 242, 248

INDEX OF AUTHORS

Meyer, H. A. W.   109, 117, 120, 123f., 125, 203, 208, 213, 214, 216, 218, 221, 242, 245, 252
Michael, J. H.   24f., 32, 34, 35, 36, 42, 46
Michaelis, W.   25, 36, 92, 218, 245
Michel, O.   142, 199, 203, 206, 211, 213, 217, 219, 220, 221, 222, 224, 240
Milligan, G.   24, 34f., 88, 121, 125, 128, 143, 147, 148, 149, 152, 155, 158, 161, 162, 175, 177, 180, 183, 190, 191, 214, 220, 249
Minear, P. S.   228
Moffatt, J.   35, 42, 52, 55, 110, 113, 121, 124, 148, 175
Molland, E.   213
Montgomery, J. A.   110
Moore, A. L.   147f., 151, 171, 175, 177, 179, 180, 182, 183, 185, 186, 187, 188, 189
Morris, L.   44, 99, 123, 147, 148, 149, 151, 159, 175, 177, 178, 180, 183, 186, 187, 188, 189, 191
Moule, C. F. D.   28, 33, 44, 48, 49, 52, 53, 55, 56, 57, 75, 77, 79, 84, 85, 86, 89, 90, 95, 99, 123, 136, 152, 154, 179, 205, 213, 227, 238, 240
Moulton, J. H.   24, 34f., 36, 88, 121, 125, 128, 158, 214, 220, 249, 250
Müller, J.   52
Mullins, T. Y.   10, 71, 108, 170, 200, 201f., 235, 248
Munck, J.   70, 111, 152, 209, 223f., 225
Murphy-O'Connor, J.   86, 189
Murray, J.   120, 206, 213, 216, 221, 222
Mussner, F.   95
Nägeli, T.   249
Neil, W.   149, 150, 151, 179, 183, 188
Neufeld, V. H.   120
Neugebauer, F.   115
Nickle, K. F.   24, 110
Nicoll, W. R.   117, 175, 203, 245
Nielen, J. M.   55, 132, 161, 205f., 251
Norden, E.   67, 71f., 73, 74, 83, 96, 244
Nygren, A.   208, 221
O'Brien, P. T.   2, 3, 89, 121, 129, 153, 259
Oepke, A.   34, 115, 143, 171, 179, 188
Oesterley, W. O. E.   241
Orphal, E.   20, 97, 205, 220, 241, 250, 258

Osty, E.   122
Pallis, A.   213, 222
Parratt, J. K.   221
Parry, R. St. J.   109, 115, 116, 117, 119, 128, 129, 132, 135, 207, 208, 209, 213, 214, 222
Pearson, B. A.   142, 143
Pedersen, J.   182
Percy, E.   58, 67, 68, 81, 87, 96, 100, 120
Pfitzner, V. C.   199, 213, 219
Piper, O.   126
Plummer, A.   113, 123, 127, 132, 143, 148, 161, 172, 185, 240, 242, 244, 245, 246, 248, 252f.
Pollard, T. E.   38
Preiss, T.   56
Procksch, O.   189
Prümm, K.   181, 185, 245, 246
Quell, G.   76
Rabin, C.   94
Rad, G. von   181
Rankin, O. S.   241
Resch, A.   220
Richardson, A.   96, 125
Richardson, P.   168, 187
Rigaux, B.   47, 143, 146, 147, 149, 150, 151, 152, 153, 154, 155, 157, 164, 169, 170, 172, 173, 176, 177, 178, 180, 181, 182, 183, 184, 187, 188, 189, 190, 191, 192, 194
Robert, A.   206
Robertson, A.   113, 123, 127, 132
Robertson, A. T.   26, 32, 36, 52, 55, 84, 88, 120, 174, 177, 181, 240, 245
Robinson, D. W. B.   80
Robinson, J. A.   32f., 110f., 184, 191
Robinson, J. M.   8, 10, 11, 12, 49, 64, 116, 130, 201, 233, 238, 239
Roller, O.   47, 76, 146, 245
Rowley, H. H.   135, 221
Sanday, W.   119, 205, 207, 213, 217, 219, 225
Sanders, J. T.   10, 12, 20, 49, 65, 71, 107, 108, 130, 143, 170, 200, 201, 235, 250, 261
Schenk, W.   160, 221f., 233, 236, 238, 239, 240

INDEX OF AUTHORS

Schermann, T. 5
Schettler, A. 204
Schippers, R. 155
Schlatter, A. 52, 119, 211, 212, 213, 218, 222, 224, 228, 248, 252
Schlier, H. 95, 96, 121, 122, 176, 177, 181f., 187, 191, 240
Schmauch, W. 19
Schmidt, K. L. 178
Schmiedel, P. W. 127, 245, 248
Schmithals, W. 119, 142
Schmitz, O. 242-244, 246, 247
Schneider, C. 60f., 62, 199, 217, 242
Schniewind, J. 209, 213
Schrenk, G. 36, 76, 77, 151, 180, 224
Schubert, P. 1, 4, 6-9, 10, 11, 12, 13, 14, 15, 20, 26, 28, 29, 42, 43, 44, 45, 49, 54, 55, 62, 63, 71, 76, 81, 89, 103, 107, 109, 113, 116, 120, 130, 136, 141, 142, 143, 144, 145, 153, 164, 167, 169, 170, 185, 200, 201, 207, 233, 250, 251, 252, 261, 262, 269
Schweizer, E. 124, 208, 212, 213, 222
Seeberg, A. 204, 205
Seesemann, H. 23, 24, 55, 132
Seidensticker, P. 212
Selwyn, E. G. 65, 73, 191, 193, 251
Sevenster, J. N. 122
Simon, W. G. H. 114
Simpson, E. K. 65
Singer, S. 130, 241
Smith, C. W. F. 128
Snaith, N. H. 110
Spicq, C. 30, 31, 32, 33, 34, 35, 51, 52, 79, 162, 174
Stacey, W. D. 163
Stählin, G. 242f.
Stanley, D. M. 155
Stauffer, E. 21, 30, 52, 174, 240
Strachan, R. H. 248
Strack, H. L. 96, 208, 211, 219, 244, 250
Strathmann, H. 120, 121, 210, 211, 212
Suhl, A. 47, 57
Sullivan, K. 32, 52, 57
Tannehill, R. C. 242, 244, 245, 246, 247, 248, 250
Tasker, R. V. G. 245, 253
Taylor, V. 56
Therrien, G. 34

Thieme, K. 142
Thomas, G. S. R. 225
Thornton, L. S. 55
Thrall, M. E. 171
Thüsing, W. 20, 37, 65, 132, 204
Trocmé, E. 224
Turner, N. 24, 36, 42, 44, 53, 76, 89, 117, 120, 123, 147, 181, 183, 240, 245
Unnik, W. C. van 122, 127, 130, 240
Viard, R. P. A. 208
Vidler, A. R. 61
Vincent, M. R. 27, 28, 29, 30, 35, 36, 43, 44, 48, 52, 55, 56, 57
Vos, G. 98
Warfield, B. B. 99
Warneck, J. 200
Wegenast, K. 154
Weiser, A. 130, 249
Weiss, B. 203, 204, 208, 240
Weiss, J. 109, 115, 118, 124, 134
Wendland, H.-D. 115, 118, 132, 252
Wendland, P. 47, 117
Westermann, C. 233f., 236, 237, 238
Wetter, G. P. 109, 119, 183, 253
White, J. L. 10, 47
Whiteley, D. E. H. 28
Wickert, U. 48, 49, 57, 200
Wiederkehr, D. 131, 179, 180, 187
Wikenhauser, A. 115
Wilckens, U. 119
Wiles, G. P. 4, 7, 9f., 13, 29, 35, 37, 38, 40, 53, 56, 69, 83, 84, 128, 135, 136, 141f., 143, 145, 146, 147, 150, 156, 157, 159, 161, 162, 163, 165, 198, 199f., 208, 210, 217, 237, 250, 252
Windisch, H. 223, 233, 241, 242, 245, 246, 252, 258
Winer, G. B. 42, 109, 240
Wobbe, J. 20, 109, 115, 124, 183f., 203, 253
Wohlenberg, G. 36, 146, 147, 175, 180, 188
Zahn, T. 42, 68, 203, 208, 222
Zerwick, M. 24, 43, 109, 178, 216
Ziesler, J. A. 36
Zimmerli, W. 110
Zuntz, G. 94, 129, 130, 249, 250
Zunz, L. 241
Zwaan, J. de 122

www.ingramcontent.com/pod-product-compliance
Lightning Source LLC
Chambersburg PA
CBHW061428300426
44114CB00014B/1589